Foundation ActionScript 3.0 with Flash CS3 and Flex

Steve Webster, Todd Yard, and Sean McSharry

D1249411

friendsof
DESIGNER TO DESIGNER™
an Apress® company

Foundation ActionScript 3.0 with Flash CS3 and Flex

ISBN-13 (pbk): 978-1-59059-815-3

ISBN-10 (pbk): 1-59059-815-6

ISBN-13 (electronic): 978-1-4302-0196-0

ISBN-10 (electronic): 1-4302-0196-7

Printed and bound in the United States of America 9 8 7 6 5 4 3 2

Trademarked names may appear in this book. Rather than use a trademark symbol with every occurrence of a trademarked name, we use the names only in an editorial fashion and to the benefit of the trademark owner, with no intention of infringement of the trademark.

Distributed to the book trade worldwide by Springer-Verlag New York, Inc., 233 Spring Street, 6th Floor, New York, NY 10013. Phone 1-800-SPRINGER, fax 201-348-4505, e-mail orders-ny@springer-sbm.com, or visit www.springeronline.com.

For information on translations, please contact Apress directly at 2855 Telegraph Avenue, Suite 600, Berkeley, CA 94705. Phone 510-549-5930, fax 510-549-5939, e-mail info@apress.com, or visit www.apress.com.

The information in this book is distributed on an "as is" basis, without warranty. Although every precaution has been taken in the preparation of this work, neither the author(s) nor Apress shall have any liability to any person or entity with respect to any loss or damage caused or alleged to be caused directly or indirectly by the information contained in this work.

The source code for this book is freely available to readers at www.friendsofed.com in the Downloads section.

Credits

CONTENTS AT A GLANCE

CONTENTS

ABOUT THE AUTHORS

Steve Webster got hooked on ActionScript back in the early days of Flash 4, when scientists still thought that the Earth was both flat and the center of the universe, and has been monkeying around with Flash and Flex ever since.

He works as a developer at Yahoo! in London, where he spends his time preaching the virtues of good Flash and Flex to his colleagues, both Flashers and standardistas alike, and occasionally attempting to practice what he preaches.

Over the years, he has written and contributed to a vast number of Flash-related books for friends of ED and somehow still possesses a modicum of sanity. He maintains a regular (OK, sporadic) blog at dynamicflash.com and runs the companion site for this book at foundationas3.com.

Todd Yard is currently a software architect at Brightcove in Cambridge, Massachusetts, where he was been working on the company's video product and service since 2005, leading the development of its Flash front end. He has contributed as an author to a dozen friends of ED books on Flash and served as technical editor on several others. His personal site, 27Bobs.com, really needs updating, but he's a busy guy.

Sean McSharry has been a Flash developer and designer since 1999 (Flash 3). Like many top developers in his field, he comes from a nonprogramming background originally (in his case, a tree surgeon). He runs the popular Flashcoder blog (flashcoder.net/blog). He has consulted in many business sectors, from oil exploration to banking to IPTV, for major industry leaders such as Microsoft and Adobe Consulting. He is an Adobe Certified Flash Developer and Designer, and has worked on everything from banners to massive RIAs. He has worked in Europe and America, and is presently freelancing in the UK. He uses the entire Flash Platform in his development (Flash, Flex, ActionScript, Flash Lite, Flash Media Server, and so on). He is a prerelease tester for many Adobe products, and is actively involved in the Flash community, most recently, getting Adobe to sponsor the poker tournaments he organizes quarterly for Adobe professionals (pokercoder.com).

Sean strongly believes that Flash developers and designers should be as comfortable with and passionate about code as they are about aesthetics and design. Pragmatic development is something he pushes very hard. Assume nothing. Don't code what you shouldn't code. Code with project maintenance in mind. These are his top rules for running a successful development team and producing successful applications.

ABOUT THE TECHNICAL REVIEWER

Mike Jones is an old man of the Flash world, having first picked up Flash in late 1996, when it was still called Futurewave Splash. For more than a decade, he has produced web applications, websites, and desktop applications using the Flash Platform, not once thinking that perhaps it was time to find something better to do.

In his spare time, Mike runs the website FlashGen.com (flashgen.com). Originally launched as a Macromedia Generator resource site in 1998, the site is now used as a blog-style repository for information based on Flash, Flex, AIR, and ActionScript. Mike lives in Haslemere, Surrey, UK, with his fiancée and their cat Figo.

ABOUT THE COVER IMAGE DESIGNER

Corné van Dooren designed the front cover image for this book. Having been given a brief by friends of ED to come up with a new design for the Foundation series, he was inspired to create this new setup, combining technology and organic forms.

With a colorful background as an avid cartoonist, Corné discovered the infinite world of multimedia at the age of 17, a journey of discovery that hasn't stopped since. His mantra has always been, "The only limit to multimedia is the imagination," which has kept him moving forward constantly.

After enjoying success after success over the past years—working for many international clients, as well as being featured in multimedia magazines, testing software, and working on many other friends of ED books—Corné decided it was time to take another step in his career by launching his own company, Project 79, in March 2005. You can see more of his work and contact him through http://www.cornevandooren.com or http://www.project79.com.

If you like his work, be sure to check out his chapter in *New Masters of Photoshop:* Volume 2, also published by friends of ED (ISBN: 1-59059-315-4).

shape.onEnterFrame = function() {
var speed =
this._width += (this.targetWidth - this._width)/speed;
this._height += (this.targetHeight - this._height)/speed;
};shape.targetHeight = shape._height;

shape.onEnterFrame = function() {
var speed = 5;
this._width += (this.targetWidth - this._width)/speed;
this._height += (this.targetHeight - this._height)/speed;

Chapter 1

GETTING STARTED WITH ACTIONSCRIPT 3.0

Steve Webster with Todd Yard

Here you stand (or sit or lie) at the very start of a long and perilous journey to becoming an ActionScript developer. Well, OK, maybe not all that perilous—it's not like there are any dragons, angry trolls, or even anything as dangerous as a mildly annoyed snail—but you can get some pretty nasty finger aches from all the typing.

Umm . . . where was I? Ah yes, ActionScript. In this chapter, we'll look at what exactly this thing called ActionScript is, the processes you'll go through to create an ActionScript project, and what ActionScript can bring to your Flash work.

Toward the end, we'll dive right in at the deep end and look at an example of an ActionScript 3.0 project in all its naked glory. Don't worry—you're not expected to understand any of what's going on at this stage. The aim of this example is to whet your geek taste buds (everyone has them, even if some people won't admit it; they're responsible for that "oooooh" sound we make when we see an iPhone or any other shiny new device). The idea is that once you've seen the potential of ActionScript, you'll be hooked and inspired enough to want to read the rest of this book in one sitting.

Before we get that far, though, I thought it might be nice to take a stroll down memory lane and look at how ActionScript came to be, stopping along the way to sniff the flowers and enjoy the views.

A brief history of ActionScript

The official definition of ActionScript, directly from our grand overlords Adobe (http://www.adobe.com/devnet/actionscript/), goes something this:

ActionScript is the programming language for the Flash Player runtime environment. Originally developed as a way for Flash developers to program interactivity, ActionScript enables efficient programming of Flash applications for everything from simple animations to complex, data-rich, interactive application interfaces.

This is a good definition, as you would expect coming from the company responsible for the language, but it doesn't tell you much about how ActionScript came to be.

What we now know as ActionScript 1.0 first appeared in Flash 5. Previous versions of Flash allowed developers to add commands to their movies to control the playback and store values, but they were basic and it was arguable whether those commands could be called a programming language. ActionScript 1.0 was based on ECMAScript 262, the same family of languages that includes JavaScript.

If you're a curious type, you might be wondering about ECMAScript. ECMAScript is a programming language defined by a standards body known as Ecma International (which used to be the European Computer Manufacturers Association before it changed its name). This organization helps create, define, and promote standardization for all sorts of highly technical stuff. ECMAScript was created in 1997 with the aim of solving the incompatibilities between the different implementations of JavaScript found in Netscape and Internet Explorer. (In fact, Microsoft's version was so different that it was called it JScript rather than JavaScript.) ECMAScript has since become the de facto standard for scripting languages on the Internet, which is why Macromedia (now Adobe) decided to adopt the standard for its new Flash scripting language.

ActionScript 2.0 arrived with Flash MX 2004 and was based on a newer version of the ECMAScript standard. Although on the surface this version appeared to have a number of new language constructs—like classes, interfaces, and private and public attributes—it was really a thin veneer over the old version, still compiling down to the prototype-based programming used with ActionScript 1.0. (Not sure what a prototype is? Thankfully, with ActionScript 3.0, we don't have to go down that road.)

ActionScript 3.0 is based on and compiles with the very latest, bleeding-edge version of the ECMAScript standard—ECMAScript Edition 4 (draft) for all you trivia buffs out there—and adds a host of new language features. Because ActionScript 3.0 is fundamentally different from its predecessors and requires a completely new player to interpret it, you can use it only for projects that target Adobe Flash Player 9 and above. ActionScript 3.0 was first available as part of Flex 2, and the language has since been incorporated into Flash CS3.

Flash CS3 and Flex 2

Adobe released Flex 2 in July 2006 and with it gave the world the ActionScript 3.0 programming language. Flex 2 was designed to provide a rapid development environment for rich Internet application

(RIA) development and does not contain the notion of a timeline as in Flash. Instead, the user interface is authored using MXML files (Adobe's own markup language for defining ActionScript applications using the Flex framework) and ActionScript 3.0 code to create the final SWF files (although this is the normal course for using Flex, you also have the option of working strictly in ActionScript without using MXML or the Flex framework).

You have at least two paths for creating SWF files with ActionScript: the Flash CS3 integrated development environment (IDE) or Flex. Since the Flash IDE is the more common choice, much of the text in this book is presented from a Flash-centric view. The basic tenets of ActionScript 3.0 programming are the same whether you use Flash or Flex, so the majority of this book will be useful no matter which development environment you're using. In addition, toward the end of the book, you'll find a couple chapters on authoring ActionScript 3.0 projects with Flex 2, so it's like getting two books for the price of one—a bargain!

If you've installed and worked with Flash, you know that creating SWFs is as simple as creating a new Flash file and using the File ➤ Publish menu command. For Flex, things get a little trickier—or, perhaps, more intriguing and appealing—presenting you with a number of options. If you have purchased and installed Flex Builder, either as a stand-alone application or as an Eclipse plug-in, you can use that to create a new Flex or ActionScript project. You can then run this project in order to create an SWF file. In addition to Flex Builder, you also have the option of using the free command-line compiler. This involves creating ActionScript and (perhaps) MXML files, and then using the compiler to create SWF files from this source. Often, this is accomplished with an automation tool like Ant (http://ant.apache.org/). To find out more about this approach, you can start with a tutorial such as http://www.senocular.com/flash/tutorials/as3withmxmlc.

> *For years, the term* Flash *has encompassed multiple meanings such as the Flash IDE, the Flash Player, and the ActionScript compiler. This book will include statements like, "This line tells Flash that . . . ," where* Flash *is used in a more general sense and is applicable even if you are using Flex Builder or the command-line compiler to create SWFs. For clarity, when referring specifically to a certain component in the larger Flash platform, the text will use the more precise term, such as the* Flash IDE.

All the examples in this book (with the exception of those from the Flex chapters) will be presented as Flash files. Because the ActionScript will nearly always be in external files, there's no reason you couldn't adapt these examples for use in Flex. In fact, this book's downloadable files include both Flash files and Flex ActionScript projects, where applicable, to run the ActionScript.

> *The Flex directories in this book's downloadable code are not actually what would be considered "Flex," which usually implies use of the Flex framework and MXML files to control layout. Flex Builder and the free command-line compiler not only allow for compilation of MXML and Flex projects, but also of pure ActionScript projects, which include nothing but ActionScript code. For the chapters not specifically about Flex, the samples are in ActionScript projects.*

ActionScript and object-oriented programming

Object-oriented programming might sound scary and official, but when you see and hear it shortened to the common and silly-sounding acronym OOP, it becomes much less daunting. What is OOP? Well, put simply, OOP is a programming technique. It's a way to write and organize your code to make it easier for you, as a developer, to build and maintain your applications. OOP developers break down functionality into modular pieces that interact in certain, recommended ways.

Back in the dark ages of programming, applications were written using a procedural programming methodology, which basically means that the program started running at the beginning and kept on going through the code in a linear fashion. But this method of programming did not lend itself well to the expansive applications with graphic user interfaces (GUIs) that were becoming more prevalent on the personal computers in everyone's home. A new way to program was needed to make it easier to build and maintain these types of applications, which were highly focused on user interaction.

This was when OOP appeared—something of a swashbuckling hero with a cape and sword, crashing through a lovely stained glass window, I would imagine. OOP introduced a new way to organize a program by breaking up an application into small pieces called *objects*, each with distinct functionality. These objects then took care of interacting with each other to create a seamless program. The beauty of this approach is threefold:

- It's easy to break down a problem into small pieces and tackle each separately.
- It's easier to reuse functionality from one project to another.
- It's a heck of a lot easier to debug a well-written OOP application if something goes wrong.

As you might have guessed, since this is a book on ActionScript and I'm spending a bit of time talking about OOP, ActionScript is an OOP language. When you code in ActionScript 3.0, you will be practicing OOP, whether you know it or not. Of course, there are degrees of adherence to true OOP methodology, and there are certainly open debates within the OOP community about how certain things should be done. But generally, there is consensus on some of the root tenets of OOP. ActionScript 3.0 helps to enforce these OOP principles, whereas ActionScript 2.0 and 1.0 were much less strict (that's not necessarily a good thing). So as you are learning ActionScript through this book, you will also be learning OOP, which is a heck of a good deal.

The development process

If you have never worked with ActionScript, it is important to understand what exactly will change in your workflow for producing SWF files once you make the decision to add ActionScript to your projects. The changes will differ depending on the amount of code you want to add. If you are an animator and want to add a simple preloader to your movie and a replay button upon its completion, the amount of code you will need and the changes to your workflow will be significantly less than if you are creating a game or an online application. In addition, where you add your code and how you incorporate it into your projects will also vary from project to project.

For Flash users, ActionScript's simplest integration involves adding some code to the timeline using the Actions panel in the Flash IDE. This was the way it was accomplished for many previous versions and still has its uses. For instance, the preloader and replay button mentioned in the previous paragraph might be implemented in such a way, as they are small pieces of functionality that are largely independent of the rest of the movie. In such cases, you can often continue to work as you normally would within the application and add the necessary code to your file once the main content has been completed. It's a great way to learn the ins and outs of ActionScript without diving headfirst into hardcore OOP programming in external class files.

If you are a Flex user or have more complex interaction to code in Flash, your best bet is to use external ActionScript files that you can reference in the Flash IDE or, in the case of Flex, through MXML. In this case, you'll need to do much more planning, and the diagramming of code beforehand is an important step. What does this diagramming mean to your workflow?

For animation development, you'll start with a storyboarding phase. In a storyboard, you mock up the proposed animation in still frames in order to determine storytelling and flow. Figure 1-1 shows an example of a simple storyboard. Including this step in the process helps to ensure that the work on the animation does not go astray. You avoid going down a path where you waste time and need to redo work based on issues that you didn't foresee.

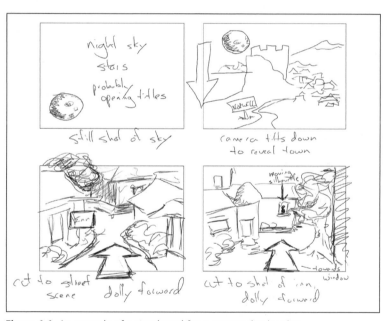

Figure 1-1. An example of a storyboard for a proposed animation

If you're developing a game or application using ActionScript to control its logic and interactions, you'll start by mapping out how code will interact. This helps to flush out problems in the logic and ensure that development stays on track (well, as much as possible). Unified Modeling Language (UML) is a common technique used for diagramming an application's programming logic, as shown in Figure 1-2.

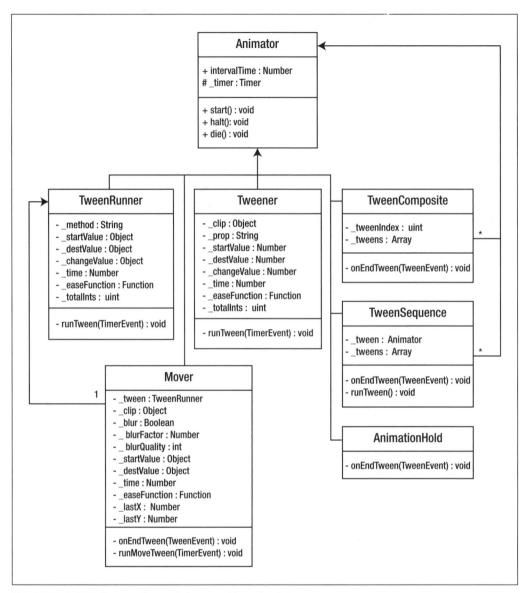

Figure 1-2. A UML diagram of several classes and how they interact

The extent you need to diagram can change from project to project, and the level of detail at which you diagram is a subjective topic. However, in any case, when planning a Flash or Flex project that will include ActionScript, planning the code before you start programming should be considered within your workflow. As tempting as it is to just dive right in and start coding, you can quickly become lost in your code and lose sight of your overall objective (if you even know what it is in the first place).

> *That's not to say that coding from the hip doesn't have its place. Sometimes before starting a more formal design process, you just need to know if something is even possible. The only way to discover that is to sit down and build a rough version that tests all the key elements of your project. This technique is known as* rapid prototyping, *and the idea is to test all the key functionality without necessarily worrying about best practices or tidy code. Once you know your ideas are possible, you either throw away the code and start again, or refactor the code into something that's a little more refined.*

Once you have done the proper planning and design, and you've created the necessary visual elements using the Flash IDE, you can write your code, testing as you go along to make sure that you're still on the right track. For an animation, you might continually test the movie to see how a motion plays out. In a similar way, with code, you might test a small piece of functionality within the larger application. Instead of tweaking graphics and animation in a timeline, you will be tweaking code to fix errors and add new functionality.

Many of the animations I work on now are all done through ActionScript. I used to build animations in a timeline, small pieces at a time. Now I build animations through code, programming small pieces at a time. The workflow has stayed very similar. Only the method I use to create the animations—code instead of timeline—has changed.

Organizing your files

Before you start writing any ActionScript code, you should consider where you are going to store your files. Your ActionScript files should go in the same directory as the main FLA file for your project for Flash users, or in your project root directory for Flex users. This might be individual ActionScript files, or, more often than not, entire subdirectories of ActionScript files divided into packages. However, having a common project root directory is usually a good rule to follow. (Of course, there are exceptions, such as when you're creating code that will be used by more than one project.)

Modern operating systems have user-specific directories where they can store personal files. On Windows 2000, XP, and Vista systems, this is C:\Documents and Settings\[*username*]; on Mac OS X, this directory is /Users/[*username*]. Personally, I like to create a Projects directory in my user directory, with subdirectories for each of my individual projects. That way, I can back up all my projects in one go without needing to hunt for them.

Since all the projects for this book are related, you'll probably want to create a subdirectory for the book (named Foundation AS3 or similar), and then have a subdirectory for each chapter. If you download the sample files from the book's website (www.foundationAS3.com), you'll find that they are already organized in this way.

Throughout the book, I'll refer to the *project directory* as the directory in which you want to store the files for that project. If you're following the suggested organization scheme, that will be the directory of the current chapter; if you're using your own scheme, then project directory can be wherever you want it to be. It's completely up to you where you want to keep your project files and how you want to organize them.

Adding ActionScript to your projects

You can add ActionScript to your projects, in several different ways:

- Place code on the timeline.
- Import code from an external file.
- Specify a document class.
- Link library assets to external classes.

Each approach has benefits and drawbacks. Here, we'll look at each option individually, using the classic "Hello, world" example, which is often the first exercise when learning a programming language—getting your program to come alive, wake up to the world, and greet you.

Placing code on the timeline

It used to be quite acceptable for developers to write their ActionScript code directly onto the timeline in their FLA files. Even now, there are times where it's useful to place code on the timeline, so it's worth knowing how to do this. Follow these steps:

1. Create a new Flash ActionScript 3.0 file and save it with the name `timeline.fla` in the project directory.

> *It's a good idea to get into the habit of saving files just after creating them (even before you've actually made any changes), and then saving periodically as you're working. As with any application, Flash could experience problems. By saving regularly, you reduce the chances of losing your work.*

2. Select the first frame of Layer 1 of your movie in the timeline.

3. Open the Actions panel by selecting Window ➤ Actions from the main menu. (To save your mouse some traveling time, you can also open the Actions panel using a keyboard shortcut: F9 if you're using Windows and Option+F9 if you're using Mac OS X.) You should now see the Actions panel in all its naked, brazen glory, looking just like Figure 1-3.

4. The big white expanse on the right side of the window is where you write your ActionScript 3.0 code if you want to place it directly on the timeline. Go ahead and click there. Then type the following:

```
trace("Hello, world");
```

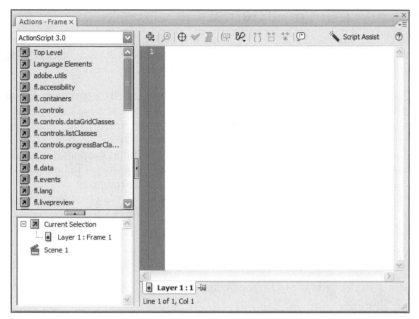

Figure 1-3. The Actions panel in the Flash IDE

5. Test your movie by selecting Control ➤ Test Movie from the main menu. You'll see the Output panel with your ActionScript's output, as shown in Figure 1-4.

Don't worry too much about what the text you've just typed in means—you'll find out in the next chapter. However, don't let that detract from the fact that you've just crafted your first piece of ActionScript 3.0 code. You're now officially an ActionScript developer. Groovy, baby!

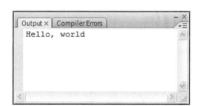

Figure 1-4. The classic "Hello, world" using ActionScript to trace to the Output panel

Unfortunately, writing your code into the frames of your Flash movies is not considered best practice. If you can imagine that the code could be on any frame of any movie clip in your Flash movie, you might guess that it's not a great deal of fun hunting down a specific piece of code if you need to change it. This makes it difficult when a new developer joins a project and needs to discover how things are done (believe me, I speak from experience). In addition, if you are using any type of version control, code directly in an FLA file cannot be versioned and compared easily. In a large software development group, this coding approach also makes it impossible for multiple developers to be working on the same file, which can be done with text files.

Still, timeline code has its place for simple projects or one-person shops. Flash developers have worked this way for years.

Importing code from an external file

One step up from placing code directly on the timeline is pulling the code into a frame from an external file. Importing code from an external file doesn't affect how your the ActionScript is incorporated into the final SWF file. It just separates your code from the FLA file.

This technique might be useful if the code you're writing is designed to be part of more than one SWF file, allowing you to make changes just once (to the external file) and have them incorporated into multiple SWF files. Without the ability to import code from an external file, you would need to copy and paste the code into each FLA file that needs to be updated. You'll still need to publish each movie that makes use of the external file when you make a change; the import happens only at compile time, not at runtime. On the plus side, this means that you don't need to upload the external ActionScript file to your server along with the SWF file(s), as it has already been compiled.

I'm sure you're itching to get your code imported from an external file. To do so, follow these simple steps:

1. Create a new Flash ActionScript 3.0 file and save it with the name import.fla to the project directory.

2. Select the first frame of the movie, open the Actions panel, and enter the following code in the area on the right:

   ```
   include "import.as";
   ```

3. Select File ➤ New from the main menu. Then select ActionScript File from the list in the New Document dialog box, as shown in Figure 1-5, and click OK.

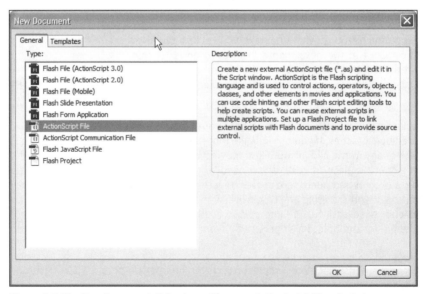

Figure 1-5. The New Document dialog box with a new ActionScript file selected

4. Enter the following line of code into the text editor:

```
trace("Hello, world");
```

5. Save your file as import.as in the project directory.

6. Switch back to the import.fla file in the Flash CS3 IDE.

7. Test your Flash movie by selecting Control ➤ Test Movie from the main menu. You should see the same result as when you placed the code on the timeline, as shown in Figure 1-4, but this time, the code is being pulled in from an external file.

While this method is better than placing all your code directly on the timeline, you still needed to add the include statement in the FLA file, which, once again, makes it difficult to find and manage. Not only that, but although the code was in an external file, it was actually compiled into the first frame of the SWF file as though you had written it on the timeline.

Thankfully, Flash CS3 provides two other, interrelated methods for adding ActionScript to your projects, both of which allow for better management of your code.

Specifying a document class

Flash CS3 introduces the concept of a *document class*. You haven't learned about ActionScript 3.0 classes yet, but what this concept basically means is that you're telling Flash which piece of ActionScript you want to be executed as soon as the movie starts to play by associating an external class with the main timeline.

OK, it's not easy talking about classes before introducing classes, but consider that everything in an SWF file is an object (like a graphic, a button, a text field, a movie clip). These objects are all made from a blueprint called a *class*. For example, all movie clips are built from a MovieClip class, so they all have similar functionality, like having a timeline, knowing how to rotate, and so on.

Well, the main timeline in Flash is actually a movie clip itself, it just happens to be one that holds everything in your movie. A document class is a movie clip, too, but a movie clip that has some extra functionality that you, as a developer, can code. So perhaps the additional code might be kicking off the loading of a series of animations and managing the playback. In that case, you would associate this class with the main timeline of your movie, so that when the SWF file is loaded into the Flash Player, it will immediately run your additional functionality.

This is actually a pretty advanced topic to bring up in Chapter 1, but to demonstrate the different ways ActionScript can be used, specifying a document class must be noted here. And actually, in execution, it's pretty easy to do, as the following set of steps demonstrates.

1. Create a new Flash ActionScript 3.0 file and save it with the name document.fla in the project directory.

2. Open the Property inspector (if it's not already visible) by selecting Window ➤ Properties ➤ Properties from the main menu, or by pressing F3 on Windows or Command+F3 on Mac OS X.

3. Toward the bottom-right side of the Property inspector, locate the text box labeled Document class and enter the text **Document**, as shown in Figure 1-6.

Figure 1-6. The Property inspector with the document class added

4. Save the changes to your Flash movie.

5. Create a new ActionScript file and save this file into your project directory with the name Document.as. (Note the capital *D*, which is a common and recommended practice for classes and class files.) This means both document.fla and Document.as will be in the same directory in your file system.

6. Enter the following text into your new ActionScript file:

```
package {

  import flash.display.MovieClip;

  public class Document extends MovieClip {

    public function Document() {
      trace("Hello, world");
    }

  }

}
```

7. Switch back to the document.fla file in the Flash CS3 IDE and test your movie by selecting Control ➤ Test Movie from the main menu. Once again you should see the same result in the Output panel (Figure 1-4).

Don't worry too much about what all the stuff you typed means. I promise that by the end of Chapter 3, you'll know it backwards and forwards.

Linking library assets to external classes

Linking library assets to external classes in order to use ActionScript in your Flash movie is very similar to using a document class. Remember when I mentioned that the main timeline was a movie clip? Well, there can obviously be a lot of examples of movie clips in your FLA—ones that you create and store in the Library and can then drag onto the stage and timeline or attach using ActionScript. In much the same way that the main timeline as a movie clip can have a class associated with it, so, too, can you have a movie clip symbol in the library associated with a class. When this is done, any instance of that symbol that is added to the stage, either in the IDE or at runtime through code, will run the additional code that you have added using the external class file.

To test this, you can reuse the ActionScript file you created in the previous example. Let's take a look at how this works.

1. Resave the Document.as file from the previous section as Symbol.as.

2. Change the references in the file from Document to Symbol, as in the following code.

```
package {

    import flash.display.MovieClip;

    public class Symbol extends MovieClip {

        public function Symbol() {
            trace("Hello, world");
        }

    }

}
```

3. Create a new Flash ActionScript 3.0 file and save it with the name symbol.fla in the project directory.

4. Select Insert ➤ New Symbol from the menu to open the Create New Symbol dialog box. Click the Advanced button in the bottom right to get the expanded dialog box, as shown in Figure 1-7.

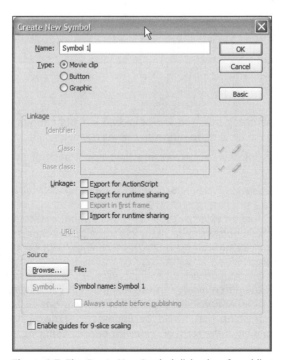

Figure 1-7. The Create New Symbol dialog box for adding new library assets

5. In the Create New Symbol dialog box, enter Symbol as the name of the symbol and set the symbol type to Movie clip. In the Linkage section, select the Export for ActionScript option. A number of fields will then be filled in automatically, as shown in Figure 1-8. You've specified that this symbol will actually create instances of the Symbol class you coded.

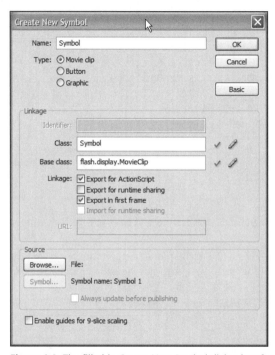

Figure 1-8. The filled-in Create New Symbol dialog box for this exercise

6. Click OK to exit the dialog box. You will be placed in editing mode for the symbol. Click the Scene 1 button on the timeline to return to the main timeline.

7. Open your Library (Window ➤ Library) and drag an instance of Symbol anywhere onto the stage.

8. Test your movie by selecting Control ➤ Test Movie from the main menu.

In this example, you associated an external class file with a symbol in the Library. You can do this for any number of symbols, having instances of many different classes represented by instances in the Library. The components that come with Flash use this technique, with each component mapped to a class and its ActionScript file.

Now that you know about the different ways to use ActionScript, you may recall that I promised you a more complex example of an ActionScript project. As I'm never one to go back on my word, next you're going to create something that would be impossible to do in Flash without the help of ActionScript: random animation in the form of hundreds of balls bouncing around the screen.

Bouncing balls

Building a Flash movie with balls bouncing all over the screen is something of a rite of passage in the ActionScript world—everyone seems to build one at some stage to test coded animation and basic physics. It's a great way to see some ActionScript in action as you start out on your programming path.

As I mentioned at the beginning of the chapter, you shouldn't try to understand the code behind this example. I promise that by the time you've completed Chapter 5, you'll understand every single line of code, but for now, you'll have to trust me that the steps you follow will produce the desired result.

Figure 1-9 shows what we're going to produce. Unfortunately, a printed screenshot isn't the ideal medium for showing animation. Just think of these balls whizzing in random directions, and you'll get the idea.

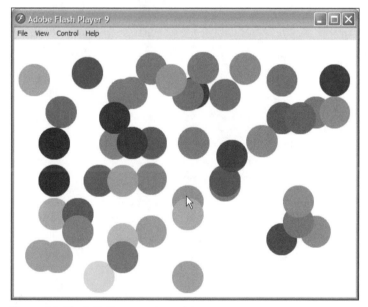

Figure 1-9. The balls they are a-bouncin'.

Without further ado, let's get cracking. You'll need Flash CS3 installed to play along, though Flex Builder users can find a Flex-tastic example in the downloadable files.

Creating the Flash file

As in the previous short examples, you begin by creating a Flash file.

1. Create a new Flash ActionScript 3.0 file and save it with the name bouncing.fla in the project directory.
2. Draw a filled circle on the stage with a diameter of roughly 50 pixels.

3. Using the Selection tool, select the circle and convert it to a symbol by selecting Modify ➤ Convert to Symbol from the main menu, or by pressing F8.

4. In the Convert to Symbol dialog box, give your symbol a name of **Ball**. Set the registration point to the center. Check the Export for ActionScript check box. Enter **Ball** in the Class field. You might need to switch to advanced mode by clicking the Advanced button to see all of the options. Your dialog box should match Figure 1-10.

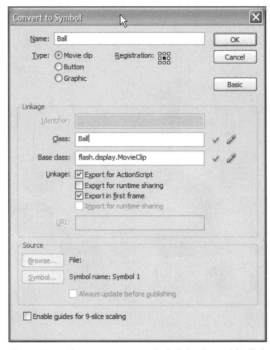

Figure 1-10. The Convert to Symbol dialog box with all the necessary fields filled in for the Ball class

5. Click the OK button. An ActionScript Class Warning dialog box will pop up, telling you that Flash couldn't find the class you have specified, and that a class will be generated for you when you publish your SWF, as shown in Figure 1-11.

Figure 1-11. This warning lets you know that no class was found and so one will be created behind the scenes upon compiling.

18

6. You know that the Ball class doesn't exist because you haven't created it yet, so it's safe to click OK and ignore the warning. Generally, it's better to create the class first before trying to associate a symbol with it, but there is no harm in creating the symbol first as long as you understand the warning.

7. Save the changes to your Flash file.

That's it for the Flash file for now. Next you need to create the Ball class that Flash was looking for and couldn't find.

Creating the Ball class

Ball is going to be an external class file. It will be similar in structure to the Document and Symbol classes you created earlier, but a little more complex since you want the ball to bounce around the screen and not just say "hello."

1. Create a new ActionScript file and save it with the name Ball.as in the project directory.

2. Enter the following code, which is the code that makes the ball bounce around the stage. Again, you don't need to understand it now, but by all means, read through it. ActionScript is quite readable for a programming language, and you don't necessarily need to understand it all to get a rough idea of what a particular piece of code is doing.

```
package {

    // Import necessary classes
    import flash.display.MovieClip;
    import flash.events.Event;
    import flash.geom.ColorTransform;
    import flash.geom.Rectangle;

    public class Ball extends MovieClip {

        // Horizontal speed and direction
        public  var speedX:int = 10;

        // Vertical speed and direction
        public var speedY:int = -10;

        // Constructor
        public function Ball() {
            addEventListener(Event.ENTER_FRAME, onEnterFrame);
            // Colors the ball a random color
            var colorTransform:ColorTransform = new ColorTransform();
            colorTransform.color = Math.random()*0xFFFFFF;
            transform.colorTransform = colorTransform;
        }

        // Called every frame
        private function onEnterFrame(event:Event):void {
```

```
// Move ball by appropriate amount
x += speedX;
y += speedY;

// Get boundary rectangle for ball
var bounds:Rectangle = getBounds(parent);

// Reverse horizontal direction if collided with left or right
// of stage.
if (bounds.left < 0 || bounds.right > stage.stageWidth) {
  speedX *= -1;
}

// Reverse vertical direction if collided with top or bottom
// of stage.
if (bounds.top < 0 || bounds.bottom > stage.stageHeight) {
  speedY *= -1;
}
      }

    }

  }
```

3. Save the changes to your ActionScript file.

4. Switch back to the bouncing.fla file in Flash CS3 and test your movie.

If everything has gone as planned, you should see the instance of the Ball symbol that is on the stage bouncing around, as in Figure 1-12. It might be a surprise to you to see the ball colored differently than what you created on the stage, but that is due to some code that colors the ball randomly when the movie starts (look for the lines with ColorTransform). If you do not see this or get an error, check your file against the Ball.as file included with this chapter's downloadable files.

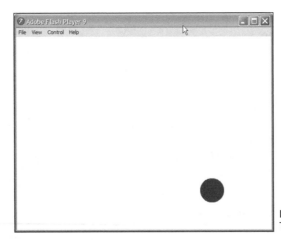

Figure 1-12.
The ball is bouncing.

You have one ball bouncing around the screen, but that's not exactly going to set the world on fire, is it? Let's scale it up.

Adding more balls

Your goal is to get 50 balls bouncing around the screen in random directions at random speeds. To do this, you first need to set up a document class for your bouncing.fla file. Then you'll create the Bouncing class so that it produces the Ball instances, places them at random points around the stage, and sets them off at random speeds and in random directions.

1. Switch back to the bouncing.fla file in Flash CS3 and save the file as multibounce.fla.
2. Delete the single instance of the Ball symbol from the stage. You're going to create all the balls using ActionScript, so you don't need anything on the stage for this example to work.
3. Create a new ActionScript file and save it with the name MultiBounce.as in the project directory.
4. Enter the following code. Again, feel free to look through and see if you can guess what might be going on here.

```
package {

    import flash.display.MovieClip;
    import flash.events.MouseEvent;

    public class MultiBounce extends MovieClip {

        // Number of balls to create
        private static const NUM_BALLS:uint = 50;

        // Constructor
        public function MultiBounce() {
            stage.addEventListener(MouseEvent.MOUSE_DOWN, onStageClick);
        }

        // Handler for when stage is clicked, creates balls
        private function onStageClick (pEvent:MouseEvent):void {
            stage.removeEventListener(MouseEvent.MOUSE_DOWN, onStageClick);
            // For each ball to be created
            for (var i:uint = 0; i < NUM_BALLS; i++) {
                // Create new Ball instance
                var ball:Ball = new Ball();

                // Places ball at mouse click
                ball.x = pEvent.stageX;
                ball.y = pEvent.stageY;

                // Specify random speed and direction
                ball.speedX = (Math.random() * 30) - 15;
                ball.speedY = (Math.random() * 30) - 15;
```

```
        // Add new Ball to stage
        addChild(ball);
      }
    }

  }

}
```

5. Save the changes to the MultiBounce.as file.

6. Switch back to the multibounce.fla file.

7. In the Property inspector, enter **MultiBounce** in the Document class field, as shown in Figure 1-13.

Figure 1-13. Setting the document class for the FLA

8. Save the changes to your Flash file.

9. Test your movie. The stage should initially be blank. Click the stage, and you should see 50 pretty little balls of different colors bouncing all over the stage (as in Figure 1-9).

There's much more you could have done with this example, but I didn't want the bells and whistles to get in the way just yet. What you did create, with only a little code, is a movie that required user interaction, then responded to that user interaction by creating and animating a large number of graphics that were positioned and colored through code.

ActionScript in action

I hope the bouncing balls example has done enough to convince you that reading the rest of this book will be worthwhile (or to buy this book if you're reading this in the "try-before-you-buy" public libraries that are Borders or Waterstones). But if it hasn't, here's a short list of just some of the cool things that you will be able to accomplish with a newfound knowledge of ActionScript:

- Websites that invite interaction
- Online video games
- Interactive banners
- Dynamic animation
- Complex visual effects
- RIAs (a *very* big category)

If you are using Flash and would like to create any of these, ActionScript is your ticket on the bus, so to speak. It is a necessary tool for any Flash developer, and, believe me, a lot of fun to play around with. In fact, I envy you a little the thrill of discovery of what can be done with ActionScript. I remember when I first started out and experimented with creating an animated star field that you could fly through. I stayed up all night working it out for myself and, in the end, it was exhilarating as I flew through the stars on my screen. Now if that isn't a metaphor that belongs in a book on learning code, I'm not sure what is!

Summary

This was a brief chapter, intended to give you an insight into what ActionScript is and what it can do. You learned the definition of ActionScript and had a brief look at its history. I explained how Flash CS3 and Flex 2 are related, and how both of them make use of ActionScript 3.0 to provide interactivity and advanced features. Finally, you created some very basic ActionScript code to demonstrate the various ways in which you can integrate ActionScript into your Flash projects.

You have already begun your journey toward becoming a full-fledged ActionScript developer. In the next chapter, you'll learn about the fundamental building blocks of the ActionScript 3.0 language. It's going to be a wild ride, so if you want to grab a coffee, be sure to put it in a mug that won't spill, then head on back to your computer and the book for some exciting chapters ahead.

Chapter 2

ACTIONSCRIPT 3.0 FUNDAMENTALS

Steve Webster with Todd Yard

This chapter covers how to:

- Store information in your projects using variables
- Choose the right data type for the information you need to store
- Create constants to store information that never changes
- Perform arithmetic and make decisions
- Perform a set of actions repeatedly using loops
- Separate common parts of code into functions
- Comment your code so that you and others know what it does

In this chapter, you will learn about the basic, fundamental building blocks of the ActionScript 3.0 language.

I'll warn you in advance that this chapter is probably the most challenging chapter in the whole book for new programmers, as there is a wealth of information covered, but it is also the single most important chapter if you're new to the ActionScript 3.0 language. The knowledge you pick up in this chapter will be used throughout the rest of the book and in every single project you work on as a fully fledged ActionScript developer. I'll try my best to make the process as fun and as light-hearted as possible, but you'll need to put in a bit of effort too.

> *If you've already dabbled with a bit of basic ActionScript 3.0, you might just want to skim this chapter or skip it completely. It'll always be here if you get stuck later on and need a little refresher.*

It might help to imagine that reading this chapter is like learning to walk. It will be hard work and even confusing at times, and you'll fall down occasionally, but once you've mastered the basics of walking you can go anywhere you want. Once you're mobile, you can then turn your attention to all the other fun stuff— like examining the contents of the cookie jar that was hitherto out of reach—and the hard slog will have been worthwhile.

Right, that's enough of the metaphors—on with the show!

Statements and expressions

Everything in ActionScript, and really, any programming language, can be broken down into **statements**. Just as a book is a series of sentences strung together, so too is a program a series of statements. Here is one statement in ActionScript:

```
var age:Number = 30;
```

Here is another:

```
trace(age);
```

And one more:

```
if ((year - age) < 2000) trace("You were born last millennium.");
```

All three of these look pretty different, but have a couple of things in common. First, and perhaps most obvious visually, is that they all are terminated with a semicolon. This is known in ActionScript as a **statement terminator** and lets the ActionScript compiler know that the statement is complete, just like a period at the end of a sentence. Although this is not necessarily required, it is good form, best practice, and from here on out we'll pretend it *is* a requirement as we present the examples. No one likes a sentence that doesn't end with the proper punctuation

The second common factor with the preceding statements is that they all form a complete command, or even a number of commands, like an instruction for ActionScript. The first line creates a number variable and gives it a value. The second line of code sends the value to be displayed in the Output panel in the Flash IDE or to the Console in Flex Builder. The third line of code traces a series of characters to the Output panel or the Console, but only if a certain condition is met. Don't worry about understanding any of this code at this time, just know that a statement is a complete instruction in ActionScript, and you're all set.

An expression, on the other hand, is not a complete instruction, but a value or values that can be evaluated to determine a single resultant value. For instance, three simple expressions follow:

```
true
1
"hello"
```

In these cases, since there is nothing more than a single value to evaluate, these expressions are unchanged upon evaluation, sort of like multiplying a number by 1. If more values are added to these expressions, though, the compiler must evaluate the series of values using the specified **operators** (more on those in a bit) to determine the resultant value.

```
true && false
1+1
"hello" + ", there"
```

Expressions can be as simple or as complex as you need them to be, but in the end, Flash will determine their single value upon evaluation. As a final example, consider the following lines:

```
var price1:Number = 55;
var price2:Number = 10 + 15 + 30;
```

In both of these cases, the expression to evaluate is on the right of the equals sign. In the first line, the expression is a single number, 55. This evaluates, unsurprisingly, to 55 and is assigned to the price1 variable on the left of the equals sign (variables and assigning values are in the next section—don't worry!). The second line is very similar to the first; it evaluates the expression to the right of the equals sign and assigns it to the price2 variable on the left, but in this case, the expression takes a little more evaluation. The numbers are added together before they are assigned to the variable. The end result is the same, with price2 getting assigned a value of 55.

If you understand the concept of statements and expressions, you're off to a great start, as these pieces will be involved in every bit of code you write from here on out.

Introducing variables

The next step on our journey is to take a look at the humble **variable**. If you've every written any kind of program before, you'll probably already know that a variable is a named container in which we can store information to be used at a later stage in the program. The type of information we can store in an individual variable is governed by the variable's assigned data type. If you didn't know that before, well, you do now.

Before we can store any information in a variable, we first have to create, or declare, it. Let's jump right in at the deep end and take a look at a variable declaration:

```
var bookTitle:String;
```

OK, that's not too scary, but what does it all mean?

We start with the var keyword, which tells ActionScript that you're about to create a new variable.

Next, we've got the variable name, or identifier, bookTitle, which is a unique name for this variable. We can use this identifier in future code to read or change the value of the variable. Note that ActionScript is a case-sensitive language, so booktitle and bookTitle would be two completely different variables. If the name looks altogether odd to you, squished together like that into a single word with odd capitalization, know that there are many ways you can name a variable as well as a few limitations and requirements. A section is coming up that dives more fully into naming conventions, so jump ahead if you need to, or just go with it for the next page or so and all your questions will be answered.

Finally, we have the data type of the variable, String, which is separated from the identifier by a colon character. When you specify a data type, you're telling Flash what kind of information can be stored in this variable. In this case, the variable is designed to hold String data, which is a character or sequence of characters such as a person's name, a stanza from a poem, or even the entire text of *War and Peace* if that's your bag. I'll talk more about data types in a few pages' time.

> *If you try to store a different type of information in this variable, such as a person's age, you would get an error when you try to publish your Flash movie. This is known as a compile-time error, which is the compiler's handy way of telling you something needs to be fixed in the code.*

Assigning a value to a variable

Now that we have a variable, we can assign it a value by writing the variable name, followed by a single equals sign, which is known as the **assignment operator**, and then the value.

```
var bookTitle:String;
bookTitle = "Foundation ActionScript 3.0";
```

This tells the Flash Player to take the string "Foundation ActionScript 3.0 " and store it in the bookTitle variable we created earlier. Simple.

Notice how the string value is enclosed in double quotes? This is how you tell that a particular sequence of characters is a **string literal** and not a bunch of program statements that it should try to make sense of and execute. You can actually use either single or double quotes; the only rule is that the closing quote must be the same as the opening quote.

A little trick you can use to cut down the number of lines of code in your ActionScript documents is to assign a value to a variable at the same time as creating it. Using this technique we can cut the previous example down to just a single line of code:

```
var bookTitle:String = "Foundation ActionScript 3.0";
```

Of course, this is only possible if the value is known at the time of the variable declaration. Not only does this require less typing than the previous example—the value of which is directly proportional to the amount of code you write, as you'll no doubt discover—but it's easier to understand. You know what the value of your variable is as soon as it is created, because you've explicitly told Flash what you want that value to be.

Retrieving the value of a variable

Once you've created a variable and given it a value, you'll want to be able to make use of that value at some point later in your code. Let's face it—if you couldn't use the value of a variable once it's been set then variables would be about as useful as a chocolate fireguard, and nowhere near as tasty.

Thankfully, you can get the value of a variable just by using its name in a statement. How that value is used depends on the nature of the statement in which it appears. This might seem a bit confusing, so let's look at an example:

```
var bookTitle:String = "Foundation ActionScript 3.0";
trace(bookTitle);
```

Here we've added one statement to our earlier example. You can see the bookTitle variable there, but I can almost hear you asking, "What's the trace stuff all about?" trace is the name of a function that is part of the Flash framework, and its sole purpose is to display information in the Output panel in the Flash IDE or the Console window in Flex Builder (from here on out we'll just refer to the Output panel for traces—readers who are testing in Flex Builder please assume that this refers to the Console in that application as well). I don't want to dwell on functions here (they're covered in more detail later in the chapter) except to say that they are reusable pieces of code that can be invoked using the name of the function followed by parentheses (or rounded brackets for those of you who didn't swallow a dictionary) passing the function any information it needs to do its thing within the parentheses.

To test this small fragment, the easiest thing to do is to put it directly in your timeline. However, since Flex users don't have a timeline, let's create a couple of files that use a Document class so that both Flash and Flex users can try out the code.

> *If you are using Flex Builder, you can follow along with these steps, except instead of creating a FLA and compiling through Flash you can create a new ActionScript project in Flex Builder and use the document class code that follows as the default application class. If you are uncertain how to create an ActionScript project in Flex Builder and test your applications, please consult the Flex Builder's documentation. I'll assume a similar proficiency for Flex users as we do for Flash users and concentrate not on the applications, but the ActionScript code.*

1. If you haven't created a project directory for Chapter 2, you should do so now. You can place this project directory in the same place where you stored the Chapter 1 project directory.

2. Create a new ActionScript file, and save it into the new Chapter 2 project directory as ActionScriptTest.as. Enter the following code:

```
package {

    import flash.display.MovieClip;

    public class ActionScriptTest extends MovieClip {

        public function ActionScriptTest() {
            init();
        }
```

```
   private function init():void {
     // chapter code will go here
   }

 }

}
```

For the rest of this chapter, you should be able to reuse this same file, just replacing the comments within the init() method. Don't yet know what comments or the init() method are? No worries (it is the beginning of the book, and we haven't covered that much!). That just means to replace the following line with the code presented in each section:

```
   // chapter code will go here
```

3. OK, for this first example, replace the comment line with the following bold code. Just this once, I will present the entirety of the code, but from here on out, you should know the section of code to replace in order to run these tests:

```
package {

  import flash.display.MovieClip;

  public class ActionScriptTest extend MovieClip {

    public function ActionScriptTest() {
      init();
    }

    private function init():void {
      var bookTitle:String = "Foundation ActionScript 3.0";
      trace(bookTitle);
    }

  }

}
```

4. Now, create a new Flash document, and save it as actionScriptTest.fla into the same directory as the ActionScript file. In the Property inspector for the document, add **ActionScriptTest** as the Document class, as shown in Figure 2-1.

Figure 2-1. Entering the document class for our test file

5. If you test your movie now, you should see the Output panel pop up with the name of this book, as shown in Figure 2-2.

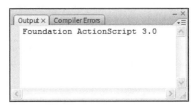

Figure 2-2.
A variable's value traced to the Output panel

Well done! You now can create a variable, set its value, and retrieve it again. Using variables is actually a major part of programming, so although this might seem fairly insignificant, it will be something you use over and over.

Naming your variables

Before you set off creating variables with careless abandon, I would be failing in my duty as your guide if I didn't talk to you about how to name your variables. There are three things you need to keep in mind when dreaming up names for the variables in your applications, one of which is required while the other two are recommendations born out of decades of experience from the entire development community.

The first thing to keep in mind is that ActionScript needs to understand what you've entered as a valid variable name. There are a few rules you should follow when constructing your variable names if you don't want Flash to throw an error and refuse to publish your movie.

A variable name must

- Consist only of letters, digits, the underscore character, and the dollar symbol
- Not start with a number
- Not be a reserved word
- Be unique

If you're wondering what a reserved word is, it's a name that has special meaning in the ActionScript 3.0 language, such as var or String. You can find a complete list of reserved words in Adobe's ActionScript documentation.

You should also make sure that your variable names bear some relation to the information that you intend on storing in them. If you're creating a variable to store the name of your favorite computer game, call it favoriteComputerGame and not thingamabob. You'll thank yourself for doing so when you come to update your code in four months' time and don't have to spend an hour trying to figure out what purpose a variable named doohickey might serve. Trust me; I've been there.

The final thing you need to consider is that your variable names should be consistent. ActionScript is a case-sensitive language, so currentbalance, currentBalance, and CURRENTBALANCE will refer to three different variables. What this means is that you should choose a naming convention for your variable names and stick to it throughout the project (if not across projects).

Although you're free to invent your own, there are many existing naming conventions, the most common of which (at least in the ActionScript world) is called **camel case**.

In camel case notation, the first letter of each word in a variable name is capitalized. When several words are joined together to make one variable name (and if you squint real hard) you get a camel-hump-like effect created by the capital letters:

    MyFavoriteColor

There is a variant to this where the first letter of the first word in a variable name is lowercase:

    myFavoriteColor

I'll be using this variant camel case notation for variable names throughout this book, as it is the most common form of notation for ActionScript developers and Flash and Flex themselves use this notation for their supported ActionScript classes, but feel free to pick your own style if you prefer something else. It doesn't matter which notation you use, so long as your use of that notation is consistent throughout your code.

> Many companies have an in-house coding standards document with a section on variable naming conventions that all developers should follow. This makes it easier for multiple developers to work on the same project without having to worry about which naming convention the other developers are using. If you're writing code within a company, see if it already has a designated naming convention.

Understanding data types

ActionScript 3.0 has a small number of basic data types—known as **primitive data types**—that you can choose from to store different types of information in your variables. All of the other more complex data types in ActionScript 3.0 are made up from these primitive data types, so we're going to spend some time discussing what they are and how they are used.

> In addition to the more complex data types (which you'll learn about as you work your way through the rest of this book), you can create your own data types from these primitive building blocks. If that sounds like fun to you, you're in luck, as that's one of the things we'll be looking at in the next chapter.

I've listed the primitive data types in Table 2-1, along with a description of the sort of information they are designed to represent.

Table 2-1. ActionScript 3.0 primitive data types

Data type	Represents
String	A single character or sequence of characters
Boolean	true or false values
int	Positive and negative whole numbers
uint	Positive whole numbers
Number	Positive and negative whole and real (i.e., fractional) numbers

> *If you're wondering why* int *and* uint *are all lowercase and the rest start with an uppercase letter, you'll have to spend some quality time reading the ECMAScript standard, which ActionScript complies with.* int *and* uint *are actually low-level numeric types that are a subtypes of* Integer *(which does not exist in ActionScript), and the lowercase denotes this and also follows syntax shared by other languages like Java, C++, and C#. Inconsistencies like this within the language seem designed to make our jobs harder, but thankfully, there are so few primitive data types that it's relatively easy to remember which ones start with a lowercase letter, and with code hinting and code completion there to help you out, most of the time you don't have to type them out fully anyway!*

We've already used the String data type, so I won't go over that one again, but the others are quite interesting so we'll spend some time looking at them in more detail.

Boolean data type

The Boolean data type is designed to represent values of either true or false. If you were to create an ActionScript program to simulate a room, whether the light in that room was on or off could probably be stored as a Boolean value (let's not dwell on dimmer switches for the moment).

```
var lightsOn:Boolean = true;
```

There isn't much more to say about Boolean variables, except that they are commonly used to make decisions in your code based on one of two states, as you'll discover later in the chapter.

Numeric data types

The ActionScript 3.0 language has three numeric data types: int, uint, and Number. ActionScript 2.0 only had the Number data type in which to store numerical data, something that was both a blessing and a curse. It was a blessing because you didn't have to worry about which numerical data type you should use, and a curse because its flexibility came at a cost: it used twice as much memory as neces-sary if all you wanted to store were whole numbers. Whether that was a real issue depended on how many variables you had in your code, but it always felt a little wasteful to me.

To counter this problem, ActionScript 3.0 introduced the int (short for "integer") and uint (short for "unsigned integer") data types, allowing you to create variables to store whole numbers without wast-ing memory. If you're creating a program to track how much money is in your bank account, you'll still have to use a Number variable to keep track of your balance, as the money will require two decimal places, but you might use a uint to store the number of transactions, as they will be whole numbers. Similarly, if you were creating a darts game, you would use int rather than Number variables to keep track of the scores.

Unfortunately, choosing the right data type isn't just about whether you want to store positive or negative numbers, or even whole or real numbers—it's also about how big a number you're trying to store.

In Table 2-2, you can see the minimum and maximum values that can be stored in the new integer data types.

Table 2-2. Minimum and maximum values for the integer data types

Data type	Minimum value	Maximum value
int	−2,147,483,648	2,147,483,647
uint	0	4,294,967,295

As you can see (well, if you do a little math in your head), both can store the same amount of num-bers, but whereas uint, being unsigned, stores only positive integers, int stores both positive and negative integers. The result is that the maximum number a uint can store is double that of an int, but it can't store negative numbers. This means that you'll have to choose wisely and be sure what val-ues you're going to have to store before deciding on the data type of a given variable.

> You might be wondering what happens if you try to store a negative number in a vari-able of type uint, or a real number in an int. If you are, get down with your inner geek and try it out—half the fun of learning something new is going off and experimenting.

What happens if you want to store a number higher than 4,294,967,295 or a negative number less than −2,147,483,648? You have to switch to using a Number variable instead. I've not listed the values for Number, since they're so gargantuan that I'd wear out the keyboard typing all the digits. If you really want to know the minimum and maximum values (and you dig scientific notation), enter the following lines of code into a new movie and see what you get in the Output panel:

```
trace("Minimum: " + Number.MIN_VALUE);
trace("Maximum: " + Number.MAX_VALUE);
```

If you give this a go, you'll see that Number can handle some seriously big numbers. If you're feeling lazy, imagine the number 179 with 305 zeroes after it (in both positive and negative directions), and you wouldn't be far off.

Having to store such a huge range of numbers, it's inevitable that the Number data type has at least one quirk, and this one's a doozy: 0.1 plus 0.2 will not equal 0.3, at least not exactly. Seemingly flying in the face of basic mathematics, 0.1 plus 0.2 will give you 0.300000000000004. The reason for this inaccuracy has to do with the way the information is represented in the computer's memory and has caused many developers to spend all night searching for bugs in their code. Don't think ill of ActionScript though; this problem plagues most modern programming languages including JavaScript, PHP, Python, and Ruby.

Constants

Constants are similar to variables in that they have an identifier, a type, and a value, but their value cannot be changed once they have been set. Constants are declared using the const keyword:

```
const DAYS_PER_WEEK:uint = 7;
```

As illustrated in the preceding line, it is an established convention that the names of constants are specified in all uppercase letters and words are separated with an underscore. This makes it easy to distinguish between constants and variables at a glance wherever they are used (it is also common convention to have constants be static properties of a class, but since I haven't covered classes or properties yet, I'll save elaborating on that until a later example).

Deciding what should be a constant and what should be a variable can sometimes be tricky, but generally, any value that is not to be changed at runtime and will be consistent throughout the life cycle of the application is a good candidate for a constant. Often, I might even separate this out further, keeping values that will always be the same each time a program is run as constants while making into variables those values that can change each time a program is run even though they are consistent during a single session. For instance, we know that DAYS_PER_WEEK in a calendar will always be seven (even if we display less), so that, I feel, would make a good constant. However, currentYear, even though it would be consistent through a single session (well, unless the program was run on New Year's Eve, but let's not quibble) would be better served as a variable value.

One common use for constants is to replace magic values in your code to aid readability, particularly if they are used in more than one place in your code. Magic values are hard-coded values within larger statements where the purpose of the value or how it was derived may not be immediately apparent. For example, take a look at the following code:

```
var totalAmount:Number = amount + (amount * 0.175);
```

This example performs some simple arithmetic (which we'll cover in a moment) to calculate the total cost for a hypothetical shopping basket full of goodies. You might be able to deduce that the number 0.175 represents the tax rate as a decimal fraction, but you'd only know that by looking at the whole statement. It's much better to replace this magic number with a constant:

```
const TAX_RATE:Number = 0.175;
var totalAmount:Number = amount + (amount * TAX_RATE);
```

Now that's much more readable. It also means that if we ever need to change the tax rate, we'd only have to change the line where the tax rate constant is defined, rather than having to search for every occurrence of our magic number.

Performing operations

No, you haven't accidentally replaced your ActionScript book with a medical text. Operations in programming are expressions evaluated using a set of common **operators**. You will be familiar with many of these operators from the world of mathematics, and their functionality remains mostly consistent with what you learned back in early schooling. Let's take a look at the common operators used for arithmetic before we take a look at some of the unique operator usage with programming.

Arithmetic operators

You've already seen a few examples of how to do basic arithmetic in the previous section. In ActionScript (or in fact in any programming language), the symbols used for arithmetic are referred to as **arithmetic operators**.

Table 2-3 describes the complete set of arithmetic operators in ActionScript 3.0.

Table 2-3. Basic arithmetic operators

Operator	Description
+	Addition
-	Subtraction
* (asterisk)	Multiplication
/	Division
%	Modulo

The function of most of these arithmetic operators should be familiar to you; even if the symbols are slightly different, they're essentially the same ones you learned to use at school when you were eight years old. Each of these operators requires two **operands** arranged in the following way:

[operand 1] [operator] [operand 2]

An example of each of the operators using the same operand values follows:

```
trace(10 + 4);
trace(10 - 4);
trace(10 * 4);
trace(10 / 4);
trace(10 % 4);
```

Test this code in a new Flash movie, and it will (rather unsurprisingly) give you the following in the Output panel:

```
14
6
40
2.5
2
```

> *The one that may seem a little quirky (and the one I hadn't heard of before I started programming) is the modulo operator. This operator gives you the remainder after the second operand has been divided into the first operand as many times as possible. In the preceding example, 4 goes into 10 twice with 2 left over, so the result of the expression is 2.*

Because each of these operators requires two operands, these are all known as **binary operators**. There are also **unary operators** (one operand) and even a **ternary operator** (three operands). We will discuss unary operators shortly, but we will leave the more complex ternary operator until later in this book, once you are more familiar with the basics.

You can string multiple arithmetic operators together to form complex expressions:

```
trace(10 / 2 * 5 + 4 % 3);
```

However, this can quickly become confusing as to which of part of the overall expression is evaluated first. The value in the Output panel after running the previous line of code is 26, but I bet that like me you'd have to work hard to figure out why just by looking at the expression itself. If you want to know what you can do about it, read on.

Specifying precedence

The order in which the arithmetic operators are evaluated is also the same as you probably learned in school. In the United Kingdom, they teach children the BODMAS acronym, which gives the order in which arithmetic operators should be evaluated: **B**rackets, **O**rders, **D**ivision/**M**ultiplication, **A**ddition/**S**ubtraction. In the United States, this is known as PEMDAS, which uses different terminology for the same thing: **P**arentheses, **E**xponents, **M**ultiplication/**D**ivision, **A**ddition/**S**ubtraction.

Why is this important? Well, it's important because ActionScript 3.0 follows the same basic rules when evaluating arithmetic expressions. This means that the following expression will actually evaluate to 15 and not 10 because division is evaluated before addition:

```
trace(10 + 10 / 2);
```

Thankfully in ActionScript, as in real-life arithmetic, you can use parentheses (or brackets) to explicitly specify the order in which the various arithmetic operators in the expression are evaluated.

```
trace((10 + 10) / 2);
```

In this case, it was necessary to use parentheses to get the desired result, but I would advise always using parentheses in your expressions, even if they would work as intended without them. Doing so makes it much easier to see what's going on without having to remember the proper evaluation order for the arithmetic operators.

Using our newfound knowledge of precedence and employing our goal of using parentheses to make precedence clear, we can rewrite the complex expression we met earlier to make it clearer:

```
trace(((10 / 2) * 5) + (4 % 3));
```

I don't know about you, but I can see exactly what's going on there now. 10 divided by 2 is 5, which when multiplied by 5 gives us 25. 4 modulo 3 is 1, which when added to the 25 gives us 26. Hurrah!

String operations

One of the arithmetic operators in the previous section is also used with strings (you may hear this referred to as the operator being "overloaded," meaning it has multiple functions based on its operands), so you might see the following in code.

```
var fullName:String = "John " + "Doe";
```

Here, the plus sign is use to join together, or **concatenate**, two strings to form a single string, which is then assigned to the fullName variable. This string functionality is unique to the plus operator—you cannot use the other arithmetic operators with strings, such as trying to subtract one string from another.

Unary operations

Table 2-4. Unary operators

Operator	Description
!	Logical negation
-	Negative
+	Positive
++	Increment
--	Decrement

As stated earlier, a unary operation involves a single operand, not the two operands as used with the arithmetic operators. The most common unary operators are listed in Table 2-4.

The two you are probably familiar with are the positive and negative operators. The negative operator will change positive values to negative and negative values to positive, as demonstrated in the following example.

```
var number:int = 10;
trace(number);
number = -number;
trace(number);
number = -number;
trace(number);
```

This produces the result:

```
10
-10
10
```

The positive operator, which is equivalent to multiplying a number by positive one, does not really have much effect in its operations and is more useful in making code more legible by specifying clearly that a number is positive.

Another unary operator that is often used is the **logical negation** operator (!). This operator works with Boolean values and, similar to how the negative operator works with numbers, causes true values to become false and false values to become true. When is this useful? Often, you might have Boolean variables or functions named based on positive assertions, like isSignedIn or editAllowed(). It makes more sense logically when reading code to have these positive assertions as opposed to negative assertions (isNotSignedIn, for instance). However, if you needed to check whether someone wasn't signed in before performing some necessary action, the easiest way to determine this is to use the logical negation operator on the isSignedIn variable. We will look into this more when we cover conditional statements later in this chapter, but the basic syntax follows:

```
if ( !isSignedIn ) {
  statements
}
```

This can be read as, "If the user is *not* signed in, run these statements."

The other unary operators listed above include the **increment** and the **decrement** operators. These are most useful in loops, so we will leave their discussion until that coming section.

Introducing arrays

Variables and constants are all well and good, but sometimes the information you need to store is better organized in an Array object. An Array is one of the more complex data types I mentioned earlier, and it is designed to store sequential information in a more convenient fashion than using a series of variables. An example may help to make this clear.

Suppose you were creating an address book application and you needed to store the names of all your contacts. You could create several variables—contactName1, contactName2, contactName3, and so on—but you would need to know how many entries there will be in the address book in advance, so you could create the correct number of variables. Instead of going through all that pain, we could use an Array to store all the contact names in a single variable, where each individual contact was kept separate but accessible. So contactName might be an array, or list, of values, and we could then use special Array syntax to retrieve individual contacts from this list.

If you are still having some trouble understanding what an array is, it might help to imagine an array as a filing cabinet where you can only store one item in each drawer.

Imagine that each drawer in this filing cabinet holds the information about one of our contacts (OK, so we collect a *lot* of data on our contacts—we're paranoid). So although we have multiple contacts, the data for all of these contacts is stored in single filing cabinet. If we wanted to refer to the collection of contacts, we could point to the filing cabinet as a single entity and say, "That is our collection of contacts." But if we needed information on a single contact within that collection, we could refer to a single drawer and access that information.

Figure 2-3. An array is like a filing cabinet that stores something in each drawer.

There are several ways you can create an Array object. The simplest is to use the Array constructor using the new operator.

```
var myArray:Array = new Array();
```

The new operator is something you will become familiar with very quickly, as it is the way to create almost any type of ActionScript object. You simply place it before the name of the object you wish to create an instance of followed by parentheses (this is actually a class's constructor, but we'll get to that next chapter) and—voilà!—you get your object.

You can also pass some values within the parentheses (called parameters) to give special instructions to or populate your array. For instance, if you pass in a number this tells the array that it will be of a certain length, meaning that it will contain a certain number of items in its list.

```
// an array with five "slots" ready to hold data
var myArray:Array = new Array(5);
```

If you pass in something other than a number or if you pass in more than one value, these will be the initial values stored in the array.

```
// an array holding a single string initially
var charArray:Array = new Array("one");

// an array holding five numbers
var numArray:Array = new Array(5, 23, 35, 52, 100);
```

The way we most often create an array, though, is by using an **array literal**, which is a comma-separated list of values enclosed in square brackets:

```
var myArray:Array = [value1, value2, value3, ... valueN];
```

Continuing our contacts collection example, creating an array to hold contact names might look like this:

```
var contactNames:Array = ["Rod", "Jane", "Freddy"];
```

If you want to find out the contents of an array, you can just pass it to the trace() function:

```
var contactNames:Array = ["Rod", "Jane", "Freddy"];
trace(contactNames);
```

This will give you a comma-separated list of all the values in the array:

```
Rod,Jane,Freddy
```

You can also tell how many values are in the array using the Array object's length property. I'll talk more about objects and their properties in the next chapter, so don't worry if this is confusing. All you need to know is that objects can have properties, which are like preassigned variables specific to the object, and you access the properties of an object using dot notation. To get the property of an object, you specify the name of the object, followed by a period, followed by name of the property.

If we work this into our example, we can find out how many elements are in the contactNames array:

```
var contactNames:Array = ["Rod", "Jane", "Freddy"];
trace(contactNames.length);
```

The values in an array are stored sequentially, by number, with the first value at index 0, the next at index 1, and so on. You can read the individual values from an array using subscript notation, which is a fancy way of saying you put the index of the desired value between square brackets after the variable name. Using subscript notation, we could change the previous example to output only the second contact name in the address book:

```
var contactNames:Array = ["Rod", "Jane", "Freddy"];
trace(contactNames[1]);
```

If you test the preceding code, you should see Jane in the Output panel. If you were expecting to see Rod, remember that the index of an Array object starts at zero—in geek parlance, Array objects are **zero indexed**.

Manipulating arrays

One of the benefits of arrays over sequentially named variables is that an array can store a nearly unlimited number of values. Once you have created an array, you can update or add a value using subscript notation in the same way you would set a normal variable's value.

For example, if we wanted to update Rod's name to Rodney we could do this:

```
var contactNames:Array = ["Rod", "Jane", "Freddy"];
contactNames[0] = "Rodney";
trace(contactNames);
```

Running the preceding code would now produce the following in the Output panel:

```
Rodney,Jane,Freddy
```

Adding a value to the array is also easy to do. Actually, you have several ways to add a new value to an array: you can do so using subscript notation, or you can use one of the Array object's many insertion methods, one of the easiest to use being the push() method, which adds the value to the end of the array. For our contactNames example, this means that the following two statements are identical:

```
contactNames[3] = "Bungle";
contactNames.push("Bungle");
```

Either of the preceding statements will result in the string Bungle being added as the fourth element in the contactNames array.

```
var contactNames:Array = ["Rod", "Jane", "Freddy"];
trace(contactNames);
contactNames.push("Bungle");
trace(contactNames);
```

So that's how you update existing values and add new ones to an array, but how do you remove them? Again, you have several choices, depending on your desired result. If you simply want to clear a value in an array, you can use the delete keyword:

```
var contactNames:Array = ["Rod", "Jane", "Freddy"];
trace(contactNames);
delete contactNames[1];
trace(contactNames);
```

If you trace the value of the contactNames variable after using the delete keyword on one of its elements, you'll get the following in the Output panel:

```
Rod,Jane.Freddy
Rod,,Freddy
```

Pay very close attention to this output—notice that although Jane has been deleted, there is still a place reserved for her in the array as indicated by the two commas between Rod and Freddy in the output. So delete clears a value, but leaves its place in the array.

If you want to obliterate Jane completely (poor Jane—what did she ever do to you?), the easiest way is to use the splice() method of the Array object. This method removes a number of items from the specified position in the array and (optionally, though we won't be using it in this case) inserts one or more values in their place.

If we replace the delete statement with a call to the splice() method instead, we can completely remove Jane from our contactNames array:

```
var contactNames:Array = ["Rod", "Jane", "Freddy"];
trace(contactNames);
contactNames.splice(1,1);
trace(contactNames);
```

This can be read in English as "starting at index 1, remove one element from the contactNames array," and that's exactly what it does.

Running our example will now produce the following result in the Output panel:

```
Rod,Jane,Freddy
Rod,Freddy
```

There, Jane's completely gone. I don't know what she did to fall out of favor with you, but it's now as though you tore the page from your address book rather than just scribbling her details out. Remind me not to get on your bad side.

That's just about all you need to know about arrays for the moment. There are quite a few more methods for manipulation, if you care to peruse the ActionScript documentation, but we'll introduce these as we need them for our examples. If you can't get enough, the good news is that we'll be revisiting them shortly when we look at looping a little later in the chapter. Loops and arrays go together like birds of a feather, or something like that anyway.

Making decisions

Up until this point, all the code you've written has been of a sequential nature—program statements that execute one after another until the end of the code is reached. In your ActionScript projects, there will be points at which you want to decide to do either one thing or another based on some condition. For example, if a user accidentally has entered his age as 234 instead of something more sensible like 23, you'd want to show him a nice error message (or ask him what the secret to longevity is).

To allow for this kind of scenario, we need to be able to make decisions in our projects, and thankfully, ActionScript provides a number of solutions to this problem: the decision-making, or **conditional**, statements.

Introducing the if statement

The simplest conditional statement in ActionScript is the if statement. Similar to its namesake in the English language, you can use the if statement to qualify that a particular block of ActionScript is only executed if a given condition is true.

An if statement takes the following form:

```
if (condition) {
  statements
}
```

If the condition (which is a Boolean expression) evaluates to true, the statements inside the following block will be executed. If not, they'll be skipped. The code block is determined by the opening and closing curly braces, if there are multiple lines of code to be run within the conditional. Fancy an example?

```
trace("Before");
if (true) {
  trace("Condition is true");
}
trace("After");
```

If you enter the preceding example and then run it, you'll get the following in the Output panel:

```
Before
Condition is true
After
```

The condition portion of the if statement evaluated to true, so the trace() statement within was executed.

> In practice, the condition of an if statement is more complex than the example shown previously. We'll look at how to build more complex condition expressions later in the chapter.

If we now change the example so that the condition evaluates to false:

```
trace("Before");
if (false) {
  trace("Condition is true");
}
trace("After");
```

we can see that the trace() statement within the if statement is skipped:

```
Before
After
```

We can spice things up a bit by adding an else block to the if statement. The else block tacks into the end of the closing brace of the if statement like this:

```
if (condition) {
  statements
} else {
  statements
}
```

The statements in the else block are only executed if the condition in the if statement is false. If we incorporate this into the previous example, we can have a nice message in the Output panel either way:

```
trace("Before");
if (false) {
  trace("Condition is true");
} else {
  trace("Condition is false");
}
trace("After");
```

This produces the following output:

```
Before
Condition is false
After
```

Now, I've cheated slightly with the preceding examples by hard-coding either true or false. The real power of the if statement becomes apparent when you use a Boolean expression in the condition.

Forming Boolean expressions

A Boolean expression is one that evaluates to either true or false. Indeed, the keywords true and false are themselves the simplest form of Boolean expressions. More complex Boolean expressions are formed using conditional or equality operators. Table 2-5 contains a list of the most common.

Like the arithmetic operators we saw earlier, these operators require an operand on either side:

```
[operand] [operator] [operand]
```

Table 2-5. Common conditional and equality operators

Operator	Description
==	Is equal to
!=	Is not equal to
<	Is less than
>	Is greater than
<=	Is less than or equal to
>=	Is greater than or equal to

Each of them compares the left operand against the right operand to produce either a true or false answer.

```
10 > 4
```

The preceding line could be read as "10 is greater than 4." A Boolean expression could be either true or false (in this case it is true). The great thing is that Flash takes care of determining whether the expression is true or false. So an expression (20 < 10) (which can be read "20 is less than 10") is evaluated by Flash to be false. So in the following lines of code, the variable canBuy is set to true, since Flash will determine that the price is less than the cash:

```
var cash:Number = 20;
var price:Number = 5;
var canBuy:Boolean = (price < cash);
```

The expression on the right of the last line, (price < cash) is evaluated to be (5 < 20), which is further evaluated by Flash to be a true statement, so a value of true is assigned to the variable canBuy.

Let's see an example of all the operators in action:

```
trace(10 == 4);
trace(10 != 4);
trace(10 < 4);
trace(10 > 4);
trace(10 <= 4);
trace(10 >= 4);
```

This will produce the following output. If you're unsure as to why a particular expression evaluates to true or false, try reading each expression aloud, replacing the operator with the description from Table 2-5.

```
false
true
false
true
false
true
```

One operator to definitely watch out for is the equality operator (==). This is how you check to see if one value is equal to another. This should not be (but often is) confused with the assignment operator (=) which you have already seen in action when assigning values to variables. Where this really can bite you is within a line that you expect to be true or false by using the equality operator, but you instead assign a value, as in the following example:

```
var age:Number = 30;
if (age = 16) {
  trace("You can drive a car (legally)!");
}
trace(age);
```

Although you might think that the contents within the if block would be skipped and the age would be traced as 30, what actually happens here is that the expression (age = 16) evaluates to (16) since 16 is first assigned to the age variable using the assignment operator, then the resulting value of age is evaluated. Any nonzero number will evaluate to true within a conditional, so the end result is that not only will age be assigned a new value, but the contents of the if block will be run. Bad news! (Thankfully, Flash will give you a warning when you do this.) The lesson here is to always be aware of the difference between the equality operator and the assignment operator.

Booleans in conditionals

Earlier, I mentioned that we might want to show a polite error message if the user has entered an impossible value for their age. In more concrete terms, we would like to show an error message if the age entered is greater than 130. To do this we need to construct a Boolean expression to test this, and then plug that into an if statement. Looking at the list of operators available, we can see that one of them fits our needs perfectly:

```
var age:uint = 159;
if (age > 130) {
  trace("I think you made a mistake");
}
```

Running the preceding example, you should see that the expression evaluates to true and the trace() statement is executed:

```
I think you made a mistake
```

Now that we can see Boolean expressions working in conditional statements, we can add just a little more to your conditional repertoire, as it were. You already know that you can follow an if conditional with an else. But you should also know that you can nest if statements within any other code block, including other conditionals. For instance, see if you can follow the logic in the following example:

```
var language:String = "ActionScript";
if (language == "Java") {
  trace("You need a Java book!");
} else {
  if (language == "ActionScript") {
    trace("You're in the right place!");
  } else {
    trace("I don't know what you're reading.");
  }
}
```

Notice here that within the else we have put another if else conditional. This can continue on to be as nested as you need. In the preceding example, though, we can actually employ another conditional variant, which is the if else if. The following lines have the same result as the ones from the previous example:

```
var language:String = "ActionScript";
if (language == "Java") {
  trace("You need a Java book!");
} else if (language == "ActionScript") {
  trace("You're in the right place!");
} else {
  trace("I don't know what you're reading.");
}
```

Even though the last two examples have the same result, it is important to note the difference. When you have an `if else` statement, at least one of conditional code blocks will be run, since if the first `if` condition evaluates to `false`, the `else` block will run. However, with an `if else if` statement, a block will only be run if its conditional is met, which makes it possible that *neither* block could be run.

Sometimes, nesting of conditionals is necessary; sometimes, a series of `if else if` statements will work; sometimes, you need a combination of both—it all depends on what you need to accomplish with the conditions at that point in your code. There's also a handy little structure called the `switch` statement that will also handle conditionals, but we'll roll that out when we need it later in the book (I'm throwing enough at you as it is!).

Using Boolean operators

You can form more complex Boolean expressions by logically joining them together using Boolean operators, which are listed in Table 2-6.

Table 2-6. Boolean operators

Operator	Description
&&	AND. Evaluates to `true` if both operands are true, otherwise evaluates to `false`.
||	OR. Evaluates to `true` if either operand is true, otherwise evaluates to `false`.

Using these Boolean operators, you can join together two or more Boolean expressions to form a larger Boolean expression.

For example, let's say that you wanted to go to the movies, but only if you had enough money, weren't working, and had someone to go with. The conditions under which you would go to the movies could be written as a Boolean expression using English like this:

```
have enough money AND not working AND have company
```

This can be translated into ActionScript simply if we assume that we have Boolean variables defined for each part of the decision:

```
haveEnoughMoney && notWorking && haveCompany
```

We can then plug this expression into an if statement to see whether we can go to the movies:

```
var haveEnoughMoney:Boolean = true;
var notWorking:Boolean = true;
var haveCompany:Boolean = true;

if (haveEnoughMoney && notWorking && haveCompany) {
  trace("Go to the movies");
} else {
  trace("Go another time");
}
```

You can only go to the movies if all three parts of the Boolean expression evaluate to true.

We can also revise the expression to say that you might consider going to the movies on your own, but only if the film is really good. In English this would be:

have enough money AND not working AND either have company OR good movie

Translated to ActionScript, this looks like:

haveEnoughMoney && notWorking && (haveCompany || goodMovie)

Working this into our example, we get this:

```
var haveEnoughMoney:Boolean = true;
var notWorking:Boolean = true;
var haveCompany:Boolean = false;
var goodMovie:Boolean = true;

if (haveEnoughMoney && notWorking && (haveCompany || goodMovie)) {
  trace("Go to the movies");
} else {
  trace("Go another time");
}
```

Now, we can go to the movies so long as both haveEnoughMoney and notWorking are true, and one or both of haveCompany or goodMovie are true.

Looping the loop

So far, we've had to manually type out every single line of ActionScript that we wanted to be executed. If I were to ask you right now to write some code that would output the numbers 1 to 5 to the Output panel, you'd probably come up with something like this:

```
trace(1);
trace(2);
trace(3);
trace(4);
trace(5);
```

This would do the job as adequately as any other solution I could come up with, but it's not the most efficient method. Imagine if, instead of 1 to 5, I had asked you to output 1 to 1000 to the Output panel. Assuming you didn't ignore me completely (and I wouldn't blame you if you did) it would take you a while to write out all the individual trace() commands.

Thankfully, programming languages have the concept of loops to take away a lot of the tedium, and ActionScript is no different. Loops allow you to define a series of actions that will be performed again and again as long as a given condition is met.

ActionScript 3.0 has three basic looping statements: while, do . . . while and for, which we'll look at individually in a moment. If you're wondering why it's necessary to have three different ways of repeatedly executing a block of statements, the answer is that they each work in a slightly different way. This means that sometimes a while loop would be a better choice than a for loop, or a do . . . while loop better than a while loop.

The while loop

The first stop on our whirlwind tour of looping constructs is the humble while loop. At first glance, the while loop looks remarkably similar to the if statement we met earlier:

```
while (condition) {
   statements
}
```

The similarity is no accident. The while loop, like the if statement, has a condition that is tested to see if it evaluates to true. If it does, the statements within the loop are executed repeatedly, with the condition being checked again at the start of each iteration of the loop. If the condition ever evaluates to false, the loop is exited and execution continues with any statements that appear after the while loop.

To a while loop, the business of printing out a series of numbers is but a moment's work:

```
var number:uint = 1;
while (number <= 1000) {
   trace(number);
   number = number + 1;
}
```

It's important to note that the condition for the while loop is checked at the start of each iteration. Like the if statement, the condition portion of the while will be evaluated, and the statements within the while loop will only be executed if the condition evaluates to true. The statements within the while loop will be executed repeatedly until the condition evaluates to false.

Where the while loop differs from the if statement is that the statements within the while loop will be executed repeatedly while the condition evaluates to true, as opposed to only once.

> It stands to reason that if the condition always evaluates to `true`, the statements in the loop will run forever. However, like a petulant child, the Flash Player will get bored after 15 seconds stuck in one loop and ask the user if they want to halt the movie, which is a good thing since nothing will appear to be happening in the movie while the loop is infinitely running—no animation will be occurring, and no interaction will be allowed as Flash continues to evaluate the condition as `true` and run the loop.
>
> It goes without saying that you should avoid this at all costs. if you need to have code run continually within your movie, there are better ways to handle this, such as `Timers` and `onEnterFrame` handlers, both of which we will discuss later in the book.

The condition of a while loop is evaluated at the start of each iteration. This means that if the condition initially evaluates to `false`, the statements within the loop will never be executed. In other words, the statements in a while loop will be executed *zero or more* times depending on the condition.

Let's look once more at the while loop that was just presented, with a slight alteration, that will trace the numbers 1 to 1000 and break down exactly what is happening. Try out this code in a Flash movie:

```
var number:uint = 1;
while (number <= 1000) {
  trace(number);
  number++;
}
```

Here, we first declare a uint variable named number and initialize it with the value of 1. We then set as a condition in our while loop that as long as number holds a value that is less than or equal to 1000, we should trace its current value to the Output panel, then add 1 to its value. At this point, the loop's contents are complete, and the condition is tested once more. If number is still less than or equal to 1000, the loop's contents are run yet again.

Running the preceding example would give you the following in the Output panel:

```
1
1
2
3
...
998
999
1000
```

There—the same result and much better than 1000 lines of code!

> In the preceding example, the number variable is often referred to as the **loop control variable**, because it alone controls when the loop stops. You don't always have a single loop control variable—your conditions may be made up of complex Boolean expressions such that no one variable controls the loop.

No doubt you noticed the slight alteration of the last line of the while loop code block. What's up with the odd ++ notation? This is known as the **increment operator**, which you might recall from the earlier discussion on unary operations; it simply adds 1 to the value of the variable specified and assigns this new value back to the variable. It is the equivalent of writing the following (which it replaced in our example):

```
number = number + 1;
```

As you can see, though, it is the same result with less code and actually (as you program more) is easier to read. There are two ways to use the increment operator, postfix and prefix, meaning the operator can appear either after or before the variable. Each produces slightly different results, as the following should demonstrate:

```
var postfix:uint = 1;
trace( postfix++ );
trace( "postfix is now:", postfix );

var prefix:uint = 1;
trace( ++prefix );
trace( "prefix is now:", prefix );
```

The lines result in the following output:

```
1
postfix is now: 2
2
prefix is now: 2
```

The first trace of the first block uses a postfix increment, which increments the postfix variable *after* it has been evaluated in its current expression. This means that the value of 1 will be traced the Output panel, since that is the current value of postfix, and only then will be the postfix value be incremented.

The first trace of the second block uses the prefix increment, which first increments the variable *before* it is used in its expression. The result in this case is that 2 is traced to the Output panel. In both cases, though, you can see that the next time each variable is accessed it has its new value.

You will get a lot of mileage out of this operator, as well as from its companion, the decrement operator, which uses a double minus sign postfix-- or --prefix. One place these are used most often? Loops! In fact, we can make our number tracing routine with fewer lines if we take even more advantage of this operator:

```
var number:uint = 1;
while(number <= 1000) {
  trace( number++ );
}
```

The while loop is often used when there is a condition to be met that is not easily managed by a fixed set of iterations but is more variable in nature. If a condition could be true for one iteration, or a thousand iterations, and this will all be determined by the contents of the loop, then this would probably call for a while statement. I often use while loops to determine the nesting of objects in an application. For instance, to step through all of the parent `DisplayObjects` of a movie clip named `myClip`, you might use a loop like the following one:

```
var clip:DisplayObject = myClip;
var parentClip:DisplayObject = clip.parent;
while (parentClip != null) {
  trace(parentClip.name);
  parentClip = parentClip.parent;
}
```

As long as the parent object is not null, Flash will trace its name to the Output panel, then check to see if there is a parent higher up the display list hierarchy. The loop will continue to run until there are no more parent objects left, which occurs once the stage is reached, which has no parent, being at the top of the display list.

The do . . . while loop

There is a variation of the while loop called the do . . . while loop:

```
do {
  statements
} while (condition);
```

This is exactly the same as the while loop except that the condition is evaluated at the end of each iteration rather than at the beginning. What this means in practice is that the statements in the loop are always executed at least once, even if the condition initially evaluates to false:

```
do {
  trace("Hello");
} while (false);
```

To prove that the while and do . . . while loops are basically the same, you can rewrite the previous number-counting example as a do . . . while loop instead:

```
var number:uint = 1;
do {
  trace(number++);
} while (number <= 1000);
```

All we've really done here is to move the furniture about a bit and add a nice new side table in the form of the do keyword, and in this case, it hasn't made a single difference to the output. In your code, you should be aware of the subtle difference between while and do . . . while loops and use the appropriate one for your needs. Remember, while will give you zero or more iterations; do . . . while will give you one or more, so do . . . while should be used in place of while when you need to ensure the contents of the loop run at least one time.

The for loop

The Grand Poobah of all the loop statements is the for loop, of which there are a few varieties. The most commonly used allows you to initialize your loop control variable, specify the loop condition, and perform some action after every iteration all in a single statement. It's like one of those multi slice 'n' dice, bash and baste kitchen tools they're always trying to peddle on the late-night shopping channels.

The for loop looks like this:

```
for (initializer; condition; action) {
    statements
}
```

The initializer statement is executed only once before we start looping. Next, the condition is checked. If this evaluates to true then the statements in the body of the for loop are executed. The action statement is executed at the end of each iteration, after which the next iteration begins by evaluating the condition again.

Like the while loop, the for loop evaluates the condition at the start of each iteration. You would use a for loop when you are counting through a finite range of something, like the number of characters in a string or the number of elements in an Array.

Using the for loop, we could rewrite our previous example like this:

```
for (var number:uint = 1; number <= 1000; number++) {
    trace(number);
}
```

If you look closely, you can see that the various statements have shifted around but they're all there, and we get exactly the same output in the Output panel:

```
1
2
3
...
998
999
1000
```

Looping through an array

The for loop is particularly handy for looping through all of the values in an Array object. Actually, any of the loop statements would work, but the for loop was designed specifically to loop through sequences such as the elements in an array.

Recall earlier that we created an array to hold the names of all the contacts in an imaginary address book. If we wanted to say hello to each of those contacts, we could write out a trace() statement for each of the contacts, but that would be both a waste of time and a code maintenance nightmare if we had 100 contacts in the address book.

Instead of messing around with 100 trace() statements, we could use a for loop to go over each of the contacts in the contactNames array starting at index 0 and ending once we've processed the last one. We know how many entries are in the address book by looking at the value of contactNames.length, so we now have all the information we need to create a for loop:

```
var contactNames:Array = ["Rod", "Jane", "Freddy"];
var numContacts:uint = contactNames.length;
for (var i:uint = 0; i < numContacts; i++) {
  trace("Hello " + contactNames[i]);
}
```

When you're using this loop, it doesn't matter how many or few contacts you have in the address book—everyone gets a nice friendly greeting:

```
Hello Rod
Hello Jane
Hello Freddy
```

> One item to point out is that we are storing the length of the array in numContacts variables before the looping begins. It is important to remember that the condition statement of the for loop is run each iteration of the loop, so if you have any complex evaluation that occurs each iteration, that can slow things down. Now, retrieving the length of an array each iteration isn't necessarily complex, but if you have a lot of loops and very long arrays, there can be a noticeable difference in your loops' execution, as Flash has to look up the value each iteration. It's therefore best to store things like an array's length in a variable before the loop begins.

As you put arrays to work in your projects, you'll find that they go hand-in-hand with for loops. Like its very own stalker, wherever there's an array, a for loop is never far away.

More for loops

In addition to the for loop discussed previously, there are two variations, the for in loop and the for each loop. These loops are used primarily for looping through all the elements in a complex object. We will discuss these loops more later in the book as we work more with such objects, but their basic syntax is presented here:

```
for (var element:String in object) {
  trace( object[element] );
}

for each (var element:Object in object) {
  trace( element );
}
```

Breaking out of a loop

There are two basic ways to break out of a loop. One is the return statement, and it has more to do with functions than with loops, so we will leave it to the next section. The most common way to exit a loop prematurely (i.e., before all iterations have been completed) is through the use of the break statement. Executing this at any point of a loop will end any further iterations and exit the loop. This is often used when some condition within the loop has been met and it is determined that further iterations are no longer needed. For instance, if you had an array of movie clips named clips and you needed to find the clip named myClip, you could set up a for loop to iterate through an array, then exit the array once the clip has been found:

```
var clip:MovieClip;
var numClips:uint = clips.length;
for (var i:uint = 0; i < numClips; i++) {
  if (clips[i].name == "myClip") {
    clip = clips[i];
    break;
  }
}
```

Once the clip was found, no other loop iterations would be necessary, so you could break out of the loop.

A related command is continue, which causes a loop to immediately exit its current iteration and go to the next iteration. This is useful if, for instance, you were looping through an array and wanted to perform operations on only a single type of value but skip other types of value. Consider the following example:

```
var integers:Array = [1, 5, -3, 5, 2, -1];
var numIntegers:uint = integers.length;
for (var i:uint = 0; i < numIntegers; i++) {
  if (integers[i] < 0) {
    continue;
  }
  // perform complex operations only on positive values
}
```

Here, the continue statement causes the loop to continue to its next iteration every time a negative number in the array is detected. Positive numbers would not cause the loop iteration to exit and would have some complex operations (not defined here) performed on them.

Introducing functions

At the very beginning of this chapter, we used the trace() function to send the value of a variable to the Output panel. I told you that a function was a reusable piece of code, and the good news is that you're not restricted to the functions built into the Flash framework—you can actually create your own.

You'll have realized by now that I'm rather fond of analogies, so indulge me while I rattle off another one. I'm forever losing my keys. I seem to find new and increasingly creative places to leave them, like in a flowerpot or on top of the mirrored cabinet in the bathroom for example. I could solve this problem by having 100 keys cut and placing them at strategic locations all over my apartment, and that would work just fine until I had to change the key (if I had to have the locks changed, for example.) I'd then have to have 100 copies made of the new key and go hunting around my apartment until I had found and replaced all copies of the old key—not how I want to spend my weekend.

A much better solution would be to buy a key hook and always hang my keys there when I come in. I could then place post-it notes all over the apartment reminding me that my keys are now hung on the back of the door. If I need to change the keys, I just change the one set hanging on the back of the door. The post-it notes can stay, because they only point me in the direction of my single set of keys.

Functions in your programs serve the same purpose. They collect together functionality that is repeated throughout your code under a name of your choosing and can then be used wherever necessary. If you ever need to change the functionality, all you need to do is update the code in your function.

Before you can make use of a function, you have to create it. A simple function definition takes the following form:

```
function functionName():returnType {
    statements;
}
```

In the preceding example, functionName is your unique name for the function, returnType is the data type of whatever is returned by the function (which could be nothing—more on that in a bit) and contained within the curly braces is the list of ActionScript statements that will be executed whenever the function is called. When deciding on a name for your function, you need to respect the same rules as when defining a variable. A function name must

- Consist only of letters, digits, the underscore character, and the dollar symbol
- Not start with a number
- Not be a reserved word
- Be unique

Also, similar to variable names, your function names should reflect what the function does and follow some kind of convention to keep your naming consistent. To keep things simple, we'll be using modified camel case notation for both function and variable names, which is exactly what ActionScript's built-in functions use.

> For the remainder of the examples in this chapter, we will no longer be able to use the document class file to test our code (that is, if you have been using it and not just placing code directly in the timeline). This is because, as we introduce functions, it is easier to test the code directly in the timeline and not have to worry about some of the more complex issues such as scope and modifiers that would be required to test using a class file. We will cover these issues next chapter and will return to using a document then, but for now, you should create a new Flash file and enter all following code directly on the timeline. Flex users can follow along in the text, but Flex versions of the code will not be presented. Unfortunately, with Flex, any exploration of functions is automatically an exploration of objects and classes, and that is a subject presented in the next chapter.

Creating a function

Let's say that there are several places in our code where we want to output the numbers 1 to 10 in the Output panel. Forgetting the fact that you're unlikely to ever want to do this in a production project (stuff in the Output panel is only visible when viewing the SWF in the Flash IDE), you'd create a function something like this:

```
function countToTen():void {
  for (var i:uint = 1; i <= 10; i++) {
    trace(i);
  }
}
```

> Remember, this code should now go directly in your timeline, not a separate class file.

You could then call this function using the function name followed by parentheses (much like we did with trace()) wherever you need to in your code instead of copying and pasting the for loop several times:

```
trace("The numbers 1 to 10...");
countToTen();
trace("... again...");
countToTen();
trace("... and again...");
countToTen();
```

Now what the heck is that void that we have specified as a return type for our countToTen() function? Read on, young grasshopper!

Returning a value from a function

You can break all functions down into two groups, really: those that are supposed to return a value and those that are not. Our countToTen() function is a good example of the latter, where it simply performs some action but does not return any value to the place in the code from where the function was called. We can call (or **invoke**) the function and let it run its course. In such cases, you must specify void as the return type for the function to let Flash know that the function is not intended to return any value.

If a function *is* supposed to return a value to the place in the code from where the function was called, then the function needs to include the return keyword followed by the data being returned:

```
return data;
```

What exactly is meant by "return a value"? Well, you have seen a function invoked without any values returned (countToTen()). When a function *does* return a value, at runtime, it is as if the call to the function is replaced with the value returned by the function. For instance, if we had a function named getDayOfWeek() that returned the name of the current day of the week, the call to the function might appear as follows in our code;

```
var day:String = getDayOfWeek();
```

If, when the movie is run, the getDayOfWeek() function determines that it is Tuesday and returns that value as a string, then it is as if the line becomes the following at runtime:

```
var day:String = "Tuesday";
```

If a function is to return any data, when you create the function the data type for that data needs to be specified in the declaration. Take, for example, the following code, which contains a function to format the user's name:

```
var firstName:String = "John";
var lastName:String = "Doe";

function getFullName():String {
  var fullName:String = firstName + " " + lastName;
  return fullName;
}

var userName:String = getFullName();
trace(userName);
```

The getFullName() function has been given the return type of String. Inside the function, we create a string variable and assign the combined values of the firstName and lastName variables created outside the function. This new variable, fullName, is then *returned* out of the function using the return keyword back to the place in the code from where the function was called.

Because the getFullName() function has a String return type, we can assign the result of this function to a new variable, userName, that is typed as String as well. If username had been declared as a Number, Flash would throw a compile-time error, and we would know that something was wrong, that we had tried to assign a string to a variable that was intended to hold a number.

Now, the return keyword does not necessarily have to appear at the end of a function and can be used to exit a function at any point. For instance, if you had a conditional within the function that returned different data based on the condition, you might have multiple return statements. This is often used when performing checks for validity before performing a function's actions and works well because no further code in a function is run after a return statement is executed. Let's look at an example of when and how this might be used:

```
var firstName:String;
var lastName:String;

function getFullName():String {
  var fullName:String = firstName + " " + lastName;
  return fullName;
}

var fullName:String = getFullName();
trace("name is: ", fullName);
```

We have modified our previous example so that no values are assigned to the firstName and lastName variables. If you test this movie now, you will see that the name is traced as null null. That isn't right! What has happened is that a String variable, if undefined, will become null within any expression. We need to account for the fact that these variables might be undefined and return an empty string (no characters) from the function in that case.

This can be accomplished by combining a number of things we have covered in this chapter: conditionals, Boolean operations, logical negation, and the return statement. Try adding the following bold code to the previous example:

```
var firstName:String;
var lastName:String;

function getFullName():String {
  if (!firstName || !lastName) {
    return "";
  }
  var fullName:String = firstName + " " + lastName;
  return fullName;
}

var fullName:String = getFullName();
trace("name is: ", fullName);
firstName = "John";
lastName = "Doe";
fullName = getFullName();
trace("name is: ", fullName);
```

The first line in the function is now a conditional statement that checks to see if there are values assigned to the firstName or lastName variables. Any variable that is defined (and is not the number 0) will be evaluated as true within a Boolean expression, so placing the logical negation operator before a variable results in true only if the variable is *not* defined. To make it clearer, the preceding conditional could be expressed in English, "If either the firstName variable is NOT defined OR the lastName variable is NOT defined, then run these statements." So if either variable is undefined, the contents of the if block are run.

Now, what exactly happens in the if block? Since we know that either one or both of the variables are undefined, there is no need to concatenate the values as that will return null null within the string, so instead, we use the return keyword to exit the function by returning an empty string. Once the return statement is run, the function is exited and *no further code is run*. This is an important point, as it allows you to exit the function when necessary while ensuring that further code is not executed.

If you want to exit a function that does not have a return type, you can use the return keyword by itself without any data following it. Take the following as an example:

```
var firstName:String;
var lastName:String;

function traceFullName():void {
  if (!firstName || !lastName) {
```

```
      return;
    }
    trace(firstName + " " + lastName);
}

traceFullName();
firstName = "John";
lastName = "Doe";
traceFullName();
```

Using function parameters

If we want our function to make use of values from outside of the function definition, we can pass these values in, and in order to do so, we need to tell Flash what kind of information the function expects to be passed when the function is called.

You define the parameters (or **arguments**) for a function by placing them between the parentheses in the function definition. We can see how this fits into the overall function definition:

```
function functionName(parameters):returnType {
  statements;
}
```

The list of parameters is comma-separated, and each parameter has a name and a data type separated by a colon. If that sounds familiar, it's because it's very similar to how you define a variable, and that's no accident—within the body of your function, the parameters are just extra variables that you can use in the statements to perform some task or other.

Let's try an example, overhauling our earlier countToTen() function to count from 1 to a maximum number that we specify as a parameter:

```
function countTo(max:uint):void {
  for (var i:uint = 1; i <= max; i++) {
    trace(i);
  }
}
```

We can now use our countTo() function to count from 1 to any number by passing that number in as part of the function call. You know how to do this already, because we've been doing it with the trace() function: you specify the value you want to pass to the function between the parentheses in the function call—

```
countTo(5);
countTo(10);
```

Note that the max parameter is now required—you have to give the parameter a value when you're calling the function or else Flash will tell you that you haven't specified the correct number of arguments for the countTo() function. Sometimes this is undesirable, which is where default values for function parameters come in.

Providing a default value for function parameters

As we've seen, having to always pass a value for every parameter defined in the function definition isn't always desirable. Sometimes, you want to specify that particular parameters are optional and, if they are not given a value when the function is called, that they should adopt a predefined default value.

Let's suppose we needed to modify our countTo() function to count up to the specified maximum number but allow the starting number to optionally be specified when calling the function. If no starting value is specified the function should start counting from 1:

```
function countTo(max:uint, min:uint = 1):void {
  for (var i:uint = min; i <= max; i++) {
    trace(i);
  }
}

countTo(5);
countTo(10);
```

We can run the preceding example without changing the function calls, because the second parameter, min, is optional and defaults to 1 if no value was specified. However, we can tell the second call to start counting from 6 by specifying the additional parameter value:

```
countTo(10, 6);
```

One thing to be mindful of is that, although you can have as many optional parameters as you like, they can only appear at the end of the parameter list. The compiler will throw an error if you try to publish a Flash movie containing a function that has an optional parameter listed before a regular parameter in the parameter list.

Allowing for variable parameters

Because the number of arguments and their types need to be defined in the function definition (or **signature**, which consists of the function name, arguments, and return type), there is special syntax that must be used if you require functions to have a variable number of parameters passed in. When might you need such functionality? One example might be a sum() function, which adds any number of values and returns their sum. To create a function such as this that could accept any number of parameters, you would require the ...(rest) parameter. Adding these three dots, like an ellipsis, to your function definition tells Flash that from that point on in the function parameters, any number of values may be passed in. Each of those values is then placed into a single array that can be accessed using the name specified after the ...(rest) notation. Let's take a look at how that sum() function might be written with this syntax:

```
function sum(...operands):Number {
  var numOperands:uint = operands.length;
  var total:Number = 0;
  for (var i:uint = 0; i < numOperands; i++) {
    total = total + operands[i];
  }
```

```
    return total;
}

trace(sum(1, 2, 3));
trace(sum(5, 10));
```

In our function definition we have specified, by using the ...(rest) syntax, that there may be any number of parameters passed in. However many this may be, they are placed into an array that we can reference using the name operands (because that is how we have defined it—any name could be used). Within the function, we determine the number of operands using the Array.length property, and use a for loop to iterate through all of the array's elements, adding each value to the total. This total is returned from the function. The end result, as demonstrated by the two trace() statements, is that we can call sum() using different numbers of parameters without any errors.

One thing I'd like to introduce at this point is a shorthand way of taking a variable's value, altering it, and reassigning it to the same variable. This was done in the last example with the following line:

```
total = total + operands[i];
```

Here, the value of total was taken and added to the value of the current operand, and the result was placed back into total. Whenever such an operation occurs, the shorthand way of writing the exact same thing is:

```
total += operands[i];
```

When an arithmetic operator is followed by the assignment operator, the variable to the left of the operators has its value operated upon along with the operand to the right of the operators, with the calculated result assigned directly back to the variable. Here are a few more examples to help demonstrate.

```
var number:uint = 2;
number += 5; // results in 7 now being assigned to number
number -= 3; // results in 4 now being assigned to number
number *= 2; // results in 8 now being assigned to number
```

The same operation can be used with the concatenation operator (+) with strings:

```
var name:String = "John";
name += " Doe"; // results in name now holding "John Doe"
```

You will see this syntax a lot in code, and we will be using it from here on out in the text.

Passing values and references

One very important item to discuss, and one that is a frequent stumbling block for new programmers, is the difference between passing variables by value and passing variables by reference. As a rule, any variable containing a primitive data type, such as numbers, strings, and Boolean values, will only pass its value, but no reference to itself, while a complex data type, like an array, will pass its reference. The easiest way to present this, before discussing it in relation to functions, is to look at simple variable assignment.

Take as an example the following code:

```
var original:uint = 1;
var copy:uint = original;
trace( original, copy );  // outputs 1 1
original = 2;
trace( original, copy );  // outputs 2 1
```

Here, a variable original is initialized and assigned the value of 1. A second variable, copy, is then initialized and given the value of original. Tracing these values produces the expected result 1 1. On the next line, the value of original is changed to 2, and when both are traced again, the result is 2 1. As you can see, although the original variable's value was changed, it had no effect on the copy variable. This is because when the value was initially assigned to copy, no *reference* to original was made, only its *value* was retrieved and stored in copy. No connection is ever made between original and copy, so the value of either can change without any effect on the other.

With arrays and other complex objects, it is not the value that is passed, but rather a reference to the place in memory where the object is stored. Altering the variable then alters the object in memory that the variable was pointing to, which means altering one variable alters all others that reference the same object. That's a pretty heady concept, so it's definitely time for an example:

```
var original:Array = [1, 2, 3];
var copy:Array = original;
trace( original );  // outputs 1,2,3
trace( copy );  // outputs 1,2,3
original[1] = 50;
trace( original );  // outputs 1,50,3
trace( copy );  // outputs 1,50,3
```

We have a similar setup to our last example. The variable original is initialized and assigned an array of three values. copy is then assigned the value of original. At this point, original and copy are just pointing to the *same place* in memory. When these arrays are traced, the result is that both output 1,2,3. We then change the value of the second index in original and trace out both variables once more. Since both variables point to a single array, altering one alters the other as well, or, more precisely, altering one alters the array stored in memory, so that when each variable is sent to the trace method, Flash looks up the current value of the array and outputs it. In both cases, the value output is 1,50,3.

So a variable with a primitive data type is passed by value and a variable with a complex data type is passed by reference. How does this apply to functions? Well, if a variable with a primitive data type is passed to a function, only its value is passed into the body of the function. Altering that value inside the function will have no effect on the original variable. Consider the following example:

```
function square(operand:Number):Number {
  return (operand * operand);
}

var number:Number = 5;
trace( square(number) );  // outputs 25
trace( number );  // outputs 5
```

The function square() takes a single operand and returns the product of that number multiplied by itself. Our first trace() statement outputs 25, as expected. The second trace() statement outputs 5, the original value of number, since *the variable is unchanged by the function*. This is because for a variable containing a primitive value, like a number, only the value is passed to the function. The function can do whatever it likes to the value without any effect on the original variable. This is the same for strings and Boolean values as well.

If you wanted to change the value of number based on the results of the function, then you would need to assign the returned value to number after the function is invoked, as in the following (which uses exactly the same function as previously):

```
var number:Number = 5;
number = square(number);
trace(number);  // outputs 25
```

In this case, the number variable is assigned the result of the square() function performed on number, so tracing its value after the fact produces 25.

Things change a bit when dealing with complex objects, such as arrays. In the case of arrays (which is the only complex object we've dealt with so far), the array is passed by reference to the function, and so it is the reference to the array in memory that exists within the body of the function. Altering any value in this reference alters the array and so will alter any other references to the array that exist. Take a look at the following code, which demonstrates the effect:

```
function doubleAllValues(array:Array):void {
  var numItems:uint = array.length;
  for (var i:uint = 0; i < numItems; i++) {
    array[i] *= 2;
  }
}

var myArray:Array = [1, 2, 3];
trace(myArray);  // outputs 1,2,3
doubleAllValues(myArray);
trace(myArray);  // outputs 2,4,6
```

Here, we create a function doubleAllValues(), which iterates through an array and doubles the value stored in each index. To test this, we create a new array with the values 1,2,3 (which our trace() statement verifies). We then pass this array to the doubleAllValues() function. When we trace the array a second time, we find the values are now 2,4,6, since these values were altered within the body of the function. This is the result of having passed the array by reference.

Function scope

The last item to address at this time concerning functions is that of function scope. This is another issue that often causes frustration with new programmers. All of our use of variables thus far has been within the scope of our main timeline. In the cases of our examples, we have not had to worry about whether variables existed within the scope of a function since, for us, all variables have been available. This is not always the case, however.

Variables are only accessible within the scope in which they were declared. Each function, actually, has its own scope. That means that *any variable that is declared within a function is only accessible within that function*. We refer to this as a **local** variable. Once the function completes, the variable will no longer exist. Take, for example, the following:

```
function createVariable():void {
  var myVariable:uint = 5;
}
createVariable();
trace(myVariable);
```

If you try to run this code, you will get a compile-time error that states "Access of undefined property myVariable." This is because we are trying to access a variable that has only been defined within the scope of the createVariable() function. It is only within this function that the variable is initialized and assigned a value. Once the function completes, the scope of the function is terminated, and the variable is no more. Attempting to access it outside of the scope in which it existed causes the error. If we alter the code slightly, we get something that will compile:

```
function createVariable():void {
  myVariable = 5;
}
var myVariable:uint;
createVariable();
trace(myVariable);  // outputs 5
```

Since now we have declared the variable outside of the scope of the function on the main timeline, we no longer get the error. Because the createVariable() function exists within the scope of the main timeline as well, it has access to all of the variables declared on the main timeline, which includes myVariable.

What happens if we initialize a variable within one scope (a function, perhaps) that already exists in another scope (like the main timeline)? Let's take a look:

```
function createVariable():void {
  var myVariable:uint = 5;
  trace("inside function:", myVariable);
}
var myVariable:uint = 10;
createVariable();
trace("main timeline: ", myVariable);
```

The output of these lines follows:

```
inside function: 5
main timeline: 10
```

In this code, we are assigning a value (10) to myVariable on the main timeline. However, within the function, we are also creating a myVariable and assigning it a value of 5. The trace() inside the function results in 5 being output. The trace() on the main timeline outputs 10. This is because, within the function, the locally declared myVariable takes precedence over any declared outside of the function's scope. Back on the main timeline, the value of 10 is traced out, because the myVariable that existed locally within the function's scope was destroyed when the function was completed—the main timeline does not have access to any variables that were created within the scope of the function.

Taking this a step further, since local variables within a function are destroyed upon completion of a function, it follows that if you want a value to persist between calls to a function, it must therefore be declared *outside* of the function, as demonstrated in the following:

```
function buy(price:Number):void {
  total += price;
}
var total:uint = 0;
buy(1.25);
buy(5.50);
buy(10.75);
trace(total);   // outputs 16
```

Only because we have declared total outside of the scope of the buy() function can we continue to add to it each time the function is called.

Commenting your code

Before we leave this chapter, I want to talk to you about comments.

Comments in a block of program code are there to help you, the developer, and the people you work with, understand what a particular block of code is intended to do and can even be used to generate helpful documentation. This may sound odd at first; surely, it's the computer that needs to understand what the code does. You already know what it does, because you wrote it. Well, that may be true when you're writing the code, but will you remember what it's supposed to do tomorrow, or next week, or next month when you have to come back and modify it? Maybe, if you've got a brain like Albert Einstein, but the chances are that you will have moved on to new projects and won't remember a darn thing. Or worse, someone else can come onto a project after you have left and have no idea what your intention was with the uncommented code, which slows down development and can give you a bad reputation as the original author of the code.

Take it from me, you don't want to have to trawl through 500 plus lines of ActionScript code on a Monday morning to try to work out exactly what it was you or someone else was trying to do.

There are two types of comments in ActionScript 3.0: the **line comment** and the **block comment**. The line comment, as its name might suggest, creates a comment that spans a single line in your code. A line comment starts with a double forward slash, //, and ends at the end of the line:

```
// Hello, I am a line comment, and I eat peanut butter on toast for breakfast.
```

A block comment can span multiple lines. It starts with a forward slash followed by an asterisk, /*, and ends with an asterisk followed by a forward slash, */:

```
/* Hello, I am a block comment,
    and I eat line comments for breakfast */
```

Comments can be inserted almost anywhere in your code: at the start of the file, between two lines of code, on the same line as a piece of code, at the end of the file—wherever you like. The exceptions to this rule are that you can't have a comment in a string literal, because the comment is interpreted as part of the string, and you can't have a block comment within another block comment.

In addition to helping you understand your code, comments can also be used to temporarily disable parts of your code. When code appears within a comment, either after a line comment marker on the same line or between block comment delimiters, that code will not be executed by the Flash Player.

Bad vs. good comments

Given the previous commenting advice, you would be forgiven for thinking that peppering your code with as many comments as you can is a good idea. However, comments are only useful if they tell you more than a quick glance at the code would and even then only so long as they remain up to date. For example, take the following snippet of code:

```
// Set matchFound to false
var matchFound:Boolean = false;
```

The line of code in the snippet creates a new Boolean variable named matchFound and sets its initial value to false. The comment above the line of code tells you exactly the same information, and a comment like that is no good to anyone and just bloats the code. Comments should generally be at a higher level of abstraction than the code. That is, they shouldn't attempt to tell you how something will be done but why it is being done. A better comment for the previous line might be

```
// Assume that no match has been found
var matchFound:Boolean = false;
```

Now the comment tells you why the matchFound variable is being set to false, something that wasn't necessarily easy to glean from looking at the line of code itself.

Also, beware of comments that become incorrect because the code around them has been updated. There's nothing more confusing than to read a comment and assume that a block of code does one thing when, in fact, it does the complete opposite:

```
// Assume that no match has been found
var matchFound:Boolean = true;
```

When you modify your code, be sure to keep the comments updated too.

Commenting for documentation

One great result of having comments in your code is that, if done with the proper syntax, those comments can be used to generate documentation. Adobe has ASDoc, a command line tool that ships with the free Flex 2 Software Development Kit (SDK) and can be used to generate documentation from code files that use a special comment syntax. As an example of the syntax, one of our functions might have the following comments:

```
/**
* This function takes a single numeric operand
* and returns the value squared.
*
* @param operand The number to square.
*
* @returns The squared value of the specified number.
*/
function square(operand:Number):Number {
  return (operand * operand);
}
```

An ASDoc comment will begin with the notation /** and end with a closing */. Within the comment block, in addition to a description placed at the top (which can use HTML formatting), there are a number of tags that you can use that contain special meaning. For instance, the tag @param is used to describe any parameters that are to be passed to a function. The @returns tag is used to describe what is returned from a function. By placing these in front of data you let the ASDoc tool know how to place the comments within the documentation.

There is a lot more to know about ASDoc, not only additional tags but also how to run the command line tool in order to generate the documentation, but it is all covered in Adobe's documentation and is beyond the scope of this book. I present it here because it is a fairly standard way to comment code (even outside the ActionScript world), and you will undoubtedly come across such syntax as you program more. Commenting in a similar fashion is certainly a good habit to get into as you begin to program.

Summary

I've covered a monumental amount of ground in this chapter, so if you're still with me give yourself a hearty pat on the back. I feel like a particularly cruel drill sergeant putting you through this so early on, but now the basics are behind you, we're almost ready to start having some serious fun.

In this chapter, we've looked at the very basic building blocks of the ActionScript language, from variables to constants, loops to functions and beyond. Along the way, I've tried to dispense what I know about best coding practices so that you're not only writing code that works, but so that it's code you can maintain when you come back to it in six months' time.

A lot of the examples were necessarily contrived so as not to let too much get in the way. If some of the concepts are still a bit fuzzy in your head, I advise that you carry on regardless, skipping back here if any of the basic concepts continue to be a bit blurry.

That's the good news. The bad news is that we've got one more brain-busting chapter to go before we get to the really cool stuff, and it's a real doozy. Unless you're eager to get going, I'd suggest you give yourself a bit of a breather before carrying on. Go out into the big wide world and take a few gulps of good, old-fashioned fresh air to clear your head. One of the biggest mistakes you can make when learning a new subject is to try and force your brain to digest too much information in one go, and the next chapter on objects and classes in ActionScript is particularly important—I need your brain to suck it up like a sponge.

See you in Chapter 3 when you're ready.

Chapter 3

OBJECTS AND CLASSES

Steve Webster with Todd Yard

This chapter covers the how to:

- Create objects and access properties.
- Use the dynamic Object object.
- Loop over objects.
- Create a custom class and its methods and properties.
- Define constructors and getter/setter methods.
- Use packages and access modifiers.
- Take advantage inheritance and override methods.

Now that you have an understanding of the fundamentals of the ActionScript world, we can move on to looking at objects and classes. This is another of those important topics that needs to be covered before we can get to the really fun stuff.

In the real world, objects are all around us. As I sit writing this, I can see many objects: a glass, a television, a light switch and (my most favorite object of them all) a shiny new MacBook Pro—I was going to add my wife to the list, but then we'd get into the whole "men see women as objects" debate and I'd end up sleeping in the sofa again. Nevertheless, the fact remains that we live in a world full of objects.

Likewise, the ActionScript world is full of objects. It may not have glasses or televisions, but it does have movie clips, text fields, sounds, and many more. Pretty much everything other than a primitive value that you can stuff in a variable in ActionScript is an object. We describe languages that support this model as being **object oriented**.

There's more to object-oriented programming in ActionScript 3.0 than mere objects. By the time you're done with this chapter, your head will be buzzing with keywords: class, method, property, inheritance, and many more. If this list of keywords doesn't scare you, you're a far braver person than I was when I first started learning about object-oriented programming. I thought I'd never get all this stuff to stay in my head, until one day one of my lecturers explained object-oriented terminology in a way that I could understand by relating it to everyday life. What follows isn't an exact replica of that story—unfortunately my university days predated the iPod by more than a few years—but hopefully it'll serve the same purpose.

The iPod analogy

I'm a certified Apple addict. In addition to my MacBook Pro and Mac Mini, I own an iPod and an iPod Shuffle, and by the time this book is published I'll probably have snapped up a shiny new iPod Nano and iPhone.

Taking my regular iPod as an example, it fits our definition of an object perfectly: it contains data (the list of tracks, the volume level, etc.), and it can perform actions based on that data (play a particular track, upload a new track, etc). If my iPod was an ActionScript object, the various bits of data I've mentioned would be the **properties** of that object. The properties of an object are unique to that—if my wife uploads a new Robbie Williams track to her iPod, the contents of my music library are left blissfully intact.

The actions my iPod can perform—play, pause, add a new track—would be the **methods** of the object. All other objects of the same type share these methods, but they operate on the unique properties that each individual object has.

Somewhere in the world, there is a factory churning out the myriad iPod models that tempt us to spend our hard-earned cash. Each iPod is created according to a blueprint, defining what properties a particular model of iPod has (along with their factory default values) and what actions it can perform. Using a blueprint means that my iPod looks and works the same way as every other iPod of the same model and has the same set of configurable options, which I can use to make my iPod unique. The blueprint given to the factory is a **class**, which is then used to create each individual IPod object, or **instance**.

Of course, there are lots of different iPod models on the market. I'm not talking about different capacities or colors (I'd consider those to be different property values for a single iPod model rather than separate models) but about the different generations of the iPod, iPod Shuffle, and iPod Nano, which have significantly different features or functionality. Despite all these different models, they all share certain characteristics and functionality, probably using much of the same code, which is defined by a master iPod blueprint or class that every model of iPod extends. This is known as **inheritance** (yes, just as you might inherit your granny's nose of your grandfather's eyes).

As much as I'm addicted to all things Apple, I fully acknowledge that they aren't the only brand of portable music player in the world. All music players can have a library of tracks they can play, pause, and skip, and in that regard, one music player is pretty much the same as any other, even if they don't share any of the same basic code. In this case, we could say that all music player manufacturers agree that their devices will have certain properties and be able to perform certain actions, and that they'll even use the same symbol for those actions (play, pause, etc.) so that you can pick up any music player and use it without having to know who created it or how it was written. We can do the same in the ActionScript world using **interfaces**.

Working with objects

Before you get your hands dirty and create your first class, I want to dwell slightly on the subject of objects. As I said earlier, everything in ActionScript 3.0 is an object—you may not have realized it, but you were creating new objects in every single example in the previous chapter. We touched on this briefly in the section on arrays, where I told you that an array is really an object and that it has a length property that tells you how many values the array contains, and we used this to loop over all the values in an array and do something useful with them.

In this case, Array is a class, and we were creating new instances of this class using array literals, which consist of a comma-separated list of values enclosed in square brackets:

```
var myFavoriteFoods:Array = ["curry", "pizza", "pineapple"];
```

Here, we're creating a new instance of the Array class with the string values curry, pizza, and pineapple and then storing this object in the myFavoriteFoods variable. The new Array instance has all the characteristics and functionality defined by the Array class, which includes a length property and methods like splice() and join().

However, there are only a few built-in classes that you can create instances of using special literal notation. If you want to create instances of other classes in the Flash framework, or classes that you've created yourself, you'll need to get familiar with the new operator.

Creating objects using the new operator

You can use the new operator in conjunction with a class's constructor to create a new object of that type (or an instance of that class, in geek-speak). A **constructor** for a class always has the same name as the class itself and is the function used to create instances. Taking the previous Array example, we can replace the array literal with an object created using the new operator:

```
var myFavoriteFoods:Array = new Array("curry", "pizza", "pineapple");
```

The results of this are exactly the same as the previous example: a new Array instance containing three elements with the specified values. You can also apply the same technique to String objects, which we've created thus far using string literals:

```
var bookTitle:String = new String("Foundation ActionScript 3.0");
```

In both these cases, the technique you choose is a matter of personal preference as much as anything else. Some developers will tell you that their way is the one true way, but as long as you're consistent, it doesn't really matter which one you choose.

> *There is one important caveat to this piece of advice: when creating an* Array *object using the* new *operator, the number and type of the parameters you provide can affect the nature of the array you get back. If you pass in a single numeric value, you will get a new* Array *object with that number of empty elements, rather than an* Array *object with a single element with the specified value. This can lead to hours of frustration and head scratching unless a kindly author takes the time to warn you in advance. My advice would be to always use array literals unless you're creating an empty array or a certain number of empty elements.*

What's important here is that you can use this technique to create instances of any ActionScript 3.0 class, whether they're part of the Flash framework or ones you've created yourself.

Accessing properties and calling methods

I briefly touched on accessing properties and calling methods of an object using dot notation in the previous chapter (when we were talking about Array objects), and to be totally truthful, there really isn't much more to know. For completeness, though, I want to go through the motions.

The properties and methods of an object can be accessed using dot notation. You specify the name of the variable in which the object is stored, followed by a dot, followed by the name of the property you want to access or the method you want to call.

Let's take a String as an example, since it's one you're already familiar with from the previous chapter. String objects have lots of properties or methods, but we're going to concentrate on just two: the length property and the indexOf() method.

The length property of a String object gives you the number of characters that make up the string. Using this property, you might loop through all the characters in a string and output them using the trace() function:

```
var bookTitle:String = new String("Foundation ActionScript 3.0");
var titleLength:uint = bookTitle.length;
for (var i:uint = 0; i < titleLength; i++) {
  trace("Character " + i + ":  " + bookTitle.charAt(i));
}
```

The example above creates a String object and then loops through all the characters in that string using a for loop, outputting each character along with its index. Notice that we're using bookTitle.length to loop through the string, so no matter how long the string is we're sure to process all the characters.

If you enter the code above into the first frame of a Flash movie and run it, you should see the following in the Output panel:

```
Character 0:   F
Character 1:   o
Character 2:   u
Character 3:   n
Character 4:   d
...
Character 22:  t
Character 23:
Character 24:  3
Character 25:  .
Character 26:  0
```

If you look closely at the code from the preceding example, you'll see that we're using a method of the bookTitle String object, charAt(), to get the character at a specified index.

> *The built-in classes in the Flash framework have lots of properties and methods, so I'm not going to attempt to go through them all here—that's a job for a much thicker (and much less entertaining) ActionScript 3.0 reference book.*

Copying objects

In the last chapter, we discussed passing objects by value versus passing objects by reference in relation to arrays. Remember that primitive objects (numbers, strings, Booleans) are passed by value, while complex objects like arrays are passed by reference. For example, if we have two variables of type Number and we copy a value from one to the other, subsequent changes to one of those values will not affect the other one:

```
var num1:Number = 256;
var num2:Number = num1;
trace(num1 + " vs " + num2); // 256 vs 256
num2 = num2 / 2;
trace(num1 + " vs " + num2); // 256 vs 128
```

This is true of all the primitive data types we examined in the previous chapter.

However, complex data types, such as an Array or an object derived from a custom class, are passed by reference, so multiple variables can be pointing to the same object in memory and changes through one variable will affect all other variables pointing to the same object. This is most evident when you try to create a copy of a complex object in the same way you would a primitive value.

```
var array1:Array = new Array("one","two","three");
var array2:Array = array1;
trace(array1 + " vs " + array2); // one,two,three vs one,two,three
array2[3] = "four";
trace(array1 + " vs " + array2); // one,two,three,four vs one,two,three,four
```

From the preceding example, you can see that, although in the code it looks as though we were only adding "four" to array2, it appeared in array1 as well, since both variables point to the same array in memory.

If we really want to create a copy of an Array object, the quickest way is to use the Array object's slice() method. The slice() method creates a new Array object based on an existing array. If you pass in parameters, it can copy a subset of the array, but if you don't pass any parameters, you'll just get a copy of the entire Array object.

```
var array1:Array = new Array("one","two","three");
var array2:Array = array1.slice();
trace(array1 + " vs " + array2); // one,two,three vs one,two,three
array2[3] = "four";
trace(array1 + " vs " + array2); // one,two,three vs one,two,three,four
```

That's more like it.

Casting objects to a type

As stated previously, nearly everything in ActionScript is an object, and all object instances inherit from Object. As such, a String variable is an Object instance; a Number variable is an Object instance; and a Boolean variable is an Object instance. Sometimes, all your code might know is that it is dealing with an Object instance of some sort and will need to determine at runtime the type of object the instance stores, String, Number, or Boolean, for instance.

As an example, imagine that you needed to determine whether a variable held a valid value or not, but depending on the type of object the variable held, the definition of what was valid would change. For a Boolean variable, only true values would be valid. For a String variable, a valid value would be anything that wasn't an empty string. For a Number variable, any positive value would be valid.

What you might do in this case is create a function that received an Object instance, since that can be any of the types, and return true or false based on whether the value is valid. Of course, inside the function you will require code that can find out the type of the variable passed in and return validity based on that type. Let's look at one possible solution, and then discuss the syntax.

```
public function getIsValid(testObject:Object):Boolean {
  if (testObject is String) {
    var testString:String = (testObject as String);
    return testString.length > 0;
  } else if (testObject is Number) {
    var testNumber:Number = (testObject as Number);
    return testNumber > 0;
  } else if (testObject is Boolean) {
    return (testObject as Boolean);
  }
  return false;
}
```

There are two new operators introduced in the preceding code. The first is the operator is. This can be used to test whether an object is of a certain type and will return either true or false. The first conditional (testObject is String) can be read aloud as, "Is testObject a String?" If it is, then the block within the conditional is run.

The second new operator above is as. This operator evaluates the operand on its left and determines whether it is of the data type specified on its right. If that is the case (i.e., if testObject is a String), then the expression evaluates to the object cast as the data type. If not, then the expression evaluates to null.

What do we mean by "cast"? That means that, although the object was initially of one data type (Object), it can be assigned to a new variable of a different data type, in this case String. This is actually known as a downcast, since the cast is going from a type higher up on the class hierarchy (Object) to one lower (String, which is a type of Object).

Once we have cast the object and placed the result within a new variable, we can perform operations supported by the new data type. In the case of String, that means we can retrieve its length property. For Number, we can check to see whether it is greater than zero. For Boolean, since that is the type returned by the function, we can simply return the argument cast as a Boolean.

There is one other way to cast, demonstrated in the following code:

```
public function getIsValid(testObject:Object):Boolean {
  if (testObject is String) {
    var testString:String = String(testObject);
    return testString.length > 0;
  } else if (testObject is Number) {
    var testNumber:Number = Number(testObject);
    return testNumber > 0;
  } else if (testObject is Boolean) {
    return Boolean(testObject);
  }
  return false;
}
```

In this case, we do not use the as operator and instead simply have the desired type followed by the object wrapped in parentheses. The results for this and the previous example would be the same, but there are some subtle differences between the two forms of casting. Whereas the as operator returns null if the object is not of the data type, the type wrapping the object form of casting will actually try to do an automatic conversion of the object to the new data type. For complex data types like arrays, this will throw a runtime error. For primitive data types, the conversion will occur according to fixed set of rules. For instance, a String "1" cast as a Number will become the number 1. A String "hello" will become NaN, or "not a number." Any nonzero Number when cast as a Boolean will become true. 0 will become false.

Sometimes, the automatic conversion that occurs with casting is what you want. Other times, it is merely a matter of downcasting an object you know is of a type, in which case the as operator works great. In fact, we could rewrite the function one more time without the is operator and rely solely on the as operator and its behavior of returning null for objects not of the specified type.

```
public function getIsValid(testObject:Object):Boolean {
  var testString:String = (testObject as String);
  if (testString) {
    return testString.length > 0;
  }
  var testNumber:Number = (testObject as Number);
  if (testNumber) {
    return testNumber > 0;
  }
  return (testObject as Boolean);
}
```

Since as will return null if the object is not of the specified type, you can use the result in a conditional statement to test whether it exists (null evaluates to a Boolean false).

Which method of testing type and casting can depend on the context of the code, but generally, you can choose the method that works best for you.

The Object object

As I've mentioned previously, everything you deal with in ActionScript is an object. The base of all objects in ActionScript is actually the Object class, which means it is possible to make what is referred to, though seemingly redundant, as an Object object. An instance of the Object class is the simplest sort of object you can make, with only a couple properties and a handful of methods, which are inherited by every other class in the ActionScript language, including Array, Number, String, and any custom class you create. Some of the more useful are hasOwnProperty(), which returns whether a property exists on an object (calling a property that doesn't exist results in a runtime error), and toString(), which returns a string identifying the object. This last method is actually automatically invoked when you pass an object to the trace() function.

To create an Object instance, you can use the new operator with the constructor:

```
var myObject:Object = new Object();
```

Object instances are actually dynamic, which means that you can then assign whatever properties you need without worry of a compile-time error. Note that this only works for Object instances and not for subclasses like Array and Number and custom classes unless those classes have been specifically identified as dynamic.

```
var myObject:Object = new Object();
myObject.name = "Simple Object";
myObject.ID = 12345;
```

Just like an array, you can also create a new Object instance by assigning an object literal, which uses curly braces:

```
var myObject:Object = {};
```

You can even include the properties you wish to define within this object literal. This is done using a comma-separated list of name/value pairs, with the name and value separated by a colon:

```
var myObject:Object = { name:"SimpleObject", ID:12345 };
```

If there are more than one or two properties and you would still like to use the object literal, I would suggest actually breaking this up over multiple lines to make it more legible.

```
var myObject:Object = {
  name: "SimpleObject",
  ID: 12345
};
```

Object instances are very versatile, but you should be careful of using them too often in your code, since their dynamic nature prevents them from having any strong data typing and so hides errors that might have otherwise been caught by the compiler. For instance, the preceding example has a name and ID property, but there is nothing that forces the name to be a string, so an error in the code could actually assign an array for this value, which could cause larger issues and runtime errors. More often than not, I will use Object instances to hold references to other objects.

For instance, suppose you had an application with a number of users and you wanted to store those users based on their IDs. In this case, an array is not a great way to store the users, since the IDs might not be numbers. In this case, storing the collection of users in an object is a great alternative. Here is an example of how you might set that up:

```
var user0:Object = {name:"John", ID:"A111"};
var user1:Object = {name:"Paul", ID:"A112"};
var user2:Object = {name:"George", ID:"A113"};
var user3:Object = {name:"Ringo", ID:"A114"};

var users:Object = {};
users[user0.ID] = user0;
users[user1.ID] = user1;
users[user2.ID] = user2;
users[user3.ID] = user3;
```

Here, we have created four unique Object instances, each containing a name and ID property. We then create another new Object instance and assign it to the variable users. Using the IDs as the property names, we assign each user to a property in our users object. If this bracket notation syntax appears odd to you, consider that the three following lines are equivalent:

```
users[user0.ID] = user0;
users["A111"] = user0;
users.A111 = user0;
```

The benefit of using the first line in the code is that this line does not rely on us hard-coding the ID value from the line above, so if we need to change that ID, we only have to do so in one place, not two.

Now, we have a users object that stores all of our users based on their IDs (the ID would be referred to as the **key** in this scenario). If we ever wanted to retrieve a user, we could find that user using her ID to look her up in the users object.

```
trace( users["A111"] );
```

> Something to note in the preceding example is that these lines could be easily condensed using an array to hold the initial user objects and then looping through this array to populate the users object. This was avoided to keep the example very clear about what it was doing, but the example is not very scalable as you gain many more users. If you are up to it, try to rewrite the preceding example using an array to see if you can figure out how to optimize those lines using a loop. That will be a great segue into the next section on looping through objects.

Iterating over objects

Since an Object instance does not have a nice length property like an Array does, how would you loop through an object if you wanted to process every property value? The answer is to use one of the two for loop variations that we introduced, but did not explore, last chapter: the for in and for each loops. Either of these looping mechanisms allows you to loop through all the **iterable** properties in an object, which means any properties that have been defined in the class as those can be surfaced during a loop. For an Object instance, this is any property you assign. Let's take a look at an example using our users object from the last section.

If you wanted to loop through all the users and output their names and IDs, you could first try it using the for in loop. This loop uses the following syntax:

```
for (var property:String in object) {
  // loop statements
}
```

This is handy when it is important to see the name of the property in the object each iteration of the loop, as that name will actually be accessible through the property variable (this variable can be named anything; often it is just the loop iterator i). Here is how you might trace out all IDs and names of the users:

```
for (var prop:String in users) {
  trace(prop + ": " + users[prop].name);
}
```

Remember that the only properties we defined on users were the IDs for each user, so using this loop will iterate over each of those properties (the IDs). In each loop iteration, prop will hold the ID of the particular user being accessed. That user can be referenced using the object[property] bracket notation, which is how we retrieve the name of the user in our loop example.

This works fine for our example, but a new looping mechanism introduced in ActionScript 3.0 is the for each loop. This loop works similarly to the for in loop, but instead of using the properties to iterate over an object, which are always cast as String, this loop allows you to iterate over the actual objects, whatever they may be, that are stored at each property. The following syntax is used:

```
for each (var iterator:DataType in object) {
  // loop statements
}
```

Applied to our users example, we could trace out the names and IDs with the following:

```
for each (var user:Object in users) {
  trace(user.ID + ": " + user.name);
}
```

This looping type has at least a con and a pro argument. The con is that you cannot access the name of the property (or key) as you iterate, as we could in the previous example with the prop value. However, the pro is that we can cast our iterator as whatever type the object contains. This works fantastically if you have assigned only a single type of instance to the object, like numbers or arrays, as you can then access properties and methods of those objects without additional casting within the loop and will receive compile-time errors if there are problems. For our users example, this benefit is not immediately apparent, since the users object contains other Object objects without any strong data typing. As an example of the loop's benefits, though, consider the following:

```
for each (var user:User in users) {
  user.sendNotification();
}
```

Here, we loop through all users, but in this scenario, we have a custom class created named User. We can type to this in the loop and then call directly a specific method that belongs to User, sendNotification(). If, at a later time, the User code changes to require a token to be passed to sendNotification(), or perhaps a message body, Flash will give us a nice compile-time error letting us know we need to update our code in the loop. This would *not* happen with the following code:

```
for (var prop:String in users) {
  users[prop].sendNotification();
}
```

In this case, the type of the object is not known at compile time, so this would only cause an error at runtime for the user when the loop was run, perhaps even after you have deployed the application (hey, this is one way bugs slip by). You could avoid this by casting within the loop, but which of the following two loops would you like to see in your code?

```
for each (var user:User in users) {
  user.sendNotification();
}
for (var prop:String in users) {
  (users[prop] as User).sendNotification();
}
```

My vote's for the first one!

Creating your first class

Assuming you've been following along faithfully since the beginning, you've already created your first class, though you probably didn't realize it at the time. In the very first chapter where we were discussing the different ways in which you can integrate ActionScript 3.0 code into your projects, you created a class to explore the new document class feature of Flash CS3 (hint: it was the stuff I told you to ignore until later).

From the iPod analogy, we know that a class is like a blueprint where you define the methods and properties that instances of that class will have. We'll get to how you create methods and properties in a moment, but for now, let's look at a class definition with no methods or properties and conveniently ignore the fact that such a class is completely useless, literally.

```
public class IPod {
}
```

Yes, it really is that simple. Well, almost. There are a couple more things we need to worry about if we want to be able to actually use this class.

First, all classes in ActionScript 3.0 must be part of a **package**. We're going to look at packages in more detail later in the chapter, so for now, just think of them as collections of classes. Thankfully, there is a default package that you can use for your classes, and making the IPod class part of that package is as simple as wrapping the class definition in a package block:

```
package {

  public class IPod {
  }

}
```

The other thing you need to know is that class definitions must appear in a separate ActionScript document, and that document must have the same name as the class name. This means that you can't add the class definition to a frame of your Flash document using the Actions window in the Flash IDE.

> *If you're wondering what the public bit is all about, it is technically known as a class access control namespace attribute. That's quite a mouthful, but in essence, it means that, as an ActionScript developer, you get to decide what other classes can make use of your class by using these access control attributes. Here, I've used the* public *namespace attribute, which means that the IPod class is available to everything. There are three other namespace attributes—*private, protected *and* internal—*which I'll cover as part of the wider topic of namespaces in the "Controlling access to properties and methods" section later in the chapter.*

Just so you can see that you've actually accomplished something with the preceding code (because on paper it doesn't look like much), follow these steps to integrate it into a simple example:

1. Create a new ActionScript document, and save it with the name IPod.as in the project directory for this chapter. Enter the code listed previously, and save the file.

> *When creating an ActionScript 3.0 class, the filename needs to be the same as the class name; otherwise, the ActionScript compiler will throw an error.*

2. Create a new Flash document, and save it with the name IPodExample.fla in the project directory.

3. Select the first frame from the timeline, open the Actions panel, and enter the following code:

```
var myIPod:IPod = new IPod();
trace(myIPod);
```

4. Save the Flash document, and test it by selecting Control ➤ Test movie from the main menu. If all goes according to plan, you should see the following in the Output panel:

```
[object IPod]
```

It's not that profound, but what it does tell you is that you've just created an instance of the IPod class you've just written. It doesn't actually do anything yet; we'll get to that shortly, but before we get there, I want to talk to you about the rules and general guidelines for choosing a name for your classes.

Choosing suitable names for your classes

As with variable and function names, ActionScript 3.0 imposes some rules that you need to follow when naming your classes. Class names must

- Consist only of letters, digits, the underscore character, and the dollar symbol
- Not start with a number
- Not be a reserved word
- Be unique

Class names should be specified in camel case notation. This is the granddaddy of the notation we've adopted for variable and function names (modified camel case) and differs only in that the first letter of the first word is always uppercase (like IPod.) The only other piece of guidance I want to give here is that you should try to make your class names nouns; after all, nouns are things, and objects are also things.

Sorry if I'm getting a little repetitive with all this naming convention; if there's one thing you take away from this book (in addition to superior ActionScript 3.0 skills), it's that consistent naming is important and will stop you from going insane. If it helps, this is the second to last time I'm going to mention naming conventions in this book. Scout's honor.

Adding properties

So far, you've created an IPod class and created an instance of it, but we've already discovered that it's completely useless as it is. It's like an annoying socialite factory capable of churning out an endless parade of celebrity wannabes who are famous just for being famous, despite being completely devoid of both substance and talent. I'm sure you can think of a few media personalities who fit this bill, and we refuse to let your IPod class become one of them.

Anyway, where was I? Ah, yes—properties. As we discussed earlier, the class definition dictates what properties objects of that class will have, so it stands to reason that if you want IPod objects to have certain properties, you're going to have to add them to the class definition.

Let's dig right in and give the IPod class a volumeLevel property. I figure that the appropriate data type is probably uint, since I don't know what a negative volume level might mean:

```
package {

  public class IPod {

    public var volumeLevel:uint = 10;

  }

}
```

From the preceding example, you can see that property definitions look pretty similar to variable definitions, and that's no accident—properties are essentially variables that belong to an object rather than floating in the global primordial soup. The property has been made public for the same reason the class itself is public: to tell the Flash Player that we want the volumeLevel property to be available to all and sundry.

> If you look closely, you'll see we were even able to give the property a default value, meaning that new IPod objects will automatically have their volume levels set to ten.

Every instance of the IPod class will now have a volumeLevel property that can be set and read back. If you now modify the code on the first frame, you can fiddle with the volume level of the IPod object we created and stored in the myIPod variable:

```
var myIPod:IPod = new IPod();
trace(myIPod.volumeLevel);
```

If you test this in the Flash IDE, you'll see the value 10, the default value for the volumeLevel property, in the Output panel. Just to prove we can also change the value of this property, add a line setting the volumeLevel to 11 so that it's one level louder (and if you haven't seen *This is Spinal Tap*, stay after class) and then trace the value out again:

```
var myIPod:IPod = new IPod ();
trace(myIPod.volumeLevel);
myIPod.volumeLevel = 11;
trace(myIPod.volumeLevel);
```

Testing the movie now should yield 11 in the Output panel.

Of course, you're not just limited to a single property: objects can have as many properties as you like, and they can be of any data type. Let's add some more likely looking properties to our class:

```
package {

  public class IPod {

    public var name:String = "";
    public var volumeLevel:uint = 10;
    public var tracks:Array;
    public var currentTrack:uint = 0;
    public var shuffle:Boolean = false;

  }

}
```

Here, we've added a name property to hold the name given to the iPod (e.g., "Steve's iPod"), a tracks array to hold all the music tracks, a currentTrack property so we can tell which track is being played and change it, and a shuffle property indicating whether the tracks will be played in a random order.

So now, instances of the IPod class are able to keep track of several different pieces of information. You can now make use of these properties:

```
var myIPod:IPod = new IPod ();
myIPod.name = "Steve's iPod";
myIPod.volumeLevel = 11;
myIPod.tracks = ["Guns 'n' Roses - Estranged", "Muse - ➡
Super MassiveBlackholes", "Evanescence - Good Enough"];
myIPod.shuffle = true;
```

All I've done here is to give my iPod a suitable name, and then populated it with the names of some of my favorite songs (no poking fun at my taste in music!) using array literal notation. Go ahead and do the same with yours, though feel free to use different values. (Unless you're some kind of copycat stalker, in which case, where have you been all my life? I've always wanted a stalker.)

At the moment, testing this in the Flash IDE won't produce any kind of output, but it's worth doing anyway just to make sure you've not made any errors. What we need is for our IPod instance to be able to do something with the information it contains, which is where methods come in.

Adding methods

As I mentioned at the start of this chapter, methods are basically functions that belong to an object. If you follow good object-oriented design principles, the method will be related to the purpose of your object, which is a long-winded way of saying that if you had a Pig class you wouldn't give it a fly() method—that belongs with the Bird class.

You add method definitions to a class in much the same way you did with properties: by adding them to the class definition. Since they're functions, you declare them using the function keyword as you would a regular function, but like properties, you need to specify an access attribute. We'll deal with these in more detail later in the chapter, but for now, you can just make all your methods publicly available using the public access attribute.

> *Method names need to follow the same rules and guidelines as function names. I won't bore you with yet another lecture on good naming practice and trust that you can look up how functions are named in the previous chapter should you need a refresher.*

Our IPod class is currently bereft of any functionality at all, so let's give it a play method that outputs the name of the current track (if we were dealing with real music files rather than just track names, it would play the MP3):

```
package {

  public class IPod {

    public var name:String = "";
    public var volumeLevel:uint = 10;
    public var shuffle:Boolean = false;
    public var currentTrack:uint = 0;
    public var tracks:Array;

    public function play():void {
      trace("Playing: " + tracks[currentTrack]);
    }

  }

}
```

Now, any instance of the IPod class will have a play method that traces out the current track title in the Output panel. Let's give that a try by modifying the code on the first frame of the IPodExample.fla file to call this method once we've set all the properties of our object:

```
var myIPod:IPod = new IPod ();
myIPod.name = "Steve's iPod";
myIPod.volumeLevel = 11;
```

```
myIPod.tracks = ["Guns 'n' Roses - Estranged", "Muse - ➡
Super MassiveBlackholes", "Evanescence - Good Enough"];
myIPod.shuffle = true;
myIPod.play();
```

If you test the movie now, you should see Playing: Guns 'n' Roses - Estranged in the Output panel. Hurrah, your first method is born!

Of course, just being able to play one track isn't going to help us sell millions of iPods (I don't think even the mercurial Steve Jobs could get away with that one), so we need to add some more methods that might make our class a little more useful. Let's start by giving our IPod class the ability to skip to the next track:

```
package {

  public class IPod {

    public var name:String = "";
    public var volumeLevel:uint = 10;
    public var shuffle:Boolean = false;
    public var currentTrack:uint = 0;
    public var tracks:Array;

    public function play():void {
      trace("Playing: " + tracks[currentTrack]);
    }

    public function next():void {
    }

  }

}
```

Remember that our IPod class has a shuffle attribute, so what we want to do is to choose a random track if this is set to true. To do this, we'll use the Math.random() method, which will return us a number between 0 and 1 that can be multiplied by the number of tracks and rounded down to the nearest whole number with the Math.floor() method (rounded down because the tracks array is zero indexed) to get a random track number:

```
...
    public function next():void {
      if (shuffle) {
        currentTrack = Math.floor(Math.random() * tracks.length);
      }
    }
...
```

> *This isn't true shuffle functionality, since the equation we're using to generate the next track number is random, meaning that you could get the same track several times in a row (which would get old in a hurry if the track in question was some kind of Robbie Williams compendium). To mimic the iPod's shuffle mode, you'd need to clone the tracks array, sort all the tracks randomly, and then play through them in sequence. That's quite tricky, however, and I didn't want to distract you from learning about methods. If you're feeling brave, feel free to have a stab at this yourself (maybe once you've finished the book), and don't be afraid to make mistakes.*
>
> *By the way, I've omitted the lines of code we created in the previous section here, because I get annoyed when programming books fill page after page with source code listings—not only does it waste trees, it also makes my eyes hurt trying to look for the one or two lines that have changed.*

If the shuffle property is set to false, we can just increment the currentTrack property or reset it to zero if we've reached the end of the track listings:

```
...
    public function next():void {
      if (shuffle) {
        currentTrack = Math.floor(Math.random() * tracks.length);
      } else {
        if (currentTrack == tracks.length - 1) {
          currentTrack = 0;
        } else {
          currentTrack++;
        }
      }
    }
...
```

Finally, we want to play the next track:

```
...
    public function next():void {
      if (shuffle) {
        currentTrack = Math.floor(Math.random() * tracks.length);
      } else {
        if (currentTrack == tracks.length - 1) {
          currentTrack = 0;
        } else {
          currentTrack++;
        }
      }
      play();
    }
...
```

To take our new method for a test drive, give the following steps a whirl:

1. In the IPodExample.fla file, draw a circle (or a fancy Next-type button if you're more graphically-oriented than I am) on the stage, select it, and convert it into a movie clip symbol by pressing F8. Name the symbol circle, and click the OK button.

2. Now, select your new instance on the stage, and give it an instance name of nextButton.

3. Add the following code to the first frame above the existing code:

```
import flash.events.MouseEvent;

nextButton.addEventListener(MouseEvent.CLICK, onNextButtonClick);
function onNextButtonClick(event:MouseEvent):void {
  myIPod.next();
}
```

We haven't gotten to event-based programming yet (that'll have to wait until Chapter 5), but all this bit of code does is call the next() method of the myIPod object when the nextButton on the stage is clicked.

Go ahead and test the movie. Clicking the button should result in the track being changed randomly (since we set the shuffle property to true a while back).

There are still a few bits of functionality missing from the IPod class, so if you are feeling particularly adventurous, see if you can add your own previous method to skip backward through the track list and anything else you can think is missing.

Initializing your objects with a constructor method

When you create custom classes, most likely you will want to perform some initialization on instances when they are created, before there is any interaction through the properties and methods. Sometimes, this will be assigning values based on properties existing in the movie or application or instantiating more complex objects that aren't as easily initialized in a property declaration. Any actions to be taken care of immediately when an object is created need to be handled within, or at least kicked off from, the class's **constructor**.

A constructor is a special method of your class that is executed on each new instance of your class as it is created. It has the same name as the class to which it belongs, and the parameters of the constructor dictate what information needs to be provided when creating a new instance of that class. The idea is that you could use the constructor in conjunction with the parameters passed to it to initialize the object and its properties so that it's ready to go to work.

> In ActionScript, there can only ever be one constructor per class, which differs from some other languages, and if you don't write one, then Flash creates a default constructor for you behind the scenes.

One of the problems with our IPod class at the moment is that, once we've created a new instance, we have to initialize all of the properties one after the other. It would be much more convenient to allow a developer to pass in values for the name, volumeLevel, and shuffle properties when creating a new IPod instance, only assigning the default values if no user-defined values are passed in. This will move the assigning of property values from the property declarations into the constructor. To keep things consistent (always a good idea), we'll actually move all of the property assignments to the constructor, even currentTrack, which will always default to 0.

Let's create a simple constructor for the IPod class to accept parameters. Remember, a constructor is just a method that has the same name as the class. The only different between its definition and any other method (well, other than the name) is that it cannot specify a return data type or return a value.

```
package {

  public class IPod {

    public var name:String;
    public var volumeLevel:uint;
    public var shuffle:Boolean;
    public var currentTrack:uint;
    public var tracks:Array;

    public function IPod(
      name:String="",
      volumeLevel:uint=10,
      shuffle:Boolean=false
    ) {
      this.name = name;
      this.volumeLevel = volumeLevel;
      this.shuffle = shuffle;
      currentTrack = 0;
      tracks = new Array();
    }
  ...
  }
}
```

What I've done here is to add three parameters to the constructor that allow you to specify the name, volumeLevel, and shuffle values, which are then copied to the appropriate properties within the body of the constructor. Each of these three parameters is given a default value, so they are optional for a developer when creating a new instance. For instance, if I don't specify the second parameter when creating a new IPod object, it will get the default volumeLevel of 10. In addition, we also instantiate our tracks array and assign 0 to currentTrack.

One new keyword that is introduced in the preceding code is this. this within a class refers to the instance of the class that is running the code. We use it here within the constructor since we are passing in local variables (in the parameters) that use the same names as our class properties, so we need some way to differentiate between the parameters and the properties, and this works perfectly for this purpose (note that we also could have simply named the parameters passed in something slightly different).

Now, if I wanted to create a new IPod with a name of Steve's Shuffle and a volume level of 11, I could now do so like this:

```
var myIPod:IPod = new IPod("Steve's Shuffle", 11);
trace(myIPod.name);
trace(myIPod.volumeLevel);
```

It's good practice to make your constructors as flexible as possible and to make sure that the parameters are in a sensible order. I've decided that I'm most likely to want to set the name of an IPod instance when creating it, so I made that the first parameter of the constructor. Similarly, it's unlikely that I'll want to set the currentTrack property to anything other than the first track, so I've not included it in the constructor parameters. Being judicious when deciding what should become a constructor parameter and what should just be a property with a default value makes your classes much easier to understand.

Controlling access to properties and methods

As it currently stands, all the properties and methods of our IPod class are publicly accessible, meaning that they can be read and modified from any other part of the code. This might not always be desired. For example, my iPod undoubtedly has a serial number that uniquely identifies that particular iPod, which we could store in a property names serialNumber. However, the serial number that Steve's iPod was given when it was created cannot be changed, so we need some way of hiding the serialNumber variable from the outside world, which is where access attributes come in.

We've already met one access attribute, public, and defined what it means, but Table 3-1 provides a complete rundown of the access attributes available in ActionScript 3.0 along with their meanings.

Table 3-1. The access attributes available in ActionScript 3.0

Access attribute	Meaning
private	Can be accessed only by methods of the class itself
public	Can be accessed from any other part of the code in the entire application in which the class exists
protected	Can be accessed only by methods of the class itself and any classes that extend this class
internal	Can be accessed by any class defined in the same package

Some of these (namely protected and internal) may not make too much sense at the moment, since they are only useful when you're dealing with inheritance and packages, which we've not covered yet in this chapter.

Despite that, you can see that the private access attribute is a good candidate for our serialNumber property. The plan is to pass the serial number as a String into the constructor method, which can then set the value of the private serialNumber variable appropriately (remember, private variables are visible to methods of the class itself).

```
...
    public var currentTrack:uint;
    public var tracks:Array;

    private var _serialNumber:String;

    public function IPod(
      serialNumber:String,
      name:String="",
      volumeLevel:uint=10,
      shuffle:Boolean=false
    ) {
      _serialNumber = serialNumber;
      this.name = name;
      this.volumeLevel = volumeLevel;
      this.shuffle = shuffle;
      currentTrack = 0;
      tracks = new Array();
    }
...
```

I have chosen to start the new _serialNumber property with an underscore character, which is common notation within ActionScript files to mark a property as private. That way, it is very easy within our class to know which properties are private (they'll contain an underscore) and which are public (no underscore). This also frees us from having to use this when assigning the property within the constructor, as the name of the property now differs from the name of the parameter passed in.

> I've made this parameter mandatory (by not providing a default value for it in the method definition), since all iPods have a serial number (with the possible exception of James Bond's, but I'm guessing he's not among the target audience for our application).

You'll also need to change the code on the first frame of the IPodExample.fla file to pass in the extra parameter to the constructor method when creating an instance of the IPod class.

```
var myIPod:IPod = new IPod("A101", "Steve's Shuffle", 11);
trace(myIPod.name);
trace(myIPod.volumeLevel);
```

Perfect. If you try to trace out the value of the _serialNumber property of the myIPod object, you'll get an error from the ActionScript compiler telling you that you cannot access a private property from outside the class. This demonstrates that the property, set as private, is not accessible to outside classes or code.

Adding getter/setter methods

Hiding properties using the access modifiers is all very well, but sometimes that isn't enough. What if all you wanted to do was to make sure that when a property was set it was given a sensible value? What would it mean, for example, for the currentTrack property of an IPod instance to be set to be greater than the number of tracks in the tracks array? In fact, setting the currentTrack property at the moment doesn't do anything at all; we certainly don't get a nice message traced to the Output panel telling us which track is being played now.

We could, of course, make the currentTrack property private and create two public methods getCurrentTrack() and setCurrentTrack() that can be used to manipulate the value of that property. These are referred to as **explicit** getter/setter methods, as they explicitly provide two methods for reading from and writing to a single property, respectively. I don't know about you, but that just doesn't feel right; ideally, I'd like currentTrack to still be a property but just be able to intervene whenever the value is being set. Thankfully, ActionScript 3.0 gives us **implicit** getter/setter methods for that exact purpose.

Implicit getter/setter methods allow you to create properties that behave like functions. They come as a pair of methods with the same name, with the getter function being called whenever the property value is read, and the setter function being called whenever a value is assigned to the property. These are known as implicit getter/setter methods since they are methods that act, on the outside, like a single public property that in fact call two separate read/write methods for a single private property.

A getter method looks almost like any other method of your class, except that it has the get keyword between the function keyword and the function name. The getter method cannot take any parameters and must return a value of the data type specified by the return type of the function, which will be the data type you want for your public property (in the case of our currentTrack property, this would be uint):

```
public function get propertyName():ReturnType {
   // needs to return a value of the appropriate type
}
```

A setter method is similar but uses the set attribute in place of the get attribute, and it's passed the new value assigned to the property as its one and only parameter. The data type of this parameter should be the same as the data type returned by the getter method. The return type of the setter method is always void.

```
public function set propertyName(value:Type):void {
   // the new value for the property is in the value variable
}
```

Before you rush off and add a getter/setter pair to our IPod class, there's one small issue we need to address: you can't have a property and a method of the same name. This means that you'll need to rename the old currentTrack property to something else so that you can create a getter/setter pair of that name. You'll also want to make it private rather than public; otherwise, there's nothing to stop other code from using the renamed public property rather than the getter/setter pairs, which rather

93

defeats the purpose. As with _serialNumber, we will give our private property _currentTrack the underscore prefix to differentiate it from the public getter/setter methods.

> *Not all getter/setter methods need to relate to a private property of the class. They could be a convenient method of setting the value of several properties (think about a* name *getter/setter pair that splits the value into* firstName *and* lastName *properties, which themselves may or may not be public) or not actually set any properties at all and just be functional.*

With that in mind, go ahead and make the currentTrack property private and prefix an underscore to its name. Here, I've grouped it with _serialNumber, as I like to keep my public and private properties separate:

```
package {

  public class IPod {

    public var name:String;
    public var volumeLevel:uint;
    public var shuffle:Boolean;
    public var tracks:Array;

    private var _serialNumber:String;
    private var _currentTrack:uint;

    public function IPod(
      serialNumber:String,
      name:String="",
      volumeLevel:uint=10,
      shuffle:Boolean=false
    ) {
      _serialNumber = serialNumber;
      this.name = name;
      this.volumeLevel = volumeLevel;
      this.shuffle = shuffle;
      _currentTrack = 0;
      tracks = new Array();
    }
    ...
```

Now, create the currentTrack getter/setter methods. The getter method just needs to return the value held in the private _currentTrack property, but we need to do something trickier with the setter method. The whole aim of this exercise was to prevent the currentTrack property from being greater than the number of tracks we have in the tracks array. We can use the Math.min() method to set the value to the smaller of the value passed in or the index of the last track in the tracks array (which is the length of the array minus one, because arrays are zero indexed). Of course, we also need to make sure that the current track is not set to be less than 0, and the Math.max() method takes care of that for us. Normally, I put getter/setter methods at the end of a class definition (just personal preference), so below you can see the methods after the next() method:

```
...
    public function next():void {
      if (shuffle) {
        currentTrack = Math.floor(Math.random() * tracks.length);
      } else {
        if (currentTrack == tracks.length - 1) {
          currentTrack = 0;
        } else {
          currentTrack++;
        }
      }
      play();
    }

    public function get currentTrack():uint {
      return _currentTrack;
    }
    public function set currentTrack(value:uint):void {
      value = Math.max(0, value);
      value = Math.min(value, tracks.length - 1);
      _currentTrack = value;
    }
...
```

You can see this magic in action by changing the code on the first frame of the IPodExample.fla file to add a couple of tracks and then try setting the currentTrack property to 55 and see what you get:

```
var myIPod:IPod = new IPod("A101", "Steve's Shuffle", 10);
myIPod.tracks.push("Guns 'n' Roses - Estranged");
myIPod.tracks.push("Muse - Supermassive Black Hole");
myIPod.tracks.push("Evanescence - Good Enough");
trace(myIPod.currentTrack); // 0
myIPod.currentTrack = 55;
trace(myIPod.currentTrack); // 2
```

If you test this movie, you'll see 0 and 2 in the Output panel in the Flash IDE, confirming that the getter/setter methods are working as planned.

Note that in the preceding example we are manipulating the tracks *array directly by calling the* push() *method. This is possible because we have made the array publicly accessible. The problem with this is that it is then possible for any outside code to manipulate that array (remember, arrays are passed by reference, so any manipulation of that array outside the class affects the array inside the class).*

Here is a great example of when you should make a property private and instead provide either implicit or explicit getter/setter methods to allow for outside classes to manipulate data. Allowing access only through the getter/setter methods provides a way to ensure that only a class will directly alter its properties, which is generally good object-oriented programming practice. In fact, in nearly all cases, I make properties private or protected and only allow access through getter/setter methods. For tracks, *a good exercise for you is to make it private and provide perhaps* addTrack() *and* removeTrack() *methods managed by the class.*

Creating read-only properties with getter methods

So far, we've discussed getter/setter methods used as a pair, but that doesn't always have to be the case. Using just a getter method with no equivalent setter, you can create properties that are read-only from outside of your class. If some other part of the code attempts to assign a value to that property, the ActionScript compiler will throw an error, and your project won't compile.

This is a great way of exposing internal private properties to the outside world without allowing them to be changed, which would be ideal for the _serialNumber property we added to the IPod class a while back.

In the following code, below the currentTrack getter/setter methods add a solitary serialNumber getter method that returns the value of the private _serialNumber property:

```
...

    public function get currentTrack():uint {
      return _currentTrack;
    }
    public function set currentTrack(value:uint):void {
      value = Math.max(0, value);
      value = Math.min(value, tracks.length - 1);
      _currentTrack = value;
    }

    public function get serialNumber():String {
      return _serialNumber;
    }
...
```

Finally, rewrite the code in the first frame of the IPodExample.fla file to trace the serialNumber of the iPod to the Output panel;

```
var myIPod:IPod = new IPod("A101", "Steve's iPod", 11);
trace(myIPod.serialNumber); // A101
```

Ta da! You can now get at the serial number of an IPod instance without being able to change its value. If you're feeling adventurous, feel free to try setting the value of the serialNumber property and see what error you get from the ActionScript compiler—it'll help you to work out what's going on the next time you get this error.

Static properties and methods

Grouping variables and functions together into logical objects is all well and good, but not all pieces of data or functionality belong to a particular instance of an object. Utility functions and pieces of data that don't logically belong to a single instance of a class, but are nonetheless related to the class, can be added to the class as static properties and methods.

Static properties and methods are part of the class definition, but are identified by the static attribute being used as part of their definition:

```
public class StaticExample {

  public static const PI:Number = 3.1415;
  public static function doStaticStuff():void {
    // take some actions
  }

}
```

> Technically, ActionScript 3.0 is somewhat flexible as to the order of the attributes applied to a class or method. When looking at code that's out there in the wild, you'll sometimes see static specified before the access attribute and sometimes see them the other way around. It's the collective meaning of the attributes that matters, not the order in which you specify them. However, you'll make life easier for yourself if you pick a convention and stick to it.

When accessing a static property or calling a static method of a class, you don't need to create an instance as the property is actually a part of the class, not of any individual object created from that class, so just use dot notation with the class name and the property or method name (just as we did with the Math.random() earlier in the chapter):

```
trace(StaticExample.PI);
StaticExample.doStuff();
```

Sometimes, you have utility functions that don't logically belong to a class at all. Take the Math class for example: you can't create an instance of the Math class (what would a math be?) and it's just used as a container for a whole bunch of mathematical constants and utility functions.

Oh, and you can even have static getter/setter methods, should you think of a good use for them.

Taking advantage of inheritance

No, I'm not going to give you advice on how to invest granny's millions (though I know a very grateful author who could take very good care of it for you). I'm talking about object-oriented inheritance.

Inheritance allows you to create new classes using an existing class as a foundation, adding or changing functionality as necessary. For example, a basic Car class might have a licensePlate property and accelerate() and brake() methods, which every car has, and there's no sense in duplicating all that stuff for every different type of car. Instead, the DeLorean class can extend the Car class and add its own functionality—a fluxCapacitor property and a travelThroughTime() method, for example.

The key to understanding inheritance is that it is an "is a" relationship. A DeLorean is a Car; a Cat is a Mammal; and an Apple is a Fruit. Each of those subclasses is a specialization of its base class, adding in its own properties and methods but inheriting the basic functionality. The idea of inheritance is to write common functionality once in the base class and then specialize that functionality for the different subclasses.

In ActionScript 3.0, you specify that one class extends another using the extends keyword as part of the class definition:

```
public class SubClass extends BaseClass {
    ...
}
```

An instance of *SubClass* will now inherit all the features and functionality defined in *BaseClass* as though they were defined in *SubClass* itself.

In the constructor of your subclass, you can call a special method named super(), which invokes the base class's constructor method. If you need to pass any parameters from the subclass constructor to the base class constructor, you can do so just as you would a normal method call:

```
public class SubClass extends BaseClass {
  public function SubClass(someParam:String) {
    super(someParam);
  }
}
```

> If you forget to call the super() method, the ActionScript compiler will attempt to invoke the constructor of your base class with no arguments. If your base class is expecting to receive parameters (i.e., it has parameters that are not optional) the ActionScript compiler will throw an error like this: 1203:   No default constructor found in base class BaseClass.
>
> If you ever get this error, make sure you're calling the super() method in the subclasses constructor and passing the necessary parameters.

Relating this back to our IPod class, we could say that there are different types of iPod. There's the iPod Shuffle, the iPod Nano, and the regular photo iPod. Each of these types of iPod supports the same basic functionality we've set up in the IPod class, but they each also add something extra. Let's create a PhotoIPod class that has a collection of photos and the ability to cycle through them:

1. Create a new ActionScript file named PhotoIPod.as, and save it in the project directory.

2. Create the basic class definition in the default package, remembering to extend the base IPod class along the way:

```
package {

  public class PhotoIPod extends IPod {
  }

}
```

3. Next, create a duplicate of the constructor method from IPod that takes the same parameters and passes them through to the super() method to let the base class initialize itself:

```
package {

  public class PhotoIPod extends IPod {

    public function PhotoIPod(
      serialNumber:String,
      name:String="",
      volumeLevel:uint=10,
      shuffle:Boolean=false
    ) {
      super(
        serialNumber,
        name,
        volumeLevel,
        shuffle
      );
    }

  }

}
```

4. Now, you can start to add the extended functionality of the PhotoIPod class. The first thing you'll need is an array to keep the list of photos in and a property to keep track of the current photo:

```
package {

  public class PhotoIPod extends IPod {

    public var photos:Array;
    public var currentPhoto:uint;
```

```
public function PhotoIPod(
  serialNumber:String,
  name:String="",
  volumeLevel:uint=10,
  shuffle:Boolean=false
) {
  super(
    serialNumber,
    name,
    volumeLevel,
    shuffle
  );
  photos = new Array();
  currentPhoto = 0;
}

}

}
```

> Notice I've been a bit lazy here and just made the currentPhoto property public. If left
> like this, it would face the same problem as the currentTrack property that we added
> getter/setter methods for earlier—namely that something could set the currentPhoto
> property to be greater than the number of entries in the photos array. If this is nagging
> at your conscience as much as it is mine, feel free to embellish this with getter/setter
> methods.

5. Add a showPhoto() method that displays the title of the current photo from the photos array:

```
public function PhotoIPod(
  serialNumber:String,
  name:String="",
  volumeLevel:uint=10,
  shuffle:Boolean=false
) {
  super(
    serialNumber,
    name,
    volumeLevel,
    shuffle
  );
  photos = new Array();
  currentPhoto = 0;
}

public function showPhoto():void {
  trace("Showing: " + photos[currentPhoto]);
}
```

6. Finally, add a nextPhoto() method to cycle through the photos sequentially, looping back round to the beginning if you get to the end:

```
public function showPhoto():void {
  trace("Showing: " + photos[currentPhoto]);
}

public function nextPhoto():void {
  if (currentPhoto == photos.length - 1) {
    currentPhoto = 0;
  } else {
    currentPhoto++;
  }
  showPhoto();
}
```

With that done we can create a new instance of the PhotoIPod, which can play music and view photos at the same time:

7. Save your IPodExample.fla file as PhotoIPodExample.fla.

8. Change the code on the first frame of the PhotoIPodExample.fla file to reflect the following changes in bold:

```
var myIPod:PhotoIPod = new PhotoIPod("A101", "Steve's iPod", 10);
myIPod.tracks.push("Guns 'n' Roses - Estranged");
myIPod.tracks.push("Muse - Supermassive Black Holes");
myIPod.tracks.push("Evanescence - Good Enough");

myIPod.photos.push("Steve with streamers on his head");
myIPod.photos.push("Nicki asleep by the fire");
myIPod.photos.push("Steve a little worse for wear");

myIPod.play();
myIPod.showPhoto();
```

Feel free to add another button to the stage to cycle through the photos. Follow the same basic instructions as the button we added to skip through the music tracks, but call the nextPhoto() method instead.

Overriding methods of the base class

Sometimes when extending a base class, you want to change or enhance some piece of functionality provided by that base class to suit the subclass. This is known as **method overriding**.

In order to override a method of a base class, you need to use the override attribute. Like the static attribute, it can go anywhere before the function name, but it's probably best to put it before the access attribute, so you know up front which methods are being overridden in a class.

```
override public function methodName():void {
  ...
}
```

If you're just embellishing the functionality of the base class (or you want to run some additional checks before the method is called) you can always use the super keyword to call the original method from the base class from within the override method:

```
override public function methodName():void {
  super.methodName();
}
```

Notice that, rather than just calling a method named super() as we did with the constructor, super is actually a reference to the base class object, and we just call the method of the same name on that object.

> If you try to just use this.methodName() instead, you'll be calling the same method again, which will call the same method again. Rinse; repeat. This is known as infinite recursion and actually crashes the Flash Player and causes a lovely little warning dialog to pop up on the user's screen. Needless to say, this is not something to strive for.

Let's take our simple Car versus DeLorean example. We'll probably want to override the Car classes forward function to check not only the fuelLevel (which in the case of the DeLorean would be black-market plutonium bought from Libya) but also check that a target date has been configured:

```
public class Car {

  public var fuelLevel:uint = 100;

  public function Car() {
  }

  public function forward() {
    if (fuelLevel > 0) {
      fuelLevel--;
    }

  }

}
```

So that's the basic Car class. Next, we'll tackle the DeLorean class, which has a target date that needs to be set before the car can go anywhere:

```
class DeLorean extends Car {

  public var targetDate:Date;

  public function DeLorean() {
    super();
  }
```

```
    override public function forward():void {
      if (targetDate != null) {
        super.forward();
      }

    }

  }
```

Here, we override the forward method of the Car class, only calling it through the super object if a target date has been set.

Using packages to group your classes

So far in this chapter, we've been putting all our classes into the default package. While this may be OK for very simple examples that we're just going to throw away later, it's not a good idea for code that you're going to have to organize, maintain, or share with others.

The reason it's not a good idea is that you can have only one class of a given name, so if everyone just dumps classes in the default package, the chance of a naming conflict is quite high (not too mention causing a staggering number of class files in a single directory). Instead of using the default package, we can use the packaging system in ActionScript 3.0 for the purpose it was intended: to organize our code into logical groups or packages, with a portion of package names being unique enough to differentiate our code from someone else's.

In ActionScript 3.0, you create a package by surrounding your class definition in a package block:

```
package name {
  ...
}
```

The package name is made up of parts separated by a dot, or period. These parts of the package name must be mirrored by the directory structure in which the ActionScript files are saved. For example, all the classes for this book are in the com.foundationAS3 package, which means that they are stored in the foundationAS3 subdirectory of the com directory within the main project directory. If you place an ActionScript class file in a location that doesn't match its package name, the ActionScript compiler won't be able to find it, and you'll get an error.

Naming your packages

There are two primary benefits of placing your code in packages. The first, as already mentioned, is to ensure that your classes don't clash with classes of the same name created by others. This means that the package name you choose for your classes needs to be unique—if everyone chooses the same package name, you're no better off than you were using the default package name.

The de facto method of ensuring unique package names is to reverse the domain name of the web site belonging to the company producing the code or the client for whom the code is being written. Because domain names are registered and can only be owned by one entity at any one time, there's very little chance of a naming conflict. Going forward, all of the ActionScript classes in this book will be within the com.foundationAS3 package.

> *Adobe has ignored this convention for the built-in Flash and Flex framework classes, which are spread across the* flash *and* mx *packages. They did this to save us from having to type* com.adobe *before each package path, mindful that we're likely to be using the built-in classes quite frequently.*

The second benefit of packages is that it helps you to organize your classes into logical groups according to their functions. When I'm working on a project, any class that's specific to that project goes within a package with the same name as the application, with any generic classes going into the top-level domain package. Going further, I then subdivide those classes according to their function, so utility classes will go in the utils package, and so on.

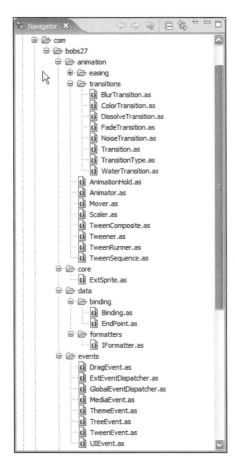

Figure 3-1. An example of a package structure for many classes

What you end up with is a structure that looks something like this the one shown in Figure 3-1.

> *You may have noticed from Figure 3-1 that you can quite happily mix classes and subpackages in the same package.*

Having said all that, you are free to ignore all this good advice and organize your code in any way you see fit. Package names need to conform to the same rules as class names but should generally be lowercase to differentiate them from classes. Other than that, you can name and structure your packages however you like. Just beware that putting all your classes for a professional project into a package named charlieBrown just for a laugh will probably get you fired. Don't say I didn't warn you.

Importing a class from a package

Once you've sectioned your classes into logical packages, you'll need to use the import statement to bring the classes into the class where you want to make use of them. Actually, you only need to do this for classes that aren't in the same package as the class you're editing—classes in the same package are automatically available to you.

When adding import statements to your code, they should go inside the package block but outside of the class definition, and you need to use the full package path and class name for the class you want to import. If we had a class that needed to make use of the MovieClip class from the flash.display package, we'd need to do something like this:

```
package {

  import flash.display.MovieClip;

  class Example extends MovieClip {
...
  }

}
```

Once the class has been imported, we can use just the class name to reference it in the code (with one small exception, which we'll get to in a bit).

Importing a class doesn't automatically mean that the class will be compiled into the resultant SWF file for your project. The ActionScript compiler is smart enough to work out if you're making use of a class and exclude it if there's no reference to that class in your code.

Importing all classes in a given package

On a large project where you have classes that use lots of classes from other packages, maintaining the import statements can become a task in itself. To help you combat this, you can use the asterisk symbol to include all the classes in a given package in a single import statement.

When we start looking at the display list in the next chapter, we're going to be using a lot of the classes from the flash.display package. Instead of importing each of these classes individually, we can import them all with a single import statement that uses the asterisk wildcard (*):

```
import flash.display.*;
```

This will only import classes directly in that package and will not include classes in any subpackages within the specified package, so you wouldn't be able to import every single class that resides in the fl.motion.easing package by importing fl.motion.*.

Resolving naming conflicts among imported classes

When importing classes from multiple packages, there's still a chance you will end up with two classes with the same name. When this happens, you won't be able to use just the name of the class in your code, as the ActionScript compiler won't be able to work out which of the classes with that name you mean.

In cases like this, you need to give the compiler a helping hand by specifying the full package name for the class wherever you use it, though you'll still need to import the classes with an import statement.

Removing dependency on timeline code

Now that you know all about classes and objects, we're going to do away with placing code on the timeline for the remainder of this book and use document classes instead.

When you specify a document class for a Flash movie, an instance of that class is created when the movie is played, and it represents the top-level MovieClip in your document (it could be a Sprite instead).

If you're dealing with timeline keyframe animation and you need something to happen on a particular frame, my advice is to place that code in a method of a class and call that method from the frame.

> There is a sneaky undocumented method that allows you to specify a function to be called when a particular frame is reached without having to put any code on the timeline: the addFrameScript() method of the MovieClip class. This method takes a frame number (starting at zero for the first frame) and a function reference, with the function you pass in being called when the movie enters the specified frame number.
>
> That said, I don't recommend using this for two reasons. The first is that the addFrameScript() method is undocumented, so Adobe could remove it at any point, and your movies would break. The second reason is that if you're shifting stuff around on the timeline (to tweak your animations, for example), you'll have to remember to change the code in the class too—at least if the code is on a frame, that frame will probably get shunted around with the animation.

Summary

The previous chapter was about basic building blocks; in this chapter, you learned how to put those building blocks together to build rooms. Classes are the foundation of everything you will do in your ActionScript projects, and thus it was important that we covered them early on.

I've kept to the basics of object-oriented programming in ActionScript, covering just enough it get you through to the end of this book. Advanced topics have been left out to spare your gray matter from imploding—I'll touch on them in the coming chapters where applicable, but I didn't want to overload you with too much information at the get-go.

Now, I promised you some fun stuff after these two chapters were over, and fun stuff you shall have. In the next chapter, we're going to look at how to create and manipulate graphics on the stage using the display list. See you there.

Chapter 4

WORKING WITH THE DISPLAY

Steve Webster with Todd Yard

This chapter covers the following topics:

- How to control movie playback
- What the display list is, and why you should care
- How to manipulate items on the display list
- How to create new display items from Library symbols
- How to load external images and SWF files
- How to animate display items
- How to live long and prosper

(Just kidding about that last one—you'll want a self-help book for that.)

This chapter is all about performing cool visual feats with ActionScript. If you're from a design background, that's no doubt music to your ears after the last two and a half chapters of techno-babble. If you rather liked all that geeky, highly technical stuff, the good news is that there's enough of that in this chapter to keep you interested, too.

Introducing the display list

In ActionScript 3.0 development, the *display list* is the term used to describe the hierarchy of visual items that make up your Flash movie. I would have called it the *display tree*, rather than the display list; the latter implies a flat list of display objects. whereas the former suggests that display objects can be arranged hierarchically. Still, I don't get to define the terms that Adobe uses, so we'll have to work with what we're given. If you've done any graphical work in Flash CS3 (or any previous version of the Flash authoring tool, for that matter), you've been creating display lists without really knowing or thinking about it. If you have a Flash movie containing a mixture of movie clips, graphic symbols, text fields (both static and dynamic), and an imported JPEG, the display list might look something like Figure 4-1.

```
stage
  layer 1
    background.jpg
  layer 2
    clouds_mc
  layer 3
    biker_mc
      bike_mc
        wheels_mc
          wheel
          wheel
        frame
      rider_mc
  layer 4
    title_tf
```

Figure 4-1. See, I told you that the display list is actually more like a tree!

The display list is made up of display objects, which all derive from the DisplayObject class in the flash.display package. However, certain display objects can hold (or nest) other display objects, and these derive from flash.display. DisplayObjectContainer. If you think about how you put graphical objects together in Flash, you should be able to come up with some examples of both DisplayObject and DisplayObjectContainer instances. MovieClip is an obvious candidate for a DisplayObjectContainer, since it can contain just about anything, and a TextField can contain only text and so would be a DisplayObject.

Many different child classes extend these two classes. Everything visual you can add to a Flash movie is represented as a class, and at least some of these should be familiar to you. Figure 4-2 shows all the display object classes and how they relate to one another.

I'm not going to go through all these classes right here, as that would be drab and boring. You'll meet most of them during the course of this chapter. I do, however, want to go over the lineage of the MovieClip class to explain what facets and features are added by each class in the hierarchy.

- DisplayObject: At the top of the hierarchy, this class provides the basic properties for all visual items in the display list, such as x, y, width, and height. Everything in the display list is an instance of one of the classes that extends the DisplayObject class, either directly or indirectly.

- InteractiveObject: This class adds various properties, methods, and events that allow users to interact with display objects using the mouse and keyboard. You'll learn more about events and how to allow users to interact with display objects in Chapter 6.

- DisplayObjectContainer: This class gives display objects the ability to contain other display objects, which can be manipulated using methods like addChild() and removeChild(). Other display list classes allow a specific number of child display objects. A good example is SimpleButton, which allows you to specify a different display object for each of the button states, but only DisplayObjectContainer instances allow you to have an open-ended number of child display objects.

- Sprite: This is a new type of object available with ActionScript 3.0, and there is no equivalent in the IDE. Basically, it is like a movie clip without a timeline, so it doesn't contain any of the timeline-controlling ActionScript necessary with MovieClip instances. You can still draw into it, add new display objects to it, and code for interactivity, but it is lighter weight in memory than a movie clip. It is the best bet if you are programmatically creating interactive graphics in your applications.

- MovieClip: This class adds the concept of frames, frame labels, and scenes, with all the properties and methods you need to query and manipulate the playhead. Note that while you can create MovieClip objects programmatically, you cannot add frames, labels, or scenes with ActionScript code.

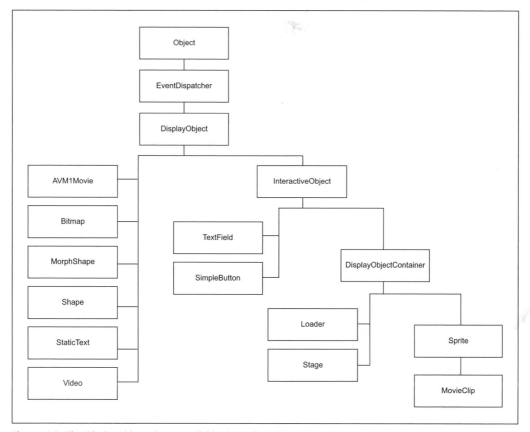

Figure 4-2. The DisplayObject classes available through ActionScript

Although DisplayObject, InteractiveObject, *and* DisplayObjectContainer *are listed in the class diagram, you can't actually create instances of any of them. These classes exist just to provide the common functionality for their descendants. Trying to create an instance of them will result in a runtime error from the ActionScript compiler such as the following:*

```
ArgumentError: Error #2012: DisplayObjectContainer$ class cannot be instantiated.
```

*Such classes are known in the trade as **abstract classes**. ActionScript 3.0 doesn't support true abstract classes. If they were true abstract classes, you should get a warning from the ActionScript compiler, rather than a runtime error from the Flash Player, but that's just me being picky.*

You also can't create an instance of the AVM1Movie *class, which is used to represent Flash movies that were created for previous versions of the Flash Player (version 8 and earlier). When you load a movie of this type, it will automatically be of type* AVM1Movie, *which is a stripped-down version of the* MovieClip *class.*

Since you're probably already familiar with the concept of a movie clip, that seems like an ideal place to start our display list journey.

Working with display objects

When you create a movie clip in the Flash CS3 IDE and place it on the stage, it becomes a property of type MovieClip in the document class specified for the Flash movie. The name of the property is the same as the instance name of the movie clip on the stage.

1. Create a new Flash movie and save it in the project directory with the name display.fla.

2. On the stage, draw a 100 × 100-pixel, light-blue square with a thick, black outline.

3. Select the square (and its outline) and convert it to a movie clip symbol by selecting Modify ➤ Convert to Symbol from the main menu or by pressing F8.

4. Enter **Square** in the Name field of the Convert to Symbol dialog box, as shown in Figure 4-3, and then click OK to create the symbol. You will get the familiar warning about the class file being created behind the scenes for you. This is OK.

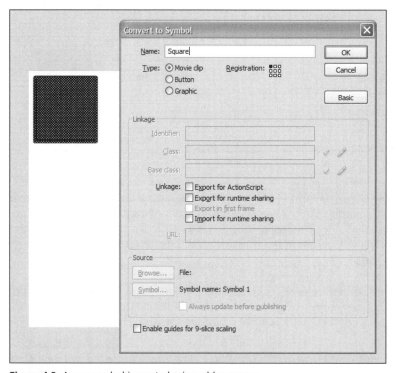

Figure 4-3. A new symbol is created using a blue square.

5. Select the instance of the Square symbol on the stage and give it an instance name of square in the Property inspector.

6. Create a new ActionScript file for the document class. As promised in the previous chapter, you're going to start organizing classes properly, so create a class named DisplayTest in the com.foundationAS3.ch4 package. This means that you'll need to create a directory structure in the project directory that mirrors this package structure. Save the file in the ch4 folder with the name DisplayTest.as.

7. Create the basic package and class definitions for the DisplayTest class with an empty constructor method. The main document class needs to extend either the Sprite or MovieClip class. Unless you have timeline animation in the root timeline of the Flash document, it's always best to use the Sprite class. It's slightly more efficient in terms of performance and memory usage, because it doesn't need to keep track of frame information. Since you don't have any timeline animation, the Sprite class will do just fine.

```
package com.foundationAS3.ch4 {

  import flash.display.Sprite;

  public class DisplayTest extends Sprite {

    public function DisplayTest() {
    }

  }

}
```

8. Once you've set this class to be the document class for the display.fla movie and published the SWF file, the instance of the Square symbol on the stage with an instance name of square will become a property of your DisplayTest instance. You can add a simple trace() statement to the constructor method to prove that the MovieClip exists:

```
package com.foundationAS3.ch4 {

  import flash.display.Sprite;

  public class DisplayTest extends Sprite {

    public function DisplayTest() {
      trace(square);
    }

  }

}
```

9. Save the changes to the DisplayTest.as file and switch back to the display.fla file.

10. You now need to specify that the display.fla movie should use the DisplayTest class as its document class. Click an empty area of the stage and enter **com.foundationAS3.ch4.DisplayTest** in the Document class field of the Property inspector, as shown in Figure 4-4.

Figure 4-4. Setting the document class

11. Save the changes to the display.fla file and test it by selecting Control ➤ Test Movie from the main menu, or by pressing Ctrl+Enter (Windows) or Command+Enter (Mac OS X).

Oops! You got your square, but nothing in the Output panel. If you look at the Compiler Errors panel, you'll see that you got an error, as shown in Figure 4-5.

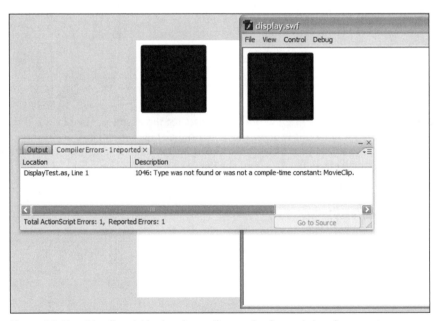

Figure 4-5. Your friendly neighborhood compiler warning for a missing class

The Flash compiler is complaining that it couldn't find the MovieClip class. But why was it looking for it if you extended the Sprite class? The answer is that the compiler tried to add the Square instance as a property of type MovieClip to the DisplayTest class, but wasn't smart enough to import the class on its own. This is a bug in the Flash compiler, but you can get around that simply by adding an import statement for MovieClip.

12. In the DisplayTest.as file, add the bold line shown in the following code.

```
package com.foundationAS3.ch4 {

  import flash.display.MovieClip;
  import flash.display.Sprite;

  public class DisplayTest extends Sprite {

    public function DisplayTest() {
      trace(square);
    }

  }

}
```

13. Save the changes to the file, switch to the display.fla movie, and test the movie again. This time, you should see the result of the trace() statement in the Output panel, as shown in Figure 4-6.

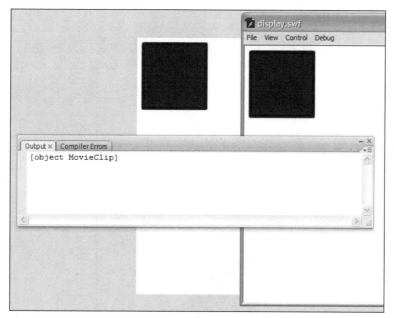

Figure 4-6. The Square instance found and traced in the DisplayTest class

Manipulating display objects

Now that you have a reference to the MovieClip instance, you can start to play around with its various properties. For example, you could move the instance of the Square symbol to (300,300) on the stage by setting its x and y properties accordingly (see Figure 4-7):

```
package com.foundationAS3.ch4 {

  import flash.display.MovieClip;
  import flash.display.Sprite;

  public class DisplayTest extends Sprite {

    public function DisplayTest() {
      trace(square);

      // Move to (300,300)
      square.x = 300;
      square.y = 300;
    }

  }

}
```

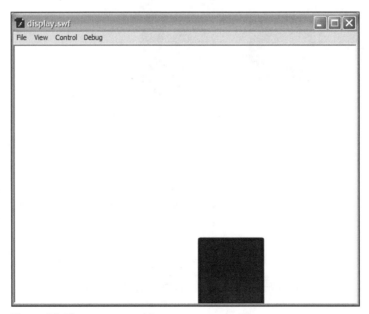

Figure 4-7. The square moved to a new screen position.

You can change the Square symbol instance's width and height by setting its width and height properties (see Figure 4-8):

```
package com.foundationAS3.ch4 {

  import flash.display.MovieClip;
  import flash.display.Sprite;

  public class DisplayTest extends Sprite {

    public function DisplayTest() {
      trace(square);

      // Move to (300,300)
      square.x = 300;
      square.y = 300;

      // Stretch horizontally and squash vertically
      square.width = 200;
      square.height = 50;
    }

  }

}
```

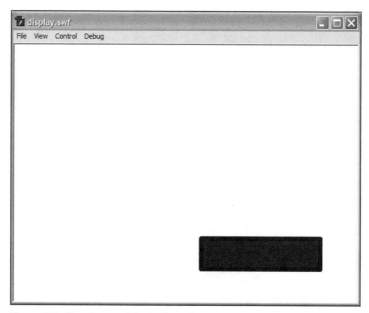

Figure 4-8. Changing an object's dimensions is a snap.

Another way to adjust a display object's height and width is by changing the scaleX and scaleY properties. These values are used to multiply the original width and height of the object to determine its scale. So, if you set scaleX and scaleY to 2, the Square instance would be twice as wide and twice as high as it was originally. Conversely, if you set scaleX and scaleY to 0.5, the Square instance would be half as tall and half as high. The following code is equivalent to the previous example, but instead of setting width and height, it scales the movie clip using scaleX and scaleY.

```
package com.foundationAS3.ch4 {

  import flash.display.MovieClip;
  import flash.display.Sprite;

  public class DisplayTest extends Sprite {

    public function DisplayTest() {
      trace(square);

      // Move to (300,300)
      square.x = 300;
      square.y = 300;

      // Stretch horizontally and squash vertically
      square.scaleX = 2;
      square.scaleY = 0.5;
    }

  }

}
```

You can change the opacity of the movie clip using the alpha property. This is a value between 0 (transparent) and 1 (opaque) that indicates the alpha level for the instance. Here's an example (see Figure 4-9):

```
package com.foundationAS3.ch4 {

  import flash.display.MovieClip;
  import flash.display.Sprite;

  public class DisplayTest extends Sprite {

    public function DisplayTest() {
      trace(square);

      // Move to (300,300)
      square.x = 300;
      square.y = 300;

      // Stretch horizontally and squash vertically
      square.scaleX = 2;
      square.scaleY = 0.5;
```

```
      // Make 50% alpha
      square.alpha = 0.5;
    }

  }

}
```

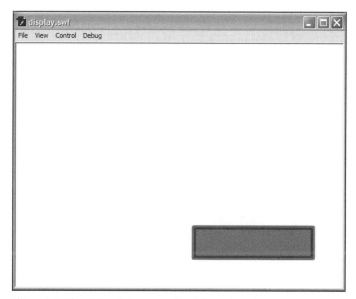

Figure 4-9. The alpha of the square is set through code.

You can also rotate the movie clip around the registration point by setting the rotation property. This is a number in degrees indicating the rotation amount of the display object. The following example rotates the Square instance 45 degrees (see Figure 4-10):

```
package com.foundationAS3.ch4 {

  import flash.display.MovieClip;
  import flash.display.Sprite;

  public class DisplayTest extends Sprite {

    public function DisplayTest() {
      trace(square);

      // Move to (300,300)
      square.x = 300;
      square.y = 300;

      // Stretch horizontally and squash vertically
      square.scaleX = 2;
      square.scaleY = 0.5;
```

119

```
        // Make 50% alpha
        square.alpha = 0.5;

        // Rotate 45 degrees
        square.rotation = 45;
      }

    }

  }
```

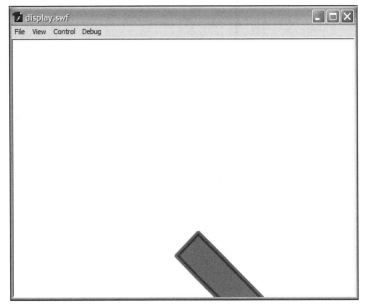

Figure 4-10. The square is rotated as well.

You'll learn about some of the other properties you can manipulate, such as blendMode and filters, throughout this chapter. Feel free to stop here and play around for a while.

Managing depth

In the Flash IDE, you may be used to controlling the depth of a visual object by using layers in the time-line or (if you like to make it harder on yourself) through the entries in the Modify ➤ Arrange menu.

In ActionScript, the depth of a display object is determined by its index in the parent display object's internal array of children. The higher the index, the further toward the front of the movie that object appears. That means if a Sprite instance has a child at index 0, that child will appear visually below a child at index 1 (or any higher number, for that matter). You can't manipulate this array directly, as it's an internal property of the DisplayObjectContainer class, but you can use the methods provided to query and manipulate the depth of a display object directly.

Discovering the depth of objects

To get the depth of a display object, you need to pass that object to its parent's getChildIndex() method. Follow these steps to see how that works:

1. Create a new ActionScript file and save it as DepthTest.as in the com.foundationAS3.ch4 directory. Add the following code to the file.

```
package com.foundationAS3.ch4 {

    import flash.display.MovieClip;
    import flash.display.Sprite;

    public class DepthTest extends Sprite {

        public function DepthTest() {
            trace(getChildIndex(square));
        }

    }

}
```

2. Save the display.fla file as depth.fla. Set the document class as com.foundationAS3. ch4.DepthTest. If you test the movie now, you should see that the square object is at depth 0. Let's make it a little more interesting by adding a few more instances of the Square symbol to the stage.

3. In the display.fla movie, drag two more instances of the Square symbol from the Library onto the stage, each in its own layer. Make sure they overlap, as shown in Figure 4-11.

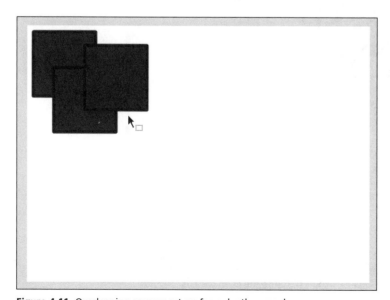

Figure 4-11. Overlapping squares set up for a depth example

4. Give these new Square symbols instance names, from back to front, of square2 and square3 (yeah, just call me Mr. Imaginative from now on).

5. Save the changes to the document, and then switch back to the DepthTest.as file.

6. Now add trace statements to get the depths of the two new instances of the Square symbol. Add string labels before them so you know which depth belongs to which instance.

```
package com.foundationAS3.ch4 {

  import flash.display.MovieClip;
  import flash.display.Sprite;

  public class DepthTest extends Sprite {

    public function DepthTest() {
      trace("square: " + getChildIndex(square));
      trace("square2: " + getChildIndex(square2));
      trace("square3: " + getChildIndex(square3));
    }

  }

}
```

7. Save the changes, switch back to the depth.fla movie, and test. In addition to seeing three squares on the stage, you should be able to see the depth of each one in the Output panel, as shown in Figure 4-12.

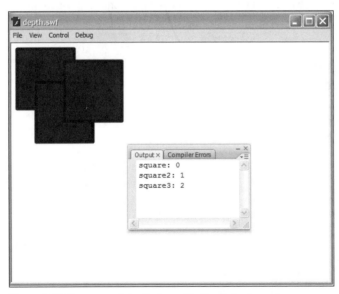

Figure 4-12. The squares' depths traced to the Output panel

As you can see, from back to front, the Square symbols are arranged from index 0 to index 2.

Manipulating the depth of objects

Now that you have several display objects on the screen, you can start to manipulate their depths using the setChildIndex() method. This method takes two parameters: the display object whose index you want to change and the index to which you want to move it.

> The specified display object must be a child of the display object on which you're calling the setChildIndex() method, and the index must not be higher than the number of children that the display object contains. Otherwise, you'll get a runtime error in the player.

Let's try moving the original square object to the front of the display list. To do this, call the parent's setChildIndex() method, passing the square object and a new depth. You could pass in 2 as the depth, but the best way to bring an object to the top of its parent's list is to use numChildren to determine the highest depth. Note that you must use (numChildren-1), since the display list is zero-indexed. So a parent with three children has a top depth of 2 (0 for the first child, 1 for the second, and 2 for the third).

```
package com.foundationAS3.ch4 {

    import flash.display.MovieClip;
    import flash.display.Sprite;

    public class DepthTest extends Sprite {

        public function DepthTest() {
            trace("square: " + getChildIndex(square));
            trace("square2: " + getChildIndex(square2));
            trace("square3: " + getChildIndex(square3));

            setChildIndex(square, numChildren-1);
        }

    }

}
```

Copy and paste the index-tracing statements below the call to setChildIndex(), so you can see what effect setting the index of a display object has on the other display objects belonging to that parent.

```
package com.foundationAS3.ch4 {

    import flash.display.MovieClip;
    import flash.display.Sprite;

    public class DepthTest extends Sprite {
```

```
public function DepthTest() {
  trace("square: " + getChildIndex(square));
  trace("square2: " + getChildIndex(square2));
  trace("square3: " + getChildIndex(square3));

  setChildIndex(square, numChildren-1);

  trace("square: " + getChildIndex(square));
  trace("square2: " + getChildIndex(square2));
  trace("square3: " + getChildIndex(square3));
}

}

}
```

Save the changes, switch to the depth.fla file, and test the movie. On the stage, you can see that the original square is now in front of the others. In the Output panel, shown in Figure 4-13, you can see why: its index is now the highest of all the display objects.

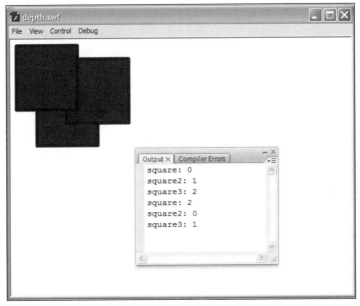

Figure 4-13. The squares with a bit of depth swapping applied using setChildIndex()

Swapping depths

The other way to alter the index of a display object is to swap its index with another display object belonging to the same parent. There are two ways to do this: call the swapChildren() method and pass the two display objects as the parameters, or call swapChildrenAt() and pass the two indexes you want to swap. Let's do both.

First swap the indexes of square2 and square3.

```
package com.foundationAS3.ch4 {

  import flash.display.MovieClip;
  import flash.display.Sprite;

  public class DepthTest extends Sprite {

    public function DepthTest() {
      trace("square: " + getChildIndex(square));
      trace("square2: " + getChildIndex(square2));
      trace("square3: " + getChildIndex(square3));

      setChildIndex(square, numChildren-1);

      trace("square: " + getChildIndex(square));
      trace("square2: " + getChildIndex(square2));
      trace("square3: " + getChildIndex(square3));

      swapChildren(square2, square3);
    }

  }

}
```

Now swap the indexes of the display objects at index 0 and 2.

```
package com.foundationAS3.ch4 {

  import flash.display.MovieClip;
  import flash.display.Sprite;

  public class DepthTest extends Sprite {

    public function DepthTest() {
      trace("square: " + getChildIndex(square));
      trace("square2: " + getChildIndex(square2));
      trace("square3: " + getChildIndex(square3));

      setChildIndex(square, numChildren-1);

      trace("square: " + getChildIndex(square));
      trace("square2: " + getChildIndex(square2));
      trace("square3: " + getChildIndex(square3));

      swapChildren(square2, square3);
      swapChildrenAt(0, 2);
    }

  }

}
```

Copy and paste the trace() statements, so you know the indexes of your Square symbols.

```
package com.foundationAS3.ch4 {

    import flash.display.MovieClip;
    import flash.display.Sprite;

    public class DepthTest extends Sprite {

        public function DepthTest() {
            trace("square: " + getChildIndex(square));
            trace("square2: " + getChildIndex(square2));
            trace("square3: " + getChildIndex(square3));

            setChildIndex(square, numChildren-1);

            trace("square: " + getChildIndex(square));
            trace("square2: " + getChildIndex(square2));
            trace("square3: " + getChildIndex(square3));

            swapChildren(square2, square3);
            swapChildrenAt(0, 2);

            trace("square: " + getChildIndex(square));
            trace("square2: " + getChildIndex(square2));
            trace("square3: " + getChildIndex(square3));
        }

    }

}
```

Finally, switch to depth.fla and test the movie. You should see in the Output panel (and on the stage) that the Square symbols have ended up in the same order in which they started. If you aren't sure why, cut up some squares of paper and perform the depth-swapping operations in the real world.

Creating new display objects

You're not just limited to the display list that is generated by the Flash IDE. You don't even need to have anything on the stage in the Flash IDE. You can create new instances of many of the display list classes and add them to the display list.

You create display list class instances in the same way as you create instances of a normal class: with the new keyword. Creating a new MovieClip object is as simple as this:

```
var myMovieClip:MovieClip = new MovieClip();
```

You now have a new MovieClip instance, but it isn't yet part of the display list. In order to add it to the display list, you need to add it as a child of a display object that's already on the display list. You can add a display object as a child of another by calling the addChild() method on the parent display object and passing the child object as the single parameter.

```
var myMovieClip:MovieClip = new MovieClip();
parentMovieClip.addChild(myMovieClip);
```

The addChild() method is part of the DisplayObjectContainer class, so only instances of classes descended from this class (Sprite, MovieClip, and so on) can have child display objects added in this way.

When you add a new child with the addChild() method, it is assigned the topmost index, and appears in front, or on top, of all other display objects belonging to the same parent. If you want to add a child at a specific depth, you can use the addChildAt() method, passing the display object to be added and the desired index.

```
var myMovieClip:MovieClip = new MovieClip();
parentMovieClip.addChildAt(myMovieClip, 4);
```

If there is already a display object at that index, the existing display object's index (and the index of all display objects above it) are incremented to make room for the new display object, as shown in Figure 4-14.

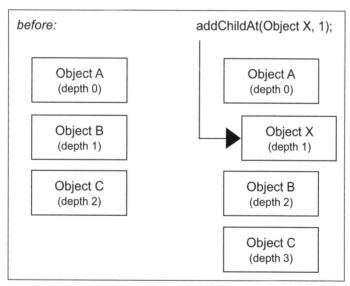

Figure 4-14. A new child is inserted into the display list, shifting all children at higher depths up a depth.

Just how useful the ability to create new display objects and add them to the display list is will become apparent when we look at using Library symbols in the "Using Library resources" section later in the chapter.

Removing display objects from the display list

You can also remove display objects from the list. The removeChild() method allows you to specify a display object to remove. The removeChildAt() method removes a display object at a specific index. Based on the previous sample code, the following two statements are equal:

```
parentMovieClip,removeChild(myMovieClip);
parentMovieClip.removeChildAt(4);
```

When you remove a display object from the display list, the index of each display object above the removed one is decremented to fill in the gap left by the removed display object, as shown in Figure 4-15.

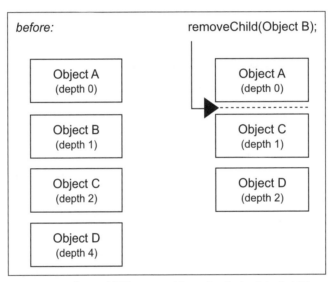

Figure 4-15. When a child is removed from the display list, all children at higher depths are shifted down a depth to fill the gap.

The display list does not allow for gaps in the depths, as was possible in ActionScript 2.0 and AVM1. You cannot add a display object at an index that is higher than the parent's number of children, and once you remove a display object, all children at higher depths shift down to fill in the gap, automatically adjusting their depths.

Specifying blend modes

You have access to the same set of blend modes in ActionScript as you have at design time in the Flash IDE. Every display object has a blendMode property, which specifies the blend mode to use to render it.

The blendMode property expects a String value, but to help you out (so you don't need to guess what the string is for each blend mode), a BlendMode class in the flash.display package has static constants for each of the blend modes.

To see this in action, go back to the DepthTest.as class from earlier and edit the constructor method to set the blendMode property of square3 to BlendMode.INVERT. Make sure to import the BlendMode class at the top.

```
package com.foundationAS3.ch4 {

  import flash.display.BlendMode;
  import flash.display.MovieClip;
  import flash.display.Sprite;

  public class DepthTest extends Sprite {

    public function DepthTest() {
      trace("square: " + getChildIndex(square));
      trace("square2: " + getChildIndex(square2));
      trace("square3: " + getChildIndex(square3));

      setChildIndex(square, numChildren-1);

      trace("square: " + getChildIndex(square));
      trace("square2: " + getChildIndex(square2));
      trace("square3: " + getChildIndex(square3));

      swapChildren(square2, square3);
      swapChildrenAt(0, 2);

      trace("square: " + getChildIndex(square));
      trace("square2: " + getChildIndex(square2));
      trace("square3: " + getChildIndex(square3));

      square3.blendMode = BlendMode.INVERT;
    }

  }

}
```

Save the changes, switch to the depth.fla file, and test the movie. The result should be as shown in Figure 4-16.

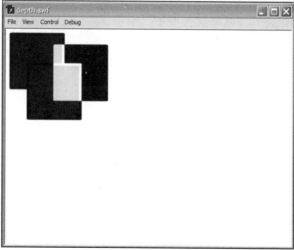

Figure 4-16. The top square in the display list is given a blend mode.

Working with filters

In addition to blend modes, you can also apply filters (or manipulate existing filters) from ActionScript. Each display object has a `filters` property, which is an array of `BitmapFilter` instances applied to the display object. Each different type of filter you can apply is represented as a subclass of the `BitmapFilter` class. Filter classes include the following:

- `BevelFilter`
- `BlurFilter`
- `ColorMatrixFilter`
- `ConvolutionFilter`
- `DisplacementMapFilter`
- `DropShadowFilter`
- `GlowFilter`
- `GradientBevelFilter`
- `GradientGlowFilter`

The filter classes live in the `flash.filters` package, and each has its own set of properties that control various facets of the filter. For example, the `BlurFilter` class has three properties—blurX, blurY, and quality—that control the amount and quality of the blur effect applied to a display object.

Applying a filter to a display object

Let's create a simple example and use the `GlowFilter`.

1. Create a new Flash document and save it to a file named `filters.fla`.
2. Draw a white 100 × 100-pixel square with a medium, black outline on the stage and convert it to a movie clip symbol named Square, as shown in Figure 4-17.
3. Drag a second Square symbol onto the stage, and position the squares next to each other in the center of the stage, as shown in Figure 4-18. Give the squares instance names of square and square2.
4. Save the changes to `filters.fla`.
5. Create a new ActionScript file for the document class. Save it as `FilterTest.as` into the `com.foundationAS3.ch4` directory.

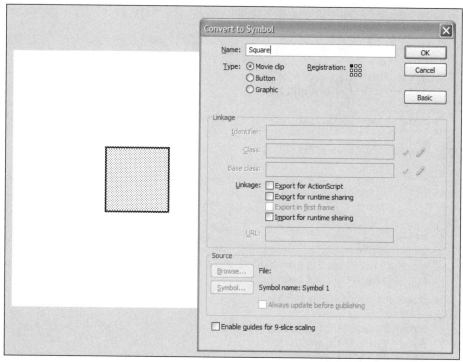

Figure 4-17. A new Square symbol

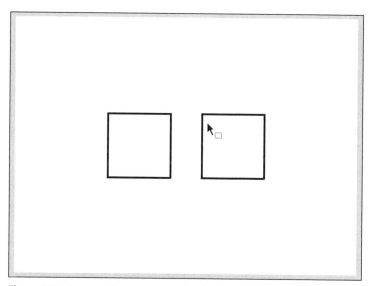

Figure 4-18. A second Square instance is added to the stage.

6. Create the basic package and class definitions for the `FilterTest` class, including an empty constructor method.

```
package com.foundationAS3.ch4 {

  import flash.display.MovieClip;
  import flash.display.Sprite;

  public class FilterTest extends Sprite {

    public function FilterTest() {
    }

  }

}
```

7. Since you will be trying out a number of filters, use the asterisk (*) wildcard to import all the classes from the flash.filters package and create a new instance of the GlowFilter class as a local variable in the class constructor.

```
package com.foundationAS3.ch4 {

  import flash.display.MovieClip;
  import flash.display.Sprite;
  import flash.filters.*;

  public class FilterTest extends Sprite {

    public function FilterTest() {
      var glow:GlowFilter = new GlowFilter();
    }

  }

}
```

8. Wrap the GlowFilter instance in an array literal, and assign that to the `filters` property of the square object.

```
package com.foundationAS3.ch4 {

  import flash.display.MovieClip;
  import flash.display.Sprite;
  import flash.filters.*;

  public class FilterTest extends Sprite {

    public function FilterTest() {
      var glow:GlowFilter = new GlowFilter();
```

```
            square.filters = [glow];
        }

    }

}
```

9. Save the changes to FilterTest.as and switch back to the filters.fla movie. Set the document class of the movie in the Property inspector to com.foundationAS3.ch4.FilterTest.

10. Save the changes to filters.fla and test the movie. You should see that one of the Square symbols on the stage has a red glow, as shown in Figure 4-19, created by the filter you've just applied.

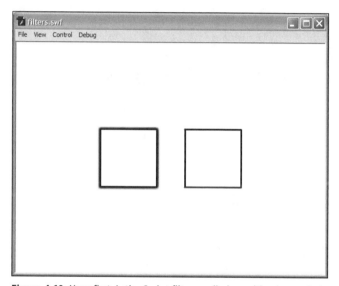

Figure 4-19. Your first ActionScript filter applied, resulting in a red glow

The GlowFilter constructor takes a whole bunch of parameters that control how the filter looks when applied to a display object. You've just used the filter with its default values. The parameters for the GlowFilter constructor are as follows:

- color: A hexadecimal value for the desired color of the glow. The default is 0xFF0000 (red).

- alpha: A value between 0 (transparent) and 1 (opaque). The default is 1.

- blurX: A Number value dictating the amount of horizontal blur applied to the glow. The default is 6.

- blurY: Same as blurX, but vertically.

- strength: A Number value between 0 and 255 indicating the intensity of the glow. The default is 2.

- quality: An int value between 1 and 15 that indicates the number of times the filter is applied. The more times a filter is applied, the better it looks, but higher-quality filters can have an impact on performance. The default is 1.

- inner: A Boolean value that, if set to true, applies the glow to the inside of a display object rather than the outside. The default is false.

- knockout: A Boolean value that, if set to true, means that the display object's fill will be transparent, leaving just the result of the filter. The default is false.

I'm not a big fan of red, and the square's glow looks a little wimpy to me, so let's change some of the properties of the filter. Let's use green (0x00FF00), with full opacity and blur values of 10 pixels. Make these changes in the FilterTest class constructor:

```
package com.foundationAS3.ch4 {

    import flash.display.MovieClip;
    import flash.display.Sprite;
    import flash.filters.*;

    public class FilterTest extends Sprite {

      public function FilterTest() {
        var glow:GlowFilter = new GlowFilter(0x00FF00, 1, 10, 10);
        square.filters = [glow];
      }

    }

}
```

Save the changes, switch back to filters.fla, and test the movie. You should now see a much bigger, green glow on the square, as shown in Figure 4-20.

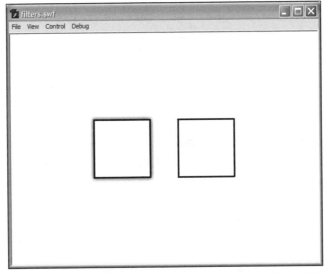

Figure 4-20. The parameters of the glow have been altered for a slightly different effect.

Applying filters in a specific order

As in the Flash IDE, the filters for a given display object are applied in the order in which they are assigned. If you apply a DropShadowFilter before a GlowFilter, the glow appears around the composite outline of the symbol and the drop shadow (which, if you ask me, just looks plain weird). Let's try it out.

In the FilterTest class constructor, create a new DropShadowFilter instance and add it as a second element in the filters array.

```
package com.foundationAS3.ch4 {

  import flash.display.MovieClip;
  import flash.display.Sprite;
  import flash.filters.*;

  public class FilterTest extends Sprite {

    public function FilterTest() {
      var glow:GlowFilter = new GlowFilter(0x00FF00, 1, 10, 10);
      var dropShadow:DropShadowFilter = new DropShadowFilter();
      square.filters = [glow, dropShadow];
    }

  }

}
```

Now assign the same filters in the reverse order to square2's filters property.

```
package com.foundationAS3.ch4 {

  import flash.display.MovieClip;
  import flash.display.Sprite;
  import flash.filters.*;

  public class FilterTest extends Sprite {

    public function FilterTest() {
      var glow:GlowFilter = new GlowFilter(0x00FF00, 1, 10, 10);
      var dropShadow:DropShadowFilter = new DropShadowFilter();
      square.filters = [glow, dropShadow];
      square2.filters = [dropShadow, glow];
    }

  }

}
```

Save the changes to the `FilterTest.as` file, switch to `filters.fla`, and test the movie. You should see the result shown in Figure 4-21.

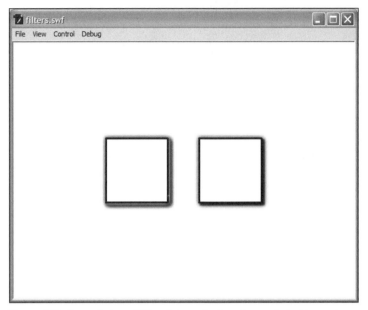

Figure 4-21. The ordering of filters is important, as demonstrated here where the same glow and drop shadow are applied to both squares in different orders for different effects.

Making changes to an existing filter

You can make changes to a `BitmapFilter` instance once it has been applied to a display object, but the process for doing so is a little trickier than you might think. Given that the `filters` array is made up references to `BitmapFilter` instances, you would think that all you need to do is get a reference to the relevant `BitmapFilter` instance, make a change, and that change would be replicated on screen in the appearance of the filter. You could try this:

```
package com.foundationAS3.ch4 {

  import flash.display.MovieClip;
  import flash.display.Sprite;
  import flash.filters.*;

  public class FilterTest extends Sprite {

    public function FilterTest() {
      var glow:GlowFilter = new GlowFilter(0x00FF00, 1, 10, 10);
      var dropShadow:DropShadowFilter = new DropShadowFilter();
      square.filters = [glow,dropShadow];
      square2.filters = [dropShadow,glow];
```

```
      // Change glow to blue
      glow.color = 0x0000FF;
    }

  }

}
```

Frustratingly, that doesn't work. It turns out that the filters property of a display object is a bit special in the way that it works.

When you assign an array of BitmapFilter instances to a display object, it clones the array and all of the BitmapFilter instances within it, meaning that making a change to one of the original BitmapFilter instances will not affect the clone that the display object is using. In order to make your changes take effect, you need to overwrite the filters property with a new array.

```
package com.foundationAS3.ch4 {

  import flash.display.MovieClip;
  import flash.display.Sprite;
  import flash.filters.*;

  public class FilterTest extends Sprite {

    public function FilterTest() {
      var glow:GlowFilter = new GlowFilter(0x00FF00, 1, 10, 10);
      var dropShadow:DropShadowFilter = new DropShadowFilter();
      square.filters = [glow,dropShadow];
      square2.filters = [dropShadow,glow];

      // Change glow to blue
      glow.color = 0x0000FF;
      square.filters = [glow,dropShadow];
    }

  }

}
```

If you test filters.fla with the preceding changes to the FilterTest class, you'll see that only one of your Square symbols has a blue glow, and the other has a green glow—job done!

This was relatively painless because you already had a reference to the BitmapFilter instance you wanted to change in the glow variable, and you had a reference to the other filter, so you could easily reconstruct the filters array. Sometimes that's not an option (maybe the filters were originally created by another part of the code). In that case, you can use the filters property of the display object to get a clone of the filters assigned to it, make your changes, and then reassign the array back to the filters property.

Let's pretend you don't have references to the BitmapFilter instances and change the angle of the drop shadow on the second Square symbol. Get a clone to the filters array from the square2 display object and loop through the BitmapFilter instances with a for each loop.

```
package com.foundationAS3.ch4 {

    import flash.display.MovieClip;
    import flash.display.Sprite;
    import flash.filters.*;

    public class FilterTest extends Sprite {

      public function FilterTest() {
        var glow:GlowFilter = new GlowFilter(0x00FF00, 1, 10, 10);
        var dropShadow:DropShadowFilter = new DropShadowFilter();
        square.filters = [glow,dropShadow];
        square2.filters = [dropShadow,glow];

        // Change glow to blue
        glow.color = 0x0000FF;
        square.filters = [glow,dropShadow];

        // Change angle of drop shadow
        var filters:Array = square2.filters;
        for each (var filter:BitmapFilter in filters) {

        }
      }
    }

}
```

Notice that the for each loop allows you to strongly type the iterator for the loop to BitmapFilter, since you know that the filters array can contain only instances of BitmapFilter.

In each iteration of the loop, you will test to see if you've found the DropShadowFilter instance and, if so, set the angle property accordingly.

```
package com.foundationAS3.ch4 {

    import flash.display.MovieClip;
    import flash.display.Sprite;
    import flash.filters.*;

    public class FilterTest extends Sprite {
```

```
    public function FilterTest() {
      var glow:GlowFilter = new GlowFilter(0x00FF00, 1, 10, 10);
      var dropShadow:DropShadowFilter = new DropShadowFilter();
      square.filters = [glow,dropShadow];
      square2.filters = [dropShadow,glow];

      // Change glow to blue
      glow.color = 0x0000FF;
      square.filters = [glow,dropShadow];

      // Change angle of drop shadow
      var filters:Array = square2.filters;
      for each (var filter:BitmapFilter in filters) {
        if (filter is DropShadowFilter) {
          (filter as DropShadowFilter).angle = 270;
        }
      }
    }

  }

}
```

Here, you are using the is operator to check to see whether the filter at the current iteration of the loop is an instance of DropShadowFilter. If it is, you then can use the as operator to cast the filter iterator as a DropShadowFilter, so that you can assign to its angle property. If you did not do this, you would get a compile-time error, since filter is typed to the abstract base class BitmapFilter in the loop—a class that does not have an angle property.

Finally, reassign the filters array to the filters property of the display object.

```
    package com.foundationAS3.ch4 {

      import flash.display.MovieClip;
      import flash.display.Sprite;
      import flash.filters.*;

      public class FilterTest extends Sprite {

        public function FilterTest() {
          var glow:GlowFilter = new GlowFilter(0x00FF00, 1, 10, 10);
          var dropShadow:DropShadowFilter = new DropShadowFilter();
          square.filters = [glow,dropShadow];
          square2.filters = [dropShadow,glow];

          // Change glow to blue
          glow.color = 0x0000FF;
          square.filters = [glow,dropShadow];
```

```
        // Change angle of drop shadow
        var filters:Array = square2.filters;
        for each (var filter:BitmapFilter in filters) {
          if (filter is DropShadowFilter) {
            (filter as DropShadowFilter).angle = 270;
          }
        }
        square2.filters = filters;
      }

    }

  }
```

Save the changes to FilterTest.as, switch to filters.fla, and test the movie. With a bit of luck, the drop shadow on the second square should have changed direction, as shown in Figure 4-22.

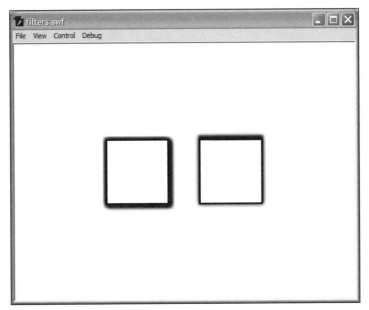

Figure 4-22. The angle of the drop shadow is changed by finding the filter in the original array, altering it, and then reassigning all the filters back to the square.

Removing an existing filter

Once you understand how to change a property of a filter, removing it from a display object is pretty straightforward. You need to get a clone of the display object's filters array, remove the element from that array containing the BitmapFilter you want to remove, and then reassign the array to the filters property of the display object.

You can remove an element from an array in several ways:

- To remove the last element in the array, the easiest method is to use pop().
- To remove the first element in the array, the easiest method to use is shift().
- To remove an element in the middle of an array, use the splice() method.

The splice() method is designed to allow you to splice two arrays together, inserting an array at a certain point in another array and replacing a specified number of the original array's values. It takes three parameters: the index into which to splice the new array, the number of elements in the original array that will be replaced, and the new array itself. However, if you leave out the last parameter, the splice() method will just remove the specified number of elements from the source array at the specified index.

Let's change the FilterTest class to remove the drop shadow filter from square. In this case, you know the index of the DropShadowFilter in the filters array (it's at index 1), so you don't need to loop through the array to find it.

```
package com.foundationAS3.ch4 {

  import flash.display.MovieClip;
  import flash.display.Sprite;
  import flash.filters.*;

  public class FilterTest extends Sprite {

    public function FilterTest() {
      var glow:GlowFilter = new GlowFilter(0x00FF00, 1, 10, 10);
      var dropShadow:DropShadowFilter = new DropShadowFilter();
      square.filters = [glow,dropShadow];
      square2.filters = [dropShadow,glow];

      // Change glow to blue
      glow.color = 0x0000FF;
      square.filters = [glow,dropShadow];

      // Change angle of drop shadow
      var filters:Array = square2.filters;
      for each (var filter:BitmapFilter in filters) {
        if (filter is DropShadowFilter) {
          (filter as DropShadowFilter).angle = 270;
        }
      }
      square2.filters = filters;

      // Remove drop shadow
      filters = square.filters;
      filters.pop();
      square.filters = filters;
    }

  }

}
```

Save the changes to FilterTest.as, switch to filters.fla, and test the movie. You should see that the first square no longer has a drop shadow, as shown in Figure 4-23.

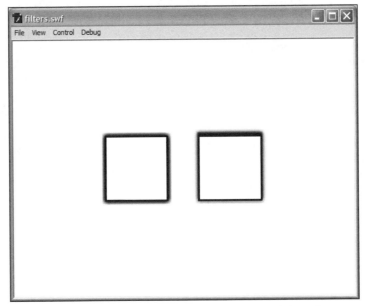

Figure 4-23. The drop shadow on the first square is removed altogether.

Introducing the advanced filters

All of the filters discussed in the previous sections are the same ones that you can create and apply visually within the Flash IDE. However, two extra BitmapFilter classes are available through ActionScript: ConvolutionFilter and DisplacementMapFilter.

When applied to a display object, the ConvolutionFilter calculates each pixel to display based on its neighboring pixels and a mathematical matrix that you supply. This is a powerful filter that enables you to achieve a number of effects, including sharpen, edge detect, emboss, and bevel. Figure 4-24 shows an example of using the ConvolutionFilter.

The DisplacementMapFilter allows you to warp a display object using a BitmapData object to calculate where and how much to warp. Using this filter, you can create fisheye, warp, mottle, and other effects. Figure 4-25 shows an example of using the DisplacementMapFilter.

If these filters sound interesting to you, many examples are available in the online help.

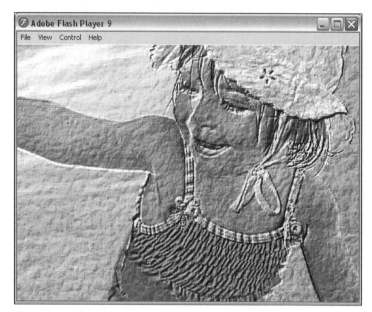

Figure 4-24. The ConvolutionFilter applied to an image to create an embossing effect

Figure 4-25. The DisplacementMapFilter applied to an image for an interesting effect

Accessing the stage

Access to the stage is done through the stage property of a display object. The Stage class is the top-most display object. This class contains a number of additional properties for the movie, such as stageWidth and stageHeight, which give you the dimensions of the entire stage (as opposed to width and height, which will tell you the combined dimensions of all the visible items in the movie).

Using Stage properties

Although the Stage class is part of the display list class diagram shown earlier in Figure 4-2, you can't actually create new instances of it—as they say in the Highlander movies, "There can be only one." In addition, many of the properties that the single Stage instance has by virtue of its class inheritance have no meaning, such as x, y, alpha, and so on; some can actually throw errors if you try to set them. However, a few useful properties of the Stage instance are worth remembering.

First, by setting scaleMode to one of the constants from the StageScaleMode class, you can change how the movie is resized when its size changes from that originally specified in the document's Property inspector. This can happen when the movie is playing in a stand-alone player and the user resizes the window, or if a developer changes the width/height of the <object>/<embed> tags used to embed the Flash movie in an HTML page.

When scaleMode is set to StageScaleMode.NO_SCALE, the stage dimensions change every time the movie is resized. That's where the stageWidth and stageHeight properties come in handy. They tell you exactly how big the stage is.

The potentially most useful Stage property is displayState, which allows you to switch the playback of the movie to full screen, either from a movie embedded in a web page or from the stand-alone player. This is great when playing back video or viewing a slide show, but has a couple of drawbacks when you're dealing with a Flash movie embedded in a web page:

- You must set the allowFullScreen parameter/attribute to true in the HTML source code for both the object and embed tags.
- You can change the Stage.displayState property only in response to a mouse click or a key press (not, for instance, when the movie loads).
- When entering full-screen mode, the Flash Player overlays a message on the screen informing the users that they are in full-screen mode and that they can press the Esc key at any time to exit.
- While the movie is in full-screen mode, keyboard input will be disabled.

This may all seem like a bit of a pain, but can you imagine how badly advertising agencies would misuse this feature if they could send users into full-screen mode without their permission? Even worse, without these precautions, scammers could use this to spoof websites and potentially steal your valuable data. Suddenly, these fail-safe measures don't seem like so much of a pain.

Making a movie full screen

Let's go through a quick example to see how you can make your movie full screen. You won't use any graphics other than a button, so this won't be much to look at, but you'll see how easy it is to get the full-screen experience.

1. Create a new Flash file and save it into your project directory as `fullscreen.fla`.

2. Draw a circle on the stage that will act as our button. Convert it into a movie clip symbol and name it Circle, as shown in Figure 4-26. Click OK to exit the dialog box and create the symbol.

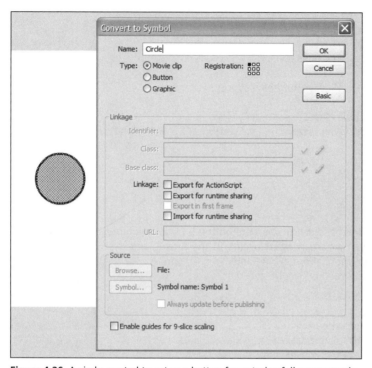

Figure 4-26. A circle created to act as a button for entering full-screen mode

3. Using the Property inspector with the Circle instance still selected, name the instance circle and save the file.

4. Create a new ActionScript file and save it into the `com.foundationAS3.ch4` directory as `FullScreenTest.as`. Add the following package information.

```
package com.foundationAS3.ch4 {
}
```

5. Add the class definition, making sure to import Sprite, which your class will extend. You also need to import MovieClip so you can access the circle on your stage.

```
package com.foundationAS3.ch4 {

    import flash.display.MovieClip;
    import flash.display.Sprite;

    public class FullScreenTest extends Sprite {
    }

}
```

145

6. Add a constructor and within it, add an event listener for the click event when the circle is clicked and released. (You'll learn about events in Chapter 6, but since you need a user event to enter full-screen mode, you get a sneak peak here.)

```
package com.foundationAS3.ch4 {

  import flash.display.MovieClip;
  import flash.display.Sprite;
  import flash.events.MouseEvent;

  public class FullScreenTest extends Sprite {

    public function FullScreenTest() {
      circle.addEventListener(MouseEvent.CLICK, onButtonClick);
    }

  }

}
```

7. You need to add the handler for when the button is clicked. A *handler* is simply a method that will be called when a certain event occurs in the movie, and is said to "handle" the event. (Again, you'll learn more about event handling in Chapter 6). For now, just know that when the circle is clicked, this method will be called.

```
package com.foundationAS3.ch4 {

  import flash.display.MovieClip;
  import flash.display.Sprite;
  import flash.events.MouseEvent;

  public class FullScreenTest extends Sprite {

    public function FullScreenTest() {
      circle.addEventListener(MouseEvent.CLICK, onButtonClick);
    }

    private function onButtonClick(event:MouseEvent):void {
    }

  }

}
```

8. Within this method, set the displayState property of Stage to full screen. It's a pretty simple procedure for a very powerful feature. Make sure you add the new import statement at the top.

```
package com.foundationAS3.ch4 {

  import flash.display.MovieClip;
  import flash.display.Sprite;
  import flash.display.StageDisplayState;
  import flash.events.MouseEvent;

  public class FullScreenTest extends Sprite {

    public function FullScreenTest() {
      circle.addEventListener(MouseEvent.CLICK, onButtonClick);
    }

    private function onButtonClick(event:MouseEvent):void {
      stage.displayState = StageDisplayState.FULL_SCREEN;
    }

  }

}
```

9. Save FullScreenTest.as. Return to fullscreen.fla and set com.foundationAS3.ch4.FullScreenTest as the document class for the movie.

10. To test full-screen mode, you need to go through the browser. Open the Publish Setting dialog box (File ➤ Publish Settings), and on the HTML tab, select Flash Only – Allow Full Screen in the Template drop-down list, as shown in Figure 4-27. Then click the Publish button at the bottom of the dialog box.

11. Save your file and find the HTML file you just published in the same directory as fullscreen.fla. Open this file in your browser, and you will find that clicking the circle takes the movie to full-screen mode, as shown in Figure 4-28. Nice!

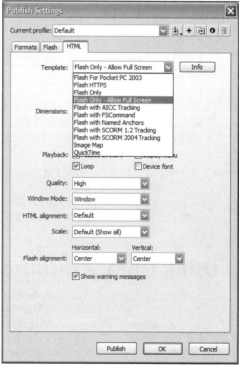

Figure 4-27. The full-screen mode is allowed using the selected template in the Publish Settings dialog box.

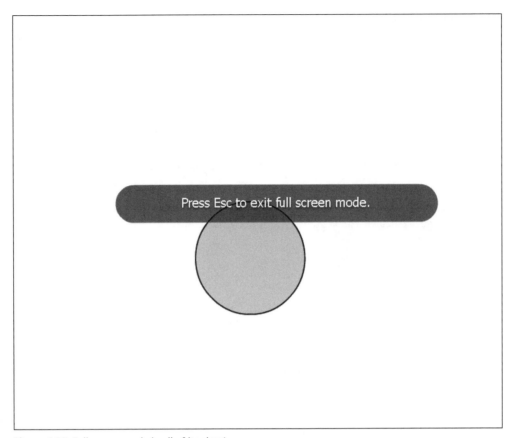

Figure 4-28. Full-screen mode in all of its glory!

You will note that the movie scales as it takes over the screen. If you wanted to maintain the same 100% scale on your objects, you would need to set the scaleMode property of the Stage instance to StageScaleMode.NO_SCALE and (usually) its align property to StageAlign.TOP_LEFT. Then you would listen for when the stage resizes, and redraw or reposition your objects accordingly.

Using Library resources

Creating instances of Library symbols in ActionScript 3.0 is much easier than it was in ActionScript 2.0. Every symbol in the Library of a Flash movie that has been exported for ActionScript is associated with a class—whether it's one you have written or one that the ActionScript compiler has created for you.

To add an instance of a symbol to your movie, you just need to create a new instance of that class and add it to the display list. Let's try it out.

1. Create a new Flash movie and save it in the project directory as library.fla.
2. On the stage, draw a 50 × 50-pixel circle.

3. Select the circle and select Modify ➤ Convert to Symbol from the main menu, or press F8. In the Convert to Symbol dialog box, enter **Ball** for the symbol name and select Movie clip for the type. Set its registration point at the top left of the graphic.

4. If the advanced options are not visible in the dialog box, click the Advanced button to reveal them. Click the Export for ActionScript check box in the Linkage options, as shown in Figure 4-29, and then click OK, accepting the default values for the Class and Base class fields.

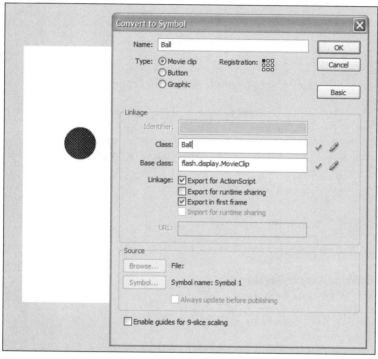

Figure 4-29. Creating the Ball movie clip symbol

That sets up the Ball symbol with a class of the same name. To finish the example, you need to create an instance of the Ball class and add it to the display list. You'll do this by adding a document class to the movie with the necessary code in the constructor.

5. Back on the main timeline, delete the Ball instance that you originally created on the stage. This example will demonstrate how to add it to a movie through ActionScript, so you want to remove this original instance.

6. Create a new ActionScript file and save it in the com.foundationAS3.ch4 directory as LibraryTest.as.

7. In the LibraryTest.as file, create the package block with the appropriate package name.

```
package com.foundationAS3.ch4 {
}
```

8. Create the LibraryTest class definition. Since this is a document class, you'll need to extend either the MovieClip or Sprite class. There's no timeline animation in this example, so you're safe to choose the Sprite class:

```
package com.foundationAS3.ch4 {

  import flash.display.Sprite;

  public class LibraryTest extends Sprite {
  }

}
```

> Don't forget to make the class public, or the ActionScript compiler won't be able to use it as the document class.

9. Add the constructor function for the LibraryTest class. In the constructor function, create a new instance of the Ball class (which is in the default package, so you don't need to import it) and add it to the display list.

```
package com.foundationAS3.ch4 {

  import flash.display.Sprite;

  public class LibraryTest extends Sprite {

    public function LibraryTest() {
      var ball:Ball = new Ball();
      addChild(ball);
    }

  }

}
```

10. Save the changes to the ActionScript file. Switch back to the library.fla file, and enter the full package and class name com.foundationAS3.ch4.LibraryTest as the document class for the Flash movie.

11. Save the Flash movie and test it. You should see an instance of the Ball symbol in the top-left corner of the movie, as shown in Figure 4-30.

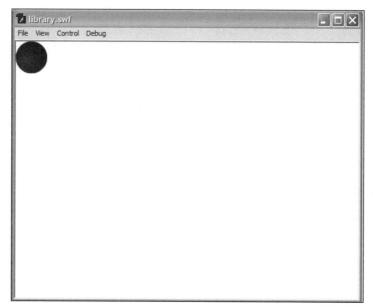

Figure 4-30. An instance of the Ball class is added to the stage through code.

Loading from external files

Needing to embed every visual asset you want to use into the Library main movie SWF file can make the SWF file unnecessarily large. Imagine an image gallery with hundreds of images where you needed to embed each image (both thumbnail and full size) into the main SWF, which could easily be 10MB or more. Visitors would need to download all the images, even if they wanted to look at only a handful. Wouldn't it be better if you could load those assets on demand from external files?

In ActionScript 3.0, loading in external visual assets is the job of the Loader class, which lives in the flash.display package and inherits from the DisplayObject class. The Loader class can load in SWF files as well as GIF, JPEG, and PNG images. Video files and sound files are handled by the Video and Sound classes, respectively.

Loading an external asset

To load an external asset, you create an instance of the Loader class, add it to the display list at the appropriate point, and then tell it to load the asset using the load() method. That sounds relatively painless, so let's give it a go.

1. Create a new Flash movie and save it in the project directory with the name loadExternal.fla.

2. Copy an image you would like to load into this same directory. If you do not have one, you can use the audrey_computer.png file that is included with this chapter's source files.

3. Next, you need to create an ActionScript file for the document class. Create a new ActionScript file and save it into the `com.foundationAS3.ch4` directory as `LoadExternalTest.as`.

4. In the `LoadExternalTest.as` file, create the package container with the appropriate package name:

```
package com.foundationAS3.ch4 {
}
```

5. Create the `LoadExternalTest` class, which should extend the `Sprite` class, since there won't be any timeline animation.

```
package com.foundationAS3.ch4 {

    import flash.display.Sprite;

    public class LoadExternalTest extends Sprite {
    }

}
```

6. In the constructor function for the document class, create a new instance of the `Loader` class in a local variable, and then add it to the display list using the `addChild()` method of the `LoadExternalTest` instance. Make sure you import the `Loader` class at the top.

```
package com.foundationAS3.ch4 {

    import flash.display.Loader;
    import flash.display.Sprite;

    public class LoadExternalTest extends Sprite {

        public function LoadExternalTest() {
            var loader:Loader = new Loader();
            addChild(loader);
        }

    }

}
```

7. You need to tell the `Loader` instance to load the image using the `load()` method. Rather than a simple string containing the URL of the asset to load, the `load()` method expects a `URLRequest` instance to be passed to it. The `URLRequest` class, which lives in the `flash.net` package, is used in most calls and requests from the Flash Player. In its simplest form, which is all that's necessary here, you just need to pass the URL address to call in the constructor. (Obviously, you should replace the `audrey_computer.png` string with the filename of whatever image you have copied into your project directory in step 2.)

```
package com.foundationAS3.ch4 {

    import flash.display.Loader;
    import flash.display.Sprite;
    import flash.net.URLRequest;
```

```
public class LoadExternalTest extends Sprite {

    public function LoadExternalTest() {
        var loader:Loader = new Loader();
        addChild(loader);
        loader.load(new URLRequest("audrey_computer.png"));
    }

}

}
```

8. Save the changes to the ActionScript file. Switch back to the loadExternal.fla file and set com.foundationAS3.ch4.LoadExternalTest as the document class in the Property inspector.

9. Save the changes to the Flash movie and test it by selecting Control ➤ Test Movie from the main menu. You should see your loaded image as part of your SWF file, as shown in Figure 4-31.

Figure 4-31. An image is loaded into the movie (and what a lovely image it is!).

If the image doesn't load, check the Output *panel for an error message. If you have an error message, double-check that the string path for the image is correct and that you've copied the image into the same directory as your FLA file. You can trap these error messages and handle them in ActionScript code, but that will need to wait until Chapter 6, where you'll learn about event handling.*

Manipulating the loaded asset

When loading an external asset through an instance of the Loader class, the asset becomes a child of that object and is accessible through the Loader's content property. This is occasionally useful when loading an image file. You can control whether the image is snapped to the nearest pixel and/or whether smoothing is used if it is resized, but it really comes into its own when you're dealing with an SWF file.

Since the Loader class can handle both image files (instances of the Bitmap class) and SWF files (either MovieClip instances or AVM1Movie instances if you're loading Flash 8 or earlier SWFs), the data type of the content property must be something that's a common ancestor of all those classes. A quick look at the display list class diagram shown earlier in Figure 4-2 will tell you that the only common ancestor for all these classes is the DisplayObject class. What this means in practice is that you'll need to cast the content property to the appropriate type before you can do anything with it that's specific to that type of asset.

```
var loadedClip:MovieClip = loader.content as MovieClip;
```

You'll need to wait at least until the asset has started loading before you can use the content property. The loaderInfo property of an instance of the Loader class dispatches a number of events that let you know when the asset begins loading, when it has been initialized (and is ready to interact with), and when it has finished loading. Again, you'll learn about the details of event handling in Chapter 6.

Making things move

When it comes to animating the position of an object on the stage with ActionScript, you have two basic choices: you can copy an animation from the timeline as ActionScript 3.0 code, or you can manually reposition the object at frequent intervals over a certain length of time. The first technique is designed for keyframe-style animation and tweening. and will be covered in detail here. The second technique is much more powerful but requires knowledge of event-based programming in ActionScript, so we'll leave that one until Chapter 6.

Copying animation from the timeline

One of the major innovations in the Flash CS3 IDE, at least from an ActionScript developer's point of view, is the ability to copy a timeline animation into the clipboard as ActionScript code. Gone are the days when developers tried to approximate animation in ActionScript from a timeline animation produced by a professional animator, only to be bashed over the head by said animator for getting it totally wrong. No, now you can just copy the animation as a reusable piece of ActionScript that can be applied to any display object.

This system has a couple of limitations. One is that you can copy only continuous frames of animation from a single layer in the Flash movie. The other is that you can have only one object on each keyframe of the animation. You can overcome both of these limitations by breaking down your animation into separate layers and copying the motion of each layer separately.

Creating the animation

Let's create a simple three-frame animation of a ball going from the left edge of the screen to the right edge and back again.

1. Create a new Flash movie and save it in the project directory with the name motion.fla.

2. Draw a 50 × 50-pixel ball on the stage.

3. Select the ball and select Modify ➤ Convert to Symbol from the main menu, or press F8. In the Convert to Symbol dialog box, name the symbol **Ball**. Give it a central registration point, and check the Export to ActionScript check box, as shown in Figure 4-32. Accept the default values for the Class and Base class fields, and then click OK.

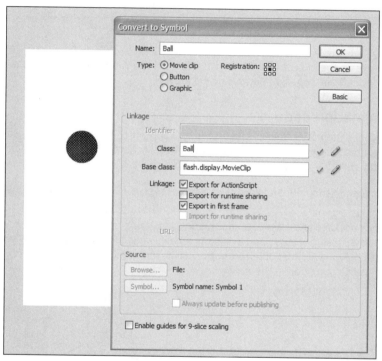

Figure 4-32. Creating a new Ball symbol

4. Position the instance of the Ball symbol on the stage at (50,50) and create two more keyframes on that layer: one at frame 13 and another at frame 24. Select frame 13 and change the location of the Ball symbol on that frame to (500,50). Right-click frame 1 and frame 13 and select Create motion tween from the context menu. Your timeline should look like Figure 4-33.

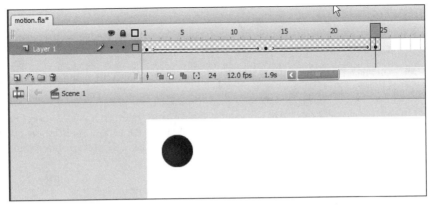

Figure 4-33. Adding some simple timeline animation

5. Save the changes to the motion.fla file and test the movie. You should see the ball moving between the top-left and top-right corners of the movie.

Copying the animation code

Now you'll copy that animation as ActionScript 3.0 code and apply it to an instance of the Ball class that you create programmatically. Then you'll take a look at the ActionScript code generated by the Flash IDE to see exactly what it's doing.

1. Create a new ActionScript file and save it as MotionTest.as in the com.foundationAS3.ch4 directory.

2. Create the basic package and class definitions. This time, you'll need to extend the MovieClip class rather than Sprite, because you have some timeline animation in the movie. If you don't extend MovieClip, you won't be able to use the playhead-related functions and properties to control the timeline animation in the movie.

```
package com.foundationAS3.ch4 {

    import flash.display.MovieClip;

    public class MotionTest extends MovieClip {

        public function MotionTest() {
        }

    }

}
```

3. Create a new instance of the Ball class, add it to the display list for the application, and then adjust its x and y properties so that its starting point is just below the existing animation at (50,150).

```
package com.foundationAS3.ch4 {
```

```
import flash.display.MovieClip;

public class MotionTest extends MovieClip {

  public function MotionTest() {
    // Create and position ball
    var ball:Ball = new Ball();
    addChild(ball);
    ball.x = 50;
    ball.y = 150;
  }

}

}
```

4. Save the changes to the MotionTest.as file, switch back to the motion.fla movie, and test it to make sure you have a static Ball instance below the one you animated from the timeline, as shown in Figure 4-34.

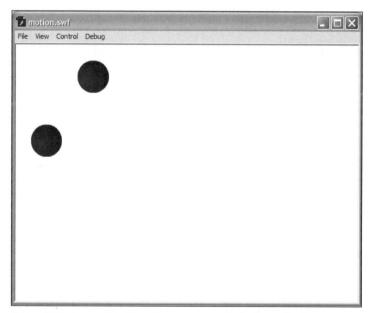

Figure 4-34. A second ball is added programmatically below the first.

5. In the motion.fla movie, select frames 1 to 23 on the timeline, right-click the selection, and select Copy Motion as ActionScript 3.0 from the context menu.

6. You'll see a Prompt window asking you for the instance name to use in ActionScript. You want to animate the ball object you created a few steps back, so enter **ball** and click OK. The ActionScript 3.0 code for the animation is now in your clipboard.

7. Switch back to the `MotionTest.as` file and paste the copied code below the existing ActionScript code in the constructor function. You should end up with something that looks like this:

```
package com.foundationAS3.ch4 {

    import flash.display.MovieClip;

    public class MotionTest extends MovieClip {

        public function MotionTest() {
            // Create and position ball
            var ball:Ball = new Ball();
            addChild(ball);
            ball.x = 50;
            ball.y = 150;

            import fl.motion.Animator;
            var ball_xml:XML = <Motion duration="24" xmlns="fl.motion.*" ➥
xmlns:geom="flash.geom.*" xmlns:filters="flash.filters.*">
 . . .
            </Motion>;

            var ball_animator:Animator = new Animator(ball_xml, ball);
            ball_animator.play();
        }

    }

}
```

> *There's a big block of animation data not shown in this code listing (indicated by the ellipsis). The reason I've omitted it here is that it's quite verbose. Right now, you don't need to worry about what the animation data looks like.*

8. Unfortunately, you're not quite finished yet. The code that was copied to the clipboard was designed to be pasted into another frame of a movie, rather than into a document class file, so you'll need to edit it in a couple of places before it will work properly. You need to move the `import` statement outside the class definition so that it's with the other import statement in this file. You also need to make the `ball_animator` variable a property of your class, rather than a local variable for the constructor method. This is because all local variables are destroyed after the constructor function has done its stuff. Since there is no reference to the Animator instance other than the local `ball_animator` variable, the object will be garbage-collected (deleted from memory) before it gets the chance to animate the ball. Making it a property of the main MotionTest class means that as long as the application is running, there will be a reference to the Animator object.

```
package com.foundationAS3.ch4 {

  import flash.display.MovieClip;
  import fl.motion.Animator;

  public class MotionTest extends MovieClip {

    private var ball_animator:Animator;

    public function MotionTest() {
      // Create and position ball
      var ball:Ball = new Ball();
      addChild(ball);
      ball.x = 50;
      ball.y = 150;

      var ball_xml:XML = <Motion duration="24" xmlns="fl.motion.*" ➥
xmlns:geom="flash.geom.*" xmlns:filters="flash.filters.*">
. . .
      </Motion>;

      ball_animator = new Animator(ball_xml, ball);
      ball_animator.play();
    }

  }

}
```

9. Save the changes to the MotionTest.as file, switch back to the motion.fla movie, and test it. You should see that you've successfully transplanted the motion from the timeline animation onto the new ball object.

Looping the animation

You may have noticed (and if you didn't, see me after class) that the animation you copied in the previous example runs only once, while the timeline animation loops continuously. This is because the code in the constructor of the MotionTest class is run only once when you first start playing the movie.

If you want the animation to loop, you need to tell the Animator class to do so by setting the autoRewind and repeatCount properties appropriately. These two properties work in tandem to control if and how many times the Animator object loops the animation. If the autoRewind property is set to true, the animation will loop, with the repeatCount property controlling how many times the animation will loop before stopping. If repeatCount is to 0, then the animation will loop continuously until you pause or stop it with the pause() or stop() method, respectively.

```
ball_animator = new Animator(ball_xml, ball);
ball_animator.autoRewind = true;
ball_animator.repeatCount = 0;
ball_animator.play();
```

Animating other properties

Using the Copy Motion as ActionScript 3.0 menu option, you can copy the following animated properties of a display object (right-click the object to access the option):

- Position
- Scale
- Skew
- Rotation
- Transformation point
- Color
- Blend mode
- Filters
- Orientation to path (as part of a tween)
- Cache as bitmap

The animation system also supports frame labels, motion guides, and custom easing equations. That's some pretty powerful, heady stuff.

Understanding the animation XML

Once you've pasted the animation into your class file, it's yours to do with as you please. It's no longer linked to the timeline animation from which you copied it, and you don't even need to have the original timeline animation in your FLA. Many animators will just create the timeline animation in a completely separate FLA file and e-mail the copied code to developers for integration into the final project FLA file.

What this means is that you can edit the animation data manually to fine-tune the animation if you understand the animation data. The animation data is represented as XML (which is covered in Chapter 11) and describes for each keyframe how the object being animated differs from its state in the initial keyframe.

The XML data starts by stating over how many frames the animation should occur, before describing the initial state (from the first keyframe) of all the properties of the object being animated.

```
<Motion duration="24" . . . >
  <source>
    <Source . . . >
. . .
    </Source>
  </source>
```

That is then followed by the bulk of the animation data, which consists of a number of Keyframe records. Each Keyframe record has details about each property of the animated object that has changed from the initial state on that keyframe. The change is stored as a delta, so if the object's x property has changed from 50 in the first keyframe to 500 in the current keyframe, the Keyframe record states that the x property changed by +450.

In addition to the property deltas, the keyframe data includes information about any tweens applied to that frame, including any easing settings (whether they are simple integer values or custom easing curves generated by the Custom Ease In / Ease Out dialog box). This information is used to transition between this keyframe and the next one in the animation data.

```
<Keyframe index="12" x="450">
  <tweens>
    <SimpleEase ease="0"/>
  </tweens>
</Keyframe>
```

When you apply the animation to another object, it applies the same set of transformations to that object, but from that object's initial state (as opposed to the state of the original animated object).

If that sounds confusing, that's because it's quite a complex idea to get your head around. If you look back at the original animation you copied, it was tweening a Ball symbol from (50,50) to (500,50), and yet somehow, when you copied it onto a Ball symbol placed at (50,150), it tweened to (500,150)—the same y value as the initial state for your new Ball symbol—rather than (500,50). It did this because the animation data said "the Ball's x position was changed by +450, and the y value wasn't changed."

The final point I want to make is that you don't even need to apply the animation to the same type of display objects. You can copy the motion of your Ball symbol and apply it to instances of any of the display list classes, including TextField, Sprite, and Shape instances. All of the properties that can be animated in this way belong to the base DisplayObject class, so they're supported by all display list classes.

Summary

Wow! What a *tour de force* of the awesome capabilities of ActionScript 3.0 when it comes to messing with the display. In fact, you've seen only the tip of the iceberg. See you across the great (page) divide for a lot more display programming fun and games, focusing on creating cool graphics from scratch using your ActionScript skills.

Chapter 5

CREATING VECTOR GRAPHICS WITH THE DRAWING API

Steve Webster

This chapter covers the following topics:

- How to draw straight and curved lines programmatically
- How to create solid and gradient-filled shapes
- How to alter a stroke's graphic style, including drawing gradient strokes
- How to combine the Drawing API methods to create a complete graphic

ActionScript 3.0 includes a Graphics class that provides a Drawing API, which you can use to create vector graphics through code. Each Sprite or Shape instance you create actually includes a Graphics instance that can be used to draw within its respective parent object. You'll learn how to use this Drawing API in this chapter.

Why we need a Drawing API

If you're from a design background, the fact that I'm getting all excited about being able to create vector graphics with ActionScript might lead you to the conclusion that I've spent too long out in the midday sun. You're wondering why on Earth you would want to create vector graphics with code when you have a perfectly good set of drawing tools in the Flash IDE, particularly if you've spent years honing your ninja-like Pen tool skills.

Having the ability to create vector graphics with ActionScript code means that you don't have to know which graphics you need in advance. Imagine putting together a Flash movie that represents the recent history of a stock price like the one shown in Figure 5-1, from Google Finance (finance.google.com). Or maybe you're building a Flash MP3 player widget for your site, and you want to have a little graphic equalizer going while the music is playing, as shown in Figure 5-2.

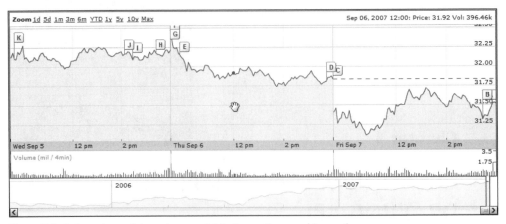

Figure 5-1. A dynamic graph is a prime candidate for runtime graphic creation.

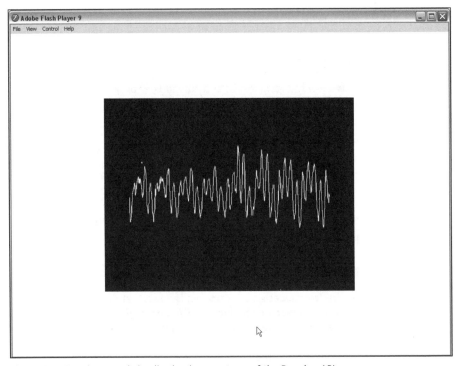

Figure 5-2. Creating sound visualization is a great use of the Drawing API.

You would require a Tolkienesque army of Flash-wielding orcs to do all the donkeywork required for the stock graph or equalizer scenario. Thankfully, there's a distinct lack of orcs in our world (they leave one heck of a stain on the carpet), but that means that we need to do this ourselves (no, thank you!) or find another solution to the problem.

Drawing API, enter stage right.

The Drawing API (or application programming interface, for the long-winded) was first introduced in Flash MX (a.k.a. Flash 6 for those of us who prefer old-fashioned numbers) but was supercharged in Flash 8 and again in Flash CS3. It provides a very powerful set of drawing tools for creating vector art-work with ActionScript. The Drawing API allows you to create, at runtime, pretty much any kind of vector graphics your twisted mind can conjure up. Developers have even used this technique to draw and animate 3D objects, as shown in Figure 5-3.

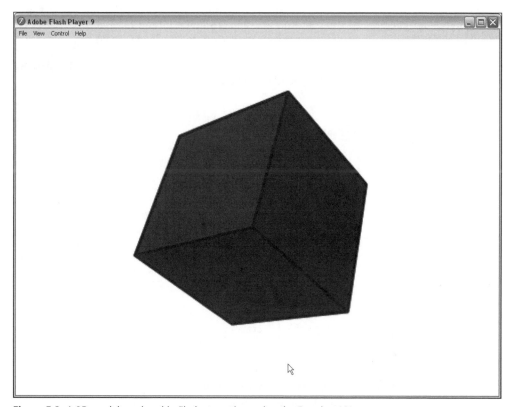

Figure 5-3. A 3D model rendered in Flash at runtime using the Drawing API

We won't be going that far in this chapter (the mathematics behind 3D drawing makes my head hurt), but you will get to play with all the features of the Drawing API. You'll then be free to pursue the whole spinning 3D cube thing yourself, if you feel so inclined.

Understanding the Drawing API

Every instance of the Sprite class (and its descendents) has a graphics property, which contains a host of methods and properties that make up the Drawing API. This property is an instance of the Graphics class from the flash.display package, and it has various methods, such as beginGradientFill() and drawCircle(), which you can use to draw vector graphics. The layer on which the vector graphics are drawn is not part of the display list and always appears below any child display objects that the sprite contains.

If you want the vector graphics to be drawn at a specific depth in the display list (in front of any other display objects belonging to the same parent display object), you'll need to create a new Sprite instance, add that to the display list at the required depth, and draw with that object's graphics property. Another alternative is to use a Shape instance, which is a direct child class of DisplayObject, meaning that it can be added to the display list but does not have the added functionality of InteractiveObject and DisplayObjectContainer. So although you cannot add children to a Shape instance or code for interactivity, you can draw into and position it on the stage. If all you want is to create a graphic without children and without interactivity, opt for the leaner Shape class.

I always recommend creating a new Sprite or Shape instance for your vector artwork. It makes positioning art a cinch, and is really helpful if you need to fill any shapes with gradient fills.

Setting up Mr. Smiley

In order to make learning about the Drawing API at least a little interesting, you'll re-create the image shown in Figure 5-4 using nothing but ActionScript code.

Figure 5-4. The image you'll create with the Drawing API

OK, so it's not fancy 3D, and it's never going to win any prizes for most original piece of artwork—poor Mr. Smiley doesn't even have a nose, for goodness' sake—but then I'm what you might call graphically challenged. Besides, this is just an exercise to help you learn all about the Drawing API. (Yes, that's my excuse, and I'm sticking to it.)

Let's set up a project for Mr. Smiley. You're going to create a new Shape instance as a child of the main document class. You could put this all into a single ActionScript class, but, ideally, you don't want your document class doing much more than acting as an entry point for your application or movie and instantiating its necessary subcomponents. Things like drawing of internal graphics, especially graphics with any complexity, are best delegated to a subcomponent, so that's what you'll set up now.

1. The main document class will instantiate and position the smiley graphic, which you will house in a separate class to make things cleaner. For this class, create a new ActionScript file and save it as Smiley.as into a new com.foundationAS3.ch5 directory that you will be using for this chapter.

2. In Smiley.as, add the necessary package and class definitions. Since the graphic will not need to hold any children or account for user interactivity, you will use the Shape class (in the flash.display package) as its base class.

```
package com.foundationAS3.ch5 {

  import flash.display.Shape;

  public class Smiley extends Shape {

    public function Smiley() {
    }

  }

}
```

3. Create a new ActionScript file for the document class. Save the file as SmileyTest.as in the same directory as Smiley.as.

4. Create the basic package and class definitions for the document class. As you may have guessed, you're going to extend the Sprite class, so you'll need to import that from the flash.display package.

```
package com.foundationAS3.ch5 {

  import flash.display.Sprite;

  public class SmileyTest extends Sprite {

    public function SmileyTest() {
    }

  }

}
```

5. In the constructor method, create a new Smiley instance, which is your custom class, and add it to the display list. Then position it in the center of the stage using the stage object's stageWidth and stageHeight properties. Note that you do not need to import the Smiley class to use it, since Smiley resides within the same package as your SmileyTest document class.

```
package com.foundationAS3.ch5 {

  import flash.display.Sprite;

  public class SmileyTest extends Sprite {

    public function SmileyTest() {
      // Create and center smiley sprite on stage
      var smiley:Smiley = new Smiley();
      addChild(smiley);
```

```
        smiley.x = stage.stageWidth / 2;
        smiley.y = stage.stageHeight / 2;
      }

    }

  }
```

6. Create a new Flash document and save it in the project directory with the name smiley.fla.

7. Set the document class of the Flash document to be the com.foundationAS3.ch5.SmileyTest class you just created.

8. Save your changes to the Flash document and test it by selecting Control ➤ Test Movie from the main menu. You should see an empty SWF file with no errors in the Output panel.

With that done, let's start drawing some lines. What fun!

Drawing lines

Imagine you have a piece of paper in front of you and you're holding a pen against the center of the paper. If you move your hand in a straight line in any direction without lifting the pen from the paper, you draw a line on the paper. However, if you lift the pen off the paper, and then move it to another location and lower it again, you have no line, but your pen is now at a new location. In the ActionScript world, these two actions are performed by the lineTo() and moveTo() methods of the Graphics class, respectively.

Creating straight lines

When a Sprite or Shape object is created, the pen is positioned at the origin (0,0) in the drawing layer. To draw a 50-pixel long horizontal line to the right of the origin, just call the lineTo() method and specify the (x,y) coordinates for the endpoint of the line as the parameters. Use the lineStyle() method to draw a line that has a visual representation (more on this in the next section).

To test this, open the Smiley.as file and add the lines shown in bold to the constructor.

```
package com.foundationAS3.ch5 {

  import flash.display.Shape;

  public class Smiley extends Shape {

    public function Smiley() {
      // Testing
      graphics.lineStyle(1);
      graphics.lineTo(50, 0);
    }

  }

}
```

Save the ActionScript file and test the movie. You should see a small, black line drawn from the center of the stage to the right, as shown in Figure 5-5. Remember that when calling the lineTo() method, the pen is kept against the paper, so a line is drawn from wherever the pen currently resides to where you've told it to go. In this case, the pen was at (0,0), and you've told the Flash Player to draw a line between there and (50,0).

Figure 5-5. Your first line

Remember that (0,0) is at the top left of the stage in Flash, as it is in most computer graphics applications. When a new Sprite or Shape instance is created, it is empty with no graphics, and therefore has no width and height, so (0,0) is merely the center of transformation (there is no concept of "top left" in an empty graphic). You can then draw graphics anywhere within the instance in relation to the origin—to the right or left, above or below.

If you are instantiating a symbol from your library, the origin is determined by what you set in the Flash IDE, which could be center, top left, bottom right, and so on.

If you were expecting the line you just added to be drawn in the top-left corner of the Flash movie, remember that we're drawing into the Smiley instance, which has been moved to the center of the stage.

After the call to the lineTo() method, the pen is in the new location, so subsequent calls to lineTo() will start at that point. Actually, what you end up with is a single line with several points along it.

Let's add a vertical line.

```
public function Smiley() {
  // Testing
  graphics.lineStyle(1);
  graphics.lineTo(50, 0);
  graphics.lineTo(50, 50);
}
```

Now you have an upside-down, back-to-front *L* shape, and the pen is at (50,50) in the drawing layer.

This is starting to look like a box, and you could finish drawing the rest of the box using the lineTo() method, but that would mean you wouldn't get to try out the moveTo() method. Instead, let's create a completely disconnected line.

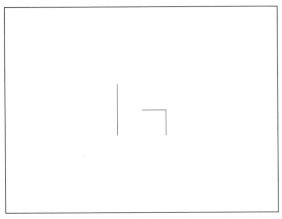

Figure 5-6. lineTo() and moveTo() at work on multiple lines

```
public function Smiley() {
    // Testing
    graphics.lineStyle(1);
    graphics.lineTo(50, 0);
    graphics.lineTo(50, 50);
    graphics.moveTo(-50, 50);
    graphics.lineTo(-50, -50);
}
```

There you have it: three distinct lines—two connected at a corner and another off on its own—all drawn by the Flash Player in response to the drawing commands you've given it (extra marks if you can tell me where the pen is after the last command). Figure 5-6 shows the result. It isn't earth-shattering, granted, but even Picasso had to start somewhere.

Controlling the line style

You probably won't want to draw everything with thin, black lines. Fortunately, it's easy to draw thick, purple lines, or anything else you desire, by specifying your choices with the lineStyle() method. This method takes up to eight parameters, each dictating a different facet of how the Flash Player will render subsequently drawn lines.

At its simplest, you can call lineStyle() with no parameters, meaning that no line will be drawn on subsequent calls to lineTo(), curveTo(), or any of the primitive shape methods. This is useful if you just want to draw a filled shape with no lines/strokes, for example. This is also the default setting for the lines drawn in a Graphics instance, so unless you explicitly set a line style using lineStyle(), you will not see any lines drawn.

The first lineStyle() parameter is thickness, and as you can guess, it controls the thickness of the lines drawn. You pass in a Number value for the desired thickness of the line in points. You can pass any whole or fractional value between 0 and 255 (which is pretty darn thick). Passing in 0 gives you a hairline, which has the special property of never scaling up, even if you scale the Graphics instance or its parent container. In contrast, a 1-point line inside a Sprite that is scaled to 300% will appear at three times its original scale. Here's an example of setting the thickness parameter to 5 (see Figure 5-7):

```
public function Smiley() {
    // Testing
    graphics.lineStyle(5);
    graphics.lineTo(50, 0);
    graphics.lineTo(50, 50);
    graphics.moveTo(-50, 50);
    graphics.lineTo(-50, -50);
}
```

As you probably have noticed, you don't need to call lineStyle() *before each line is drawn. The* lineStyle() *method is **sticky**, which means that once you've called it, the settings you provide are used for all drawing functions until you call the method again.*

You can also call the clear() *method, which wipes the graphics layer clean and resets all aspects of the pen and graphics layer to their defaults, including the line style. The* clear() *method is an important part of the Drawing API. Its most common use is when you need to redraw within a* Graphics *instance. It is important in such a case to clear any previous graphics that may have been drawn.*

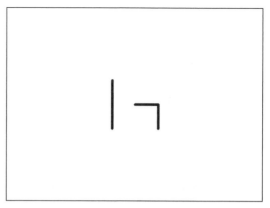

Figure 5-7. Beefier lines created by the thickness parameter in lineStyle()

The next lineStyle() parameter is color, and, unsurprisingly, it controls the color used to draw the lines. The data type for this parameter is uint, but to make it easy to work with colors, the number is usually specified in hexadecimal (base 16) format. Hexadecimal number literals in ActionScript start with *0x* followed by a number of hexadecimal digits. In the case of colors, there are six digits: two each for the red, green, and blue components of the color: 0xRRGGBB. To make it easy, you can copy this number straight from the Color panel in the Flash IDE, as shown in Figure 5-8, replacing the hash symbol (#) with 0x. If you don't supply a color, the default is black.

The third lineStyle() parameter is alpha, which controls the opacity of the lines drawn. This is a Number value between 0 (transparent) and 1 (opaque), with numbers in between offering varying degrees of semitransparency. The default alpha value is 1, or fully opaque. Here is an example of setting the lineStyle() method's color parameter to 0xFF0000 (red) and its alpha parameter to 0.5 (see Figure 5-9):

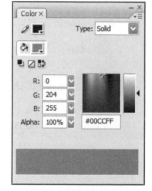

Figure 5-8. Color values can be copied directly from the Color panel in the Flash IDE into your ActionScript.

```
public function Smiley() {
  // Testing
  graphics.lineStyle(5, 0xFF0000, 0.5);
  graphics.lineTo(50, 0);
  graphics.lineTo(50, 50);
  graphics.moveTo(-50, 50);
  graphics.lineTo(-50, -50);
}
```

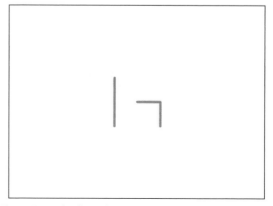

Figure 5-9. Using lineStyle() to set the color and alpha of lines

171

The other parameters for the lineStyle() method allow you to fine-tune how the Flash Player renders the lines drawn, as follows:

- pixelHinting: A Boolean value that when set to true will improve the rendering of curves and straight lines at small sizes. The default is false.

- scaleMode: A String value that determines how lines are scaled when the scaleX and scaleY properties of the DisplayObject are altered. See the LineScaleMode class in the online help for a list of possible values. The default is LineScaleMode.NORMAL.

- caps: A String value from the CapsStyle class that determines how the ends of lines are rendered. This is equivalent to the Cap setting shown in the Property inspector in the Flash IDE when drawing a line or a shape with a stroke. The default is CapsStyle.ROUND.

- joints: A String value from the JointStyle class that determines how joins between points on a line are rendered. This is equivalent to the Join setting shown in the Property inspector in the Flash IDE when drawing a line or a shape with a stroke. The default is JointStyle.ROUND.

- miterLimit: A Number value that determines the limit at which a miter is cut as a factor of the line thickness. This applies only when the joints parameter is set to JointStyle.MITER, and is equivalent to the Miter setting shown in the Property inspector in the Flash IDE when drawing a line or a shape with a stroke. The default is 3.

You can consult Adobe's documentation for examples of these more complex parameters.

Drawing curved lines

Drawing straight lines is no fun unless you're trying to draw a map of old Roman roads, or maybe a cartoon caricature of Sylvester Stallone. The rest of us live in a curvy world, and are easily offended by utilitarian straight lines and sharp angles (or is that just me?). Thankfully, we have the curveTo() method to ease our (or my) troubles.

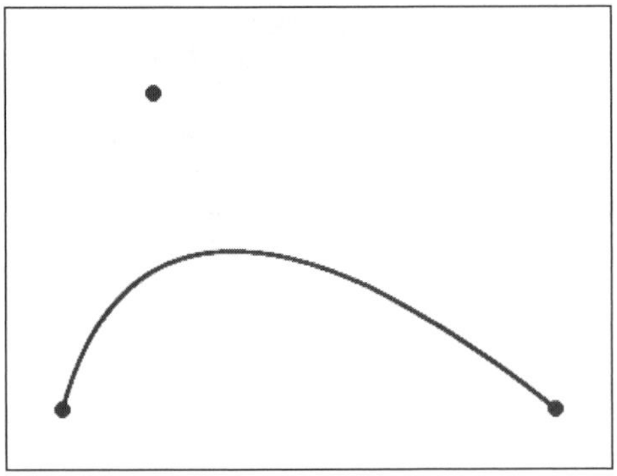

The curveTo() method is similar to the lineTo() method, in that it draws a line from the current pen location to the one you specify, but you also get to include a control point that is used to specify the curve of the line. Some seriously complex math is going on behind the scenes, but all you need to know is that the curve of the line is dragged in the direction of the control point. It's almost as if the control point were a magnet that is pulling the line toward it in order to create the curve. Figure 5-10 shows an example.

Figure 5-10. curveTo() at work to create a curved line. The control point above is not rendered; it is shown here only to illustrate how it affects the curve of a line.

The curveTo() method takes four parameters: the (x,y) coordinates of the control point, and the (x,y) coordinates of the end anchor of the line.

```
curveTo(controlX:Number, controlY:Number, anchorX:Number, anchorY:Number):void
```

Let's add the curveTo() method to the sample code to draw a curved line from the current pen position back to the Shape instance's origin, as shown in Figure 5-11.

```
public function Smiley() {
    // Testing
    graphics.lineStyle(5, 0xFF0000, 0.5);
    graphics.lineTo(50, 0);
    graphics.lineTo(50, 50);
    graphics.moveTo(-50, 50);
    graphics.lineTo(-50, -50);
    graphics.curveTo(0, -50, 0, 0);
}
```

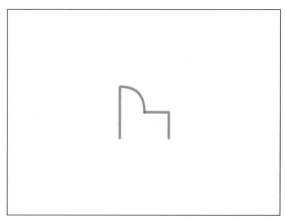

Figure 5-11. In this example, the curveTo() method draws a curved line from the current pen position back to the origin.

Drawing and filling shapes

The ability to draw straight and curved lines is undoubtedly useful, but it seems like it might be a lot of work to draw simple shapes such as rectangles and circles. Consider trying to draw a rectangle with rounded corners using various combinations of lineTo() and curveTo() calls—we're talking about 8 lines and 20 points. Thankfully, Adobe has provided a number of primitive shape drawing methods as part of the Graphics class. You can also create custom shapes.

Drawing primitive shapes

The shape-drawing methods are drawCircle(), drawEllipse(), drawRect(), and drawRoundRect()—not exactly exhaustive, but not too shabby.

You'll use two of these methods for the smiley graphic: drawCircle() for the face and the eyes, and drawRoundRect() for the glasses. You'll draw just the outlines for the moment, and then fill them in later.

The drawCircle() method takes three parameters: the (x,y) coordinate for the center of the circle and a Number value specifying the radius of the circle in pixels. Let's clear out all the test code and draw a 100-pixel radius circle in the center of the smiley object (see Figure 5-12). You'll use a 5-point black line for the outlines, some of which you'll keep and some of which you'll get rid of in favor of a fill color.

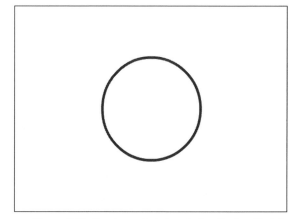

```
public function Smiley() {
    // Draw face
    graphics.lineStyle(5);
    graphics.drawCircle(0, 0, 100);
}
```

Figure 5-12. Drawing a circle is a cinch with drawCircle().

173

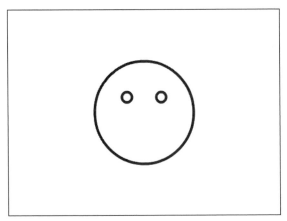

Figure 5-13. drawCircle() is used to draw the eyes as well.

Remember that this code replaces all the test drawing code you originally put into your constructor.

Next, use the same method to draw the eyes. I had to play around a bit to find the right coordinates for the eyes. Circles that were too close together made my smiley face looked untrustworthy; too far apart made him look just plain weird. In the end, I settled on 10-pixel radius circles at (-35,-30) and (35,-30) (see Figure 5-13).

```
public function Smiley() {
    // Draw face
    graphics.lineStyle(5);
    graphics.drawCircle(0, 0, 100);

    // Draw eyes
    graphics.drawCircle(-35, -30, 10);
    graphics.drawCircle(35, -30, 10);
}
```

You can use the drawRoundRect() method to draw the Woody Allen-style glasses on our little hero. This method takes six parameters:

- x: The x coordinate for the top-left corner of the rectangle
- y: The y coordinate for the top-left corner of the rectangle
- width: The width of the rectangle
- height: The height of the rectangle
- ellipseWidth: The width of the ellipse used to draw the rounded corners
- ellipseHeight: The height of the ellipse used to draw the rounded corners

Again, after a bit of experimentation, I came up with reasonable values for each of these parameters to get the look I wanted (see Figure 5-14).

```
public function Smiley() {
    // Draw face
    graphics.lineStyle(5);
    graphics.drawCircle(0, 0, 100);

    // Draw eyes
    graphics.drawCircle(-35, -30, 10);
    graphics.drawCircle(35, -30, 10);

    // Draw glasses
    graphics.drawRoundRect(-60, -50, 50, 40, 20, 20);
    graphics.drawRoundRect(10, -50, 50, 40, 20, 20);
}
```

You can see that the eyes look a little big for the glasses, but fear not. Later, you'll remove the outline from the eyes and fill them with black.

Now you can draw the remainder of the glasses (the arms and nose bridge) using a combination of moveTo(), lineTo(), and curveTo() (see Figure 5-15):

```
public function Smiley() {
    // Draw face
    graphics.lineStyle(5);
    graphics.drawCircle(0, 0, 100);

    // Draw eyes
    graphics.drawCircle(-35, -30, 10);
    graphics.drawCircle(35, -30, 10);

    // Draw glasses
    graphics.drawRoundRect(-60, -50, 50, 40, 20, 20);
    graphics.drawRoundRect(10, -50, 50, 40, 20, 20);
    graphics.moveTo(-60, -30);
    graphics.lineTo(-80, -40);
    graphics.moveTo(-10, -30);
    graphics.curveTo(0, -40, 10, -30);
    graphics.moveTo(60, -30);
    graphics.lineTo(80, -40);
}
```

Figure 5-14. drawRoundRect() is employed to create the eyeglass frames.

Lovely! Next you need to draw the mouth, which requires the use of a custom shape.

Creating custom shapes

Sometimes the primitive shape drawing functions offered by the Graphics class aren't enough, such as when you want to draw a triangle or something much more complex, like a monkey. For your smi-ley face, you need to draw the mouth, which is crescent moon shape on its side—something none of the primitive drawing functions can handle.

Figure 5-15. The glasses are completed by drawing lines with moveTo(), lineTo(), and curveTo().

In cases like this, you're left pretty much to your own devices, using the lineTo() and curveTo() methods to draw the shape. The key here is to draw the shape in one continuous series of statements, so that rather than a lot of separate lines, you have many points on a single line. This makes it possible to fill the shape with a color, gradient, or bitmap.

Drawing the mouth of the smiley face is as simple as drawing two curves—from left to right and then back again—using different control points to increase the curve for the bottom of the mouth (see Figure 5-16).

```
    public function Smiley() {
. . .

        // Draw glasses
        graphics.drawRoundRect(-60, -50, 50, 40, 20, 20);
        graphics.drawRoundRect(10, -50, 50, 40, 20, 20);
        graphics.moveTo(-60, -30);
        graphics.lineTo(-80, -40);
        graphics.moveTo(-10, -30);
        graphics.curveTo(0, -40, 10, -30);
        graphics.moveTo(60, -30);
        graphics.lineTo(80, -40);

        // Draw mouth
        graphics.moveTo(-45, 30);
        graphics.curveTo(0, 50, 45, 30);
        graphics.curveTo(0, 90, -45, 30);
    }
```

Figure 5-16. Who needs a drawCrescent() when a couple of curveTo() calls do the trick?

As you can see, you've finished the outline of the smiley face. Now it's time to add a splash of color.

Filling shapes with a solid color

Filling shapes with a solid color is as easy as calling the beginFill() method before drawing the shape, and then calling endFill() when you're finished. The beginFill() method takes two arguments: the color to fill the shape with and a Number value between 0 (transparent) and 1 (opaque) for the alpha value of the fill color. If you omit the alpha value, it defaults to 1, or fully opaque. You can call beginFill() before or after you set the line style. endFill() does not take any parameters and is just used to signify the end of the filled shape, so that a new shape (with perhaps a new fill or no fill) can be drawn.

Using the fill methods, let's give the smiley face a nice (un)healthy yellow complexion, jet-black eyes, and a super-shiny dentist's smile (see Figure 5-17).

```
public function Smiley() {
    // Draw face
    graphics.lineStyle(5);
    graphics.beginFill(0xFFFF00);
    graphics.drawCircle(0, 0, 100);
    graphics.endFill();

    // Draw eyes
    graphics.beginFill(0x000000);
    graphics.drawCircle(-35, -30, 10);
    graphics.drawCircle(35, -30, 10);
    graphics.endFill();
. . .
    // Draw mouth
    graphics.moveTo(-45, 30);
    graphics.beginFill(0xFFFFFF);
    graphics.curveTo(0, 50, 45, 30);
    graphics.curveTo(0, 90, -45, 30);
    graphics.endFill();
}
```

Figure 5-17. beginFill() and endFill() create solid color shapes.

Now let's give the glasses a slight white tint (see Figure 5-18). You can do this by filling them with pure white with an alpha value of 0.3, which equates to 30% alpha and creates a very subtle effect.

```
// Draw glasses
graphics.beginFill(0xFFFFFF, 0.3);
graphics.drawRoundRect(-60, -50, 50, 40, 20, 20);
graphics.drawRoundRect(10, -50, 50, 40, 20, 20);
graphics.endFill();
graphics.moveTo(-60, -30);
graphics.lineTo(-80, -40);
graphics.moveTo(-10, -30);
graphics.curveTo(0, -40, 10, -30);
graphics.moveTo(60, -30);
graphics.lineTo(80, -40);
```

Figure 5-18. A transparent fill is given to the glasses.

177

Mr. Smiley is looking better, but his eyes are still too big. Now that they've been filled in black, let's remove the line from them by calling lineStyle() with no parameters before drawing them. You'll also need to set lineStyle() back to 5-point thickness before drawing the glasses.

```
// Draw eyes
graphics.lineStyle();
graphics.beginFill(0x000000);
graphics.drawCircle(-35, -30, 10);
graphics.drawCircle(35, -30, 10);
graphics.endFill();

// Draw glasses
graphics.lineStyle(5);
graphics.beginFill(0xFFFFFF, 0.3);
graphics.drawRoundRect(-60, -50, 50, 40, 20, 20);
graphics.drawRoundRect(10, -50, 50, 40, 20, 20);
graphics.endFill();
graphics.moveTo(-60, -30);
graphics.lineTo(-80, -40);
graphics.moveTo(-10, -30);
graphics.curveTo(0, -40, 10, -30);
graphics.moveTo(60, -30);
graphics.lineTo(80, -40);
```

As you can see in Figure 5-19, the eyes look much better.

Figure 5-19. Calling lineStyle() with no parameters allows for shapes to be drawn without strokes.

Filling shapes with color gradients

Gradient fills (both linear and radial) are created using the beginGradientFill() method. A gradient may be a gradual progression through two or more colors, a gradual progression through two or more alpha values, or a mixture of the two, all at varying ratios. Using the beginGradientFill() method and its many parameters, you can replicate any kind of gradient fill you can create in the Color panel of the Flash IDE.

The beginGradientFill() method has eight parameters:

- type: A String value from the GradientType class that specifies whether to use a linear or radial fill (GradientType.LINEAR or GradientType.RADIAL, respectively).

- colors: An array of the colors in the gradient fill. You must have as many colors as you have alpha values, and vice versa, so if you are setting up a seven-step alpha gradient for a single color, you'll need to repeat that color seven times in the colors array.

- alphas: An array of the alpha values to use in the gradient fill. These values should be between 0 (transparent) and 1 (opaque).

- ratios: An array of values between 0 and 255 that indicate at what point in the gradient each color and alpha should be positioned. There should be the same number of elements in the ratios array as there are in the colors and alphas arrays. You can think of these values as percentages, except that they go from 0 to 255 instead of 0 to 100.

- matrix: An instance of the Matrix class from the flash.geom package. Its purpose is to describe the dimensions of the gradient (gradients don't necessarily need to be the same size as the object they're filling), the rotation of the gradient, and the (x,y) coordinates of the origin of the gradient. Confused? Imagine that the gradient fills a piece of paper underneath the paper on which you're drawing, and when you draw a shape, you're revealing the gradient underneath. The matrix determines the size, position, and rotation of the paper with the gradient. How the gradient paper is transformed affects how it fills the shape above. Thankfully, every instance of the Matrix class has a createGradientBox() method, which takes all the pain out of creating matrices for gradients. This method takes five parameters—width, height, rotation, x, and y—and sets the matrix values accordingly.

- spreadMethod: A String value from the SpreadMethod class that determines what happens if the gradient does not fill the entire shape (if it was not wide or tall enough, or was positioned outside the shape). This property maps directly to the Overflow value found in the Color Mixer panel of the Flash IDE. Figure 5-20 shows the results of each of the possible values for this parameter (as set through the IDE). This parameter is optional and defaults to SpreadMethod.PAD if omitted.

- interpolationMethod: A String value from the InterpolationMethod class that fine-tunes the method used to calculate the gradations between two colors in the gradient. This parameter is optional and defaults to InterpolationMethod.LINEAR_RGB if omitted.

- focalPointRatio: Specific to radial gradients, a Number value between -1 and 1 that specifies how far along the axis of rotation the focal point for the radial gradient will be. -1 is on the left edge of the gradient, 0 is in the center, and 1 is on the right edge; values in between are somewhere along that line. This parameter is optional and defaults to 0 (center) if omitted.

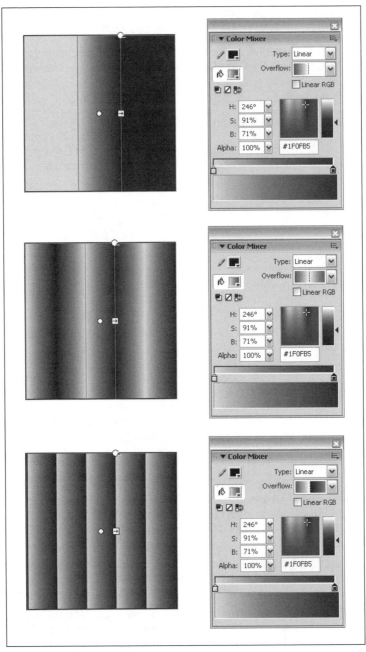

Figure 5-20. Examples of the spreadMethod (or Overflow in the Flash IDE) for a gradient

Going back to Mr. Smiley, he's looking OK but a little too flat. Let's give him some depth with a radial fill of the face.

Start with a simple radial fill between a light yellow, a moderate yellow, and a dark yellow to give the face a 3D look (see Figure 5-21). Use 100% alpha for all the colors, and spread them out evenly over the gradient.

```
package com.foundationAS3.ch5 {

  import flash.display.GradientType;
  import flash.display.Shape;

  public class Smiley extends Shape {

    public function Smiley() {
      // Draw face
      graphics.lineStyle(5);
      var colors:Array = [0xFFFF66, 0xFFFF00, 0xCCCC00];
      var alphas:Array = [1, 1, 1];
      var ratios:Array = [0, 128, 255];
      graphics.beginGradientFill(
        GradientType.RADIAL,
        colors,
        alphas,
        ratios
      );
      graphics.drawCircle(0, 0, 100);
      graphics.endFill();
```

Figure 5-21. A gradient fill is applied to the smiley face.

That looks a little better, but there's something slightly unnatural about the focal point for the gradient being dead center in the circle. You can use the focalPointRatio parameter of the beginGradientFill() method to adjust the location of the focal point. Remember that this is a number between -1 (left edge) and 1 (right edge) that specifies where the focal point should be in the gradient. Set this to -0.5 to shift the focal point from the center of the circle to halfway toward the left edge (see Figure 5-22). Because the focalPointRatio parameter comes after matrix, spreadMethod, and interpolationMethod, none of which you want to set, you can just pass null for those three parameters.

Figure 5-22. The focalPointRatio parameter can be used to offset the center of the gradient.

```
public function Smiley() {
  // Draw face
  graphics.lineStyle(5);
  var colors:Array = [0xFFFF66, 0xFFFF00, 0xCCCC00];
  var alphas:Array = [1, 1, 1];
  var ratios:Array = [0, 128, 255];
  graphics.beginGradientFill(
    GradientType.RADIAL,
    colors,
    alphas,
    ratios,
    null,
    null,
    null,
    -0.5
  );
  graphics.drawCircle(0, 0, 100);
  graphics.endFill();
```

You're nearly there, but the fill would look better with the focal point above and to the left of center, rather than just to the left. To do this, you'll need to rotate the gradient by 45 degrees. And for that, you need a matrix. Let's create a new Matrix instance and call its createGradientBox() method to build a gradient matrix.

The only tricky bit about the createGradientBox() method is that the rotation parameter is in radians, whereas we humans normally think in degrees. Thankfully, it is simple to convert degrees to radians, requiring only that you multiply the degrees value by the result of Math.PI divided by 180. You can even do this in-line in the method call:

```
matrix.createGradientBox(100, 100, 90 * (Math.PI / 180), 0, 0);
```

Remember also that Flash's degrees system is a little kooky in that 0 degrees is at 3 o'clock.

The createGradientBox() method takes five parameters: width, height, rotation, x, and y. The width, height, x, and y parameters are the dimensions and location of the matrix in the Shape's coordinate space, and rotation is how far the gradient is rotated (in radians). You need a gradient that's the same dimensions as your circle (200 × 200 pixels), but because the circle is centered at (0,0) in the sprite, you'll need to move the gradient to (-100,-100), so that the gradient is positioned correctly. For the rotation parameter, just plug 45 degrees into the little degrees-to-radians formula, and you're finished.

```
package com.foundationAS3.ch5 {

  import flash.display.GradientType;
  import flash.display.Shape;
  import flash.geom.Matrix;

  public class Smiley extends Shape {

    public function Smiley() {
```

```
// Draw face
graphics.lineStyle(5);
var colors:Array = [0xFFFF66, 0xFFFF00, 0xCCCC00];
var alphas:Array = [1, 1, 1];
var ratios:Array = [0, 128, 255];
var matrix:Matrix = new Matrix();
matrix.createGradientBox(
  200,
  200,
  45 * (Math.PI / 180),
  -100,
  -100
);
graphics.beginGradientFill(
  GradientType.RADIAL,
  colors,
  alphas,
  ratios,
  matrix,
  null,
  null,
  -0.5
);
graphics.drawCircle(0, 0, 100);
graphics.endFill();
```

Figure 5-23. With the help of a Matrix instance, the gradient fill is offset for a more 3D look for the smiley face.

Make sure that you import the Matrix class from the flash.geom package and that you pass the Matrix instance in the beginGradientFill() method. Figure 5-23 shows the result.

So there you have it: a smiley face drawn entirely with ActionScript code. You're not quite finished with the Drawing API just yet—I couldn't shoehorn all of the methods into the smiley face example—but feel free to stop here and play around. Maybe you would be kind enough to give the poor little fellow a nose, perhaps some hair, and swap the geek glasses for some cool shades.

Simplifying the code

Before continuing with another example of using the Drawing API, let's look at how you might improve the code for drawing the smiley face, to make it a little easier to work with and extend.

First, look at any common pieces and address redundancies in the code. For instance, the thickness of the lines is hard-coded in two separate places in the code. This could be moved into a private variable to make it easier to edit, especially if the number may ever be needed again in another part of the code. The same could hold true for any of the "magic numbers" throughout the code.

You may also notice that the drawing is always done through the graphics property of the Shape instance. Because of this, you can employ the with statement to nest all these lines and reduce the code. Basically, a with allows you to target a specific object to be used to execute all the code within the block. If you use with (graphics), you do not need to continually target the graphics property in each of the calls within the block. Here is the Smiley class rewritten with a with statement, so you can see how it works to simplify the code.

```
package com.foundationAS3.ch5 {

    import flash.display.GradientType;
    import flash.display.Shape;
    import flash.geom.Matrix;

    public class Smiley extends Shape {

        public function Smiley() {
            with (graphics) {
                // Draw face
                lineStyle(5);
                var colors:Array = [0xFFFF66, 0xFFFF00, 0xCCCC00];
                var alphas:Array = [1, 1, 1];
                var ratios:Array = [0, 128, 255];
                var matrix:Matrix = new Matrix();
                matrix.createGradientBox(
                    200,
                    200,
                    45 * (Math.PI / 180),
                    -100,
                    -100
                );
                beginGradientFill(
                    GradientType.RADIAL,
                    colors,
                    alphas,
                    ratios,
                    matrix,
                    null,
                    null,
                    -0.5
                );
                drawCircle(0, 0, 100);
                endFill();

                // Draw eyes
                lineStyle();
                beginFill(0x000000);
                drawCircle(-35, -30, 10);
                drawCircle(35, -30, 10);
                endFill();
```

```
        // Draw glasses
        lineStyle(5);
        beginFill(0xFFFFFF, 0.3);
        drawRoundRect(-60, -50, 50, 40, 20, 20);
        drawRoundRect(10, -50, 50, 40, 20, 20);
        endFill();
        moveTo(-60, -30);
        lineTo(-80, -40);
        moveTo(-10, -30);
        curveTo(0, -40, 10, -30);
        moveTo(60, -30);
        lineTo(80, -40);

        // Draw mouth
        moveTo(-45, 30);
        beginFill(0xFFFFFF);
        curveTo(0, 50, 45, 30);
        curveTo(0, 90, -45, 30);
        endFill();
      }
    }

  }

}
```

Creating gradient line styles

Earlier, I mentioned that the Drawing API was significantly enhanced in Flash 8. The ability to draw lines that use a gradient rather than a solid color was one of those enhancements.

Setting up a gradient line style takes two steps:

- Set up the line thickness by calling the lineStyle() method, just as you would for solid-color lines. You may as well ignore the color and alpha properties for the line style, since they will be ignored in favor of the gradient style.

- Call the lineGradientStyle() method to set up the gradient style. This method takes exactly the same arguments as the beginGradientFill() method you met earlier, and it works in exactly the same way to produce a gradient, which you can then use to render lines with the Drawing API.

Let's give this a go with a linear gradient fill that cycles through all the colors of the rainbow.

1. Create a new Flash document and save it with the name lineGradient.fla in the project directory.

2. Create a new ActionScript document for the document class. Save the file as LineGradientTest.as in the com.foundationAS3.ch5 directory.

3. Create the basic package and class definitions, including the constructor method, using Sprite as the base class. Be sure to import the Shape, Sprite, and GradientType classes from the flash.display package.

```
package com.foundationAS3.ch5 {

  import flash.display.GradientType;
  import flash.display.Shape;
  import flash.display.Sprite;

  public class LineGradientTest extends Sprite {

    public function LineGradientTest () {
    }

  }

}
```

4. As this is a simpler example than the smiley face, you'll include all the drawing code within this document class. Create a new Shape object on which you can draw, add the item to the display list, and center it on the stage.

```
package com.foundationAS3.ch5 {

  import flash.display.GradientType;
  import flash.display.Shape;
  import flash.display.Sprite;

  public class LineGradientTest extends Sprite {

    public function LineGradientTest() {
      // Create and center ellipse shape on stage
      var ellipse:Shape = new Shape();
      addChild(ellipse);
      ellipse.x = stage.stageWidth / 2;
      ellipse.y = stage.stageHeight / 2;
    }

  }

}
```

5. Set up the basic line style with a call to lineStyle(). So you can see the line gradient clearly, use a thickness of 30 pixels. Remember that the lineStyle() color and alpha parameters are ignored, so you don't need to supply them.

```
package com.foundationAS3.ch5 {

  import flash.display.GradientType;
  import flash.display.Shape;
```

```
import flash.display.Sprite;

public class LineGradientTest extends Sprite {

  public function LineGradientTest() {
    // Create and center ellipse shape on stage
    var ellipse:Shape = new Shape();
    addChild(ellipse);
    ellipse.x = stage.stageWidth / 2;
    ellipse.y = stage.stageHeight / 2;

    // Set basic line style
    ellipse.graphics.lineStyle(30);
  }

}

}
```

6. Begin to set up the properties for the gradient, starting with the colors array. You'll create an array containing all the colors of the rainbow: red (0xFF0000), orange (0xFF6600), yellow (0xFFFF00), green (0x00FF00), blue (0x0000FF), indigo (0x2E0854), and violet (0x8F5E99). You may as well deal with the alphas array here, too, since you want the gradient to be fully opaque.

```
package com.foundationAS3.ch5 {

  import flash.display.GradientType;
  import flash.display.Shape;
  import flash.display.Sprite;

  public class LineGradientTest extends Sprite {

    public function LineGradientTest() {
      // Create and center ellipse shape on stage
      var ellipse:Shape = new Shape();
      addChild(ellipse);
      ellipse.x = stage.stageWidth / 2;
      ellipse.y = stage.stageHeight / 2;

      // Set basic line style
      ellipse.graphics.lineStyle(30);

      // Set up gradient properties
      var colors:Array =
        [
          0xFF0000,
          0xFF6600,
          0xFFFF00,
```

```
                      0x00FF00,
                      0x0000FF,
                      0x2E0854,
                      0x8F5E99
                  ];
            var alphas:Array = [1,1,1,1,1,1,1];
        }

    }

}
```

7. Now you need to deal with the gradient ratios. You want the colors spaced evenly, so you need to divide 255 (the maximum ratio value) by 6 (you have seven colors, but one of them will exist at position 0, so you don't need to count it). That gives increments of 42, give or take a fraction.

```
package com.foundationAS3.ch5 {

    import flash.display.GradientType;
    import flash.display.Shape;
    import flash.display.Sprite;

    public class LineGradientTest extends Sprite {

        public function LineGradientTest() {
            // Create and center ellipse shape on stage
            var ellipse:Shape = new Shape();
            addChild(ellipse);
            ellipse.x = stage.stageWidth / 2;
            ellipse.y = stage.stageHeight / 2;

            // Set basic line style
            ellipse.graphics.lineStyle(30);

            // Set up gradient properties
            var colors:Array =
              [
                0xFF0000,
                0xFF6600,
                0xFFFF00,
                0x00FF00,
                0x0000FF,
                0x2E0854,
                0x8F5E99
              ];
            var alphas:Array = [1,1,1,1,1,1,1];
            var ratios:Array = [0,42,84,126,168,210,255];
        }

    }

}
```

8. Call the lineGradientStyle() method to set up a linear gradient using the gradient properties you've just created.

```
package com.foundationAS3.ch5 {

  import flash.display.GradientType;
  import flash.display.Shape;
  import flash.display.Sprite;

  public class LineGradientTest extends Sprite {

    public function LineGradientTest() {
      // Create and center ellipse shape on stage
      var ellipse:Shape = new Shape();
      addChild(ellipse);
      ellipse.x = stage.stageWidth / 2;
      ellipse.y = stage.stageHeight / 2;

      // Set basic line style
      ellipse.graphics.lineStyle(30);

      // Set up gradient properties
      var colors:Array =
        [
          0xFF0000,
          0xFF6600,
          0xFFFF00,
          0x00FF00,
          0x0000FF,
          0x2E0854,
          0x8F5E99
        ];
      var alphas:Array = [1,1,1,1,1,1,1];
      var ratios:Array = [0,42,84,126,168,210,255];

      // Set gradient line style
      ellipse.graphics.lineGradientStyle(GradientType.LINEAR, colors, ➥
  alphas, ratios);
    }

  }

}
```

Use the drawEllipse() method to draw the outline of an ellipse on the stage. This method takes four parameters to specify the location and size of the ellipse to draw: x, y, width, and height. Using this method, draw a 200 × 100-pixel ellipse in the center of the ellipse sprite.

> *The* drawEllipse() *method operates more like* drawRect() *than* drawCircle(). *The parameters specify the positions and dimensions of an imaginary rectangle that would contain the ellipse, rather than the center point and the horizontal and vertical radius values.*

```
package com.foundationAS3.ch5 {

  import flash.display.GradientType;
  import flash.display.Shape;
  import flash.display.Sprite;

  public class LineGradientTest extends Sprite {

    public function LineGradientTest() {
      // Create and center ellipse shape on stage
      var ellipse:Shape = new Shape();
      addChild(ellipse);
      ellipse.x = stage.stageWidth / 2;
      ellipse.y = stage.stageHeight / 2;

      // Set basic line style
      ellipse.graphics.lineStyle(30);

      // Set up gradient properties
      var colors:Array =
        [
          0xFF0000,
          0xFF6600,
          0xFFFF00,
          0x00FF00,
          0x0000FF,
          0x2E0854,
          0x8F5E99
        ];
      var alphas:Array = [1,1,1,1,1,1,1];
      var ratios:Array = [0,42,84,126,168,210,255];

      // Set gradient line style
      ellipse.graphics.lineGradientStyle(GradientType.LINEAR, colors, ➥
alphas, ratios);

      // Draw ellipse
      ellipse.graphics.drawEllipse(-100, -50, 200, 100);
    }

  }

}
```

10. Save your changes to the LineGradientTest.as document and switch to lineGradient.fla. Set the document class of the movie to com.foundationAS3.ch5.LineGradientTest.

11. Save your changes to the lineGradient.fla document and test your movie.

Et voilà, you have an ellipse drawn on the stage using a gradient for its outline, as shown in Figure 5-24.

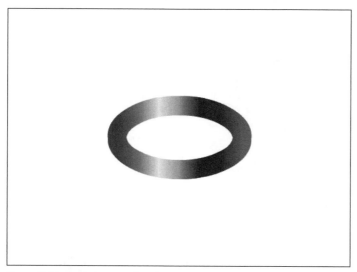

Figure 5-24. A rainbow gradient filling the stroke of an ellipse demonstrates the power of lineGradientStyle().

Summary

So, that was the Drawing API. This was a relatively brief chapter, but then there's not that much to the Drawing API. The power of the API is that it is very simple to learn, and yet you're limited in what you can create only by your artistic talents and the amount of time you have to sit and fiddle.

You'll be seeing the Drawing API again in the next chapter, when you combine it with the event model to produce a basic drawing application. Until then, get creative!

Chapter 6

USER INTERACTION AND MORE WITH EVENTS

Steve Webster

This chapter covers the following topics:

- How the ActionScript event model works
- How to work with event listeners
- How to use standard input events from the mouse and keyboard to allow for interactivity in your projects
- The event flow and why it's useful

One of the facets that makes Flash movies and Flex applications so appealing to users is that developers (you and me) can tap into the Flash Player to handle mouse and keyboard events and provide immediate feedback. All of the projects you've looked at so far in this book have been lacking one vital ingredient: user interaction. I'm going to remedy that here and now by taking you on a journey through the magical world of events and event handling.

As you might have guessed from the title, events in ActionScript 3.0 let you do more than just allow your projects to interact with the users. They are the means by which you know when an external image file has finished loading, for example, or when the Flash Player shows the next frame of your movie. We'll get to these less tangible, but no less important, uses of events and event handling later in the chapter, and begin by concentrating on user interaction.

Understanding events

In the real world, you don't need to check your microwave every 2 seconds to see when your food has finished cooking. Instead, when the timer reaches zero, the microwave beeps to let you know that your gourmet all-in-one chicken dinner (complete with artificial gravy and green things that may once have been peas) is ready to eat. The fact that your microwave will tell you when the food is ready lets you get on with other stuff while it's cooking, like searching through the bathroom cabinet for some antacid tablets to extinguish the inevitable heartburn you'll get after consuming your "gourmet" meal.

The events system in ActionScript 3.0 is made up of three types of objects: **events**, **event dispatchers**, and **event listeners**. In ActionScript 3.0 parlance, the microwave would be known as the event dispatcher. The event would be the microwave timer reaching zero and beeping frantically. You, or more specifically, the part of your brain you've tasked with listening for the beep, would be the event listener. Figure 6-1 illustrates this concept.

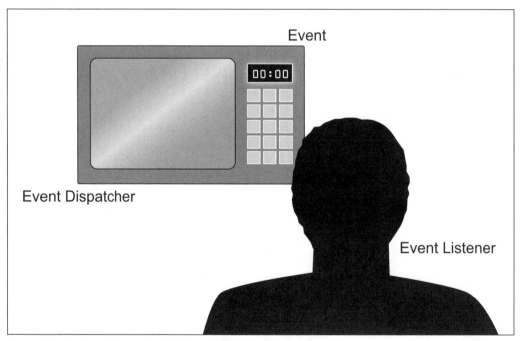

Figure 6-1. A real-world metaphor for the event model in ActionScript

An event is an instance of the Event class, which has a variety of properties that relate to the type of event that occurred. If the event in question were a mouse click, the event object would contain details about the position of the mouse pointer and which (if any) modifier keys—Shift or Ctrl—were held down at the time the event occurred.

Many different classes extend the core Event class in the Flash and Flex frameworks, each tailored to a specific type of event. For example, the mouse click is represented by the MouseEvent class, which adds stageX and stageY properties, among others, to describe the position of the mouse pointer when the event occurred. Additional event classes include KeyboardEvent for keyboard activity, NetStatusEvent for events that occur when streaming video and communicating with the Flash Media Server, and ProgressEvent for monitoring the loading of assets and data. Consult the Adobe documentation for a complete listing of all the event classes, including the additional ones in the Flex framework.

Listening for an event

If you want to be notified of a specific type of event, you register your interest in that event type with the event dispatcher using the addEventListener() method. When you set up a listener for an event using this method, you need to provide two crucial pieces of information: the type of event you are interested in and the method you want to be called when that type of event occurs (commonly called the **event handler method**).

```
someObject.addEventListener(type, listener);
```

The type parameter is the name of the event you want to listen for, in the form of a string. Rather than use a string literal, you should use the static event type constants that are part of the Event class and its descendants. These constants are provided so that you don't need to memorize the event names themselves, and they bring the added benefit that the compiler will probably catch any mistakes you might make in the event name.

The second parameter is a reference to the method you want to be called whenever an event of the specified type occurs. This method should have a single parameter, which corresponds to the class of event you want to listen for (Event for basic events, MouseEvent for mouse-related events, and so on) and have a return type of void.

```
private function methodName(event:EventClass):void {
  // Handle event in here
}
```

> Be careful when specifying the type for the handler's parameter: The Flash Player will throw a runtime error if the type of dispatched event does not match the specified data type in your event listener.

As an example, if you wanted to set up an event listener for the Event.ENTER_FRAME event, which is broadcast by all DisplayObject instances whenever a new frame is displayed, you would end up with something like this:

```
mySprite.addEventListener(Event.ENTER_FRAME, onSpriteEnterFrame);

private function onSpriteEnterFrame(event:Event):void {
  x += 2; // moves sprite 2 pixels right each frame
}
```

195

Event listeners are processed in the order in which they were added to the object, so if you added three listeners for the same event, the listeners will receive notification of the event in the order they were added as listeners.

> The addEventListener() method has a couple of extra optional parameters you can pass. Generally, you will not need to worry about these additional parameters, but it is good to understand what the options provide.
>
> First, the useCapture parameter offers a way to have listeners receive event notifications at an earlier stage of the event flow. You'll learn more about this parameter in the "Listening for events in the capture phase" section later in this chapter.
>
> The priority parameter allows you to specify an order in which listeners receive event notification. You'll learn more about this parameter in the "Stopping an event from propagating" section later in this chapter.
>
> The useWeakReference parameter specifies that an object can be garbage-collected if its only reference is as a listener for another object's events. Basically, when an object adds an event listener for an event, a reference to that object is stored and cannot be garbage-collected (removed from memory), even when that object is no longer referenced anywhere but as an event listener. At that point, it is even impossible to remove the object as an event listener, since no other reference exists, so the object is said to be "orphaned" and is really just wasted memory. Passing true for the useWeakReference parameter tells the Flash runtime that if no other references to the object exist except as the event listener, the object may be marked for garbage collection.

Removing an event listener

Should you no longer wish to listen for an event, you just need to call the removeEventListener() method, passing the exact same parameters you passed to addEventListener() to set up the event listener in the first place: the event type (preferably using one of the event type constants from the Event classes) and a reference to the event listener method:

```
someObject.removeEventListener(type, listener);
```

Once you call the removeEventListener() method, your listener will no longer receive events of the specified type from the event dispatcher.

> It's important that you remove event listeners when you're finished with them in order to prevent your project from consuming more and more memory. An object will not be garbage-collected by the Flash Player when it has event listeners registered for it, meaning that those objects will just hang around for as long as your project is running in the Flash Player. You can get around this by passing true for the useWeakReference parameter in the addEventListener() method call, but it is still strongly recommended that you remove any event listener that no longer needs notification of an event.

Naming your event listener methods

Your event handler methods can have any name you like—they are your methods, and you're telling the event dispatcher which method to call. However, to make things easier for you (and anyone else reading your code) to know at a glance what a particular event listener method is designed to handle, you can use the following convention:

on + *ObjectType* + *EventType*

For example, if you have your own DisplayObject class to represent thumbnails of photographs (named, rather cunningly, PhotoThumbnail) that users can click to view a larger version (which will be communicated by the MouseEvent.CLICK event), name your event handler onPhotoThumbnailClick. Simple, huh?

Creating a simple drawing application

Now is a good time to handle your first event in ActionScript 3.0. This example combines event handling with the Drawing API (covered in the previous chapter).

The premise is simple: when the mouse button is held down and the mouse is moved, you draw a line from the last mouse position to the current one. When the mouse button is released, you stop drawing. Granted, it's more Etch-A-Sketch than Adobe Photoshop, but everyone needs to start somewhere, right?

Setting up the canvas

Let's begin by setting up the basic framework for the simple drawing application.

1. Create a new Flash file and save it in the project folder with the name drawingApplication.fla.

2. Create a new ActionScript file for the document class, which will live in the com.foundationAS3.ch6 package. Create the appropriate package directory structure, and save the file named DrawingApplication.as in the ch6 directory.

3. Create the basic package and class definitions for the DrawingApplication class, including an empty constructor method. You'll extend the Sprite class, since you're not dealing with any timeline animation.

```
package com.foundationAS3.ch6 {

  import flash.display.Sprite;

  public class DrawingApplication extends Sprite {

    public function DrawingApplication() {
    }

  }

}
```

4. You need a surface on which to draw, so create a new Sprite display object (storing a reference to it in a new property named canvas).

```
package com.foundationAS3.ch6 {

  import flash.display.Sprite;

  public class DrawingApplication extends Sprite {

    private var _canvas:Sprite;

    public function DrawingApplication() {
      _canvas = new Sprite();
    }

  }

}
```

5. In order for the canvas to receive mouse events, it needs to have a width and a height. The easiest way to provide that, as well as present some visual surface for the user, is to draw into it. Draw a light-gray rectangle that is the same size as the stage using the Drawing API methods.

```
package com.foundationAS3.ch6 {

  import flash.display.Sprite;

  public class DrawingApplication extends Sprite {

    private var _canvas:Sprite;

    public function DrawingApplication() {
      _canvas = new Sprite();

      _canvas.graphics.beginFill(0xF0F0F0);
      _canvas.graphics.drawRect(0, 0, stage.stageWidth, stage.stageHeight);
      _canvas.graphics.endFill();
    }

  }

}
```

6. Set the line style of the canvas to be a 2-pixel black line, which will be used for all further drawing. Then add the canvas to the stage.

```
package com.foundationAS3.ch6 {

  import flash.display.Sprite;

  public class DrawingApplication extends Sprite {
```

```
    private var _canvas:Sprite;

    public function DrawingApplication() {
      _canvas = new Sprite();

      _canvas.graphics.beginFill(0xF0F0F0);
      _canvas.graphics.drawRect(0, 0, stage.stageWidth, stage.stageHeight);
      _canvas.graphics.endFill();

      _canvas.graphics.lineStyle(2, 0x000000);

      addChild(_canvas);
    }

  }

}
```

With this basic framework in place, you're ready to add the event listeners to your canvas object.

Adding event listeners

When the mouse button is pressed, communicated by the MouseEvent.MOUSE_DOWN event, you need to move the drawing pen to the current mouse location. You also need to start listening for the MouseEvent.MOUSE_MOVE event so that you can draw a line whenever the mouse moves. Finally, when the mouse button is released and a MouseEvent.MOUSE_UP event is dispatched, you need to draw a line to the current mouse position and remove the listener for the MouseEvent.MOUSE_MOVE event.

1. Create a new private method named onCanvasMouseDown() that takes a single parameter, event, of type MouseEvent, and add that method as a listener for the MouseEvent.MOUSE_DOWN event of the canvas object. You'll need to import the MouseEvent class from the flash.events package.

```
package com.foundationAS3.ch6 {

  import flash.display.Sprite;
  import flash.events.MouseEvent;

  public class DrawingApplication extends Sprite {
. . .
      addChild(_canvas);

      _canvas.addEventListener(MouseEvent.MOUSE_DOWN, onCanvasMouseDown);
    }

    private function onCanvasMouseDown(event:MouseEvent):void {
    }

  }

}
```

2. Within the onCanvasMouseDown() event, move the Drawing API pen to the current mouse position, which is contained in the localX and localY properties of the event object.

> localX and localY *are good to use when it's important to obtain the mouse positions within a sprite's own coordinate space, as when you are drawing into that sprite. In this particular case,* stageX *and* stageY, *which return the global coordinates, could have been used, since the canvas is at coordinates (0, 0) within the main document class. However, it's still a good idea to be in the habit of looking at the local coordinates, just in case the canvas was moved to a different location.*

```
package com.foundationAS3.ch6 {

  import flash.display.Sprite;
  import flash.events.MouseEvent;

  public class DrawingApplication extends Sprite {
. . .
      _canvas.addEventListener(MouseEvent.MOUSE_DOWN, onCanvasMouseDown);
    }

    private function onCanvasMouseDown(event:MouseEvent):void {
      _canvas.graphics.moveTo(event.localX, event.localY);
    }

  }

}
```

3. Create a new private method named onCanvasMouseMove() to handle the MouseEvent. MOUSE_MOVE event. Add the addEventListener() call to set up this event listener within the onCanvasMouseDown() method, meaning that you'll be notified of mouse move events only after the mouse button has been pressed.

```
package com.foundationAS3.ch6 {

  import flash.display.Sprite;
  import flash.events.MouseEvent;

  public class DrawingApplication extends Sprite {
. . .
    private function onCanvasMouseDown(event:MouseEvent):void {
      _canvas.graphics.moveTo(event.localX, event.localY);
      _canvas.addEventListener(MouseEvent.MOUSE_MOVE, onCanvasMouseMove);
    }
```

```
      private function onCanvasMouseMove(event:MouseEvent):void {
      }

   }

}
```

4. Within the onCanvasMouseMove() event, draw a line from the current pen position to the current position of the mouse pointer.

```
package com.foundationAS3.ch6 {

   import flash.display.Sprite;
   import flash.events.MouseEvent;

   public class DrawingApplication extends Sprite {
   . . .
      private function onCanvasMouseDown(event:MouseEvent):void {
        _canvas.graphics.moveTo(event.localX, event.localY);
        _canvas.addEventListener(MouseEvent.MOUSE_MOVE, onCanvasMouseMove);
      }

      private function onCanvasMouseMove(event:MouseEvent):void {
        _canvas.graphics.lineTo(event.localX, event.localY);
      }

   }

}
```

5. Create a new private method named onCanvasMouseUp() to handle the MouseEvent.MOUSE_UP event. The event listener should be added in the same place the MouseEvent.MOUSE_DOWN event was added: in the main DrawingApplication constructor method.

```
package com.foundationAS3.ch6 {

   import flash.display.Sprite;
   import flash.events.MouseEvent;

   public class DrawingApplication extends Sprite {
   . . .
      addChild(_canvas);

      _canvas.addEventListener(MouseEvent.MOUSE_DOWN, onCanvasMouseDown);
      _canvas.addEventListener(MouseEvent.MOUSE_UP, onCanvasMouseUp);
   }
```

```
        private function onCanvasMouseDown(event:MouseEvent):void {
          _canvas.graphics.moveTo(event.localX, event.localY);
          _canvas.addEventListener(MouseEvent.MOUSE_MOVE, onCanvasMouseMove);
        }

        private function onCanvasMouseMove(event:MouseEvent):void {
          _canvas.graphics.lineTo(event.localX, event.localY);
        }

        private function onCanvasMouseUp(event:MouseEvent):void {
        }

      }

    }
```

6. Within the onCanvasMouseUp() method, you need to draw a line to the current mouse location (just in case the mouse has been moved since the last MouseEvent.MOUSE_MOVE event was dispatched) and remove the MouseEvent.MOUSE_MOVE event listener using the removeEventListener() method.

```
package com.foundationAS3.ch6 {

  import flash.display.Sprite;
  import flash.events.MouseEvent;

  public class DrawingApplication extends Sprite {
  . . .
    private function onCanvasMouseMove(event:MouseEvent):void {
      _canvas.graphics.lineTo(event.localX, event.localY);
    }

    private function onCanvasMouseUp(event:MouseEvent):void {
      _canvas.graphics.lineTo(event.localX, event.localY);
      _canvas.removeEventListener(MouseEvent.MOUSE_MOVE, onCanvasMouseMove);
    }

  }

}
```

7. Save the changes to the DrawingApplication.as file and switch back to the drawingApplication.fla file.

8. Set com.foundationAS3.ch6.DrawingApplication as the document class in the Property inspector. Save the changes and test your movie.

Figure 6-2 shows an example of the drawing application in action. You'll have to forgive my (lack of) drawing skills; I'm certainly no Rembrandt. But I think you'll agree that it's not a bad application for 30-odd lines of code.

Figure 6-2. The drawing application made possible by events (and your code!)

Refreshing the screen

One thing you might notice is a lack of smoothness in the drawing interaction. This is due to the fact that the movie will update the screen only at the frame rate that you have set prior to publishing, which may be slower than the rate at which you draw. You can get around this by forcing the screen to update whenever the mouse changes its position.

Mouse events have a method named updateAfterEvent() (in ActionScript 2.0, this method was a global function). By calling this method within your mouse move handler, you can force the screen refresh and create a smoother interaction.

Add the following line of code to the end of the onCanvasMoveHandler():

```
private function onCanvasMouseMove(event:MouseEvent):void {
  _canvas.graphics.lineTo(event.localX, event.localY);
  event.updateAfterEvent();
}
```

Save the file, and then return to drawingApplication.fla. Test the movie, and you should see a much smoother result.

203

Using one event listener for multiple objects

One of the nice features of the event model is that it does not force you to have one method respond to each event (which can happen if you are using something like callback handlers—users of the version 1 Flash components may remember those days!). Multiple objects can have the same listener and handler method, if that suits your needs.

For instance, suppose that you have a group of Sprite instances that you want to scale in size when the user rolls over them. You could take care of all of this in a single method, and add it as the handler for the MouseEvent.MOUSE_ROLLOVER event. When any of the Sprite instances are rolled over, the method is called, and you can access the rolled-over Sprite instance through the MouseEvent object's target property.

```
private function onSpriteRollover(event:MouseEvent):void {
  // Get reference to rolled-over sprite
  var sprite:Sprite = event.target as Sprite;
  sprite.scaleX = sprite.scaleY = 1.5;
}
```

As shown in this snippet, you need to cast the target property to the appropriate class (Sprite in this case) using the as operator in order to use this property. This is necessary because any type of object can be the target of an event, so the data type of the target property in the Event class is Object.

Using events with the display list

Now that you know how events work in ActionScript 3.0, it's time to look at some of the more interesting events that are dispatched by the various DisplayObject classes and the different ways in which those events can be used.

Handling single and double mouse clicks

With enough time and energy, you could use the MouseEvent.MOUSE_UP and MouseEvent.MOUSE_DOWN events to handle single and double mouse clicks in your project. You would need to listen for a MOUSE_DOWN, followed by a MOUSE_UP on the same object, then wait a specified amount of time to see if another MOUSE_DOWN, MOUSE_UP sequence happened on the same object.

Thankfully, Adobe has taken pity on us poor time- and energy-deficient developers by providing us with ready-made MouseEvent.CLICK and MouseEvent.DOUBLE_CLICK events. The only small hoop you need to jump through is that display objects don't receive MouseEvent.DOUBLE_CLICK events by default. To remedy this, you just need to set the display object's doubleClickEnabled property to true.

```
myDisplayObject.doubleClickEnabled = true;
```

Once you've done that, you're ready to rock and roll, double-click style.

Let's work through a simple example to show how these two events work.

1. Create a new Flash document named click.fla and save it in the project directory.

2. Create a new ActionScript file for the document class, which will be in the com.foundationAS3.ch6 package, and save it in the appropriate location within the project directory with the name ClickTest.as.

3. Create the basic package and class definitions for the ClickTest class, which will extend the Sprite class.

```
package com.foundationAS3.ch6 {

    import flash.display.Sprite;

    public class ClickTest extends Sprite {

        public function ClickTest() {
        }

    }

}
```

4. In the constructor method, create a new Sprite object in a local variable named square and add it to the display list.

```
package com.foundationAS3.ch6 {

    import flash.display.Sprite;

    public class ClickTest extends Sprite {

        public function ClickTest() {
            var square:Sprite = new Sprite();
            addChild(square);
        }

    }

}
```

5. Use the Drawing API methods to draw a 100 × 100-pixel, red square with a black outline within the new Sprite instance.

```
package com.foundationAS3.ch6 {

    import flash.display.Sprite;

    public class ClickTest extends Sprite {
```

```
    public function ClickTest() {
      var square:Sprite = new Sprite();
      square.graphics.lineStyle(2, 0x000000);
      square.graphics.beginFill(0xFF0000);
      square.graphics.drawRect(0, 0, 100, 100);
      square.graphics.endFill();
      addChild(square);
    }

  }

}
```

6. Create two private methods named onSquareClick() and onSquareDoubleClick(), and add them as event listeners for the MouseEvent.CLICK and MouseEvent.DOUBLE_CLICK events on the new Sprite instance, respectively. You'll need to import the MouseEvent class from the flash.events package. Also, don't forget to set the doubleClickEnabled property of the Sprite instance to true; otherwise, the Flash Player will not dispatch double-click events for this object.

```
package com.foundationAS3.ch6 {

  import flash.display.Sprite;
  import flash.events.MouseEvent;

  public class ClickTest extends Sprite {

    public function ClickTest() {
      var square:Sprite = new Sprite();
      square.graphics.lineStyle(2, 0x000000);
      square.graphics.beginFill(0xFF0000);
      square.graphics.drawRect(0, 0, 100, 100);
      square.graphics.endFill();
      addChild(square);

      square.doubleClickEnabled = true;

      square.addEventListener(MouseEvent.CLICK, onSquareClick);
      square.addEventListener(MouseEvent.DOUBLE_CLICK, onSquareDoubleClick);
    }

    private function onSquareClick(event:MouseEvent):void {
    }

    private function onSquareDoubleClick(event:MouseEvent):void {
    }

  }

}
```

7. In the onSquareClick() and onSquareDoubleClick() methods, trace some string values to identify which method was clicked. I've gone for "ouch!" and "double ouch!", but feel free to be creative.

```
package com.foundationAS3.ch6 {

  import flash.display.Sprite;
  import flash.events.MouseEvent;

  public class ClickTest extends Sprite {

    public function ClickTest() {
      var square:Sprite = new Sprite();
      square.graphics.lineStyle(2, 0x000000);
      square.graphics.beginFill(0xFF0000);
      square.graphics.drawRect(0, 0, 100, 100);
      square.graphics.endFill();
      addChild(square);

      square.doubleClickEnabled = true;

      square.addEventListener(MouseEvent.CLICK, onSquareClick);
      square.addEventListener(MouseEvent.DOUBLE_CLICK, onSquareDoubleClick);
    }

    private function onSquareClick(event:MouseEvent):void {
      trace("ouch!");
    }

    private function onSquareDoubleClick(event:MouseEvent):void {
      trace("double ouch!");
    }

  }

}
```

8. Save the changes to the ClickTest.as file and switch back to the click.fla document.

9. In the Property inspector, set the document class to com.foundationAS3.ch6.ClickTest. Then save the changes to the click.fla document.

10. Test the Flash movie and go click-happy on the shiny red square.

If you click once, you'll see the string "ouch!" (or whatever you chose instead) added to the Output panel. If you click twice in quick succession, you'll see "ouch!" followed by "double ouch!," which is the initial MouseEvent.CLICK event firing, followed by the MouseEvent.DOUBLE_CLICK event. Figure 6-3 shows an example of the results.

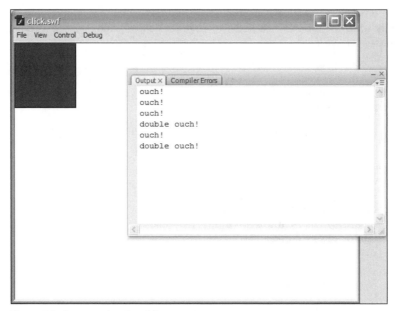

Figure 6-3. An example of enabling mouse events

For me, the MouseEvent.DOUBLE_CLICK *event behavior is a little counterintuitive. When double-clicking a* DisplayObject *instance, I would have expected a solitary* MouseEvent.DOUBLE_CLICK *event. The fact that the* MouseEvent.CLICK *event fires for the first mouse click of a double-click action means that you need to be wary when you're listening for both types of events, particularly if the actions you're performing are mutually exclusive.*

Handling mouse hover states

When the mouse pointer passes over an InteractiveObject instance in the display list, several events are fired to help you respond appropriately:

- MouseEvent.MOUSE_OVER and MouseEvent.MOUSE_OUT: These events are dispatched when the user moves the mouse pointer over and out of an InteractiveObject instance. These will fire whenever the mouse pointer moves from one InteractiveObject to another, even if that object is a descendant of the previous one.

- MouseEvent.ROLL_OVER and MouseEvent.ROLL_OUT: These have been added to make it easier to write event handlers for InteractiveObject instances that have children. They will fire only for a given InteractiveObject if the mouse pointer has moved to or from another InteractiveObject instance that is not one of its descendants.

Since using MouseEvent.MOUSE_OVER and MouseEvent.MOUSE_OUT can make it difficult to write event handlers for nested objects, I advise using MouseEvent.ROLL_OVER and MouseEvent.ROLL_OUT if you're trying to handle rollovers, even if the display objects in question have no children. On one of my projects, it took me an entire day to track down a problem with rollovers, all because the designers had changed the sprites to have children, and I was using the MouseEvent.MOUSE_OVER and MouseEvent.MOUSE_OUT events. Forewarned is forearmed, or so they say.

Responding to a rollover event

Let's change the previous example so that the square changes to blue when the mouse is over it.

1. Create a new Flash document named rollover.fla and save it in the project directory.

2. For the document class, save the previous example's ClickTest.as file as RolloverTest.as. Change the class name and constructor to use RolloverTest instead of ClickTest.

```
package com.foundationAS3.ch6 {

    import flash.display.Sprite;
    import flash.events.MouseEvent;

    public class RolloverTest extends Sprite {

        public function RolloverTest() {
            var square:Sprite = new Sprite();
            square.graphics.lineStyle(2, 0x000000);
            square.graphics.beginFill(0xFF0000);
            square.graphics.drawRect(0, 0, 100, 100);
            square.graphics.endFill();
            addChild(square);

            square.doubleClickEnabled = true;

            square.addEventListener(MouseEvent.CLICK, onSquareClick);
            square.addEventListener(MouseEvent.DOUBLE_CLICK, onSquareDoubleClick);
        }

        private function onSquareClick(event:MouseEvent):void {
            trace("ouch!");
        }

        private function onSquareDoubleClick(event:MouseEvent):void {
            trace("double ouch!");
        }

    }

}
```

3. Create two new private methods named onSquareRollOver() and onSquareRollOut(), and add them as event listeners for the MouseEvent.ROLL_OVER and MouseEvent.ROLL_OUT events, respectively.

```
package com.foundationAS3.ch6 {

    import flash.display.Sprite;
    import flash.events.MouseEvent;
. . .
        square.addEventListener(MouseEvent.CLICK, onSquareClick);
        square.addEventListener(MouseEvent.DOUBLE_CLICK, onSquareDoubleClick);
        square.addEventListener(MouseEvent.ROLL_OVER, onSquareRollOver);
        square.addEventListener(MouseEvent.ROLL_OUT, onSquareRollOut);
    }

    private function onSquareClick(event:MouseEvent):void {
        trace("ouch!");
    }

    private function onSquareDoubleClick(event:MouseEvent):void {
        trace("double ouch!");
    }

    private function onSquareRollOver(event:MouseEvent):void {
    }

    private function onSquareRollOut(event:MouseEvent):void {
    }

    }

}
```

4. Since you're going to need a reference to the square object in your new event handlers (so you can redraw it using different colors), change the local square variable to be a private property of the object instead. To follow the previous naming conventions, you'll change its name to include a preceding underscore, so make sure to update this in the code.

```
package com.foundationAS3.ch6 {

    import flash.display.Sprite;
    import flash.events.MouseEvent;

    public class RolloverTest extends Sprite {

        private var _square:Sprite;

        public function RolloverTest() {
            _square = new Sprite();
            _square.graphics.lineStyle(2, 0x000000);
            _square.graphics.beginFill(0xff0000);
```

```
      _square.graphics.drawRect(0, 0, 100, 100);
      _square.graphics.endFill();
      addChild(_square);

      _square.doubleClickEnabled = true;

      _square.addEventListener(MouseEvent.CLICK, onSquareClick);
      _square.addEventListener(MouseEvent.DOUBLE_CLICK, onSquareDoubleClick);
      _square.addEventListener(MouseEvent.ROLL_OVER, onSquareRollOver);
      _square.addEventListener(MouseEvent.ROLL_OUT, onSquareRollOut);
    }
  . . .
  }
```

5. Move the drawing code to a new private method named drawSquare(). This method accepts a single parameter, color, which specifies the fill color for the shape. Add a call to this new method in place of the old drawing code in the constructor method. Also, add a call to the graphics.clear() method at the start of this new method to clear the graphics layer, so you're not just drawing over the top of whatever was already there.

```
package com.foundationAS3.ch6 {

  import flash.display.Sprite;
  import flash.events.MouseEvent;

  public class RolloverTest extends Sprite {

    private var _square:Sprite;

    public function RolloverTest() {
      _square = new Sprite();
      drawSquare(0xFF0000);
      addChild(_square);

      _square.doubleClickEnabled = true;

      _square.addEventListener(MouseEvent.CLICK, onSquareClick);
      _square.addEventListener(MouseEvent.DOUBLE_CLICK, onSquareDoubleClick);
      _square.addEventListener(MouseEvent.ROLL_OVER, onSquareRollOver);
      _square.addEventListener(MouseEvent.ROLL_OUT, onSquareRollOut);
    }

    private function drawSquare(color:uint):void {
      _square.graphics.clear();
      _square.graphics.lineStyle(2, 0x000000);
      _square.graphics.beginFill(color);
      _square.graphics.drawRect(0, 0, 100, 100);
      _square.graphics.endFill();
    }
  . . .
  }
```

> *Don't forget to use the* color *parameter of the* drawSquare() *method in the call to the* beginFill() *Drawing API method in place of the hard-coded* 0xFF0000 *(red).*

6. Within the onSquareRollOver() and onSquareRollOut() methods, call the drawSquare() method with parameters of 0x0000FF (blue) and 0xFF0000 (red), respectively.

```
package com.foundationAS3.ch6 {
. . .
    private function onSquareRollOver(event:MouseEvent):void {
      drawSquare(0x0000FF);
    }

    private function onSquareRollOut(event:MouseEvent):void {
      drawSquare(0xFF0000);
    }

  }

}
```

7. Save the changes to the RolloverTest.as document and switch back to the rollover.fla document in the Flash IDE.

8. In the Property inspector for the document, set the document class to com.foundationAS3.ch6.RolloverTest.

9. Save the changes to the rollover.fla document, and then test your movie.

Rolling your mouse over the square and off again should change the color from red to blue and then back to red again, as shown in Figure 6-4.

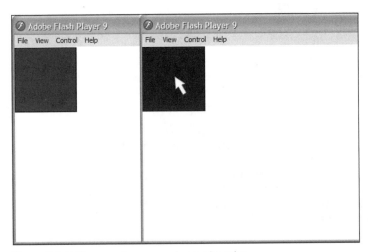

Figure 6-4. Rolling over the square changes its color.

If you were trying to turn the square *object from the preceding example into a button, you might consider using the built-in* SimpleButton *class. That class allows you to specify a different* DisplayObject *for each of the up, over, down, and hit states that a simple button has, without needing to mess with setting up events.*

Making colors constants

One final change you should make to the RolloverTest class is to move the colors into constant properties for the class, as opposed to specifying them directly in the drawSquare() calls. Why do this?

Notice that even at this simple state, red is specified in two places in the code. If you wanted a different color for the up state, you would need to make sure to update both places in the code. What if the class was twice as long, with colors in more than three places? Sure, you could do a search and replace, and hope to catch everything, but the better solution is to move items like colors into properties that are easily accessed and updated. This works great not only for values that appear in multiple places, but also for values that appear only once but may require editing at some point. Placing such values in properties, perhaps defined at the top of the class, makes it much easier to go in and tweak values—you don't need to hunt through the code to see where things are set.

Place the following constants in your RolloverTest class:

```
package com.foundationAS3.ch6 {

    import flash.display.Sprite;
    import flash.events.MouseEvent;

    public class RolloverTest extends Sprite {

        private static var UP_COLOR:uint = 0xFF0000;
        private static var ROLLOVER_COLOR:uint = 0x0000FF;

        private var _square:Sprite;
    . . .
    }
```

Now update the places in the code where the colors were hard-coded with the new constant values.

```
package com.foundationAS3.ch6 {

    import flash.display.Sprite;
    import flash.events.MouseEvent;

    public class RolloverTest extends Sprite {

        private static var UP_COLOR:uint = 0xFF0000;
        private static var ROLLOVER_COLOR:uint = 0x0000FF;
```

```
        private var _square:Sprite;

        public function RolloverTest() {
          _square = new Sprite();
          drawSquare(UP_COLOR);
          addChild(_square);

          _square.doubleClickEnabled = true;

          _square.addEventListener(MouseEvent.CLICK, onSquareClick);
          _square.addEventListener(MouseEvent.DOUBLE_CLICK, onSquareDoubleClick);
          _square.addEventListener(MouseEvent.ROLL_OVER, onSquareRollOver);
          _square.addEventListener(MouseEvent.ROLL_OUT, onSquareRollOut);
        }
    . . .
        private function onSquareRollOver(event:MouseEvent):void {
          drawSquare(ROLLOVER_COLOR);
        }

        private function onSquareRollOut(event:MouseEvent):void {
          drawSquare(UP_COLOR);
        }

      }

    }
```

Of course, there's no reason you couldn't also make the line color and thickness, as well as the width and height of the box, into properties. I will leave that as an exercise for you to do on your own.

Handling key presses

The Flash Player dispatches keyboard events in response to user input through the keyboard. In contrast to the myriad of mouse-related events, only two events are associated with keyboard input: KeyboardEvent.KEY_DOWN and KeyboardEvent.KEY_UP. The events dispatched to listeners of these events are instances of the KeyboardEvent class, which includes information about which key was pressed and whether the Ctrl and/or Shift keys were held down at the time.

The keyCode and charCode properties can be used to determine which key was pressed. keyCode will give you a numeric value that corresponds to the key on the keyboard that was pressed (and which can be compared against the constants in the flash.ui.Keyboard class). charCode will give you the numeric value for the character represented by that key in the current character set. Thus, pressing 1 on the main keyboard and 1 on the numeric keypad will return different results for keyCode but the same result for charCode.

The flash.ui.Keyboard class also has two Boolean properties named capsLock and numLock, which will tell you whether the CapsLock and NumLock keys, respectively, are enabled.

For the modifier keys, you have the ctrlKey and shiftKey Boolean properties (there is also altKey, but it is not currently implemented and is reserved for future use). If you need to differentiate between the left and right Shift or Ctrl keys, you can use the keyLocation property along with the LEFT and RIGHT properties of the flash.ui.KeyLocation class. If you are a Mac user, the Ctrl key corresponds to the Command key (as you are probably well aware, with all the Windows-centric documentation out there!).

When a key is pressed, the Flash Player uses the focus property of the Stage object to determine which InteractiveObject instance in the display list should be the target of that event. The Stage.focus property contains a reference to the InteractiveObject instance on the display list that currently has input focus. By default, this will be the main Application object for your project. The user can change the object with the focus (by tabbing to a different text field or button, for example). And you can change the object with the focus programmatically, by assigning a new value to the Stage.focus property.

Setting up a keyboard drawing application

To demonstrate using the keyboard events, you'll re-create the simple drawing application from earlier so that it can be operated using the keyboard instead. You'll listen for keyboard events from the cursor keys and the spacebar. The cursor keys will be used to move a crosshair around the screen (our keyboard-friendly equivalent of the mouse pointer). If the cursor keys are used while the spacebar is held down, you will draw a line between the last known crosshair position and the current one.

1. Create a new Flash document named keyboardDrawing.fla and save it in the project directory.

2. Create a new ActionScript document for the document class, which will belong to the com.foundationAS3.ch6 package. Save the file with the name KeyboardDrawing.as in the appropriate location in the project directory.

3. Create the basic package and class definitions for the KeyboardDrawing class, extending the Sprite class.

```
package com.foundationAS3.ch6 {

  import flash.display.Sprite;

  public class KeyboardDrawing extends Sprite {

    public function KeyboardDrawing() {
    }

  }

}
```

4. Add two private properties, _canvas and _crosshair, to the class definition, and create the Sprite and Shape instances, respectively, in the constructor method before adding them both to the display list (canvas first, so that the crosshair is on top visually). You are making the crosshair a Shape instance, since it does not need any of the interactive capabilities of Sprite.

```
package com.foundationAS3.ch6 {

  import flash.display.Shape;
  import flash.display.Sprite;

  public class KeyboardDrawing extends Sprite {

    private var _canvas:Sprite;
    private var _crosshair:Shape;

    public function KeyboardDrawing() {
      _canvas = new Sprite();
      addChild(_canvas);
      _crosshair = new Shape();
      addChild(_crosshair);
    }

  }

}
```

5. Draw the crosshair using the Drawing API. Use the lineStyle() method to set the line style to draw 1-pixel black lines, and draw two lines—from (–5,0) to (6, 0) and from (0,–5) to (0,6)—using a combination of the moveTo() and lineTo() methods. To keep things clean, you will place this code in a separate method.

```
package com.foundationAS3.ch6 {

  import flash.display.Shape;
  import flash.display.Sprite;

  public class KeyboardDrawing extends Sprite {

    private var _canvas:Sprite;
    private var _crosshair:Shape;

    public function KeyboardDrawing() {
      _canvas = new Sprite();
      addChild(_canvas);
      _crosshair = new Shape();
      drawCrosshair();
      addChild(_crosshair);
    }
```

```
    private function drawCrosshair():Void {
      _crosshair.graphics.lineStyle(1, 0x000000);
      _crosshair.graphics.moveTo(-5, 0);
      _crosshair.graphics.lineTo(6, 0);
      _crosshair.graphics.moveTo(0, -5);
      _crosshair.graphics.lineTo(0, 6);
    }

  }

}
```

6. Set the line style of the canvas to draw 2-pixel black lines, and set the stage.focus property to the canvas so it will receive keyboard events.

```
package com.foundationAS3.ch6 {

  import flash.display.Shape;
  import flash.display.Sprite;

  public class KeyboardDrawing extends Sprite {

    private var _canvas:Sprite;
    private var _crosshair:Shape;

    public function KeyboardDrawing() {
      _canvas = new Sprite();
      addChild(_canvas);
      _crosshair = new Shape();
      drawCrosshair();
      addChild(_crosshair);

      // Prepare canvas for drawing and keyboard input
      _canvas.graphics.lineStyle(2, 0x000000);
      stage.focus = _canvas;
    }

    private function drawCrosshair():void {
      _crosshair.graphics.lineStyle(1, 0x000000);
      _crosshair.graphics.moveTo(-5, 0);
      _crosshair.graphics.lineTo(6, 0);
      _crosshair.graphics.moveTo(0, -5);
      _crosshair.graphics.lineTo(0, 6);
    }

  }

}
```

With that done, you're ready to devise a strategy for handling crosshair movement.

Handling crosshair movement

Since it would be neat to allow diagonal movement as well as horizontal and vertical movement, I've decided to use two private class properties— _xDirection and _yDirection—to store how to move in the x and y position of the virtual pen. This pen's position will be set when the relevant cursor keys are pressed, and cleared when they're released. These values will then be checked in an Event.ENTER_FRAME event listener, and the crosshair will be moved by a specified amount each frame.

The final piece of the puzzle is determining whether you should be drawing or moving the Drawing API pen from its current location to the new location of the crosshair object. This will be handled by a private Boolean _isDrawing class property, which will be set to true when the spacebar is pressed, and set to false when it's released.

1. Create the _xDirection, _yDirection, and _isDrawing properties. The _xDirection and _yDirection properties need to be of type int, since they can have both positive (right/down) and negative (left/up) values, in addition to 0 (stationary). While you're there, add a constant for the pixel distance amount to draw each frame (which I've set to 2).

```
package com.foundationAS3.ch6 {

  import flash.display.Shape;
  import flash.display.Sprite;

  public class KeyboardDrawing extends Sprite {

    private const PIXEL_DISTANCE_TO_DRAW:uint = 2;

    private var _canvas:Sprite;
    private var _crosshair:Shape;

    private var _xDirection:int = 0;
    private var _yDirection:int = 0;
    private var _isDrawing:Boolean = false;

    public function KeyboardDrawing() {
    . . .
    }

  }

}
```

2. Create two private methods named onCanvasKeyDown() and onCanvasKeyUp() and set them up as listeners for the KeyboardEvent.KEY_DOWN and KeyboardEvent.KEY_UP events, respectively, on the _canvas instance. You'll need to import the KeyboardEvent class from the flash.events package.

```
package com.foundationAS3.ch6 {

  import flash.display.Shape;
  import flash.display.Sprite;
  import flash.events.KeyboardEvent;
```

```
public class KeyboardDrawing extends Sprite {
. . .
    // Prepare canvas for drawing and keyboard input
    _canvas.graphics.lineStyle(2, 0x000000);
    stage.focus = _canvas;

    // Add canvas event listeners
    _canvas.addEventListener(KeyboardEvent.KEY_DOWN, onCanvasKeyDown);
    _canvas.addEventListener(KeyboardEvent.KEY_UP, onCanvasKeyUp);
    }

    private function onCanvasKeyDown(event:KeyboardEvent):void {
    }

    private function onCanvasKeyUp(event:KeyboardEvent):void {
    }

  }

}
```

3. In the onCanvasKeyDown() listener, use the keyCode property of the KeyboardEvent object to determine which key was pressed by comparing it to the constants from the Keyboard class. You'll need to import the Keyboard class from the flash.ui package. Depending on the key pressed, set the value of the _yDirection or _xDirection variable to the appropriate value using the PIXEL_DISTANCE_TO_DRAW constant you created earlier. Remember that positive is right/down and negative is left/up. If the spacebar has been pressed, set _isDrawing to true.

```
package com.foundationAS3.ch6 {

  import flash.display.Shape;
  import flash.display.Sprite;
  import flash.events.KeyboardEvent;
  import flash.ui.Keyboard;

  public class KeyboardDrawing extends Sprite {
  . . .
    private function onCanvasKeyDown(event:KeyboardEvent):void {
      switch (event.keyCode) {
        case Keyboard.UP:
          _yDirection = -PIXEL_DISTANCE_TO_DRAW;
          break;
        case Keyboard.DOWN:
          _yDirection = PIXEL_DISTANCE_TO_DRAW;
          break;
        case Keyboard.LEFT:
          _xDirection = -PIXEL_DISTANCE_TO_DRAW;
          break;
        case Keyboard.RIGHT:
          _xDirection = PIXEL_DISTANCE_TO_DRAW;
          break;
```

```
        case Keyboard.SPACE:
          _isDrawing = true;
          break;
      }
    }

    private function onCanvasKeyUp(event:KeyboardEvent):void {
    }

  }

}
```

The onCanvasKeyDown() listener uses a construct called the switch statement. This is a conditional statement similar to the if else if construct. It allows you to run different lines of code based on whether a certain case is met.

You begin a switch statement with a value you wish to match, almost certainly contained within some variable or variable property, followed by cases with the different possible values for the variable. The one that matches the current value of the variable will have its code run. Here's an example:

```
switch (variable) {
  case value0:
    trace("run first block");
    break;
  case value1:
    trace("run second block");
    break;
}
```

If variable equals value0, then the first trace() will run. If variable equals value1, then the second trace() will run. This is equivalent to the following if else if statement:

```
if (variable == value0) {
  // run first block
} else if (variable == value1) {
  // run second block
}
```

Well, that doesn't look so bad, does it? So why use switch at all? In this case, using if else if makes sense because there are only a couple conditions. switch statements are useful when you need to test many more values. Try rewriting onCanvasKeyDown() with if else if, and you will see that the switch statement is much more readable.

Each case in the example here and in onCanvasKeyDown() has a break statement. Just as in a loop, when a break statement is encountered, the code block—in this case, the switch statement—will be exited. If a break is not included in a case, the switch statement will continue to run, and the code in the next case will be run as well, continuing until the switch block is complete or a break statement is reached. This is called **falling through** and allows for multiple cases to run a single section of code, as in the following:

```
switch (action) {
  case "run":
  case "jump":
```

```
      raiseHeartrate();
      break;
    case "sit":
    case "sleep"
      lowerHeartrate();
      break;
  }
```

In this example, if the current action is "run", there is no further code to execute for that case, and the switch statement will continue to run until it reaches the end or a break statement, which happens within case for "jump". The result is that raiseHeartrate() will be called if action equals either "run" or "jump". lowerHeartrate() will be called if either "sit" or "sleep" is the current action.

switch statements may also include the default keyword, usually at the end of a switch block, to indicate code to run if no cases have been met (or no break statement has been hit).

```
  switch (variable) {
    case value0:
      break;
    case value1:
      break;
    default:
      // default code runs
  }
```

Here, the default code will run only if variable does not equal either value0 or value1. default can be seen as similar to the final else block in an if else if else statement, which will run only if no other conditions are met.

4. In the onCanvasKeyUp() listener, do the same thing but set the relevant property to 0, since the key is no longer pressed. If the spacebar was released, set _isDrawing to false.

```
package com.foundationAS3.ch6 {
. . .
    private function onCanvasKeyUp(event:KeyboardEvent):void {
      switch (event.keyCode) {
        case Keyboard.UP:
        case Keyboard.DOWN:
          _yDirection = 0;
          break;
        case Keyboard.LEFT:
        case Keyboard.RIGHT:
          _xDirection = 0;
          break;
        case Keyboard.SPACE:
          _isDrawing = false;
          break;
      }
    }

  }
}
```

5. Add a private onCanvasEnterFrame() method, and add that as a listener for the Event.ENTER_FRAME event on the canvas Sprite. You'll use this for the actual drawing code. You'll need to import the Event class from the flash.events package.

```
package com.foundationAS3.ch6 {

    import flash.display.Shape;
    import flash.display.Sprite;
    import flash.events.Event;
    import flash.events.KeyboardEvent;
    import flash.ui.Keyboard;

    public class KeyboardDrawing extends Sprite {
. . .
        // Prepare canvas for drawing and keyboard input
        _canvas.graphics.lineStyle(2, 0x000000);
        stage.focus = _canvas;

        // Add canvas event listeners
        _canvas.addEventListener(KeyboardEvent.KEY_DOWN, onCanvasKeyDown);
        _canvas.addEventListener(KeyboardEvent.KEY_UP, onCanvasKeyUp);
        _canvas.addEventListener(Event.ENTER_FRAME, onCanvasEnterFrame);
    }
. . .
    private function onCanvasEnterFrame(event:Event):void {
    }

    }

}
```

6. Within the onCanvasEnterFrame() method, add the values of _xDirection and _yDirection to the crosshair's own x and y properties. Move the Drawing API pen to the new crosshair location using either the moveTo() or lineTo() method, depending on whether the _isDrawing property is set to true or false.

```
package com.foundationAS3.ch6 {
. . .
    private function onCanvasEnterFrame(event:Event):void {
        _crosshair.x += _xDirection;
        _crosshair.y += _yDirection;

        if (_isDrawing) {
          _canvas.graphics.lineTo(_crosshair.x, _crosshair.y);
        } else {
          _canvas.graphics.moveTo(_crosshair.x, _crosshair.y);
        }
    }

    }

}
```

7. Save the changes to the KeyboardDrawing.as document and switch back to the keyboardDrawing.fla document in the Flash IDE.

8. In the Property inspector for the document, set the document class to com.foundationAS3. ch6.KeyboardDrawing.

9. Save the changes to the keyboardDrawing.fla document and test your movie.

Use the cursor keys to move the crosshair around (it starts in the top-right corner), holding down the space-bar when you want to draw. You might end up with something like Figure 6-5.

Preventing an event's default action

Some of the events generated by the Flash Player for certain objects have default actions associated with them, and many of these default actions can be overridden programmatically by using the preventDefault() method of the Event object. When called, this method will prevent whatever default action is associated with the event.

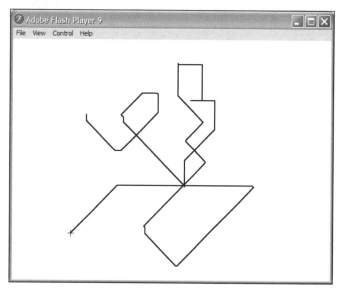

Figure 6-5. Drawing with the keyboard (look, ma, no mouse!)

Not all events have default actions, and of those that do, only some will allow you to prevent that default action from occurring. You can tell whether an event has a default action that can be prevented by checking the cancelable property of the Event object, which is a Boolean value indicating whether the event can be canceled.

One example of a cancelable event is TextEvent.TEXT_INPUT, which is dispatched when the user types a character into a TextField object while it has input focus. Unless you instruct it otherwise, the default action carried out by the Flash Player is to insert the character into the contents of the text field at the current insertion point.

If you wanted to filter the characters that can be entered into a TextField object (assuming the restrict property wasn't rich enough for your needs), you could register an event listener for that event and decide whether to allow the character to be inserted (or whether to do something else entirely) within your event handler.

Let's quickly code an example that will let you enter a particular character only once in a text field. Admittedly, this example is a little contrived—I certainly can't see this having many uses in the real world—but it does demonstrate something that can't be done using the TextField.restrict property.

1. Create a new Flash document and save it in the project directory as preventDefault.fla.

2. Create a new ActionScript document for the document class, which is going to be in the com.foundationAS3.ch6 package. Save it as PreventDefaultTest.as in the appropriate package directory in the project directory.

3. Create the basic package and class definitions, including an empty constructor method. The PreventDefaultTest class should extend the Sprite display class, since you do not have any timeline animation.

```
package com.foundationAS3.ch6 {

  import flash.display.Sprite;

  public class PreventDefaultTest extends Sprite {

    public function PreventDefaultTest() {
    }

  }

}
```

4. In the constructor method, create a new TextField object and add it to the display list. You'll need to import the TextField class from the flash.text package.

```
package com.foundationAS3.ch6 {

  import flash.display.Sprite;
  import flash.text.TextField;

  public class Application extends Sprite {
    public function Application() {
      var tf:TextField = new TextField();
      addChild(tf);
    }

  }

}
```

5. Set the width and height properties of the new TextField object to match the stage width and height. Set the type and wordWrap properties to TextFieldType.INPUT and true, respectively. You'll need to import the TextFieldType class from the flash.text package.

```
package com.foundationAS3.ch6 {

  import flash.display.Sprite;
  import flash.text.TextField;
  import flash.text.TextFieldType;

  public class PreventDefaultTest extends Sprite {
```

```
      public function PreventDefaultTest() {
        var tf:TextField = new TextField();
        addChild(tf);

        tf.width = stage.stageWidth;
        tf.height = stage.stageWidth;
        tf.type = TextFieldType.INPUT;
        tf.wordWrap = true;
      }

    }

  }
```

This will give you a TextField object that's as big as the stage, accepts user input, and will wrap the text. Next, you need to add a listener for the TextEvent.TEXT_INPUT event that cancels the event if the character entered already exists in the TextField.

6. Create a private method named onTextFieldTextInput() (which nicely follows your naming convention for event listeners) and add it as a listener for the TextEvent.TEXT_INPUT event of the TextField object you created. You'll need to import the TextEvent class from the flash.events package.

```
package com.foundationAS3.ch6 {

  import flash.display.Sprite;
  import flash.text.TextField;
  import flash.text.TextFieldType;
  import flash.events.TextEvent;

  public class PreventDefaultTest extends Sprite {

    public function PreventDefaultTest() {
      var tf:TextField = new TextField();
      addChild(tf);

      tf.width = stage.stageWidth;
      tf.height = stage.stageWidth;
      tf.type = TextFieldType.INPUT;
      tf.wordWrap = true;

      tf.addEventListener(TextEvent.TEXT_INPUT, onTextFieldTextInput);
    }

    private function onTextFieldTextInput(event:TextEvent):void {
    }

  }

}
```

7. Within the onTextFieldTextInput() handler, use the text property of the event object to get the character entered by the user, and then use the TextField object's text property in conjunction with the indexOf() method to see if that character is already present. If it is, call the preventDefault() method of the event object to prevent the character being added to the TextField object.

```
package com.foundationAS3.ch6 {

  import flash.display.Sprite;
  import flash.text.TextField;
  import flash.text.TextFieldType;
  import flash.events.TextEvent;

  public class PreventDefaultTest extends Sprite {

    public function PreventDefaultTest() {
      var tf:TextField = new TextField();
      addChild(tf);

      tf.width = stage.stageWidth;
      tf.height = stage.stageWidth;
      tf.type = TextFieldType.INPUT;
      tf.wordWrap = true;

      tf.addEventListener(TextEvent.TEXT_INPUT, onTextFieldTextInput);
    }

    private function onTextFieldTextInput(event:TextEvent):void {
      var tf:TextField = event.target as TextField;
      if (tf.text.indexOf(event.text) > -1) {
        event.preventDefault();
      }
    }
  }

}
```

> Remember that the indexOf() method of a String object takes a single parameter—another String object—and returns either the position of the latter within the former or -1 if the specified string could not be found.

8. Save the changes to the PreventDefaultTest.as file and switch back to the preventDefault.fla document.

9. In the Property inspector, set the document class to com.foundationAS3.ch6.PreventDefaultTest.

10. Save the changes to the preventDefault.fla file and test the Flash movie.

Try to type a whole bunch of characters (let your inner keyboard masher go wild). You should see that you can enter each character only once. Good job!

Capturing and bubbling: the event flow

When an event is dispatched by a DisplayObject instance on the display list, it progresses through three states: **capture**, **at target**, and **bubble**. These states are collectively known as the **event flow**, which is illustrated in Figure 6-6.

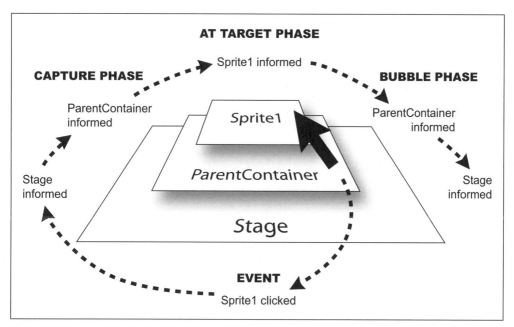

Figure 6-6. The event flow in the Flash Player

Let's use the MouseEvent.MOUSE_CLICK event as an example. When the user clicks a DisplayObject, a MouseEvent object is created by the Flash Player and dispatched from the topmost DisplayObject under the mouse pointer.

Initially, the event is in the capture phase. In the capture phase, an event works its way down the display list hierarchy through the event target's ancestors, until it reaches the target object itself. At each level of the hierarchy, any event handlers that match the event type and have been specified as capture event listeners (you'll learn how to do that in the "Listening for events in the capture phase" section, coming up soon) will be called.

Once the event reaches the target object, it is said to be in the at-target phase. (Whoever came up with that name isn't going to win any prizes for originality or creativity, but at least it's descriptive.) In the at-target phase, all the event listeners registered on the event target that match the event type are called.

After all the event listeners on the event target have been called, the event enters the bubble phase. In the bubble phase, the event travels back up through the display list hierarchy toward the Stage, calling any event listeners that match the specified event type.

If you're anything like me when I first encountered the event flow, you're probably thinking, "Well, that's interesting, but what's it useful for?" Actually, the event flow is useful for a lot of things. At any stage in the event flow, you can have an event handler respond to the event, and you get to choose whether to stop the event right there or allow it to continue its journey through the display hierarchy. You can also override some default actions associated with an event, such as text being entered into a TextField when a key is pressed.

Event objects even have a property, eventPhase, to help you determine the current phase. This property can have one of three values, for each of the event phases: EventPhase.CAPTURING_PHASE, EventPhase.AT_TARGET, or EventPhase.BUBBLING_PHASE.

> Not all events go through the bubble and capture phases. If an event is not associated with a display object, there is no display list hierarchy for the event to travel through. Effectively, the event flow consists of just the at-target phase.

Listening for events in the bubble phase

In order to listen for events in the bubble phase, you just need to attach event listeners to an ancestor of the target object using the addEventListener() method. An event fired on the descendants of a display object will automatically bubble up through the display list hierarchy toward the stage.

One of the biggest use cases for listening for events in the bubble phase is event delegation. This technique allows you to register a single event listener for all of the descendants of a display list object. Consider a grid of thumbnails where each thumbnail can be clicked. Instead of registering a listener for every single thumbnail, you could register a listener to receive events from the parent container, and then use the properties of the Event object to determine which thumbnail had been clicked.

The key to using this technique successfully is the target property of the Event object passed to the event listener. This will give you a reference to the object that dispatched the event. To elaborate on this example, suppose that the thumbnails in question are instances of a custom PhotoThumbnail class. Using the target property when the event is handled in parent container, you can make sure that the object that was clicked was actually a PhotoThumbnail using the is operator. You need to do this because the container display object will receive MouseEvent.CLICK events both for itself and for all its descendants. The following code snippet shows what I'm talking about here.

```
photoContainer.addEventListener(MouseEvent.CLICK, onPhotoContainerClick);
. . .
private function onPhotoContainerClick(event:MouseEvent):void {
  if (event.target is PhotoThumbnail) {
    // Handle event in here
  }
}
```

Using the built-in event bubbling, you are able to listen for clicks on all thumbnails with only several lines of code.

Listening for events in the capture phase

Listening for events in the capture phase is most useful when you need to prevent an event from being dispatched to other objects or when the default behavior for the event sometimes needs to be prevented. To listen for events in the capture phase, you need to use one of the extra parameters to the addEventListener() method that I hinted about earlier. The first optional parameter for this method, useCapture, is a Boolean value indicating whether the event listener should listen for events of the specified type when they're in the capture phase.

```
someObject.addEventListener(type, listener, useCapture);
```

The default value for this parameter is false. By passing true, you set up a capture phase event listener for the specified event type.

Let's rework the previous snippet of code to listen for the capture phase of an event:

```
photoContainer.addEventListener(MouseEvent.CLICK, onPhotoContainerClick, true);
. . .
private function onPhotoContainerClick(event:MouseEvent):void {
  if (event.target is PhotoThumbnail) {
    // Handle event in here
  }
}
```

When you add an event listener for the capture phase of a specific type of event, that event listener will not be called in the at-target or bubble phases. If you want to set up a single event listener for all event phases, you'll need to call addEventListener() twice: once with useCapture set to true and once with it set to false (or omitted).

```
photoContainer.addEventListener(MouseEvent.click, onPhotoContainerClick, true);
photoContainer.addEventListener(MouseEvent.click, onPhotoContainerClick);
. . .
private function onPhotoContainerClick(event:MouseEvent):void {
  if (event.target is PhotoThumbnail) {
    // Handle event in here
  }
}
```

The capture phase is the first phase of an event where it trickles down the display list hierarchy to the event target. Because capture phase event handlers are called before any at-target or bubble phase event handlers, you can use this technique, together with either stopPropagation() or stopImmediatePropagation(), to effectively suppress an event, as discussed next.

Stopping an event from propagating

You might have several event handlers for the same event attached at various points in the display list. If in one of these event handlers, you decide that the event should be ignored or has been handled sufficiently, you can prevent the event from continuing through the rest of the event flow using the stopPropagation() method of the Event object. For example, you could prevent all clicks within an application from being registered by calling stopPropagation() within a capture phase MouseEvent.CLICK event listener attached to the main document class.

> *Calling* stopPropagation() *does not mean that the default action of the event won't occur—that's the job of the* preventDefault() *method discussed earlier in this chapter.*

When you have multiple handlers for the same event on the current display object, they will all be called, regardless of when you call stopPropagation(). The stopPropagation() method prevents events from continuing through the event flow, but it doesn't stop the remaining event handlers on the current display object from being called. If you need to stop all remaining event handlers from being called, use the stopImmediatePropagation() method instead.

Remember that event listeners are processed in the order in which they were added to the object. If it is important to have a listener receive notification of the event first, add it first as a listener. Alternatively, you could use the priority argument in addEventListener() method, which determines whether certain listeners take precedence over others when the event is dispatched. For instance, consider this line, which adds two event listeners, one with a specified priority and one without:

```
object.addEventListener(Event.CHANGE, callFirst, false, Number.MAX_VALUE);
object.addEventListener(Event.CHANGE, callSecond);
```

The first line adds a listener using an extremely high priority (the highest value a number can hold). The second line adds a listener without passing a priority, so it defaults to a priority of 0. When the CHANGE event fires on the object, the listener set at the higher priority will receive notification first, no matter the order in which the listeners were added.

Removing capture phase event listeners

To remove a capture phase event listener, use the optional useCapture parameter of the removeEventListener() method.

```
someObject.removeEventListener(type, listener, useCapture);
```

Again, this is a Boolean value specifying whether the event listener you want to remove is listening for the capture phase of events of the specified type.

When removing an event listener, it's important to make sure that you use the same parameters when calling removeEventListener() as you did when you called addEventListener(). If you don't use the same parameters, your event listener won't be removed, and you'll end up with a project that consumes more and more memory, because an object will not be garbage-collected by the Flash Player when it has event listeners registered for it.

Summary

This chapter has been a whistle-stop tour of events and event handling in ActionScript 3.0. You'll meet many different types of events throughout the rest of this book, and the knowledge gleaned in these pages will help you to use them to their full effect.

In the next chapter, you'll learn how you can use ActionScript to work with video.

Chapter 7

WORKING WITH VIDEO

Sean McSharry

This chapter covers the following topics:

- Types of video format
- How to access, load, and display video
- How to control video once it has loaded
- How to send data to and from video

In this chapter, you will learn the basics of how to load and control video using ActionScript 3.0. After an introduction to encoding, delivering, and playing video, you'll build a simple video player. This example will demonstrate how to define the video location, control its loading and use, and display information about it and its state.

Video on the modern Web

We are currently in the middle of a video revolution on the Web, which is made possible, for the most part, by the availability of better Internet connections and better codecs. Video usage in rich Internet applications (RIAs) and websites is becoming very common.

A codec, in ActionScript video terms, is a device or program capable of performing encoding and decoding on a digital data stream or signal. The word codec *can be a combination of any of the following: compressor-decompressor, coder-decoder, or compression/decompression algorithm.*

The video experience

Developers are excited about the experience video allows them to give to web users, or "viewers," as they have now become. This is often as good as or better than the standard TV experience, because it can be made in high-definition (HD) video, fully interactive and integrated with multiple data sources. For example, Diesel recently did a five-day, live, multicamera, *faux* hostage broadcast (`http://www.diesel.com/lockin/splash.php`), where two underwear models kidnapped a Diesel executive and held him for ransom (see Figure 7-1). This site took more than 100,000 hits a day. The viewers could interact with the models and the hostage situation in real time and affect its outcome.

Figure 7-1. Diesel's video-based interactive site

Marketing in general is making some excellent use of web video, creating beautifully shot and produced interactive experiences. Nokia's interactive spoof "Great Pockets" clothes and online store (`http://www.greatpockets.com/index.php`), which ultimately is an advertisement for their excellent N95 phone, is a great example of this.

Other companies and individuals have gone the obvious route of creating their own "channels." They usually record digital video (DV) clips of something they have a passion for (be it a summary of their band's last concert or a video tutorial on how to create a Flash widget). Then they encode it so Flash can play it (which is very easy, as you'll see in this chapter), and then share it on their site. Many people have scheduled regular programs and streamed live content (see http://www.stickam.com for an example of a site that specializes in live webcam feeds), and their channels are beginning to gather a rather respectable number of viewers. Ask a Ninja is a permanent favorite of mine (http://www.askaninja.com/). Issy Depew, of Denver, Colorado, created a channel for mothers (http://www.mommetv.com/), which is a massive broadcasting success. I'm a big golf fan and GolfSpan is very helpful for me and thousands of other golfers for video lessons (http://www.golflink.com).

Third-party video-sharing sites like YouTube (http://www.youtube.com) and Revver (http://www.revver.com) allow anyone to share their video clips, with or without a website/host of their own. Many companies have now jumped on this bandwagon—AOL, Google, Yahoo, and blip.tv are just a few.

Finally, companies such as Eyespot (http://www.eyespot.com) and Brightcove (http://www.brightcove.com) are providing APIs and hosting services that go even further, allowing you to add special effects, events, and more to your video clips; create custom players; edit your videos online; and so on. Also check out Jumpcut (http://www.jumpcut.com), Motionbox (http://www.motionbox.com), and Crackle (http://www.crackle.com).

I think you can start to see why this is so exciting. We are all filmmakers and broadcasters now—from large companies to the man on the street with nothing more than an Internet connection and a DV camera, or even a camera phone.

Where ActionScript comes in

So where does ActionScript come into all this? Flash/ActionScript is at the center of the video revolution. This is because it provides one of the easiest and best ways to deliver video on to the Web, for the following reasons:

- Flash CS3 has an easy workflow available for video, including an easy-to-use video encoder, comprehensive support for video in ActionScript 3,0, and a video player component that can just be dropped onto the stage and wired up.

- The ubiquity of the Flash Player means that your new video application can be seen easily and quickly by almost any user. Also, with the recent introduction of support for the H.264 codec standard, repurposing existing broadcast and HD video is quick, easy, and affordable.

- It allows you to easily integrate animation, graphics, text, and even other videos, as dynamically and interactively as you can conceive.

Though a video player component is available in both Flex and Flash, using ActionScript is far more rewarding, provides for an optimal solution, and allows a greater diversity of video implementations. Often, you will want to create a more flexible or powerful video player. If you know ActionScript 3.0, creating a video player from scratch is just as quick as trying to learn about the video component for the first time. Once you have created all the class files for your video player, you have effectively the same thing as a video player component, but with none of the overhead. And you can reuse the class files any time you need to create a new video player, with very little modification of the original code (or none, if you're a good object-oriented developer). The bottom line is that using ActionScript 3.0 allows you to take advantage of all of its extended video control and modification capabilities, many of which simply aren't available or as flexible when using the built-in components and property panels within Flash or Flex.

But video players aside, video can be used in many ways that don't require the standard player layout (with play, stop, fast-forward, and rewind buttons and so on). Examples of these other uses include demos, interactive navigation, information, tutorials, banners, and backgrounds.

As I've said, the Flash Player is one of the best ways of delivering video to the Web. Let's move on to the basics of just how to do that.

Encoding your video

Until very recently, your only choice for delivering video in the Flash Player was to encode it using the Sorenson Spark codec or On2 VP6.2 codec, giving you an FLV (Flash video) file. While these codecs were optimized for web delivery, they did not support HD. From a process point of view, they were time-consuming and poorly automated, and made commercial delivery of video comparatively costly. Many suggested to Adobe that support for the industry-standard H.264 codec would be very desirable for all these reasons, and supporting that codec would open many new doors for the use of video in the Flash Player (I was among the early developers to complain about it when I was working for an Internet Protocol television project startup some years ago).

Adobe listened to the increasing requests for the H.264 codec support and implemented it in Flash Player 9. This is a huge step forward and allows for the repurposing of commercial, broadcast-quality HD video directly in ActionScript. But this does not mean that FLV is now redundant! Far from it. The FLV format has its own strengths, and even within FLV files, the choice of Spark and VP6.2 codecs is based, for the most part, on their inherent and different strengths. We simply have more choices, so that we can provide our clients with the right solutions.

So let's take a look at the process of getting your video ready for the Web. If your video source is in FLV or H.264 format, you really have to do very little with it. Supported H.264 formats include MOV, 3GP, MP4, M4V, and M4A. The Flash Player reads the file header to ascertain the file format, so provided your file has been encoded to a supported H.264 format, the filename extension doesn't matter. You could name a supported MOV file file.txt, and it would still load and play. In addition, Flash Player 9 is capable of playing back On2's VP7 content created in other software tools, provided it is saved with the .flv extension.

So, you can use a video file in a supported format directly in ActionScript. However, you may want to go on to encode the file into an FLV format for the benefits that format offers: the ability to provide cue points (timeline-related events, which are discussed in the "Cue point events" section later in this chapter) and a reduced file size. However, in some cases, the production of FLV-encoded footage takes more time, and it thus is not as cost-effective.

Now suppose you have a video in a format that is completely unsupported in the Flash Player—say an AVI file—and you want to share it with the world through the Flash Player. You have a couple of choices. The Flash Player supports H.264- and FLV-based codecs natively. You can therefore choose to encode your unsupported video format to H.264-based video or an FLV file.

H.264 is industry standard for most broadcast quality and HD format video, and this can be easily repurposed for use in the Flash Player. This approach is less time-consuming, and thus less costly. The main drawbacks of this method are that there can be licensing cost issues and you cannot place cue points into the video.

> *Although you probably won't receive FLV-formatted video from the client, you are likely to receive video source files that are H.264-encoded. In fact, many companies pay good money to have H.264-based video files reduced to something more manageable before they even try to use the footage on the Web. Thankfully, this is no longer always necessary. We can now take things like movie trailers, advertisements, and even entire programs and films, and with little or no optimization, use them directly in our applications. However, often you will need to optimize it on delivery platforms that are associated with a different aspect ratio or resolution, such as mobile phones. Or you might want to remove specific advertisements or even add some. All of these things constitute* **repurposing**.

Should you choose to deliver your video as an FLV, this requires some extra work, though to be honest, sometimes repurposing H.264 source format can require a little work, too. And you need to consider the quite legitimate need for cue points, which will require encoding.

Capturing your video

If you don't yet have your video in a digital format (for example, it's still on your DV camera), you'll need to capture it. You can use some great commercial packages, like Adobe Premier Pro, Apple Final Cut, and so on, but they all cost a lot. I'm here to tell you how it can be done on a shoestring budget.

If you have Windows, the much-underrated Windows Movie Maker is the easiest and cheapest (free) choice. It automates much of the process for you. In fact, if you use a FireWire (DV) connection, Windows will even prompt you to launch Movie Maker to rip the video. Launch Movie Maker, as shown in Figure 7-2, and you will see that it offers a host of easy-to-use features—from format conversion to automatic scene definition and special effects. Although I have had the odd problem with it, it's a great free capture and production package. However, at present, it doesn't support FLV format output. So save your final video as an .mov or .avi file, and you won't go wrong. At this point, you can just use the .mov file directly in ActionScript, as noted earlier. However, you may want to continue and encode it to an FLV file.

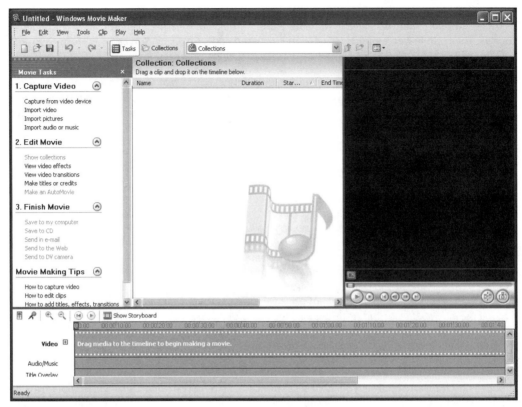

Figure 7-2. Windows Movie Maker

If you're running Mac OS X, then the obvious choice for capturing your video is iMovie HD, shown in Figure 7-3. This little baby is free, user-friendly, and ready to capture your input from your DV camera, your HDV camera, an MPEG-4 source, or even your iSight camera. We've come to expect a lot of functionality and grace from Apple media software, and though iMovie HD will never be used on the next Hollywood blockbuster, it is perfect for your web-based video ventures. Once again, if you have an H.264 source, you can just use it or repurpose it first. IMovie HD supports *full HD 1080 interlaced* input. I have no doubt Apple will add *true HD 1080 progressive* in the next full release. But this kind of geek jargon is really for another book, so let's move on.

> *Working with video in most video-capture and video-editing software often bears remarkable resemblance to working in the Flash CS3 IDE itself, and this is no accident. They share many of the same workflow processes, naming conventions, and functionalities. In fact, if you take a look at Adobe After Effects, you'll be surprised at how similar it is to the Flash IDE, and the differences are quickly being reduced as both of these software packages evolve. I foresee a time when the workflow between video applications and Flash will be seamless.*

So, now you have your AVI, MOV, MP4, or other format video file. Next, to get an FLV file, you need to take your captured video files and encode them using the Flash Video Encoder.

FIGure 7-3. Apple iMovie HD

Using the Flash Video Encoder

The Flash Video Encoder is a separate program installed along with Flash. It supports files in MOV, AVI, MP4, ASF, DV, MPG/MPEG, and WMV format. You can use any video you like if it's in one of the supported formats. If you don't have a video in one of these formats, you can use the video provided with this book's downloadable code (available at www.friendsofed.com).

To begin, open the Flash Video Encoder, as shown in Figure 7-4. You will find it in a separate directory in the same place as Flash CS3 was installed. On your PC, that will usually be in C:\Program Files\Adobe\FlashMediaEncoder\. On a Mac, it will usually be found in Macintosh HD\Applications.

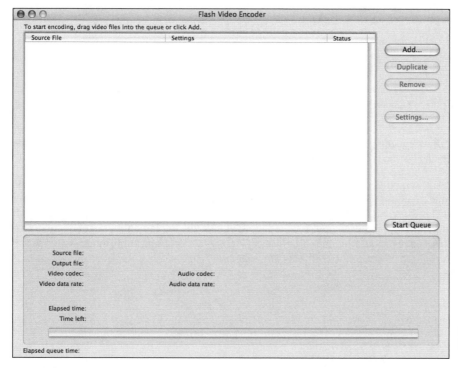

Figure 7-4.
Flash Video Encoder

To add your video file, click the Add button and search for your video. Find it and click OK. Now you will see your source video as the one and only entry in the queue, as shown in Figure 7-5.

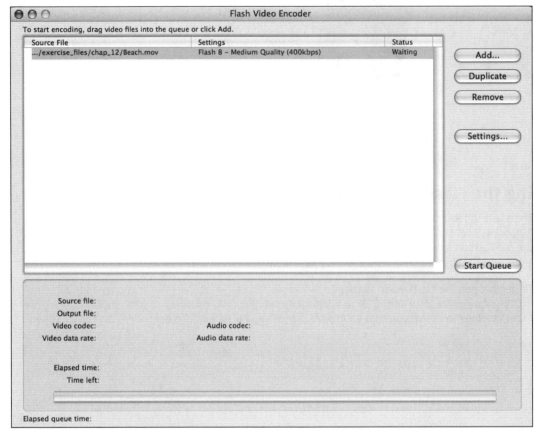

Figure 7-5. Adding a file to be encoded

To check and adjust encoding settings, if necessary, click the Settings button. This takes you to the Flash Video Encoding Settings screen, as shown in Figure 7-6.

As you can see, this screen has a number of tabs. In most cases, you won't make any changes on the Audio tab. You'll learn about the settings on the Cue Points tab in the "Cue point events" section later in this chapter. The Crop and Resize tab is one I believe has very limited use. Frankly, if you've left your video sizing and cropping until you're encoding it, you're not implementing a good video production workflow. Videos should be edited before they are encoded using tools much better suited to the job (Adobe Premier Pro or After Effects, for example). That leaves the Profiles and Video tabs to address here.

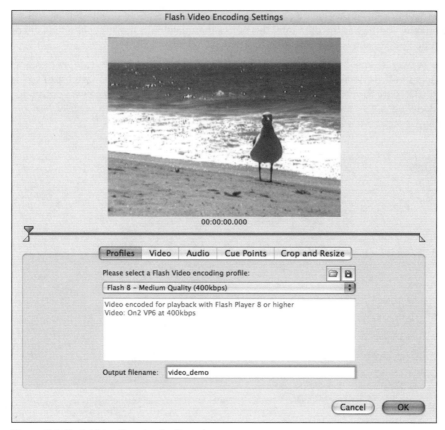

Figure 7-6. Flash Video Encoder Profiles tab

> *If you try to encode your file to a child directory and that directory doesn't exist, the encoder will generate an error, and you will have difficulty getting it to export again without first removing the entry from the encoder and starting from scratch! This appears to be a bug.*

The Video tab, shown in Figure 7-7, allows you to set the following options:

- Video codec: Choose the compression codec, either Sorenson Spark or On2 VP6. On2 provides better compression and quality as a rule. Beneath this, you can choose Encode alpha channel and/or Deinterlace, if you have video with green-screen footage, for example, or broadcast footage that needs deinterlacing.

- Frame rate: It is often best to leave this at the default (Same as Source).

- Quality: You can set the quality of the video in both a generalized quality setting and maximum data rate. The higher the data rate, the better the quality but the larger the final encoded FLV will be. It takes some experimenting to get these settings right.

- Key frame placement: The encoder will place keyframes at a variable rate, depending on the changes in the displayed video. If you want to ensure quality (and increased size) by increasing that to a more formal rate of keyframes, you can set the Key frame placement option to Custom and define a Key frame interval setting. Having more keyframes is actually less processor-intensive, so there is a benefit.

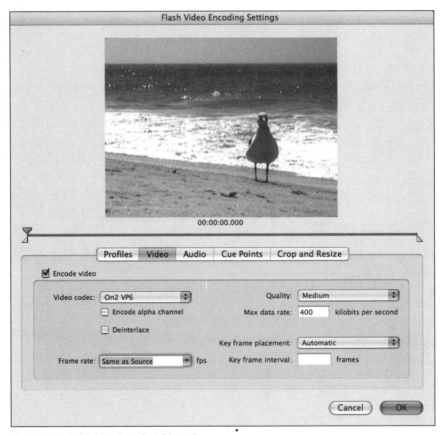

Figure 7-7. Flash Video Encoder Video tab

For this example, you will use the default settings. So return to the Flash Video Encoder queue screen and click the Start Queue button. You'll see the encoding process kick off quickly and smoothly. It should look like Figure 7-8.

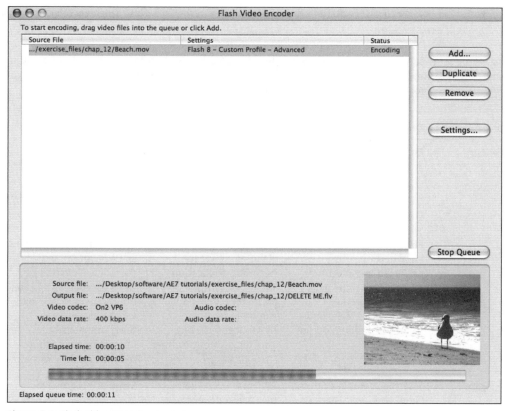

Figure 7-8. Flash video encoding in progress

You will see the video play in a preview panel. The progress bar shows the encoding status, and the elapsed time and the time left to finish encoding your video are displayed. When the video has finished encoding, you'll be notified, and that's it. You now have video encoded to FLV format.

Exactly how long it will take your video to encode depends on a lot of factors: how large your source file is, how powerful your machine is, what else is running on it, and what encoding settings you've chosen. I can say that any decent size, reasonable quality, usable video source is going to require enough encoding time to allow you to get a cup of coffee and read some more of this book. The example I used was a video of just under 6 seconds. With all of the default settings, it took 17 seconds to encode.

Delivering your video

Video can be referenced and used from a number of different places:

- From imported video embedded in the timeline or Flash Library
- From an external FLV/H.264 file, using progressive download or streamed through the Flash Media Server (FMS) or another server

■ From a webcam, live encoded and streamed to and from the FMS, Flash Video Encoder, or similar

■ From DV camera feeds, which can be streamed

So, the three methods of delivery are **embedded**, **progressive**, and **streamed**. The method you use has a direct bearing on the performance you can expect and the code you will write to access your video. Table 7-1 compares these methods, based on video delivery across the Internet.

Table 7-1. Comparison of video delivery methods

Feature	Embedded	Progressive	Streaming
Encoding	Video and audio are encoded on import into Flash using the Sorenson Spark codec. Alternatively, FLV files (encoded elsewhere) can be imported and placed on the Flash timeline (reencoding is not necessary). H.264 video cannot be embedded on the timeline.	FLV files are encoded externally from the Flash authoring system, either through the Flash Video Encoder or using a stand-alone video-encoding application such as Sorenson Squeeze. H.264 video can be used (as is or repurposed), but encoding is not essential.	Same as progressive download. In addition, you can capture and record live video feeds from client-side webcams or DV cameras and control live encoding variables such as bit rate, frames per second, and video playback size programmatically. Currently, you cannot record to H.264 format.
File size	SWF files contain both the video and audio streams as well as the Flash interface, resulting in a single large and often unusable file.	SWF and FLV/H.264 files are kept separate, resulting in a smaller SWF file size and independent video loading.	Same as progressive download.
Start time	Large SWF files often require users to wait a long time before seeing any video, for a horrible user experience.	Begins quite quickly. This can be fine-tuned by setting the buffer size programmatically.	Immediate—this offers the fastest video download and play.
Timeline access	When embedded in the Flash timeline, video appears on individual keyframes and can be treated like any other object on the stage.	Video is played back only at runtime. Timeline events (cue points) can be marked at the time of encoding and then triggered as the playhead reaches those cue points if you use FLV format.	Same as progressive download.

Feature	Embedded	Progressive	Streaming
Publishing	Each time the Flash movie is published or tested, the entire video file is republished. Changes to video files require manually reimporting files into the timeline.	FLV/H.264 files are referenced only during runtime. Publishing to the SWF format is much faster than with embedded video. Video files can be updated or modified independently of any SWF files.	Same as progressive download. You can dynamically pull FLV/H.264 files from virtual locations, such as your storage area network or the Flash Video Streaming Service content delivery network.
Frame rate	Video frame rate and SWF movie frame rate must be the same.	FLV files can have a different frame rate than the SWF files.	Same as progressive download. Live video capture has programmable control over the frame rate.
ActionScript access	Video playback and control are achieved by controlling the movie's playback on the timeline.	The NetStream class can be used to load and control external FLV/H.264 files.	Same as progressive download. Server-side ActionScript can also be used to provide additional functionality such as synchronization of streams, server-side playlists, smart delivery adjusted to client connection speed, and more.
Components	No video-specific components.	Media components can be used to set up and display external FLV/H.264 files together with transport controls (play, pause, and search).	Same as progressive download.
Seek and navigation ability	Requires the entire SWF file to be downloaded before the user can seek or navigate the video.	User can seek to only portions of the video that have been downloaded.	User can seek anywhere at any time.
Web delivery	Entire SWF file must be downloaded to the client and loaded into memory in order to play back video.	FLV files are progressively downloaded, cached, and then played from the local disk. The entire video clip need not fit in memory, and the theory is that the cache will stay ahead of the playhead.	FLV/H.264 files are streamed from the FMS, played on the client's machine, and then discarded from memory in a play-as-you-go method. This provides very secure video delivery.

Continued

Table 7-1. *Continued*

Feature	Embedded	Progressive	Streaming
Performance	Audio and video synchronization is limited after approximately 120 seconds of video. Total file duration is limited to available memory on the playback system.	Improved performance over embedded SWF video, permitting larger video files and reliable audio synchronization. Provides best image quality, which is limited only by the amount of hard drive available.	Improved efficiency from a web-delivery perspective, with optimal bit rate delivery on an as-needed basis to as many customers as necessary.
Video stream control	None.	None.	Full control over what gets delivered when.
Live video support	No.	No.	Yes.

Embedded video is hardly ever used and is considered an amateur way of delivering video content in all but the odd rare example, so you can basically ignore it. Streaming, while offering the best control in terms of content and digital rights management (DRM), requires a server-side technology to control the streaming, such as the FMS. Streaming may be the best delivery platform in many situations, but it is quite complex. The examples in this chapter will demonstrate the most commonly used method of video delivery on the Web today: progressive download. Playing external FLV/H.264 files provides several advantages over embedding video in a Flash document, such as better performance and memory management, and independent video and Flash frame rates.

> *A note about security: by default, loading and playing an audio or video file is not allowed if the SWF file is local and tries to load and play a remote file. A user must grant explicit permission to allow this. Additionally, the security sandbox must be placated by the use of a cross-domain policy file.*

Using ActionScript to play videos

Generally, four main ActionScript classes are used to access, control, and render video:

- `NetConnection`: Sets up a connection to a video source, either network or local. It also provides the ability to invoke commands on a remote application server.
- `NetStream`: Provides methods and properties for playing, controlling, monitoring, and even recording video files.
- `Video`: Allows you to create a display object for your video feeds.
- `Camera`: Allows you connect to one or more webcam feeds for viewing or recording.

Figure 7-9 illustrates the general workflow among these four classes.

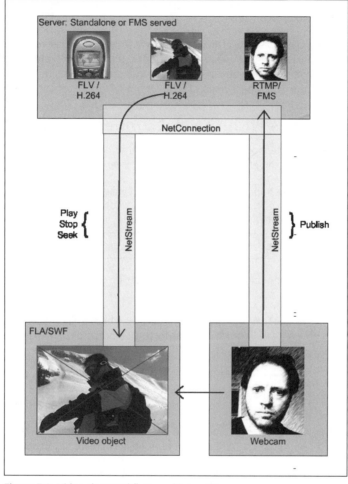

Figure 7-9. Video class workflows and interaction

As you can see, the NetConnection class is essentially a data-access class. It connects your Flash movie to the video source location. Through this class, you can access the videos you need or call server-side ActionScript. The NetStream class provides control over the video stream connection that NetConnection has set up, including play, pause, and seek functions. It also allows a video source to be recorded to a media server.

The Video and Camera class instances are display objects that actually display or capture the output and input for the end user. The Camera class is also capable of publishing back to the server (when used in conjunction with a streaming server like the FMS) or to the open page (when used in conjunction with a video object).

These four classes adhere to the Model-View-Controller (MVC) design pattern. The NetConnection class is the model (also the controller in some cases). The NetStream class is the controller. The Video and Camera classes are the view. Most Flash and Flex-based applications are developed using this pattern. Essentially, the MVC pattern dictates that developers modularize the model (data handling and facilitation), view (display handling), and controller (control code) to separate them from each other. This allows developers to work on an application together more easily and efficiently.

Before we get to building the video player application, let's look at the classes and events you'll be using in some detail. This will serve as a valuable reference section as you create your first projects. If you just want to build something and you can't wait, you can skip these sections and get straight to building the video player (the "Building a video player" section).

Managing connections with the NetConnection class

This class opens and closes connections to a video source, either network or local. It can invoke commands on a remote application server, such as the FMS or Flex server.

Table 7-2 briefly summarizes the public properties of the NetConnection class.

Table 7-2. NetConnection public properties

Property	Type	Description
client	Object	Indicates the object on which callback methods should be invoked.
Connected	Boolean	Read-only. Indicates whether Flash Player has connected to a server through a persistent Real Time Messaging Protocol (RTMP) connection (true) or not (false).
ConnectedProxyType	String	Read-only. If a successful connection is made, indicates the method that was used to make it: a direct connection, the connect() method, or HTTP tunneling.
DefaultObjectEncoding	uint	Static. The default object encoding (AMF version) for NetConnection objects created in the SWF file.
ObjectEncoding	uint	The object encoding (AMF version) for this NetConnection instance.
ProxyType	String	Determines whether native Secure Sockets Layer (SSL) is used for RTMPS (RTMP over SSL) instead of HTTPS (HTTP over SSL), and whether the connect() method of tunneling is used to connect through a proxy server.
Url	String	Read-only. The URI of the application server that was passed to NetConnection.connect(), if connect() was used to connect to a server.
UsingTLS	Boolean	Read-only. Indicates whether a secure connection was made using native Transport Layer Security (TLS) rather than HTTPS.

Here's an example of using NetConnection:

```
//Import the NetConnection class
import flash.net.NetConnection;
. . .
//Declare a NetConnection data type variable in the class header
private var ncVideoPlayer:NetConnection;
. . .
//Create a new instance of the NetConnection class and connect it in
//the class constructor
ncVideoPlayer=new NetConnection();
ncVideoPlayer.connect(null);
```

This example connects the NetConnection instance to null. You would do this if you are actually going to connect to a local FLV file. If you want to connect to an FMS service, the connection instruction would look more like this:

```
ncVideoPlayer.connect(RTMP://www.flashcoder.net/videoChatRoom, (P1));
```

where (P1) signifies any additional parameters.

Loading and controlling video with the NetStream class

The NetStream class provides methods and properties for playing, controlling, and monitoring FLV files from the local file system or from an HTTP address. Using the NetStream class gives you a conduit through which to load and control video files (FLV or MPEG-4 files) to a Video object from a NetConnection object. The video you are working with through the NetStream instance can be changed dynamically at any time.

> *Event handlers need to be in place to handle* onMetaData *and, if they exist,* onCuePoint *events, as discussed in the "Handling video events" section later in this chapter. If they are not, then the compiler will issue error warnings. This will not prevent the code from compiling successfully, nor prevent the final SWF from working properly. But be aware of this, as it is pointing out poor convention on your part as an object-oriented programmer.*

Table 7-3 briefly summarizes the public properties of the NetStream class.

Table 7-3. NetStream class public properties

Property	Type	Description
bufferLength	Number	Read-only. The number of seconds of data currently in the buffer.
bufferTime	Number	Read-only. The number of seconds assigned to the buffer by NetStream.setBufferTime().

Continued

249

Table 7-3. *Continued*

Property	Type	Description
bytesLoaded	Number	Read-only. The number of bytes of data that have been loaded into the player.
bytesTotal	Number	Read-only. The total size in bytes of the file being loaded into the player.
checkPolicyFile	Boolean	Specifies whether Flash Player should attempt to download a cross-domain policy file from the loaded FLV file's server before beginning to load the FLV file itself.
currentFps	Number	Read-only. The number of frames per second being displayed.
time	Number	Read-only. The position of the playhead, in seconds.

Initially, you need to import, declare, and instantiate the NetStream class, but you also need to give it a reference to an existing NetConnection object, so it will have access to the video source.

```
//Import the NetStream class
import flash.net.NetStream;
. . .
//Declare a NetStream data type variable in the class header
private var nsVideoPlayer:NetStream;
. . .
//Create a new instance of the NetStream class and pass it a reference
//to the NetConnection object we created for it.
nsVideoPlayer=new NetStream(ncVideoPlayer);
```

Now you want to be able to play, pause, stop, and otherwise control the FLV file. The NetStream instance needs to be assigned to an actual Video display object before you will see anything happening, as discussed in the upcoming section about the Video class. As previously mentioned, the NetStream class represents the controller part of the MVC pattern.

Buffering your video

FLV buffering should definitely be a consideration. By default, the FLV you try to access and play will start playing as soon as the player receives one-tenth of a second of the file. For obvious reasons, you will probably want to allow a buffer of the video to load before you start playing it, to avoid jerky playback as much as possible. For very small videos, this is not so important; but these days, hardly anyone is showing small videos.

You can set the bufferTime parameter of your NetStream instance to tell the player how many seconds of FLV video to load before beginning playback. This is, of course, entirely individual to the project. It's worth experimenting with this value to get it right for your expected bandwidth, FLV size, and so on. Here is an example of buffering 10 seconds of video before it starts to play.

```
//Set buffer load before playing
nsVideoPlayer.bufferTime=10;
```

Playing your video

Playing the video couldn't be simpler:

```
//Tell the NetStream instance what FLV file to play
nsVideoPlayer.play("video_final.flv");
```

You can easily make references to local or remote FLV files. However, remember that if they are on another domain, you will need to address the cross-domain security policy before you do that.

Pausing your video

Pausing the video requires another simple command:

```
nsVideoPlayer.pause();
```

From a display point of view, it's important to remember to toggle the play button to be the pause button and vice versa when going from play to pause to play again.

Stopping your video

Use close() to stop playing the video:

```
nsVideoPlayer.close();
```

Stopping the video does not clear it from the cache (though it *does* unload it from the player). It automatically resets the NetStream.time property to 0, and It makes this NetStream instance available for use by another video, but not by another Video object.

The video will stop exactly where it is. This will make it appear as if it has paused at the point where you stopped it. This is not aesthetically or functionally pleasing. When the user clicks the play button again, because the NetStream.time property has been set to 0, your video will start again from the beginning. A better solution is to set the NetStream.seek() function to 0 first. If you still want the video to continue loading after you have stopped it, don't use the NetStream.close() function. Instead, use the NetStream.pause() function after the NetStream.seek(0) function.

Fast-forwarding and rewinding your video

Fast-forwarding and rewinding are slightly less straightforward than the other functions (no single line of code here. I'm afraid). This is because these functions need to loop through incremental or decremental seek methods using a timer. You will need to decide on the size of the seek increment/decrement steps (in seconds) for the fast-forward (FF) and rewind (RW) functions to use.

```
//Set the seek increment/decrement in seconds
private var seekIncDec:Int;
private var playHeadPosition:Int;
private var timerFF:Timer;
private var timerRW:Timer;
...
seekIncDec=3;
timerFF=new Timer(100, 0);
timerRW=new Timer(100, 0);
```

Fast-forwarding is simply a matter of seeking through the video feed in the specified increments (set in the seekIncDec variable; 3 seconds in this example), incrementing the playHeadPosition variable based on this, and *seeking* to that position while the fast-forward button is selected (I have not included the button code here, as this is not about the button classes).

```
Private function onClickFF():void{
   timerFF.addEventListener(TimerEvent.TIMER, FFward);
   timerFF.start();
}

private function FFward():void {
   playHeadPosition = Math.floor(ns1.time)+seekIncDec;
   nsVideoPlayer.seek(playHeadPosition);
}
```

When the fast-forward button is released, simply clear the timer and tell the NetStream object to play(), and it will play from the new playhead position.

```
Private function onReleaseFF():void {
   timerFF.reset();
   nsVideoPlayer.play();
}
```

Rewinding your video is almost the same as fast-forwarding, but in reverse:

```
Private function onClickRW():void {
   timerRW.addEventListener(TimerEvent.TIMER, RWind);
   timerRW.start();
}
private function RWind():void {
   playHeadPosition = Math.floor(ns1.time)-seekIncDec;
   nsVideoPlayer.seek(playHeadPosition);
}
```

When the rewind button is released, simply clear the timer and tell the NetStream object to play(), and it will play from the new head position.

```
Private function onReleaseRW():void {
  timerRW.reset();
  nsVideoPlayer.play();
}
```

Creating video objects with the Video class

In previous versions of ActionScript, the Video class didn't exist (at least not in the same way it does in ActionScript 3.0). You needed to create a physical video object and drag it on screen, then give it an instance name, which you would then use to link the NetStream instance to it. This meant that the development cycle of a video-based application could not be done by code alone (not something I mind to be honest, as you can't make syntax errors with a physical object). This was, however, a bit of a glaring inconsistency in the way we develop video-based applications, and it has now been addressed with the Video class.

Table 7-4 briefly summarizes the public properties of the Video class.

Table 7-4. Video class public properties

Property	Type	Description
deblocking	int	Indicates the type of filter applied to decoded video as part of postprocessing.
smoothing	Boolean	Specifies whether the video should be smoothed (interpolated) when it is scaled.
videoHeight	int	Read-only. Specifies the height of the video stream, in pixels.
videoWidth	int	Read-only. Specifies the width of the video stream, in pixels.

Create a Video object like this:

```
//Import the Video class
import flash.media.Video;
. . .
//Declare a Video data-typed variable in the class header
private var vid1:Video;
. . .
//Create an instance of the Video class in the class constructor
vid1=new Video();
```

The Video class is a display object. As mentioned earlier, in respect to the MVC pattern, it represents the view. This means it displays and can modify what it displays; however, it doesn't have any control over the content it displays. Remember to add your Video object instance to the display list also.

```
//Add Video instance to display list
addChild(vid1);
. . .
//Set display properties

vid1.x=166;
vid1.y=77;
vid1.width=490;
vid1.height=365;
```

Since the Video instance has no control over the video it displays, you must attach a NetStream control object to the Video instance, as follows:

```
vid1.attachNetStream(nsVideoPlayer);
```

When your video is stopped using the NetStream.close() function, the video display object does not clear. To get around this cleanly, use the Video.clear() function once the video has stopped playing. You can also remove the Video object from the display list:

```
vid1.clear();
removeChild(vid1);
```

That's pretty much it for setting up the Video class. It can be modified in other ways to alter how it is displayed, but that would be overkill for this example. Its work is done, and now the NetStream class will do all the controlling.

Creating camera objects with the Camera class

The Camera class provides access to and control of the user's webcam, so it can be used as the video source. Generally, the Camera class is used in conjunction with the FMS; however, it can be used without any back-end communication requirements.

When using the Camera class to call the camera in question, the user will be challenged for access to the camera. This is a security feature, and the user must agree to allow access in the pop-up box that appears.

> The pop-up challenge box is 215 × 138 pixels, so the SWF in which you publish the FLV must be this size as a minimum.

Table 7-5 briefly summarizes the public properties of the Camera class.

Table 7-5. Camera class public properties

Property	Type	Description
activityLevel	Number	Read-only. Specifies the amount of motion the camera is detecting.
bandwidth	int	Read-only. Specifies the maximum amount of bandwidth the current outgoing video feed can use, in bytes.
Constructor	Object	A reference to the class object or constructor function for a given object instance.
currentFps	Number	Read-only. The rate at which the camera is capturing data, in frames per second.
fps	Number	Read-only. The maximum rate at which you want the camera to capture data, in frames per second.
height	int	Read-only. The current capture height, in pixels.
index	int	Read-only. A zero-based integer that specifies the index of the camera, as reflected in the array returned by the names property.
keyFrameInterval	int	Read-only. Specifies which video frames are transmitted in full (called keyframes) instead of being interpolated by the video compression algorithm.
loopback	Boolean	Read-only. Specifies whether a local view of what the camera is capturing is compressed and decompressed (true), as it would be for live transmission using FMS, or uncompressed (false).
motionLevel	int	Read-only. Specifies the amount of motion required to invoke the activity event.
motionTimeout	int	Read-only. The number of milliseconds between the time the camera stops detecting motion and the time the activity event is invoked.
muted	Boolean	Read-only. Specifies whether the user has denied access to the camera (true) or allowed access (false) in the Flash Player Privacy panel.
name	String	Read-only. Specifies the name of the current camera, as returned by the camera hardware.
names	Array	Static, read-only. Retrieves an array of strings reflecting the names of all available cameras without displaying the Flash Player Privacy panel.

Continued

255

Table 7-5. Continued

Property	Type	Description
prototype	Object	Static. A reference to the prototype object of a class or function object.
quality	int	Read-only. Specifies the required level of picture quality, as determined by the amount of compression being applied to each video frame.
width	int	Read-only. The current capture width, in pixels.

Creating a Camera object is very simple. However, just as with the NetStream object, it needs to be assigned a Video object in order to display it:

```
private var cam1:Camera;
. . .
cam1=new Camera();
. . .
//Load camera source
public function loadCamera():void {
  addChild(vid1);
  vid1.x=40;
  vid1.y=70;
  vid1.width=500;
  vid1.height=375;
  cam1=Camera.getCamera();
  vid1.attachCamera(cam1);
}
```

The Camera class has a number of useful methods, which are summarized in Table 7-6.

Table 7-6. Camera class methods

Method	Description
getCamera(name:String = null):Camera [static]	Returns a reference to a Camera object for capturing video
setKeyFrameInterval(keyFrameInterval: int):void	Specifies which video frames are transmitted in full (called keyframes) instead of being interpolated by the video compression algorithm
setLoopback(compress:Boolean= false):void	Specifies whether to use a compressed video stream for a local view of the camera

Method	Description
setMode(width:int, height:int, fps:Number, favorArea:Boolean = true):void	Sets the camera capture mode to the native mode that best meets the specified requirements
setMotionLevel(motionLevel:int, timeout:int = 2000):void	Specifies how much motion is required to dispatch the activity event
setQuality(bandwidth:int, quality:int):void	Sets the maximum amount of bandwidth per second or the required picture quality of the current outgoing video feed

Handling video events

A number of useful events are associated with video. These include mouse events, status events, metadata events, and cue point events.

Mouse events

All of the buttons for standard video player functionality—such as play, pause, fast-forward, rewind, and stop—require listeners for their mouse-based events to be handled. To set up these listeners, you need to import both the SimpleButton class and the MouseEvent class:

```
import flash.display.SimpleButton;
import flash.events.MouseEvent;
```

Then create the button instances:

```
//Rewind, Play, Pause, Stop and Fast Forward buttons
private var butRW:SimpleButton;
private var butPlay:SimpleButton;
private var butPause:SimpleButton;
private var butStop:SimpleButton;
private var butFF:SimpleButton;
```

Add MouseEvent listeners. Here's an example of adding listeners for the CLICK event:

```
//Add button listeners
butRW.addEventListener(MouseEvent.CLICK, doRewind);
butPlay.addEventListener(MouseEvent.CLICK, doPlay);
butPause.addEventListener(MouseEvent.CLICK, doPause);
butStop.addEventListener(MouseEvent.CLICK, doStop);
butFF.addEventListener(MouseEvent.CLICK, doFastForward);
```

In some cases, you will also need to listen for the MouseEvent.UP event, such as with the fast-forward and rewind buttons.

Status events

Status events will be broadcast about any existing NetStream instance when it has a change in status. The event will tell you information such as if the NetStream stops or pauses, if the buffer is full, and if it errors out.

```
import flash.events.NetStatusEvent;
. . .
//Add a listener for any status events (playing, stopped, etc.)
nsVideoPlayer.addEventListener(NetStatusEvent.NET_STATUS, nsOnStatus);
. . .
private function nsOnStatus(infoObject:NetStatusEvent) :void {
  for (var prop in infoObject.info) {
    trace("\t"+prop+":\t"+infoObject.info[prop]);
  }
}
```

The nsOnStatus function will trace through the infoObject and its contents whenever a status event is broadcast.

Table 7-7 summarizes the NetStream onStatus events and errors.

Table 7-7. NetSteam onStatus events and errors

Event/Error	Description
NetStream.Buffer.Empty	Data is not being received quickly enough to fill the buffer. Data flow will be interrupted until the buffer refills, at which time a NetStream.Buffer.Full message will be sent and the stream will begin playing again.
NetStream.Buffer.Full	The buffer is full and the stream will begin playing.
NetStream.Buffer.Flush	Data has finished streaming, and the remaining buffer will be emptied.
NetStream.Play.Start	Playback has started.
NetStream.Play.Stop	Playback has stopped.
NetStream.Play.StreamNotFound	The video file passed to the play() method can't be found.
NetStream.Seek.InvalidTime	For video downloaded with progressive download, the user has tried to seek or play past the end of the video data that has downloaded thus far, or past the end of the video once the entire file has downloaded. The Error.message.details property contains a time code that indicates the last valid position to which the user can seek.
NetStream.Seek.Notify	The seek operation is complete.

The Camera class has the same onStatus event as the NetStream class, and should be handled in the same way. Camera also has a unique activity event (ActivityEvent.ACTIVITY), which is fired whenever the camera detects or stops detecting motion.

First, import the event class.

```
import flash.events.ActivityEvent;
```

Then, once you have created a Camera instance, add a listener for any activity.

```
Cam1.addEventListener(ActivityEvent.ACTIVITY, activityHandler);
```

Metadata events

You can use the onMetaData callback handler to view the metadata information in your video files. Metadata includes information about your video file, such as duration, width, height, frame rate, and more. The metadata information that is added to your FLV or H.264 file depends on the software you use to encode it, or the software you use to add metadata information after encoding. You can use the metadata to do things like work out and display the video length, The metadata gives you a way to interrogate the video file prior to playing it, and gives the user this feedback as soon as the video file is accessible.

ActionScript 3.0's metadata callback handler is considerably different from that of ActionScript 2.0, and indeed, from the callback handlers of just about any other class. It uses a client object, to which the onMetaData handler method is assigned. The callback method is invoked on whatever is set with the client property.

```
var objTempClient:Object=new Object();
objTempClient.onMetaData=mdHandler;
nsVideoPlayer.client=objTempClient;

//This function cycles through and displays all of the video file's
//metadata, so you can see what metadata it has and get used to
//seeing the sort of metadata that is attached to video files.
private function mdHandler(obj:Object) :void {
  for(var x in obj){
    trace(x+" : "+obj[x]);
  }
}
```

Using the previous code snippet to trace the returned metadata information object in the mdHandler() method creates the following output on the included FLV file:

```
width: 320
audiodatarate: 96
audiocodecid: 2
videocodecid: 4
videodatarate: 400
canSeekToEnd: true
duration: 16.334
audiodelay: 0.038
height: 213
framerate: 15
```

Table 7-8 shows the possible values for video metadata in FLV files.

Table 7-8. Video metadata in FLV files

Parameter	Description
audiocodecid	A number that indicates the audio codec (code/decode technique) that was used. Possible values are 0 (uncompressed), 1 (ADPCM), 2 (MP3), 5 (Nellymoser 8kHz mono), and 6 (Nellymoser).
audiodatarate	A number that indicates the rate at which audio was encoded, in kilobytes per second.
audiodelay	A number that indicates what time in the FLV file "time 0" of the original FLV file exists. The video content needs to be delayed by a small amount to properly synchronize the audio.
canSeekToEnd	A Boolean value that is true if the FLV file is encoded with a keyframe on the last frame that allows seeking to the end of a progressive download movie clip. It is false if the FLV file is not encoded with a keyframe on the last frame.
cuePoints	An array of objects, one for each cue point embedded in the FLV file. The value is undefined if the FLV file does not contain any cue points. Each object has the type, name, time, and parameters.
duration	A number that specifies the duration of the FLV file, in seconds.
framerate	A number that is the frame rate of the FLV file.
height	A number that is the height of the FLV file, in pixels.
videocodecid	A number that is the codec version that was used to encode the video. Possible values are 2 (Sorenson H.263), 3 (screen video; SWF 7 and later only), 4 (VP6.2; SWF 8 and later only), and 5 (VP6.2 video with alpha channel: SWF 8 and later only).
videodatarate	A number that is the video data rate of the FLV file.
width	A number that is the width of the FLV file, in pixels.

Table 7-9 shows the video metadata reported on H.264 files.

Table 7-9. Video metadata in H.264 files

Parameter	Description
duration	Shows the length of the video. (Unlike for FLV files, this field is always present.)
videocodecid	For H.264, avc1 is reported.
audiocodecid	For AAC, mp4a is reported. For MP3, mp3 is reported.
avcprofile	The H.264 profile. Possible values are 66, 77, 88, 100, 110, 122, and 144.
avclevel	A number between 10 and 51.
aottype	Audio type. Possible values are 0 (AAC Main), 1 (AAC LC), and 2 (SBR).
moovposition	The offset in bytes of the moov atom in a file.
trackinfo	An array of objects containing various information about all the tracks in a file.
chapters	Information about chapters in audiobooks.
seekpoints	You can directly feed into NetStream.seek();.
videoframerate	The frame rate of the video if a monotone frame rate is used. Most videos will have a monotone frame rate.
audiosamplerate	The original sampling rate of the audio track.
audiochannels	The original number of channels of the audio track.
width	The width of the video source.
height	The height of the video source.

"The time has come," the Walrus said, "to talk of many things." Of moov atoms and seekpoints, of cabbages and kings. Well, OK, perhaps we won't get into vegetables and royalty, but now is a good time to talk about a couple of interesting differences when interrogating H.264-based video files, which involve moov atoms and seekpoints.

Atoms are metadata in their own right. Specifically, you can get information about the moov atom. The **moov atom** is movie resource metadata about the movie (number and type of tracks, location of sample data, and so on). It describes where the movie data can be found and how to interpret it.

Since H.264 files contain an index, unlike FLV files, you can provide a list of **seekpoints**, which are times you can seek to without having the playhead jump around. You'll get this information through the onMetaData callback from an array with the name seekpoints. Some files, however, are not encoded with this information, which means that these files are not seekable at all. This works differently from keyframe-based FLV files. which use cue points, rather than seekpoints. H.264-based video cannot use cue points.

Cue point events

Cue points are video-based broadcast events. You will need the Flash Video Encoder, at the very least, to be able to create and add cue points to your movies as you encode them to an FLV file. Once again, cue points are not available in H.264-based video.

Each cue point event fires with it an information object. When you scrub through your video in the Flash Video Encoder and find a point where you want to add a cue point, open the Flash Video Encoding Settings screen, and click the Cue Points tab, shown in Figure 7-10.

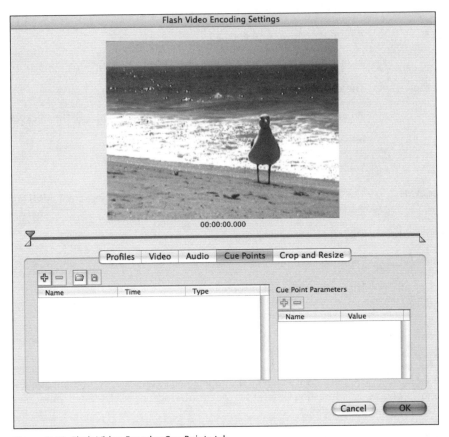

Figure 7-10. Flash Video Encoder Cue Points tab

The Cue Points tab has two entry boxes: one for the cue point's name and the other for the cue point's parameters. These parameters are passed to any event handler listening for the onCuePoint event when it fires. You can make the parameters anything you want, but they are essentially name/value pairs.

For example, if you wanted to add a cue point to a point where a particular seagull landed and then pass information about that bird to the listener, you would do it as shown in Figure 7-11.

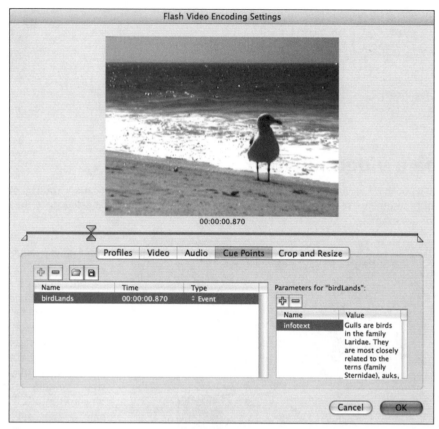

Figure 7-11. Adding cue points with the Flash Video Encoder

Handling cue points is very similar to handling metadata events. The following code sets up the client object of the NetStream instance and assigns the onCuePoint event handler to point at a method called cpHandler. In this case, the example simply cycles through the attached information object to find all the parameters for each cue point event that is broadcast:

```
var objTempClient:Object=new Object();
objTempClient.onCuePoint=cpHandler;
nsVideoPlayer.client=objTempClient;

private function cpHandler(obj:Object) :void {
  //First we cycle through the cue point information object's
  //variables, which include 'time', 'type', 'name' and most
  //importantly to us, 'parameters'
  for (var c in obj){
    trace("CP "+c+" is "+obj[c]);
    //When we find the 'parameters' object, we can then cycle through
    //it to see all the cue point names and values
```

```
        if (c == "parameters"){
          for (var p in obj[c]){
            trace("*** "+p+" is "+obj[c][p]);
          }
        }
      }
    }
  }
```

Building a video player

So now that you have all the theory, let's build an actual video player application. You will eventually end up with something like the player shown in Figure 7-12. All the physical assets have already been created for the example.

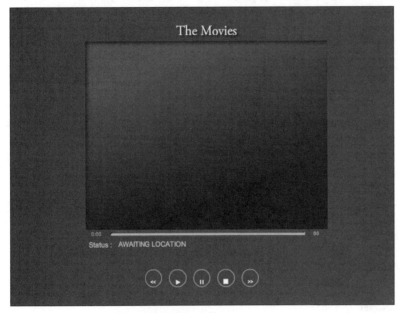

This simple video player will have a loading progress bar incorporated into the scrubber bar. Beneath that is a status text field to tell the user when a video is loading, playing, paused, and so. At the bottom are the standard play, pause, stop, rewind, and fast-forward buttons. The video play length will be displayed on the right of the scrubber bar, and the position of the playhead will be displayed on the left of the scrubber bar.

You'll use four class files for the video player:

Figure 7-12. The final video player

- `Main.as`: This class will contain the instances of the video and button controls. You will need to create, address, and display buttons, video, and text fields so you need to import the Flash classes for these.

- `Videos.as`: This class will handle the video control, which will load the video, read its metadata, and respond to button-control commands.

- `ButtonManager.as`: This class will handle the interactive controls.

- `MediaControlEvent.as`: This class will allow us to fire off bespoke events for button presses.

A number of "manager" classes that I use really should be made into single-tons. A **singleton** is a pattern as well as a code implementation, which enforces the convention of creating only one instance of a given class. With the release of ActionScript 3.0, Adobe has chosen to comply with the ECMA 262 standard, and thus has been forced to disallow private constructors. These were essential for the Java standard way of implementing singletons. Without private constructors, implementing a singleton-based class is a sticky-tape and elastic-band quality build proposition that is doomed to lack consistency, and has my object-oriented spidey senses tingling away like crazy. Bring back the private constructor!

Setting up the project

I have created the physical assets and initial FLA file (videoDemo_final.fla) to save you some time on this example. You can find the starting point for this exercise in this book's downloadable code. You will also find all the class files (in case you have the urge to cheat).

Open videoDemo_final.fla in Flash. You will see all the graphical assets are already laid out on the stage for you, as shown in Figure 7-13. They also already have instance names for your convenience. Save this file to a new work directory of your choice. This is where you will create all your other class files.

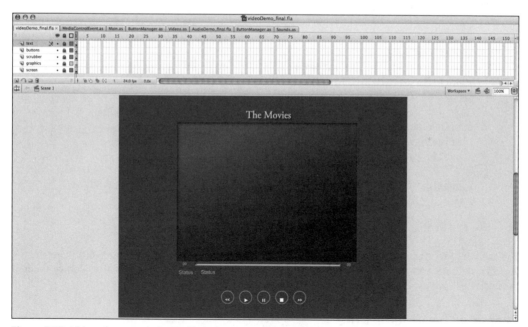

Figure 7-13. Video player assets inside Flash

Creating the Main.as file

The FLA has a document class called Main.as, and this is where you will start. Let's get to work.

1. Create a new .as file, and add the following code to it:

```
package com.fas3.smc{

    import flash.display.MovieClip;
    import com.fas3.smc.Videos;
    import com.fas3.smc.ButtonManager;
    import flash.text.TextField;
    import flash.display.SimpleButton;

    public class Main extends MovieClip {

    }
}
```

2. Save the file in a subdirectory called com.fas3.smc as Main.as. You have created the class and imported the external classes you will be using.

3. Add the code to declare the Video and ButtonManager classes and create the Main constructor. These will take care of the video and the button control and functionality. Your file should look like this:

```
package com.fas3.smc{

    import flash.display.MovieClip;
    import com.fas3.smc.Videos;
    import com.fas3.smc.ButtonManager;
    import flash.text.TextField;
    import flash.display.SimpleButton;

    public class Main extends MovieClip {
        private var vids:Videos;
        public var buts:ButtonManager;

        public function Main(){
        }
    }
}
```

The Main.as FLA document class is complete. This won't do much at the moment, but never fear—you'll come back and put the calls for the Videos and ButtonManager classes in after you've created those classes.

Creating the Video.as file

Now it's time to turn our attention to another class file: Videos.as. You will start by importing all the classes you will need for this file. I will explain what these are for as we go along.

> *The qualified constructor you will create is designed so you can pass references for the scrubber movie clip and the text fields I have physically put on the stage so the class can directly update these. I could have created these within the Videos class file in code, as they are specifically for the video player, but for the sake of simplicity (less code), I have chosen to create these physically and reference them. There is nothing wrong with this approach (no matter what strict object-oriented purists may tell you).*

1. Create another new .as file and save it as Videos.as in your com.fas3.smc directory.

2. Add the following code to the Videos.as file, and then save it. You'll notice that it declares a number of variables—all of the variables you will use in the code. This is to save time, so you don't need to later go back to the top of the class to create them.

```
package com.fas3.smc{
import flash.net.NetConnection;
import flash.net.NetStream;
import flash.media.Video;
import flash.display.MovieClip;
import flash.events.TimerEvent;
import flash.events.NetStatusEvent;
import flash.utils.Timer;
import flash.text.TextField;
import com.fas3.smc.MediaControlEvent;

public class Videos extends MovieClip {
private var vid1:Video;
private var ncVideoPlayer:NetConnection;
private var nsVideoPlayer:NetStream;
private var flvTarget:String;
private var vidDuration:Number;
private var trackLength:int;
private var timerLoading:Timer;
private var timerPlayHead:Timer;
private var timerFF:Timer;
private var timerRW:Timer;
private var txtStatus:TextField;
private var txtTrackLength:TextField;
private var txtHeadPosition:TextField;
private var bytLoaded:int;
private var bytTotal:in;
private var opct:int;
private var movScrubber:MovieClip;
private var ns_minutes:Number;
private var ns_seconds:Number;
private var seekRate:Number=3;
private var headPos:Number;
```

```
// CONSTRUCTOR
public function Videos(movScrubber:MovieClip, txtStatus:TextField,
txtHeadPosition:TextField, txtTrackLength:TextField) :void {
}
}
}
```

3. Now assign the references you sent to the constructor to local variables. Also set the loading progress bar to its initial size, turn off the scrubber playhead (until you have loaded enough video to play), and set the initial status message. Among other things, these initial settings prove your references are working. Add the following code to the constructor:

```
// Set movies and text fields to local references and to start
// positions and contents
movScrubber=movScrubber;
txtStatus=txtStatus;
txtHeadPosition=txtHeadPosition;
txtTrackLength=txtTrackLength;
movScrubber.movLoaderBar.width=1;
movScrubber.movHead.alpha=0;
txtStatus.text="AWAITING LOCATION";
```

4. Set up the netConnection and netStream classes, and set the video target file. To do so, add the following into the constructor, just before the closing curly brace:

```
//Instantiate vars, connect NC and NS
ncVideoPlayer=new NetConnection();
ncVideoPlayer.connect(null);
nsVideoPlayer=new NetStream(ncVideoPlayer);
flvTarget="video_final.flv";
```

> Although you are targeting an FLV file in this example, you could just as easily target an H.264-encoded file at this point.

5. Before playing the video, you want to set up the buffer so that you will have preloaded an acceptable amount of video into buffer before you play it. Set the buffer to 5 seconds. Add the following to the constructor:

```
nsVideoPlayer.bufferTime=5;
```

6. Instantiate the Video display object, like so (add this to the constructor):

```
vid1=new Video();
```

7. You're finally ready to call and play your video file. Add the following line to the constructor:

```
loadFLV();
```

But hang on—that's a function call isn't it? Yes, it is. This keeps the call to action modularized. The specifics of which video to load, where to place it, and how big to make it, along with the actual instructions to play it, are all in this one function. In a refactored future version, you can easily make this method public and allow the user to pass the video target and extend the video object settings when it is called.

8. Add the function the constructor calls to your Video.as file:

```
//Load FLV source
  private function loadFLV():void {
  addChild(vid1);
  vid1.x=166;
  vid1.y=77;
  vid1.width=490;
  vid1.height=365;
  vid1.attachNetStream(nsVideoPlayer);
  nsVideoPlayer.play(flvTarget);
  }
```

For the moment, you have hard-coded the dimensions and position of the Video instance and added it to the display list, before attaching the NetStream instance to it. Then you simply issue the NetStream play() command. Now you will see that the video source will load and play when you publish your file.

You now need to address a number of important and complementary issues in order to make use of the event handling and the control functionality that the NetStream class affords. You can see the buttons on the screen, and although they will respond when you click them, they do not have any control over the actual video yet.

This section leaves you with a lot of the basic code set up, although you still have a way to go. Next, you'll turn your attention to the control of the video player.

Controlling the video player

Now we will add the status text field, loading progress bar, and playhead bar. You'll also handle the metadata and the cue points.

Setting up the status text field

Let's start by setting up a listener and handler for the NetStream onStatus event. This event is fired off whenever the NetStream starts playing, stops playing, the buffer fills, and so on (see Table 7-7 for the NetStream events).

Using the NetStream onStatus event is a great way of populating the status text field initially. You might think the button event listeners would be the most consistent way to do that, but they are only command events and do not reflect if the video actually responded to those commands.

First, add the following event listener in the constructor, just before the closing curly brace:

```
nsVideoPlayer.addEventListener(NetStatusEvent.NET_STATUS, nsOnStatus);
```

You have set up your NetStream instance to listen for the NetStatus event NET_STATUS and call the nsOnStatus function when it receives an event object of that type. It will automatically send the event object with it when it calls the handler.

Next, create the following event handler in the Videos.as file, outside the Videos.as constructor, as a function in its own right:

```
public function nsOnStatus(infoObject:NetStatusEvent) :void {
for (var prop in infoObject.info) {
//This trace will show what properties the NetStatus event contains
trace("\t"+prop+":\t"+infoObject.info[prop]);
//This If checks to see if it is a code property and if that contains
//a stop notification. If it is, then it displays this in the status
//text field
if (prop=="code" && infoObject.info[prop]=="NetStream.Play.Stop"){
txtStatus.text="Stopped";
//This If checks to see if it is a code property and if that contains
//a start notification. If it is, then it displays this in the status
//text field and makes the scrubhead movie clip visible
}else if(prop=="code" && infoObject.info[prop]== ➡
"NetStream.Play.Start"){
txtStatus.text="Playing";
movScrubber.movHead.alpha=100;
}
}
}
```

The received object is of type NetStatusEvent. To give you a better idea of the sort of things the NET_STATUS event reports, the code includes a for in loop to cycle through all the contents of the code array of the returned NetStatusEvent and trace them. When you next publish your SWF, you will see a lot of NET_STATUS events being reported to the Output panel of your IDE, like the following:

```
level:     status
code:      NetStream.Play.Start
```

Of course, you really need the NET_STATUS event to confirm a few important things at the moment: when the video starts playing and when it stops, for example, because you need to adjust the status text, the playhead, and so forth. It would be better if you could get pause, fast-forward, and rewind status events also. However, although the NET_STATUS can provide seek event notification, it cannot report which way it's going and it has no concept of pausing at all. So for these functions, you will need to rely on the buttons themselves dispatching these events. This is less satisfactory, as it tells you only that the command was sent, not that it has been executed, but it's the best you're going to do until Adobe extends the NetStream events.

Now you will implement the loading progress bar of your video player.

Implementing the loading progress bar

The loading progress bar will display how far the video is through the loading process. This should complement the playhead bar, and indeed, it will operate within the scrubber movie clip. I have already created the physical asset. You will need to loop the check at regular intervals until the load is complete. In ActionScript 2.0, you would have used setInterval or an onEnterFrame. In ActionScript

3,0, it is more powerful and elegant to use the new Timer class. You have already imported this and declared it in the constructor, so let's instantiate it, add a listener, and start the timer running.

Add the following code to your Videos.as constructor, just before the closing curly brace:

```
// Add Timers
timerLoading=new Timer(10, 0);
timerLoading.addEventListener(TimerEvent.TIMER, this.onLoading);
timerLoading.start();
```

The first line instantiates the new Timer instance with the parameters of interval and number of loops. You have set a 10-millisecond interval and told it to loop indefinitely. You will be a good programming citizen and stop the timer when it has finished its job.

Now that you have defined an event listener and started the timer, let's take a look at the event handler code. Create the following function at the bottom of the Videos.as class file:

```
private function onLoading(event:TimerEvent) :void {
 bytLoaded=nsVideoPlayer.bytesLoaded;
 bytTotal=nsVideoPlayer.bytesTotal;
 opct=((nsVideoPlayer.bytesTotal)/100);
 movScrubber.movLoaderBar.width=(Math.floor(bytLoaded/opct))*4;
 if(bytLoaded == bytTotal){
  timerLoading.stop();
 }
}
```

This is all fairly self-explanatory. The first few lines work out the amount loaded and the total size of the video in bytes. You then calculate what 1% of the total value would be. After this, it is a simple matter of setting the scrubber movie clip's loader bar movie clip to be the appropriate width based on these calculations and taking into account that the entire bar is 400 pixels wide. Finally, you check if the video has completed loading (if the bytes loaded equal the bytes total), and if so, stop the loading Timer instance.

Now publish your FLA, and you will see the loading progress bar fill as the video loads.

> *The movie loading will seem instantaneous if the file is being loaded locally. To see the loading progress bar in action, you really need to load a video from a web server.*

Let's follow this by creating the playhead bar.

Creating the playhead bar

The playhead bar will show where the playhead is when you are watching the video. Once again, I have already created the graphical object on the stage, within the scrubber movie clip. This will be coded very similarly to the loading progress bar. You already have the necessary variables defined in the Videos.as class file, so let's go ahead and create a Timer instance for this function in its constructor.

Add the following code to the Videos.as constructor, again just before the closing curly brace:

```
timerPlayHead=new Timer(100, 0);
timerPlayHead.addEventListener(TimerEvent.TIMER, this.headPosition);
timerPlayHead.start();
```

The first line instantiates the new Timer instance with the parameters of interval and number of loops. You have set a 100-millisecond interval and told it to loop indefinitely.

Now that you have defined an event listener and started the timer, let's look at the event handler code. Create the following function at the bottom of the Videos.as class file:

```
private function headPosition(event:TimerEvent) :void {
 //Set Head movie clip to correct width but don't run till we get the
 //track length from the metadata
 if(trackLength>0){
  movScrubber.movHead.width=(nsVideoPlayer.time/(trackLength/100))*4;
 }
 //Format and set timer display text field
 ns_minutes = int(nsVideoPlayer.time/60);
  ns_seconds = int(nsVideoPlayer.time%60);
  if (ns_seconds<10) {
  txtHeadPosition.text=ns_minutes.toString()+":0"+ ns_seconds.toString();
  }else{
  txtHeadPosition.text=ns_minutes.toString()+":"+ ns_seconds.toString();
  }
```

As you can see, you don't set the playhead movie clip width until you have received the duration metadata to establish the track length. You will learn how to handle the metadata in the next section.

The playhead movie clip calculations differ from the loader bar movie clip in that they cannot make use of the bytes loaded to give an indication of the playhead position, nor the bytes total to give an indication of the total track length. This is because you are working in chronological time units here, not bytes as you did with the loading progress bar. So you need the NetStream.Time information, which tells you the playhead position in seconds, and the duration metadata, which tells you the total duration of the video in seconds. Once you have the necessary calculation from the figures, you need to do a little formatting to show this in *minutes:seconds* format. Once the *minutes:seconds* formatting is done, you display it in the head position text field. Because this is on a timer, this will update in real time for the user.

> *I have deliberately not shown the duration in* hours:minutes:seconds *format. For these examples, you will not be playing anything that stretches into hours. If you need to do this, the calculation is simple and obvious.*

Handling the metadata

Now you need to get the duration of the video from the video's metadata. Although you need only the duration, you will use a for in loop in the metadata event handler to see what metadata your video contains (see the "Metadata events" section earlier in the chapter for more information).

> With FLV video that was encoded in versions before Flash CS3, often the duration metadata was missing, and you would need to use some third-party software to specifically add the duration metadata. You may still find this is the case in any video you have not encoded yourself or not encoded in the most recent versions of the available video encoders. This is why it is important to specifically check for the duration metadata in early testing of any video you will play. It is a relatively simple matter to add the duration information to the metadata after the fact.

Let's set up the metadata event listener. Again, you have already imported and defined any necessary classes and variables. Add the following lines of code to the Videos.as class file constructor:

```
//Create a metadata event handling object
var objTempClient:Object=new Object();
objTempClient.onMetaData=mdHandler;
nsVideoPlayer.client=objTempClient;
```

Metadata (and for that matter, cue point) handling is quite different in ActionScript 3.0 than it was in ActionScript 2.0. You now use NetStream's client property (discussed in the "Metadata events" section earlier in the chapter).

Now that you've assigned the NetStream client property and set the metadata handler, let's look at the event handler itself. You have assigned the mdHandler function to deal with all metadata events. Add this function to your Videos.as class file:

```
private function mdHandler(obj:Object) :void {
    for (var x in obj){
        trace("METADATA "+x+" is "+obj[x]);
        //If this is the duration, format it and display it
        if(x=="duration"){
           trackLength=obj[x];
          var tlMinutes:int = trackLength/60;
          if (tlMinutes<1){
             tlMinutes=0
          }
          var tlSeconds:int = trackLength%60;
          if (tlSeconds<10) {
             txtTrackLength.text=tlMinutes.toString()+":0"+ tlSeconds.toString();
          }else{
             txtTrackLength.text=tlMinutes.toString()+":"+ tlSeconds.toString();
          }
        }
    }
}
```

You loop through the properties of the object that this function receives. You check specifically for only the duration property. Once you find it, you format it for use in the track length text field and store it for use in the playhead calculations. Now when you publish your movie, you will see all the metadata information in the Output panel.

Handling cue points

Cue point handling is very similar to metadata handling. As explained in the "Cue point events" section earlier in the chapter, not all videos have cue points, and it's up to you or your production team to add them. You generally use them to add enhanced interactivity to video. This is an incredibly powerful feature of ActionScript.

So let's set up the cue point event listener. As usual, you have already imported and defined any necessary classes and variables. Add the following line of code to the Videos.as class file constructor just below where you defined your metadata listener:

```
objTempClient.onCuePoint=cpHandler;
```

This should now leave this small section of the constructor looking like so:

```
//Create a metadata and cue point event handling object
var objTempClient:Object=new Object();
objTempClient.onMetaData=mdHandler;
objTempClient.onCuePoint=cpHandler;
nsVideoPlayer.client=objTempClient;
```

As you can see, both the cue point and metadata events use the same NetStream Client object. They only differ in the handler function.

Now add the following function to your Videos.as class file to handle the cue points:

```
private function cpHandler(obj:Object) :void {
 for (var c in obj){
  trace("CUEPOINT "+c+" is "+obj[c]);
  if(c=="parameters"){
   for (var p in obj[c]){
    trace("        PARAMETER "+p+" is "+obj[c][p]);
   }
  }
 }
}
```

This function will for in loop through the returned cue point object to display the standard cue point information (time, type, and name). Most important, when it finds the parameters array within it, it will for in loop through this also to output any extra parameters you defined and set during the cue point encoding process.

```
CUEPOINT time is 5.38
CUEPOINT type is event
CUEPOINT name is onMary
```

```
CUEPOINT parameters is
        PARAMETER activity is snowboarding
        PARAMETER with is Fluffy
        PARAMETER name is Mary
        PARAMETER location is Chamonix
```

> For the purposes of this demo, you do not actually use cue points to enhance the interaction with the video. I have added some simply to show the sort of output you can expect and that you can set.

OK, so you've loaded, played, monitored, and event-handled the video. Now you really need to exercise some control over it. You have a full complement of buttons on the stage, but as of yet, no control is exercised using them. So let's change that now.

Controlling the video on the stage

Now you will create another class called ButtonManager, which will deal with all the button-based events in the video player.

Create a new file inside your com.fas3.smc directory called ButtonManager.as. Add the following code, which takes care of all the classes you need to import and the variable definitions you will need.

```
package com.fas3.smc{
 import flash.net.*;
 import flash.display.Sprite;
 import flash.display.SimpleButton;
 import flash.events.MouseEvent;
 import flash.events.EventDispatcher;
 import flash.events.Event;
 import com.fas3.smc..MediaControlEvent;

 public class ButtonManager extends Sprite{
  private var butRW:SimpleButton;
  private var butPlay:SimpleButton;
  private var butPause:SimpleButton;
  private var butStop:SimpleButton;
  private var butFF:SimpleButton;
  private var eventDispatcherButton:EventDispatcher;
  private var evtButRW:String;
  private var pauseOn:Boolean=false;

 public function ButtonManager(butRW:SimpleButton, butPlay:SimpleButton,
 butPause:SimpleButton, butStop:SimpleButton, butFF:SimpleButton) :void {
    butRW=butRW;
    butPlay=butPlay;
    butPause=butPause;
```

```
  butStop=butStop;
  butFF=butFF;
 }


 }

}
```

Because I have deliberately not added extra code to create the buttons for this example, and instead opted to create them graphically on the stage, you will see you have passed references to them into the class file constructor. You also immediately pass these references to your local variables so you can access them in the scope of the class.

To instantiate the ButtonManager class and pass in the button instance references, you need to return to the Main.as FLA document class file and add the following line after the line that adds the Videos.as class instance to the display list:

```
addChild(vids);
buts=new ButtonManager(butRW, butPlay, butPause, butStop, butFF);
```

Adding button functionality

Now let's add the button functionality. You need to start by adding event listeners to the ButtonManager.as class file constructor for each button to listen for MOUSE_DOWN events. These will tell you as soon as a button is pressed; you do not want to wait until the button is released to be notified. It is especially important with functions like fast-forward (FF) and rewind (RW), which rely on the user pressing and holding down the button to execute them. The FF and RW buttons use a Timer class instance to continue to run while the button is pressed, and they need a release event handler so you can stop them from executing when the user releases the mouse. You will use the CLICK mouse event rather than the more obvious MOUSE_UP event.

> The MOUSE_UP event is fired on any button, even if it is not the one that fired the MOUSE_DOWN event. If you moved your mouse during the press, you could easily get an erroneous release function call for another button. The CLICK event registers the button that was pressed and registers a mouse release against only that button, no matter where the mouse may have slid before it was released.

In the ButtonManager.as constructor, add the following listener definitions:

```
//Add button listeners
butRW.addEventListener(MouseEvent.MOUSE_DOWN, doRewind);
butRW.addEventListener(MouseEvent.CLICK, stopRewind);
butPlay.addEventListener(MouseEvent.MOUSE_DOWN, doPlay);
butPause.addEventListener(MouseEvent.MOUSE_DOWN, doPause);
butStop.addEventListener(MouseEvent.MOUSE_DOWN, doStop);
butFF.addEventListener(MouseEvent.MOUSE_DOWN, doFastForward);
butFF.addEventListener(MouseEvent.CLICK, stopFastForward);
```

In the constructor, you also need to set the initial state of the buttons. By default, the enabled state of all the buttons is true. However, as the video will automatically begin playing, you really don't need the play button to be enabled initially. In fact, it would be very poor usability to make it so. This also applies to other buttons based on the status of the video. If the video is paused, for example, then none of the other buttons need to be enabled. So, let's start by adding the following to the end of the ButtonManager.as constructor before coding the other relational button states:

```
butPlay.enabled=false;
```

The event handling itself could have been done in a number of ways, and I spent considerable time deciding on the best way to do it here. I chose to use good convention over poor code. In principle, you need to fire off notification that a button has been pressed or released to the Video.as class instance so it can execute that command on the video it is controlling. The simpler way might have been to add a function for every button and every press within the Videos.as class instance, and then add each one of these as event listeners to each button and each event. Long-winded, but it would look pretty simple and it would work. But that calls for a lot of functions and is really not great convention, so I decided to use button event handlers within the ButtonManager.as class instance. So add the following functions to the body of your ButtonManager.as class file:

```
private function doRewind(evnt:MouseEvent) :void {
        dispatchEvent(new MediaControlEvent("RW"));
}

private function stopRewind(evnt:MouseEvent) :void {
        dispatchEvent(new MediaControlEvent("RWEND"));
}

private function doPlay(event:MouseEvent) :void {
        butPlay.enabled=false;
        butPause.enabled=true;
        butRW.enabled=true;
        butFF.enabled=true;
        butStop.enabled=true;
    dispatchEvent(new MediaControlEvent("PLAY"));
}

private function doPause(event:MouseEvent) :void {
        if (pauseOn){
            butRW.enabled=true;
            butFF.enabled=true;
            butStop.enabled=true;
            pauseOn=false;
        } else {
            butRW.enabled=false;
            butFF.enabled=false;
            butStop.enabled=false;
            pauseOn=true;
        }
        dispatchEvent(new MediaControlEvent("PAUSE"));
}
```

277

```
        private function doStop(event:MouseEvent) :void {
            butPlay.enabled=true;
            butPause.enabled=false;
            butRW.enabled=false;
            butFF.enabled=false;
            butStop.enabled=false;
            dispatchEvent(new MediaControlEvent("STOP"));
    }

        private function doFastForward(event:MouseEvent) :void {
         dispatchEvent(new MediaControlEvent("FF"));
        }
        private function stopFastForward(event:MouseEvent) :void {
         dispatchEvent(new MediaControlEvent("FFEND"));
        }
```

Let's look at the Pause functionality for a moment before we move on. Notice that you have set a Boolean variable in the class called pauseOn. You need to use this because there is no easy way to detect whether the video is paused or unpaused when the pause button is pressed, as it toggles. You know that, by default, when the application loads, the video starts playing and the video is not paused. Therefore, the first time through, you know the pauseOn is false, so you can toggle the status within the pause event handler based on this knowledge, as you will see.

Next, notice that these functions are dispatching their own event: MediaControlEvent. This is an event that you will create by extending the Event class, in order to fire off notifications of stop, play, pause, and so on when the buttons are clicked. You'll create the custom event after finishing the three class files, but let's look at the reasoning for handling events this way.

You want to allow for simple, modular, extendable event handling and registration for any classes that need to use the media control buttons created in the ButtonManager class. Also, you want to allow for the possibility to add parameters to be sent with the returned object, which can be read by interrogation when it is received. You will include a string that shows what the button command was ("Rewind" or "Rewind End," for example). You could, because of the design of this solution, refactor it to send any amount of data that the event handler might need in the future, or indeed allow for any other type of class that might need to use these media control buttons but need extended event data. Additionally you can assign a single event handler function in the listening class to handle any events for which it receives notification. (In a stricter object-oriented project, you would be looking at supporting the use of interfaces through this approach, but that's a subject for another book.)

So let's add an event listener for the new event you are going to create. Add this function into the ButtonManager class. It will register an external handler for any MediaControlEvent.CONTROL_TYPE events.

```
    //This function adds any external objects to the listener list
    //for the mediaControl event
      public function addMediaControlListener(funcObj:Function) :void {
        addEventListener(MediaControlEvent.CONTROL_TYPE, funcObj);
      }
```

> *Adding the listener now is a little back to front, as you should really create the event class first. However, it wouldn't have meant that much to you if you had created the event class first, with no frame of reference to its purpose. Also, I wanted to keep the* ButtonManager *class code all together, as it's a simple class.*

And that's it for the ButtonManager class. You will call this function from the FLA document class, Main.as. This will be the last line of code in the Main.as class:

```
buts.addMediaControlListener(vids.onControlCommand);
```

As you can see, you have defined the Videos.as class function onControlCommand to handle the MediaControlEvent.CONTROL_TYPE events, and you'll add that next.

Save and close both the Main.as and ButtonManager.as classes. They are complete.

Your Main.as file should look like this:

```
package com.fas3.smc{

  import flash.display.MovieClip;
  import com.fas3.smc.Sounds;
  import com.fas3.smc.Videos;
  import com.fas3.smc.ButtonManager;
  import flash.text.TextField;
  import flash.display.SimpleButton;

  public class Main extends MovieClip {
   private var sound1:Sounds;
   private var vids:Videos;
   public var buts:ButtonManager;

  public function Main(){
  vids=new Videos(movScrubber, txtStatus, txtHeadPosition, txtTrackLength);
  addChild(vids);
  buts=new ButtonManager(butRW, butPlay, butPause, butStop, butFF);
  buts.addMediaControlListener(vids.onControlCommand);
  }
  }
  }
```

And your ButtonManager.as file should look like this:

```
package com.fas3.smc{
  import flash.net.*;
  import flash.display.Sprite;
  import flash.display.SimpleButton;
  import flash.events.MouseEvent;
```

```
import flash.events.EventDispatcher;
import flash.events.Event;
import com.fas3.smc.MediaControlEvent;

public class ButtonManager extends Sprite{
 private var butRW:SimpleButton;
 private var butPlay:SimpleButton;
 private var butPause:SimpleButton;
 private var butStop:SimpleButton;
 private var butFF:SimpleButton;
 private var eventDispatcherButton:EventDispatcher;
 private var pauseOn:Boolean=false;

public function ButtonManager(butRW:SimpleButton, ➥
butPlay:SimpleButton, butPause:SimpleButton, butStop:SimpleButton, ➥
butFF:SimpleButton) :void {
    butRW=butRW;
    butPlay=butPlay;
    butPause=butPause;
    butStop=butStop;
    butFF=butFF;

    //Add button listeners
    butRW.addEventListener(MouseEvent.MOUSE_DOWN, doRewind);
    butRW.addEventListener(MouseEvent.CLICK, stopRewind);
    butPlay.addEventListener(MouseEvent.MOUSE_DOWN, doPlay);
    butPause.addEventListener(MouseEvent.MOUSE_DOWN, doPause);
    butStop.addEventListener(MouseEvent.MOUSE_DOWN, doStop);
    butFF.addEventListener(MouseEvent.MOUSE_DOWN, doFastForward);
    butFF.addEventListener(MouseEvent.CLICK, stopFastForward);
        butPlay.enabled=false;
}

//This function adds any external objects to the listener list for
//the mediaControl event
public function addMediaControlListener(funcObj:Function) :void {
 addEventListener(MediaControlEvent.CONTROL_TYPE, funcObj);
}

private function doRewind(evnt:MouseEvent) :void {
 dispatchEvent(new MediaControlEvent("RW"));
}

private function stopRewind(evnt:MouseEvent) :void {
 dispatchEvent(new MediaControlEvent("RWEND"));
}
```

```
private function doPlay(event:MouseEvent) :void {
  butPlay.enabled=false;
  butPause.enabled=true;
  butRW.enabled=true;
  butFF.enabled=true;
  butStop.enabled=true;
 dispatchEvent(new MediaControlEvent("PLAY"));
}

private function doPause(event:MouseEvent) :void {
  if (pauseOn){
      butRW.enabled=true;
      butFF.enabled=true;
      butStop.enabled=true;
      pauseOn=false;
  } else {
      butRW.enabled=false;
      butFF.enabled=false;
      butStop.enabled=false;
      pauseOn=true;
  }
  dispatchEvent(new MediaControlEvent("PAUSE"));
}

private function doStop(event:MouseEvent) :void {
    butPlay.enabled=true;
  butPause.enabled=false;
  butRW.enabled=false;
  butFF.enabled=false;
  butStop.enabled=false;
  dispatchEvent(new MediaControlEvent("STOP"));
}

private function doFastForward(event:MouseEvent) :void {
 dispatchEvent(new MediaControlEvent("FF"));
}

private function stopFastForward(event:MouseEvent) :void {
 dispatchEvent(new MediaControlEvent("FFEND"));
 }
 }
}
```

Finishing the Videos.as class

Open the Videos.as class file and add the following function to it to handle the
MediaControlEvent.CONTROL_TYPE events:

```
public function onControlCommand(evt:MediaControlEvent) :void {
 switch(evt.command){
  //---- PAUSE ----
  case "PAUSE":
  nsVideoPlayer.togglePause();
  txtStatus.text=(txtStatus.text=="Playing")? "Paused" : "Playing";
  break;
  //---- PLAY ----
  case "PLAY":
  nsVideoPlayer.play(flvTarget);
  break;
  //---- STOP ----
  case "STOP":
  nsVideoPlayer.seek(0);
  nsVideoPlayer.pause();
  txtStatus.text="Stopped";
  break;
  //---- RW ----
  case "RW":
  nsVideoPlayer.pause();
  timerRW.start();
  txtStatus.text="Rewind";
  break;
  //---- RW END ----
  case "RWEND":
  nsVideoPlayer.resume();
  timerRW.stop();
  txtStatus.text="Playing";
  break;
  //---- FF ----
  case "FF":
  timerFF.start();
  txtStatus.text="Fast Forward";
  break;
  //---- FF END ----
  case "FFEND":
  timerFF.stop();
  txtStatus.text="Playing";
  break;
 }
}
```

You have used a single switch/case statement to deal with every possibility or delegate it, as appropriate. As previously mentioned, dispatching your own custom event allows you to send extra parameters in the dispatched object, and you are going to be interrogating it for a variable called command. This is a String that contains they type of command that a particular button fired off (such as STOP, RW, FF, or FFEND). Once a case has been made, it will set the status text field to reflect this change and execute the appropriate NetStream function.

The PAUSE case needed some special handling. In ActionScript 2.0, you used the NetStream.pause() function (using true or false as parameters to pause or resume playing). In ActionScript 3.0, the pause() command still works to pause, but it does not resume play if pressed again, and it does not support the use of a Boolean parameter. ActionScript 3.0 has togglePause() and resume() functions, and for the example, you need only the togglePause() function. This doesn't, however, fire off any event or give any indication as to what state it's in, so you need to add some sort of logic to determine what the status text field should show based on whether the video is toggled to paused or resumed. This can be done by checking the status text field's present text every time the pause button is clicked and toggling it accordingly, using the simplified if else statement:

```
txtStatus.text=(txtStatus.text=="Playing")? "Paused" : "Playing";
```

The fast-forward (FF) and fast-forward end (FFEND) events, along with their rewind counterparts (RW and RWEND), also require special consideration. These need to continue to fire and implement as long as the FF or RW buttons are pressed. In order to accommodate this functionality, you must use a couple of Timer class instances for them. Add the following timer code into the constructor of the Video.as class file:

```
timerFF=new Timer(100, 0)
timerFF.addEventListener(TimerEvent.TIMER, this.runFF);
timerRW=new Timer(100, 0)
timerRW.addEventListener(TimerEvent.TIMER, this.runRW);
```

You may notice that these Timer instances are not told to start yet. That is because they should start when the appropriate button is clicked, and this functionality will be dealt with by the onControlCommand event handler. If the case is RW or FF, the appropriate timer gets started, which in turn calls the timer event handlers. Add the following FF and RW timer handler functions to the bottom of the Videos.as class file:

```
private function runFF(event:TimerEvent) :void {
 headPos = nt((nsVideoPlayer.time)+seekRate);
 nsVideoPlayer.seek(headPos);
}

private function runRW(event:TimerEvent) :void {
 headPos = int((nsVideoPlayer.time)-seekRate);
 nsVideoPlayer.seek(headPos);
}
```

Basically, the runFF() function increments the seekRate variable amount to set the headPos number, and then seeks that position in order to fast-forward the playhead. The runRW() function simply decrements this number in order to rewind the playhead. When the FF or RW button is released, the case changes to FFEND or RWEND, the timers are stopped, and the status text is changed to reflect this.

> *This example uses* seek *to fast-forward and rewind through a video, However, H.264-encoded video does not* seek *in the same way as FLV-encoded video. There is a parameter in the metadata of an H.264-encoded file called* seekpoint, *which is an array of saved seekpoints. You can seek directly to these time points, provided that that part of the video has downloaded when you try. However, there are presently a large number of encoded files that do not have this information embedded and are thus not seekable (that is, you cannot fast-forward or rewind through them in this way). This is a limitation of using H.264-based video at this time; however, I have no doubt that this issue will be addressed very soon.*

So finally, you are also finished with the Videos.as file, which looks like this:

```
package com.fas3.smc{
 import flash.net.*;
 import flash.net.NetConnection;
 import flash.net.NetStream;
 import flash.media.Video;
 import flash.display.MovieClip;
 import flash.events.TimerEvent;
 import flash.events.NetStatusEvent;
 import flash.utils.Timer;
 import flash.text.TextField;
 import com.fas3.smc.MediaControlEvent;

 public class Videos extends MovieClip {
  private var vid1:Video;
  private var ncVideoPlayer:NetConnection;
  private var nsVideoPlayer:NetStream;
  private var flvTarget:String;
  private var vidDuration:Number;
  private var trackLength:int;
  private var timerLoading:Timer;
  private var timerPlayHead:Timer;
  private var timerFF:Timer;
  private var timerRW:Timer;
  private var txtStatus:TextField;
  private var txtTrackLength:TextField;
  private var txtHeadPosition:TextField;
  private var bytLoaded:int;
  private var bytTotal:int;
  private var opct:int;
  private var movScrubber:MovieClip;
  private var ns_minutes:Number;
  private var ns_seconds:Number;
  private var seekRate:Number=3;
  private var headPos:Number;
```

```
    // CONSTRUCTOR
    public function Videos(movScrubber:MovieClip, txtStatus:TextField,
 txtHeadPosition:TextField, txtTrackLength:TextField) :void {
    //Set movies and text fields to local references and to start
    //positions and contents
     movScrubber=movScrubber;
     txtStatus=txtStatus;
     txtHeadPosition=txtHeadPosition;
     txtTrackLength=txtTrackLength;
     movScrubber.movLoaderBar.width=1;
     movScrubber.movHead.alpha=0;
     txtStatus.text="AWAITING LOCATION";

     //Instantiate vars and connect NC
     ncVideoPlayer=new NetConnection();
     ncVideoPlayer.connect(null);
     nsVideoPlayer=new NetStream(ncVideoPlayer);
     nsVideoPlayer.bufferTime=3;
 flvTarget="video_final.flv";

 //Add event listeners and handlers
 nsVideoPlayer.addEventListener(NetStatusEvent.NET_STATUS, nsOnStatus);

 //Instantiate display objects
 vid1=new Video();

 // Create a metadata and cue point event handling object
 var objTempClient:Object=new Object();
 objTempClient.onMetaData=mdHandler;
 objTempClient.onCuePoint=cpHandler;
 nsVideoPlayer.client=objTempClient;

 // Add Timers
 timerLoading=new Timer(10, 0);
 timerLoading.addEventListener(TimerEvent.TIMER, this.onLoading);
 timerLoading.start();
 timerPlayHead=new Timer(100, 0);
 timerPlayHead.addEventListener(TimerEvent.TIMER, this.headPosition);
 timerPlayHead.start();
 timerFF=new Timer(100, 0)
 timerFF.addEventListener(TimerEvent.TIMER, this.runFF);
 timerRW=new Timer(100, 0)
 timerRW.addEventListener(TimerEvent.TIMER, this.runRW);

 loadFLV();
 }
```

```
//Load FLV source
  public function loadFLV():void {
   addChild(vid1);
   vid1.x=166;
   vid1.y=77;
   vid1.width=490;
   vid1.height=365;
   vid1.attachNetStream(nsVideoPlayer);
   nsVideoPlayer.play(flvTarget);
  }

//------------- FLV's metadata -----------------------------
  private function mdHandler(obj:Object) :void {
   for (var x in obj){
    trace("METADATA "+x+" is "+obj[x]);
    //If this is the duration, format it and display it
    if(x=="duration"){
     trackLength=obj[x];
      var tlMinutes:int = trackLength/60;
     if (tlMinutes<1){
      tlMinutes=0
     }
      var tlSeconds:int = trackLength%60;
      if (tlSeconds<10) {
     txtTrackLength.text=tlMinutes.toString()+":0"+ tlSeconds.toString();
      }else{
      txtTrackLength.text=tlMinutes.toString()+":"+ tlSeconds.toString();
      }
    }
   }
  }

//------------- FLV's cue points -----------------------------
  private function cpHandler(obj:Object) :void {
   for (var c in obj){
    trace("CUEPOINT "+c+" is "+obj[c]);
    if(c=="parameters"){
     for (var p in obj[c]){
      trace("        PARAMETER "+p+" is "+obj[c][p]);
     }
    }
   }
  }

//--------------- ON STATUS LISTENER -------------------------
  public function nsOnStatus(infoObject:NetStatusEvent) :void{
   for (var prop in infoObject.info) {
      trace("\t"+prop+":\t"+infoObject.info[prop]);
    //If end of video is found, then stop the movHeadSlider moving.
```

```
    if (prop=="code" && infoObject.info[prop]=="NetStream.Play.Stop"){
    txtStatus.text="Stopped";
                    }else if(prop=="code" && infoObject.info[prop]== ➥
"NetStream.Play.Start"){
    txtStatus.text="Playing";
    movScrubber.movHead.alpha=100;
    }
    }
 }


//----------------- HEAD POSITION & COUNT --------------------
private function headPosition(event:TimerEvent) :void {
 //Set Head movie clip to correct width but don't run till we get the
 //track length from the metadata
 if(trackLength>0){
  movScrubber.movHead.width=(nsVideoPlayer.time/(trackLength/100))*4;
 }
 //Set timer display text field
 ns_minutes = int(nsVideoPlayer.time/60);
   ns_seconds = int(nsVideoPlayer.time%60);
   if (ns_seconds<10) {
    txtHeadPosition.text=ns_minutes.toString()+":0"+ ns_seconds.toString();
   }else{
    txtHeadPosition.text=ns_minutes.toString()+":"+ ns_seconds.toString();
   }
}


//------------------- FILE LOADER ----------------------------
// --- Load bar calculations & text field settings----------

  private function onLoading(event:TimerEvent) :void {
   bytLoaded=nsVideoPlayer.bytesLoaded;
   bytTotal=nsVideoPlayer.bytesTotal;
   opct=((nsVideoPlayer.bytesTotal)/100);
   movScrubber.movLoaderBar.width=(Math.floor(bytLoaded/opct))*4;
   if(bytLoaded == bytTotal){
    timerLoading.stop();
       }
      }

//----------------- CONTROL BUTTONS -------------------------

  public function onControlCommand(evt:MediaControlEvent) :void {
    switch(evt.command){
      //---- PAUSE ----
      case "PAUSE":
      nsVideoPlayer.togglePause();
      txtStatus.text=(txtStatus.text=="Playing")? "Paused" : "Playing";
```

```
      break;
      //---- PLAY ----
      case "PLAY":
      nsVideoPlayer.play(flvTarget);
      break;
      //---- STOP ----
      case "STOP":
      nsVideoPlayer.seek(0);
      nsVideoPlayer.pause();
      txtStatus.text="Stopped";
      break;
      //---- RW ----
      case "RW":
      nsVideoPlayer.pause();
      timerRW.start();
      txtStatus.text="Rewind";
      break;
      //---- RW END ----
      case "RWEND":
      nsVideoPlayer.resume();
      timerRW.stop();
      txtStatus.text="Playing";
      break;
      //---- FF ----
      case "FF":
      timerFF.start();
      txtStatus.text="Fast Forward";
      break;
      //---- FF END ----
      case "FFEND":
      timerFF.stop();
      txtStatus.text="Playing";
      break;
    }
  }

  private function runFF(event:TimerEvent) :void {
  headPos = Number(Math.floor(nsVideoPlayer.time)+seekRate);
  nsVideoPlayer.seek(headPos);
}

                 private function runRW(event:TimerEvent) :void {
  headPos = Number(Math.floor(nsVideoPlayer.time)-seekRate);
  nsVideoPlayer.seek(headPos);
             }
         }
       }
```

Creating a custom event

Finally, let's code the custom event class. You'll be amazed how short and very simple it is to create a custom event, so don't panic.

Open a new ActionScript file and save it in com.fas3.smc as MediaControlEvent.as. Now put this code inside it:

```
package com.fas3.smc{
  import flash.events.Event;

  public class MediaControlEvent extends flash.events.Event {
    public static const CONTROL_TYPE:String = "headControl";
    public var command:String;

    public function MediaControlEvent( command:String ) {
      super( CONTROL_TYPE);
      this.command = command;
    }
  }
}
```

This class simply needs to extend the Event class. You add a static constant String variable to identify the event type when you interrogate the returned event object. In this case, you want it to identify itself as type headControl. Then you add as many variables as you want to be able to pass to it and get from it when the event is fired. In this case, you just want to set up a String variable called command. (Remember that you interrogated the returned event object in the MediaControlEvent event handler for the command variable in order to determine which command button was pressed.)

As you saw earlier, a MediaControlEvent instance is created on the fly when you dispatch the event in the ButtonManager.as class, like this:

```
dispatchEvent(new MediaControlEvent("button command"));
```

And that's it. You're finished! Save all your classes and publish your FLA. You'll have a working video player. If you find it doesn't work and you want to see the working version before you track down your bugs, just check it against the complete code you downloaded for this book.

Summary

This chapter covered the basics of video—enough to begin to use it in your own projects. An entire book could be written on the subject, so I've concentrated on the essentials. You've learned how to do the following:

- Load a video or access the camera
- Encode your videos
- Monitor and report on video load and play status

- Read metadata
- Create and read cue point data
- Control video loading and play back

You can experiment with the video player you built in this chapter and see what else you can do with it. For example, you could add filter effects, have multiple sources, or look at live streaming and recording.

We've done video, so now let's trip into sound. Onward!

Chapter 8

USING AUDIO

Sean McSharry

This chapter covers the following topics:

- How to load sound files
- How to control audio behavior
- How to read and display audio ID3 information
- How to display the sound spectrum
- How to control sound volume and panning

The value of sound is subtle and undervalued. Often, it makes the difference between a good site and a great site. Sound is similar in many ways to video in ActionScript 3.0. It contains overhauled properties and functionality, which were long overdue in ActionScript 2.0.

In this chapter, you will learn about the basics of using sound, including how to load, play, and control audio, as well as some of the new, funky sound capabilities that are exposed in ActionScript 3.0. By the end of this chapter, there won't be a dry eye in the house, and you'll be using audio in every site you make (although you probably shouldn't—the watchword is *appropriate*).

For this chapter's example, you'll build a basic audio player that will play any MP3 file. You'll create a comprehensive control and display system for the player.

Importing and converting sound files

ActionScript 3.0 supports files encoded in MP3 or AAC format. But for our examples, we'll look at using MP3 files. Just as with video, there are numerous ways to import sound files before converting them to MP3, but we will stick with loading external MP3 files as we need them. There may be times when pragmatism demands that you load the sound file directly into the timeline; however, these are fairly rare for all the same reasons that they are when considering loading a video into the timeline. Just be aware that although all the examples in this chapter use MP3 files externally, that is not the only choice, although it is usually the best choice.

There are many sound encoders available, both as freeware and to purchase. Here, I'll cover the ubiquitous and freely available iTunes, as well as a sound editor called Soundbooth.

Using iTunes

Though WAV and AIFF formats are very popular, most of the files in your iTunes directories will have been ripped off your CDs or downloaded from the iTunes Store in M4A format. iTunes has the facility to convert unprotected M4A files to MP3. iTunes also has a useful little ID3 editor.

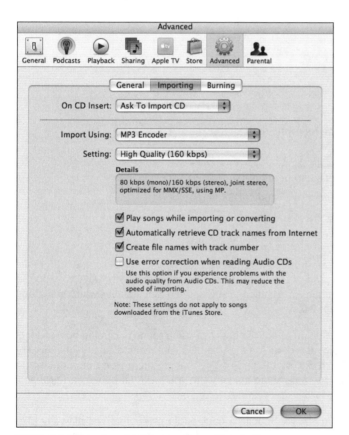

Converting to MP3 format

Here are the steps to convert your sound files to MP3 format:

1. In iTunes, select Edit ➤ Preferences from the main menu, and then choose the Advanced tab in the dialog box that appears.

2. Select the Importing tab. In the Import Using field, choose MP3 Encoder, as shown in Figure 8-1. Then click OK.

3. Go back to your iTunes Library and select the files you want to convert from M4A to MP3.

4. Select Advanced ➤ Convert Selection to MP3 from the main menu, as shown in Figure 8-2.

This will export an MP3 version of the selected sound track to your iTunes directory.

Figure 8-1. PC version of MP3 conversion settings in iTunes

Figure 8-2. Mac version of MP3 conversion settings in iTunes

Adding ID3 information

ID3 information is the MP3 metadata, including the name of the artist, song title, name of the album, and so on. When you convert a file to MP3, it often has no ID3 information attached. You can add ID3 information to your MP3 files in several ways, including by using the iTunes ID3 editor, as described here.

Once you have converted your file to MP3 inside iTunes, you will see a second version of the same track. This is the MP3 version. You can add ID3 information to it as follows:

1. Select the MP3 version, right-click (Control-click on a Mac) it, and choose Get Info from the menu that pops up.

2. in the next window that appears, select the Info tab, as shown in Figure 8-3. Here you can fill in all the ID3 information. After you have entered all the information you want in the fields provided, click the OK button.

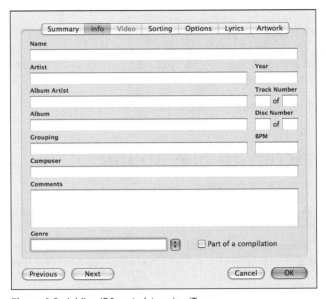

Figure 8-3. Adding ID3 metadata using iTunes

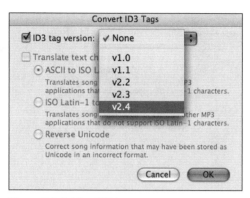

Figure 8-4. Adding ID3 tags

3. With your track still selected, select Advanced ➤ Convert ID3 Tags.

4. In the Convert ID3 Tags dialog box, check the ID3 tag version check box. From that option's drop-down list, shown in Figure 8-4, choose v2.4. Version 2.4 is the latest version of the ID3 tagging standards, and ActionScript 3.0 has no problems reading these tags. Click the OK button.

Your MP3 file will now be saved again with all the ID3 information in place. ActionScript 3.0 will be able to read it.

Using Soundbooth

Recently, Adobe brought out a sound-editing product called Soundbooth (http://www.adobe.com/products/soundbooth/). I saw a demo of this software at the New York Adobe CS3 launch party. It is excellent for your application and website needs, incorporating much of the familiar interface functionality from some Adobe products and taking inspiration from others.

For example, you can look through a sound waveform to see a graphical representation of the sound. If there's an aberration present (a mobile phone ringing for example), you can remove it from the sound waveform graphically—yes, graphically! You can literally cut out (select and cut) the section of the waveform pattern that represents the aberration and then play back the track, and the section is gone. It's obviously not perfect, as you can still lose some of the sound's required waveform at the same time if the frequencies overlap, but it's a great feature and one of many intuitive tools that Soundbooth makes available. It's also full of easy-to-use effects and tasks. I recommend you download it and try it out.

For the task at hand of converting audio files to MP3s, Soundbooth offers a remarkably easy-to-use and quick tool (I did it in about 5 seconds). You can import a music file of any format and encode a version to MP3 format. Just open Soundbooth, open your sound file (WAV file, for example), and save it as type MP3. That's it!

With your MP3 files ready, you can now use ActionScript to play them.

Using ActionScript to play sound

Seven main classes are associated directly with sound:

- Sound: Makes it possible to create a Sound object to load, control, and access metadata from the MP3 file you are loading.

- SoundChannel: Allows you to treat each sound you load as a separate channel, so you can control the sound, get/set its playhead position, and assign a SoundTransform object.

- SoundLoaderContext: Provides contextual information for the Sound class at load time.
- SoundTransform: Allows you to control the volume and panning of your loaded sound.
- SoundMixer: Provides global sound control.
- ID3Info: Contains properties that reflect ID3 metadata.
- Microphone: Lets you capture audio from a microphone attached to the computer that is running Flash Player.

There are some other classes without which we couldn't use sound, such as the URLRequest class, which we use to load the sound file. You'll see how to use those classes in the examples, but the following sections concentrate on the direct sound classes.

Accessing sound files with the Sound class

The Sound class (flash.media.Sound) lets you create a new Sound object, load and play an external MP3 file into that object, close the sound stream, and access data about the sound, such as information about the number of bytes in the stream and ID3 metadata. More detailed control of the sound is performed through the sound source—the SoundChannel or Microphone object for the sound—and through the properties in the SoundTransform class that control the output of the sound to the computer's speakers. Table 8-1 briefly summarizes the public properties of the Sound class.

Table 8-1. Sound class public properties

Property	Type	Description
bytesLoaded	uint	Returns the currently available number of bytes in this Sound object
bytesTotal	int	Returns the total number of bytes in this Sound object
id3	ID3Info	Provides access to the metadata that is part of an MP3 file
isBuffering	Boolean	Returns the buffering state of external MP3 files
length	Number	Returns the length of the current sound in milliseconds
url	String	Returns the URL from which this sound was loaded

Controlling sound channels with the SoundChannel class

The SoundChannel class (flash.media.SoundChannel) controls a sound in an application. Each sound playing is assigned to a sound channel, and the application can have multiple sound channels that are mixed together. The SoundChannel class contains a stop() method, properties for monitoring the amplitude (volume) of the channel, and a property for setting a SoundTransform object to the channel. Table 8-2 briefly summarizes the public properties of the SoundChannel class.

Table 8-2. SoundChannel class public properties

Property	Type	Description
leftPeak	Number	The current amplitude (volume) of the left channel, from 0 (silent) to 1 (full amplitude)
position	Number	The current position of the playhead within the sound
rightPeak	Number	The current amplitude of the right channel, from 0 (silent) to 1 (full amplitude)
soundTransform	SoundTransform	The SoundTransform object assigned to the sound channel

Doing security checks with the SoundLoaderContext class

The SoundLoaderContext class (flash.media.SoundLoaderContext) provides security checks for SWF files that load sound. SoundLoaderContext objects are passed as an argument to the constructor and the load() method of the Sound class, and specify things like preload buffer size. Table 8-3 briefly summarizes the public properties of the SoundLoader class.

Table 8-3. SoundLoader class public properties

Property	Type	Description
bufferTime	Number	Returns the number of seconds to preload a streaming sound into a buffer before the sound starts to stream; set to 1000 milliseconds by default
checkPolicyFile	Boolean	Specifies whether Flash Player should try to download a cross-domain policy file from the loaded sound's server before beginning to load the sound; set to false by default

Controlling volume and panning with the SoundTransform class

The SoundTransform class (flash.media.SoundTransform) allows control of volume and panning. Microphone, NetStream, SimpleButton, SoundChannel, SoundMixer, and Sprite objects all contain a SoundTransform property, the value of which is a SoundTransform object. Table 8-4 briefly summarizes the public properties of the SoundTransform class.

Table 8-4. SoundTransform class public properties

Property	Type	Description
leftToLeft	Number	A value ranging from 0 (none) to 1 (all), specifying how much of the left input is played in the left speaker
leftToRight	Number	A value ranging from 0 (none) to 1 (all), specifying how much of the left input is played in the right speaker
pan	Number	The left-to-right panning of the sound, ranging from -1 (full pan left) to 1 (full pan right), with 0 (the default) as equal panning left and right, for central, balanced sound
rightToLeft	Number	A value ranging from 0 (none) to 1 (all), specifying how much of the right input is played in the left speaker
rightToRight	Number	A value ranging from 0 (none) to 1 (all), specifying how much of the right input is played in the right speaker
volume	Number	The volume, ranging from 0 (silent) to 1 (full volume)

Controlling sounds globally with the SoundMixer class

The SoundMixer class (flash.media.SoundMixer) contains static properties and methods for global sound control. The ActionScript 3.0 documentation states that "The SoundMixer class controls embedded streaming sounds in a SWF; it does not control dynamically created Sound objects (that is, Sound objects created in ActionScript)," However, this is not strictly true. Although the public properties reflect this position, the public methods it exposes do not. In fact, one of the public methods is extremely useful for any sound you create. This is the computeSpectrum() method, which you will use in this chapter's example to good effect. The only problem with the public methods is that because they are global, they affect every sound that is playing, whether embedded, dynamically loaded, or part of a video sound track.

The public properties of the SoundMixer class are specifically directed at embedded sound, and you probably won't use them often. In contrast, the SoundMixer class's public methods are generic and useful. Table 8-5 describes the public methods of the SoundMixer class.

Table 8-5. SoundMixer class public methods

Method	Type	Description
areSoundsInaccessible()	Boolean	Determines whether any sounds are not accessible due to security restrictions.
computeSpectrum (outputArray,FFTMode, stretchFactor)	void	Takes a snapshot of the current sound wave and places it into the specified ByteArray object. outputArray is a ByteArray, FFTMode is a Boolean (false by default), and stretchFactor is an int (0 by default).
stopAll()	void	Stops all sounds currently playing.

Getting ID3 data with the ID3Info class

The ID3Info class (flash.media.ID3Info) contains properties that reflect ID3 metadata. Essentially, it translates native ID3 tags into something more legible. For example, it allows you to access the TPE1 tag, which contains the artist name, by allowing you to reference it as ID3Info.artist. This translation is not strictly necessary, but it makes things a little easier on the eyes and the brain. You can get additional metadata for MP3 files by accessing the id3 property of the Sound class; for example, mySound.id3.TIME. For more information, see the Sound.id3 entry in Table 8-1 and the ID3 tag definitions at http://www.id3.org. Table 8-6 briefly summarizes the public properties of the ID3Info class.

Table 8-6. ID3Info class public properties

Property	Type	Description
album	String	The name of the album; corresponds to the ID3 2.0 tag TALB
artist	String	The name of the artist; corresponds to the ID3 2.0 tag TPE1
comment	String	A comment about the recording; corresponds to the ID3 2.0 tag COMM
genre	String	The genre of the song; corresponds to the ID3 2.0 tag TCON
songName	String	The name of the song; corresponds to the ID3 2.0 tag TIT2
track	String	The track number; corresponds to the ID3 2.0 tag TRCK
year	String	The year of the recording; corresponds to the ID3 2.0 tag TYER

Using a microphone with the Microphone class

The Microphone class (flash.media.Microphone) is primarily for use with a server, such as the Flash Media Server (FMS) or the Flex server. However, you can also use the Microphone class in a limited fashion without a server—for example, to transmit sound from the microphone through the speakers on the local computer. You attach a Microphone object to a NetStream object to stream audio from a microphone. Table 8-7 briefly summarizes the public properties of the Microphone class.

Table 8-7. Microphone class public properties

Property	Type	Description
activityLevel	Number	The amount of sound the microphone is detecting
gain	Number	The microphone gain; that is, the amount by which the microphone should multiply the signal before transmitting it
index	int	The index of the microphone, as reflected in the array returned by Microphone.names

Property	Type	Description
muted	Boolean	Specifies whether the user has denied access to the microphone (true) or allowed access (false)
name	String	The name of the current sound-capture device, as returned by the sound-capture hardware
names	Array	The names of all available sound-capture devices
rate	int	The rate at which the microphone is capturing sound, in kilohertz
silenceLevel	Number	The amount of sound required to activate the microphone and dispatch the activity event
silenceTimeout	int	The number of milliseconds between the time the microphone stops detecting sound and the time the activity event is dispatched
soundTransform	SoundTransform	Controls the sound of this Microphone object when it is in loopback mode
useEchoSuppression	Boolean	Returns true if echo suppression is enabled; false otherwise

Understanding the basics of a sound player application

For a sound player, the first thing you want to do is define and load an external audio source (an MP3 file). Let's break down the most basic list of definitions and commands:

```
var audioLocation:String;        //Define the audio source
var URLReq:URLRequest;        //Define a URL request object
var snd1:Sound;          //Define a new Sound object

//Instantiate audio location string
audioLocation = "song1.mp3";
//Instantiate URLrequest to call audio source
URLReq = new URLRequest(audioLocation);
//Instantiate Sound instance
snd1 = new Sound();

//Call the Sound object's load function to load audio source, using the
//URLrequest
snd1.load(URLReq);

snd1.play();        //Finally play the audio source. Phew!
```

> *Some download manager software can cause the Flash Player to fail to load the MP3 file you are calling, as it will intercept the response and bypass Flash. There is a way around this. As with video files, the Flash Player reads the file header, not the file suffix, to assess the file type. This means you can give your audio file any suffix type you like. So, for example, you might rename a file called* sound.mp3 *to* sound.fsf, *and this would load and play just fine.*

Preloading a buffer

The previous code is the basic implementation, from defining the audio source to playing it. It doesn't take into consideration the use of a buffer to partially preload the sound file both before and as it plays, which on the whole, is usually essential. As with video, sound can be of low or high quality, and these days, for the sake of an exceptional experience, we err toward much better quality. This is why you need to consider and test buffer size. For seamless playback, you want to allow enough of the sound file to download before beginning to play it, to prevent the playhead from catching up with the progressive download head. To create a buffer that you can pass to the Sound class's load() function, you must use the SoundLoaderContext class.

> *Using the* Sound.load() *function can allow you to truly preload the entire audio source before commanding it to* play(). *Add an event listener on the* Sound *object to listen for the* Event.COMPLETE *event before playing. Although this offers little in the way of runtime buffering, if your site/application has enough time due to its design, consider preloading as many of your sound files as possible this way.*

Here's the basic code with the buffer preloader added:

```
//Define the audio source
private var audioLocation:String;
//Define a URL request object
private var URLReq:URLRequest;
//Define new Sound object
private var snd1:Sound;
//Define a buffer
private var buffer:SoundLoaderContext;
//Instantiate audio location string
audioLocation = "song1.mp3";
//Instantiate URLrequest to call audio source
URLReq = new URLRequest(audioLocation);
/Instantiate Sound instance
snd1 = new Sound();/
//Create audio buffer size (in seconds)
buffer = new SoundLoaderContext(5000);
```

```
//Call the Sound object's load function to load audio source,
//using the URLrequest and setting a buffer
snd1.load(URLReq, buffer);

//Finally play the audio source. Phew!
snd1.play();
```

This version strictly separates the declarations, definitions, and commands from one another. These classes could be defined, instantiated, and given much of the information they need all in one go, condensing ten lines of code into four:

```
//Define new Sound object
private var snd1:Sound;
//Pass the length of the buffer in milliseconds to the new instance of
//the SoundLoaderContext object as it is instantiated.
var buffer:SoundLoaderContext=new SoundLoaderContext(5000);
//Call the Sound object's load function implicitly at instantiation by
//loading the audio source in the  URLrequest object instantiation
//and set the buffer
snd1=new Sound(new URLRequest(song), buffer);

//Play (offset , number of loops)
snd1.play(30000,2);
```

However, for the sake of practicality, good convention, and easy maintenance, I don't recommend condensing the process quite this much, and you will see that I have taken the middle ground in the code for this chapter's example.

OK, so you've seen how to define a sound source, load it, and play it, but you're probably going to want to be able to stop it, pause it, rewind, and fast-forward it, not to mention control the volume and panning of the audio. And believe it or not, you can even display its sound spectrum. Well, relax—these things are all pretty easy to do.

Pausing sound

Pausing is one of a few areas of sound usage in ActionScript 3.0 that shows that Adobe needs to address this functionality a little more seriously. There is no actual pause functionality in the Sound class, nor in any other sound-related classes. You therefore need to use a simple hack. Because you will need to stop the sound playing to make it appear that it is paused, you will need to use the play() command to start it again. But you want to play from the point where the user clicked the pause button the first time, right? And simply playing it again will just start the sound file from the beginning. Luckily, the SoundChannel class has a property called position, which you can use to get the position of the playhead when the pause button is clicked the first time. You store the position before calling the SoundChannel.stop() method, and then use that as an offset when the pause button is clicked again, and restart playing from this offset.

So let's consider the variables you need for the pause functionality to work. You need to set a Boolean variable to store the status of the pause button and a Number variable to store the position of the playhead:

```
private var pauseStatus:Boolean;
private var playHeadPosition:Number;
```

Now you need the code to use these when the pause button is toggled:

```
if (pauseStatus){
    sc = snd1.play(playHeadPosition,1);//Play offset , number of loops
    pauseStatus=false;
} else {
    playHeadPosition=sc.position;
    sc.stop();
    pauseStatus=true;
}
```

As you can see, you check to see if the status of pause is true. If it's not, then you store the playhead position, stop() the SoundChannel, and set the pause status to true. If it is true, you play the sound file from the offset position stored in the playHeadPosition variable, and then set the pause status to false. So, even though you have no built-in, native pause functionality, you can emulate it relatively easily and reliably.

Stopping sound

Stopping a sound file playing is very straightforward. Let's assume you have a Sound instance called snd1. You can stop it as follows:

```
Private var snd1:Sound;
. . .
snd1.close();
```

However, you should consider that you cannot use the Sound.close() method once the sound file has finished loading. If you try, you will get the following error:

```
Error: Error #2029: This URLStream object does not have a stream opened
```

This is because it is designed to close the sound file download stream, and this will execute without error only if the sound file is still in the process of downloading. Once it has finished downloading, issuing the Sound.close() command will have no effect on the playing sound file. Also, in order to restart a sound file downloading once the Sound.close() method has been successfully executed on it, you must reissue the load() command first. Whatever amount of the sound file that had downloaded at the point where you issued the Sound.close() command will remain in memory and can be played as normal.

The simple, reliable, and generally best choice is to use the SoundChannel.stop() function. as described in the previous section. It will still keep the channel open and the sound file loading into memory, but loading another sound file will replace it.

If you want to be thorough, you can have the stop button execute Sound.close() if the file is still downloading and SoundChannel.stop() if it has finished downloading.

> As your code becomes more advanced, it will be important for you to learn about the try...catch method of error handling for checking if a file is still downloading. I suggest you look into this in more detail when you finish this book. You might check out Adobe's excellent MXNA blog aggregator (http://weblogs.macromedia.com/mxna/) to start learning more about topics such as error handling. This aggregator provides links to the blog sites of some of the most talented developers in the world.

Fast-forwarding and rewinding sound

For fast-forward (FF) and rewind (RW) functionality, you need to define timers, so they can run continuously while the user is pressing the FF or RW button. You will notice that you don't start these timers right away.

```
timerFF=new Timer(100, 0)
timerFF.addEventListener(TimerEvent.TIMER, this.runFF);
timerRW=new Timer(100, 0)
timerRW.addEventListener(TimerEvent.TIMER, this.runRW);
```

When the FF or RW button is pressed or released, it will start or stop the timer. So, for example, when the user presses the RW button, you will start the timer:

```
timerRW.start();
```

and when the user releases the RW button, you stop the timer:

```
timerRW.stop();
```

The important thing is what the timer handler code does.

```
On FF press:
  playHeadPosition=sc.position;
  sc.stop();
  timerFF.start();
```

First, you store the present playhead position. Then you stop the track playing (otherwise, you'll hear multiple versions of the track playing when you release the FF button and it starts playing the track again). Finally, start the FF timer. The FF Timer event handler will simply carry out the calculation of the increment of the playhead position by whatever increment you choose (in milliseconds) and move the playhead bar to represent the present position:

```
playHeadPosition+=1000;
movScrubber.movHead.width= ➥
((Math.floor(playHeadPosition)/trueChronoLength)*100)*4;
```

305

Once the FF button is released, the timer is stopped, and the SoundChannel plays the sound from the offset position defined by the new playHeadPosition variable.

```
timerFF.stop();
sc = snd1.play(playHeadPosition,1);//(Play offset , number of loops)
```

The rewind code is exactly the same, except that the Timer event handler decrements the playhead position.

```
playHeadPosition-=1000;
```

Obviously, these are the bare bones of the functionality. In a real-world application, you need to address the fast-forwarding and rewinding not extending beyond the beginning or end of the actual play time. Also, you need to take care of little details, like preventing the FF and RW buttons from being engaged if the sound is not already playing, and making sure the modified volume and pan values are stored and reapplied once the sound is restarted.

Controlling volume

So now you need to control how loud the sound file plays back. For this, you need to create some form of graphical volume-control mechanism for the user. This can be as simple as an input text field or as smooth as a volume dial with meter display.

The important things here are the SoundTransform and the SoundChannel classes. The SoundTransform class allows you to set the volume and pan settings for the SoundChannel instance to which it is assigned. Remember that, in turn, the SoundChannel instance will already be assigned to a Sound class instance.

```
//Import required classes
import flash.media.SoundChannel;
  import flash.media.SoundTransform;
  . . .
  //Declare SoundTransform variable
  private var sc:SoundChannel;
private var stVolume:SoundTransform;
  . . .
  //Instantiate SoundTransform object
stVolume=new SoundTransform();
  . . .
  //Set up SoundChannel
  sc = snd1.play(0,1);//Play offset , number of loops
  sc.soundTransform=stVolume;
```

You will fire off the volume adjustment event by whatever means are appropriate, based on the type of volume-control interface you have implemented. For example, if you used volume-up and volume-down buttons, you would assign an event listener to those buttons for when a MouseEvent.MOUSE_DOWN event is fired. The event handler code would look like this:

```
stVolume.volume=soundVariable;
sc.soundTransform=stVolume;
```

Notice that this takes soundVariable as a number. This will be a number you feed in directly, or it will be factored on the scale of your volume slide, depending on how you have developed your volume control. Once you have set it, you must reapply the SoundTransform to the SoundChannel class's own SoundTransform property, which expects a value in the range 0.0 to 1.0. In this chapter's example, you will see what this process looks like using a slider to set the volume.

And that's it. That's how easy controlling the volume is. Next, we'll look at controlling the sound panning.

Controlling panning

Controlling the panning of the sound that is playing is almost exactly the same as controlling its volume. You use the same classes (SoundChannel and SoundTransform) and instantiate them as shown in the preceding section. You actually use the same SoundTransform instance to control both the volume and panning on its assigned SoundChannel object. The only difference is that you need a different event handler, as a different control is being used. But inside the event handler, the only difference is that you set the pan and not the volume.

```
stVolume.pan=soundVariable;
sc.soundTransform=stVolume;
```

Remember that the pan has a range of -1.0 to 1.0 (with 0 the default central setting), unlike the volume range. You should take this into account when deciding what values to send to the event handler for the pan functionality.

Displaying the sound spectrum

So would you like to visualize the sound? I'm sure you've dreamed of being able to make graphic equalizers to represent the sound file you were playing, or of being able to interpret the sound file waveform frequencies into beautiful aesthetic patterns. I know I have. I even faked a graphic equalizer in one of my early portfolio sites. Well, I'm not much of a back-end coder, so I couldn't mash one up properly. It looked OK, but it didn't do anything magical because it couldn't read the sound frequency data. Well, you'll be pleased to know that's all changed with the advent of ActionScript 3.0 and the introduction of the SoundMixer.computeSpectrum() function.

Now I won't lie; the SoundMixer class doesn't do all the work. In fact, to be fair, it really just produces all the frequency information and populates the ByteArray it must be passed, with 512 floating-point values representing either the high to low sound frequencies of both the left and right channels or a fast Fourier transform (FFT) algorithm of the sound signal. The first 256 floating-point values represent the left channel, and the second 256 represent the right channel.

> If you want to understand more about the FFT algorithm, I suggest you dust off your advanced mathematics degree and Google it. Or you can just accept that we can use this algorithm.

Adobe's choice of 512 floating-point values was probably driven by optimization, as FFT algorithms can be represented by a range of return values above and below 512. Additionally, you should be aware that it samples *all* the sounds playing globally as one sound sample, and not any one specific sound file you have loaded. All the sexy stuff is done by the ByteArray, BitmapData, or whatever display vehicle class you decide to use.

> *A tip for improving the performance of the spectrum computation is to just use the first or last 256 floating-point values (left or right side only), duplicating the data. The audio data will often be very similar, and you skip 256 iterations per timed interval.*

You will need to import these classes:

```
import flash.media.SoundMixer;
import flash.display.BitmapData;
import flash.utils.ByteArray;
```

Declare the ByteArray variable:

```
private var baSpectrum:ByteArray;
```

Then instantiate the ByteArray class to pass to the SoundMixer.computeSpectrum() function:

```
baSpectrum = new ByteArray();
```

This ByteArray will be populated with the 512 values, representing the frequencies from the snapshot the computeSpectrum() function has taken. Each one of these frequency entries has a value range of -1.0 through 1.0. You need this to happen repeatedly for as long as the sound file is playing, and as you will want to update the visual representation of the playing sound wave constantly, you will need to put this on a Timer event.

```
timerSpectrum=new Timer(100, 0);
timerSpectrum.addEventListener(TimerEvent.TIMER, onSpectrum);
```

Notice you haven't started the timer yet. This is because you don't want to run the computeSpectrum() function when the sound isn't playing and there is consequently no spectrum to compute. Also, this would lead to unnecessary processor overhead. So you'll need to start the timer every time the sound file is played, and stop it every time it is paused. fast-forwarded, rewound, or stopped. (You'll see the code permutations for the various play statuses in this chapter's example.) You need to add the following code where appropriate in the command control function:

```
timerSpectrum.start();
. . .
timerSpectrum.stop();
```

So now let's look at the onSpectrum Timer event handler function code, as this is where the action is. You will pass the ByteArray instance to the computeSpectrum() function every time you loop through. As I mentioned earlier, this will be populated with the 512 frequencies that the spectrum snapshot has taken at that moment:

```
SoundMixer.computeSpectrum(outputArray, FFTMode, stretchFactor);
```

This function accepts the following parameters:

- outputArray: A ByteArray object that holds the values associated with the sound. If any sounds are not available due to security restrictions (areSoundsInaccessible == true), the outputArray object is left unchanged. If all sounds are stopped, the outputArray object is filled with zeros. This parameter is mandatory.

- FFTMode: A Boolean value indicating whether an FFT is performed on the sound data first. The default is false. Setting this parameter to true causes the method to return a frequency spectrum instead of the raw sound wave. In the frequency spectrum, low frequencies are represented on the left and high frequencies are on the right.

- stretchFactor: An int value indicating the resolution of the sound samples. With the default value of 0, data is sampled at 44.1 KHz; with a value of 1, data is sampled at 22.05 KHz; with a value of 2, data is sampled at 11.025 KHz; and so on.

This takes care of constant sound wave frequency data gathering. Now it's time to look at the other side of the coin: displaying this data aesthetically. There are innumerable ways to display such a large amount of frequency data, and indeed this is one of the features that makes the computeSpectrum() function so powerful.

Let's consider a couple of the simpler display implementations: an equalizer bar chart and a sound wave display. For the purposes of this example, assume you have created a new Sprite instance called grFrequency. So let's look at the Timer event handler function code:

```
//----------------COMPUTE SPECTRUM -----------------------
    private function onSpectrum(evt:Event):void{
      SoundMixer.computeSpectrum(baSpectrum, false);
      grFrequency.graphics.clear();
      grFrequency.graphics.beginFill(0x00FF00);
      grFrequency.graphics.moveTo(0, 0);
      for (var i:int=0; i<512; i+=1) {
        grFrequency.graphics.drawRect(i, 0, 1, (baSpectrum.readFloat() * 150));
      }
    }
```

The first line of the function deals with actually computing the spectrum and passing it into the baSpectrum ByteArray. I have set the false value on the FFTMode simply as a reminder that this is the type of display I want (as noted earlier, by default, the FFTMode is already false). As a simplification, if the FFTMode is set to false, you will produce a sound wave visualization; if it is set to true, you will produce a bar chart visualization.

The next three lines are all initializing the graphics to display the sound wave or bar chart. You clear the graphic, set the color, and move to the start position, before beginning the drawing cycle.

Following this, you simply loop through the 512 ByteArray values by calling the ByteArray.readFloat() method to get the value, and then display it using the graphics.drawRect method, which takes the x and y coordinates and the width and height as parameter values:

```
public function drawRect(x:Number, y:Number, width:Number, height:Number):void
```

You calculate the bar height as a factor of the -1.0 through 1.0 value that the readFloat() function returns. This needs to take into account the size of the display area you have available and be adjusted accordingly.

Handling ID3 events

Even though the recommended standard for ID3 metadata is not always fully implemented, what we do have from most MP3 files is still very useful. You can get data like the artist name, the track name, the album title, year of production, and so on. Table 8-8 lists commonly available ID3 tags, which ActionScript allows for access to through the ID3Info class.

Table 8-8. Common ID3 tags

ID3 2.0 tag	Corresponding ActionScript property
COMM	Sound.id3.comment
TALB	Sound.id3.album
TCON	Sound.id3.genre
TIT2	Sound.id3.songName
TPE1	Sound.id3.artist
TRCK	Sound.id3.track
TYER	Sound.id3.year

Table 8-9 lists ID3 tags that *are* supported but do *not* have predefined properties in the ID3Info class (you could extend the ID3Info class in order to add them). You can access these directly by calling Sound.id3.TFLT, Sound.id3.TIME, for example.

Table 8-9. Supported ID3 tags without predefined properties

ID3 2.0 tag	Description
TFLT	File type
TIME	Time
TIT1	Content group description
TIT2	Title/song name/content description
TIT3	Subtitle/description refinement

ID3 2.0 tag	Description
TKEY	Initial key
TLAN	Languages
TLEN	Length
TMED	Media type
TOAL	Original album/movie/show title
TOFN	Original filename
TOLY	Original lyricists/text writers
TOPE	Original artists/performers
TORY	Original release year
TOWN	File owner/licensee
TPE1	Lead performers/soloists
TPE2	Band/orchestra/accompaniment
TPE3	Conductor/performer refinement
TPE4	Interpreted, remixed, or otherwise modified by
TPOS	Part of a set
TPUB	Publisher
TRCK	Track number/position in set
TRDA	Recording dates
TRSN	Internet radio station name
TRSO	Internet radio station owner
TSIZ	Size
TSRC	International Standard Recording Code (ISRC)
TSSE	Software/hardware and settings used for encoding
TYER	Year
WXXX	URL link frame

Now that you know the kind of information the ID3 metadata tags can contain, let's look at how you go about getting that information out of the tags.

First, make sure you have imported the Sound and ID3Info.

```
import flash.media.Sound;
import flash.media.ID3Info;
```

Next, set up your ID3 event listener:

```
snd1.addEventListener(Event.ID3, id3Handler)
```

Finally, add the ID3 event-handling code. I have written this with two possibilities in mind: you might simply want to loop through all the fields in the ID3 metadata, just to see what's in there, and you might want to represent a few of the more common (and indeed, essential) pieces of information in on-screen text fields (in this example, the artist and song name):

```
function id3Handler(event:Event):void {
  var song:Sound = Sound(event.target);
  var songInfo:ID3Info = ID3Info(song.id3);
  for (var xx in songInfo){
    trace("ID3 - "+xx+" is "+songInfo[xx]);
  }
  txtArtist.text=songInfo.artist;
  txtTitle.text=songInfo.songName;
}
```

You will use these techniques in the sound player you'll build next, to see what is in the ID3 metadata and to display the artist name and track title while an MP3 file is playing.

Building a sound player

Now that you've been introduced to the basics of manipulating sound in ActionScript 3.0, including the relevant classes and common functionality, let's put this all together to create an MP3 player. The MP3 player will look like Figure 8-5. As you can see, it has all the typical features you would expect in an MP3 player.

You'll use the following files for the sound player:

- AudioDemo_final.fla
- Main.as
- Sounds.as
- ButtonManager.as
- MediaControlEvent.as

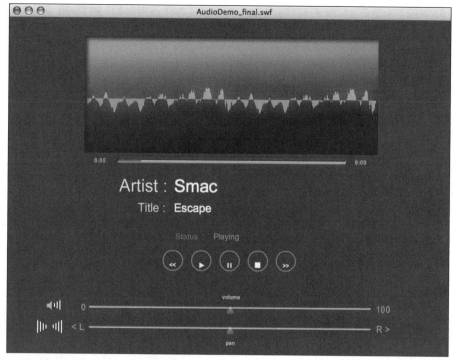

Figure 8-5. The finished MP3 player

Setting up the project

As with the video player, I have created the physical assets and initial FLA file (AudioDemo_final.fla) to save you some time on this example. To begin, locate the AudioDemo_final.fla in the code you downloaded for this book and open it.

Now you need to do a quick check, The document class is Main.as, and you need to make sure it is selected. In the Flash IDE, select File ➤ Publish Settings. In the window that appears, click the Settings button to open the ActionScript 3.0 Settings screen, as shown in Figure 8-6.

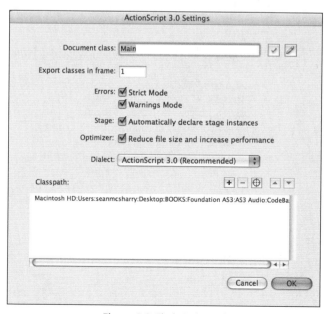

Figure 8-6. Flash ActionScript 3.0 Settings screen

313

In the Document class text field, enter **Main**, if it's not already there. This will load the Main.as file as the document class.

Next, click the target button to the right of the Classpath: heading and navigate to the directory location where you have stored your class files. When you select it, it should appear very much as mine does in Figure 8-6.

Creating the Main.as file

In the Main.as file, you will create the instances of the Sounds class and button controls. You will need to create, address, and display buttons, an audio spectrum, and text fields, so you need to import the Flash classes for these.

> It is common practice to keep your class and resource files in a deeper directory structure that reflects the domain under which it is stored and served. For example, if this book's files were on a domain called www.fas3.com, the classes on this domain would be stored in a directory structure that most competent object-oriented developers would expect to be com.fas3.classes (or similar). Indeed, this is almost the exact package structure I have used. This is to avoid class namespace clashes. A package declaration for the domain would look like this:

```
package com.fas3.smc{
  class. . .
}
```

> This is an approach you would be well advised to start using regularly.

First, create a new .as file and add the following code to it:

```
package com.fas3.smc{
    import flash.display.MovieClip;
    import com.fas3.smc.Sounds;
    import com.fas3.smc.ButtonManager;
    import flash.text.TextField;
    import flash.display.SimpleButton;

    public class Main extends MovieClip {

    }
}
```

Save this file as Main.as in your work directory.

Now it's time to declare the Sound and ButtonManager classes and create the Main constructor, as follows:

```
package com.fas3.smc{
  import flash.display.MovieClip;
  import com.fas3.smc.Sounds;
  import com.fas3.smc.ButtonManager;
  import flash.text.TextField;
  import flash.display.SimpleButton;

  public class Main extends MovieClip {
    private var soundManager:Sounds;
    private var buts:ButtonManager;

    public function Main(){
    }
  }
}
```

This completes the base Main.as FLA document class. This won't do much at present, but you'll add the calls for the Sounds and ButtonManager classes after you've created them.

Creating the Sounds.as file

The Sounds.as class will handle all the sound requirements. Create this file now and save it in your project folder.

Now, let's add the import and variable declaration statements. As with the video player example in the previous chapter, you're creating these all in advance, so you don't need to repeatedly return to the top of the class file and import a class or define a variable. The naming convention should give you some clues as to the code you will be creating. Add the following to your Sounds.as class:

```
package com.fas3.smc{
  import flash.media.Sound;
  import flash.media.SoundChannel;
  import flash.media.SoundLoaderContext;
  import flash.media.SoundTransform;
  import flash.media.ID3Info;
  import flash.events.Event;
  import flash.display.MovieClip;
  import flash.net.URLRequest;
  import flash.text.TextField;
  import flash.utils.Timer;
  import flash.events.TimerEvent;
  import fl.controls.Slider;
  import fl.events.SliderEvent;
```

```
public class Sounds extends MovieClip {
  private var snd1:Sound;
  private var sc:SoundChannel;
  private var buffer:SoundLoaderContext;
  private var timerLoading:Timer;
  private var timerPlayHead:Timer;
  private var timerFF:Timer;
  private var timerRW:Timer;
  private var barWid:int = 200;
  private var barHi:int = 5;
  private var bytLoaded:int;
  private var bytTotal:int;
  private var pctLoaded:int;
  private var trueChronoLength:Number;
  private var txtStatus:TextField;
  private var txtTrackLength:TextField;
  private var txtHeadPosition:TextField;
  private var txtArtist:TextField;
  private var txtTitle:TextField;
  private var movScrubber:MovieClip;
  private var multiplier:Number;
  private var nsMinutes:Number;
  private var nsSeconds:Number;
  private var pauseStatus:Boolean;
  private var playHeadPosition:Number;
  private var volumeSlider:Slider;
  private var panSlider:Slider;
  private var stVolume:SoundTransform;
  private var tempVol:Number=0.5;
  private var tempPan:Number=0;
  private var trackEnd:Boolean;
  private var trackStart:Boolean;

  }
}
```

There's quite a lot there I know, especially in the variable definitions. The sound manager needs to define text fields, components, temporary minders, multiple integers and numbers for calculations, timers, and so on. It's a busy bunny. But don't let this put you off. Everything will become clear as you step through each part of the process of creating an MP3 player.

Let's continue with the constructor for your Sound.as class file. This class needs to be passed references to the physical movie clips and text fields on the stage, which I have created for your convenience. Add the constructor function at the bottom of the file:

```
public function Sounds(movScrubber:MovieClip, txtStatus: ➡
TextField, txtHeadPosition:TextField, txtTrackLength:TextField, ➡
txtArtist:TextField, txtTitle:TextField, volumeSlider:Slider, ➡
panSlider:Slider){
```

```
//Set movies and text fields to local references and to start
//positions and contents
this.movScrubber=movScrubber;
this.txtStatus=txtStatus;
this.txtHeadPosition=txtHeadPosition;
this.txtTrackLength=txtTrackLength;
this.txtArtist=txtArtist;
this.txtTitle=txtTitle;
this.volumeSlider=volumeSlider;
this.panSlider=panSlider;
}
```

As you can see, you're already starting to use your defined variables. In this case, you're using them to store a local reference to the movie clip, text field, and component references passed into the constructor.

Now you need to define a function to play the sound file you pass to it and listen for any events. Add the following to the bottom of the file:

```
public function loadSong(song:String):void{
  snd1=new Sound(new URLRequest(song));
  snd1.addEventListener(Event.ID3, id3Handler)
}
```

In this example, you will listen only for the ID3 events, as you will display some important ID3 metadata. The first line of this function is a compound load statement. It declares a new Sound instance, using a URLRequest instance it creates on the fly, to load the song you have passed to it.

Loading the sound file

I have provided a sample sound file to use with this application, called song1.mp3 (not very original, I know). Check out your downloaded code for this file, and see the Creative Commons license with which it is issued (http://www.videojournal.tv/FAS3/licence.html). You can, of course, use your own sound file instead.

Now let's return to the Main.as file and add the instantiation of the Sound.as class file and subsequently call its loadSong() function. Add the following to the bottom of the file:

```
soundManager=new Sounds(movScrubber, txtStatus, txtHeadPosition, ➥
txtTrackLength, txtArtist,
txtTitle, volumeSlider, panSlider);
  soundManager.loadSong("song1.mp3");
  addChild(soundManager);
```

As you can see, when you instantiate the Sounds class, you pass in all the references to the objects on the stage that this class will need to work with. Then you pass the song1.mp3 reference to its loadSong() function. This loads the sound file but doesn't play it. Finally, you add the soundManager instance to the display list.

Buffering sound

When you load the sound file, you need to define a buffer for the sound to load into before playing. So first instantiate the buffer variable in the Sound.as class file constructor:

```
//Song buffer size in milliseconds
buffer=new SoundLoaderContext(5000);
```

In the example, 5 seconds of the song will need to load into the buffer before it will commence playing. You need to pass this information to the loader, and you do this during the load command. In the Sound.as file, modify the first line of the loadSong() function accordingly:

```
snd1=new Sound(new URLRequest(song), buffer);
```

This will start the song1.mp3 file loading.

Adding display items

The sound player will display a loading progress bar, playhead bar, sound spectrum, and sound track information. Let's start by adding the loading progress bar.

Creating the loading progress bar

The loading bar will display the progress of the sound file load process. This should complement the playhead bar, and indeed it will operate within the scrubber movie clip. I have already created the physical asset as a white bar.

You will need to loop the check at regular intervals until the load is complete. So you'll instantiate a timer, add a listener, and start the timer running.

Add this code to your Sounds.as constructor:

```
timerLoading=new Timer(100, 0);
timerLoading.addEventListener(TimerEvent.TIMER, onLoading);
timerLoading.start();
```

The first line instantiates the new Timer instance with the parameters of interval and number of loops. You have set the timer to a 100-millisecond interval and told it to loop indefinitely. You will stop the timer when it has finished its job.

Now that you have defined an event listener and started the timer, let's add the event handler code for the timer event. Add the following function to the bottom of the Sounds.as class file:

```
private function onLoading(event:TimerEvent):void{
  bytLoaded = snd1.bytesLoaded;
  bytTotal = snd1.bytesTotal;
  if ((bytTotal >= bytLoaded)&&(bytLoaded>0)){
    if(txtStatus.text!="Playing"){
      txtStatus.text="Loading";
    }
```

```
movScrubber.movLoaderBar.width=((bytLoaded/bytTotal)*100)*4;
if(bytLoaded == bytTotal){
  if(txtStatus.text=="Loading"){
    txtStatus.text="Load Complete";
  }
  timerLoading.stop();
}
}
}
```

This is all fairly self-explanatory. The first few lines work out the amount loaded and the total size of the sound in bytes. You check that the file hasn't completed loading and that it has actually started loading before you try representing the information and issuing status notifications to the status text field. Provided this is all in order, you then set the width of the loading bar to represent the percentage loaded times four (as the movie clip is 400 pixels wide). Finally, you perform another check to see if the total bytes loaded are equal to the total number of bytes in the sound file. If it is, then the sound file has finished downloading, and you need to stop the associated timer and alert the user through the status text field.

Now if you publish your FLA file, you will see the loading progress bar fill as the sound loads.

> *The sound file loading will seem instantaneous if the file is being loaded locally. To see this in action, you really need to load a sound file from a remote Internet server.*

Creating the playhead bar

The playhead bar will show where the playhead is when the sound file is playing. Once again, I have already created the graphical object on the stage, within the scrubber movie clip, and you already have the necessary variables defined in the Sounds.as file.

So let's go ahead and create a Timer instance for this function in the Sounds.as class constructor. Add this to the bottom of the file:

```
timerPlayHead=new Timer(500, 0);
timerPlayHead.addEventListener(TimerEvent.TIMER, this.headPosition);
```

The first line instantiates the new Timer instance with the parameters of interval and number of loops. You have set it to a 500-millisecond interval and told it to loop indefinitely.

Now that you have defined an event listener, you need to think about the event handler code. This is not as simple as when you are working with a video file. The basic principle of displaying an accurate graphical representation of the playhead position is that you take the total length of the sound or video track in a chronological format and compare it against the track's playhead position chronological information. The goal is to create a relative and accurately scaled playhead graphic, and possibly display the total track length and playhead position in minutes and seconds in appropriate text fields.

For video, you get the track's chronological head position from the NetStream.Time property. The SoundChannel.position property gives the same information about a sound file, so that's all good.

Next, you need to get the total track length, so that you can use it to work out how far the track playhead has advanced relative to the total track length. This is where the problem lies. You get video track length from the duration information in the metadata, which is encoded into the FLV file. However, Sound class–loaded MP3s often do not have that information. You can interrogate the track's ID3 metadata for the TLEN property, which is set aside for the declaration of the track's length; however, this is far too rarely used to be of reliable value.

The other option is to get the chronological track length by interrogating the length property of the Sound class into which the sound file was loaded. Unfortunately, the Sound.length property is a chronological representation of only the amount of the sound file (in milliseconds) that has been downloaded at the time the property is interrogated, so it will never be accurate until the sound file has completely finished downloading. As you can imagine, that will change the playhead position ratio during the load process, and possibly quite dramatically. It might even look like the track playhead was going backward, as the ratio of percent loaded to playhead position changed. So you would seem to have no reliable way of getting the track length.

There is, however, a cunning way around this, which is certainly accurate enough to represent the playhead position acceptably. You can use the information you have about the track load status to extrapolate the track length information. "How?" I hear you ask. "You're a madman!" I hear you say. Well, it's simple, if not perfect. As you have the total number of bytes in the sound file and can compare that to the bytes loaded, you can get an accurate representation of the percentage of the file that has been loaded. As this is exactly the information the Sound.length property uses, you can use that percentage as a multiplier on that property. This will give you an accurate representation of the true chronological track length. Of course, you will need to do a little tweaking and formatting to get it in seconds and initially, while the factors are at their highest, the calculations could be a little off.

The following code gets the playhead to display the count in minutes and seconds, the total track length to display in minutes and seconds, and the graphical representation of the playhead position, using the work-around for the total track length time. These three distinct requirements are separated into the three commented sections within the function. Add this function at the bottom of your Sounds.as file:

```
        private function headPosition(event:TimerEvent):void{
          //Set playhead position graphic
          multiplier=(1/(snd1.bytesLoaded/snd1.bytesTotal));
          trueChronoLength=snd1.length*multiplier;
          if(txtStatus.text=="Playing"){
            if(trueChronoLength>0){
    movScrubber.movHead.width=((Math.floor(sc.position)/ trueChronoLength)*100)*4;
            //Set head position display text field
            nsMinutes = Math.floor((sc.position/1000)/60);
              nsSeconds = Math.floor((sc.position/1000)%60);
              if (nsSeconds<10) {
              this.txtHeadPosition.text=nsMinutes.toString()+":0"+ nsSeconds.toString();
              }else{
              this.txtHeadPosition.text=nsMinutes.toString()+":"+ nsSeconds.toString();
              }
          }
```

```
    //Set track length display text field
      var tlMinutes:int = Math.floor((trueChronoLength/1000)/60);
    if (tlMinutes<1){
      tlMinutes=0
    }
      var tlSeconds:int = Math.floor((trueChronoLength/1000)%60);
      if (tlSeconds<10) {
        txtTrackLength.text=tlMinutes.toString()+":0"+ tlSeconds.toString();
    }else{
        txtTrackLength.text=tlMinutes.toString()+":"+ tlSeconds.toString();
      }
    }
```

The first section takes care of displaying the correct position of the playhead, as the function comment suggests. However, it will skip the display process if you do not yet have the full chronological length of the track worked out when this function fires. The playhead numerical position display text field will, once you have the information, format and display it in the appropriate text field. The same it true of the total track length text field, and a great amount of code is devoted to formatting the display in this function.

Adding the sound spectrum

Now let's add the code to compute the spectrum. This goes in the Sounds.as file, where you have already imported the SoundMixer, ByteArray, BitmapFilterQuality, and GlowFilter classes. You have also declared the Timer for the spectrum calculation, the ByteArray to hold the returned 512 frequency variables, and the Sprite that will be used to display the frequency information in its final state. Additionally, you have declared a width uint and a spread Number for the display sizes, and a GlowFilter to polish the display a little.

Add these variable declarations to your Sounds.as class file:

```
private var timerSpectrum:Timer;
private var baSpectrum:ByteArray;
private var grFrequency:Sprite;
private var w:uint = 1;
private var spread:Number;
private var glow:GlowFilter;
```

Next, you need to instantiate these variables. Add the following code to the bottom of your Sounds.as class constructor:

```
baSpectrum = new ByteArray();
grFrequency = new Sprite();
grFrequency.x = 0;
grFrequency.y = 200;
movScreen.movSpectrum.addChild(grFrequency);
glow = new GlowFilter()
```

Here, you have instantiated the ByteArray GlowFilter and the Sprite. You have also set the Sprite's x and y position and added it to the movScreen.movSpectrum display list, as this is the movie clip set up in the FLA file to display it.

Finally, initialize and add an event listener to the spectrum timer. You won't start it, as it should run only when the sound file is playing. You'll add that to the button event handler later in the code. For now, just add the following to the Sounds.as constructor:

```
timerSpectrum=new Timer(100, 0);
timerSpectrum.addEventListener(TimerEvent.TIMER, onSpectrum);
```

It seems natural to add the Timer event handler function onSpectrum() now. Add this function into your Sounds.as file:

```
//------------------COMPUTE SPECTRUM ----------------------
   private function onSpectrum(evt:Event):void{
      SoundMixer.computeSpectrum(baSpectrum, false);
      grFrequency.graphics.clear();
      grFrequency.graphics.beginFill(0x00FF00);
      grFrequency.graphics.moveTo(0, 0);
      var i:int;
      for (i=0; i<512; i+=w) {
        spread = (baSpectrum.readFloat() * 150);
        grFrequency.graphics.drawRect(i, 0, w, -spread);
      }
   }
```

The first line within the function does the important work of computing the sound spectrum and passing it to the baSpectrum ByteArray you defined earlier. You then set up the graphic to display the sound frequencies by setting its color and start position. Once this is done, you loop through the 512 frequency values in the ByteArray by using the readFloat() method, applying a factoring number of 150 to allow for the display size, and then draw the rectangle that represents these calculations and settings.

After the basic drawing to screen is done, you need to add a little polish. The setting of the color is bright green. This is a color traditionally used by manufacturers to display graphic equalizer information, where it is so bright against the usually black background that it seems to glow. So you're going to add a simple glow filter. You have already imported the GlowFilter class and instantiated it. Add the following code to the bottom of the onSpectrum function, after the for-next loop:

```
//Apply the glow filter to the grFrequency graphic.
glow.color = 0x009922;
glow.alpha = 1;
glow.blurX = 25;
glow.blurY = 25;
glow.quality = BitmapFilterQuality.MEDIUM;
grFrequency.filters = [glow];
```

The last line adds the newly configured glow filter to the Sprite's filters array.

Displaying ID3 track metadata

You need to be able to display track information about the artist's name and the name of the track, at the very least. As explained earlier in the chapter, you can interrogate for more ID3 information, but you'll stick with these two reasonably reliable and simple fields in this example.

Add the following event listener to the loadSong() function in the Sounds.as file:

```
snd1.addEventListener(Event.ID3, id3Handler);
```

Now you can add the event handler code to the Sounds.as file, like so:

```
//---------------- ID3 information event handler ----------------
    function id3Handler(event:Event):void {
      var song:Sound = Sound(event.target);
      var songInfo:ID3Info = ID3Info(song.id3);
      trace("ID3 loaded");
//We now loop over the songs metadata so you can see how much
//there is; we'll just trace it
      for (var xx in songInfo){
        trace("ID3 - "+xx+" is "+songInfo[xx]);
      }
      txtArtist.text=songInfo.artist;
      txtTitle.text=songInfo.songName;
    }
```

You extract the sound file target from the returned object and store it in a Sound variable, so that you can interrogate its ID3 information. You'll notice you're feeding even the song's ID3 information into another class: the ID3Info class. As noted earlier in the chapter, essentially, this class takes the fairly nondescript ID3 tags and translates them into something legible to call. For example, the ID3 tag TPE1 becomes the ID3Info property artist. You don't have to use the ID3Info class, and indeed, you loop through the ID3 metadata in this function to give you some idea of what data you can find in any MP3 files you choose to use.

You assign the artist and songName properties of the ID3Info instance to the appropriate text fields, which, once again, I have already put on the stage for you. As you can see, getting ID3 information is pretty simple.

Controlling the audio as it plays

The ButtonManager class will deal with all the button-based events. Create that class file now and save it as ButtonManager.as.

Add the following code to the ButtonManager.as file. This covers all the classes you need to import and the variable definitions you will need later on.

```
package com.fas3.smc{
  import flash.net.*;
  import flash.display.Sprite;
  import flash.display.SimpleButton;f
```

```
import flash.events.MouseEvent;
import flash.events.EventDispatcher;
import flash.events.Event;
import com.fas3.smc.MediaControlEvent;

public class ButtonManager extends Sprite{
   private var butRW:SimpleButton;
   private var butPlay:SimpleButton;
   private var butPause:SimpleButton;
   private var butStop:SimpleButton;
   private var butFF:SimpleButton;
   private var eventDispatcherButton:EventDispatcher;
        private var pauseOn:Boolean=false;

   //Simply instantiate your button manager class by passing it the
   //names of your Rewind, Play, Pause, Stop and Fast Forward
   //button instances
   public function ButtonManager(butRW:SimpleButton, butPlay :➡
SimpleButton, butPause:SimpleButton, butStop:SimpleButton, ➡
 butFF:SimpleButton){
        this.butRW = butRW;
        this.butPlay = butPlay;
        this.butPause = butPause;
        this.butStop = butStop;
        this.butFF = butFF;
   }
  }
 }
```

Because I have deliberately not added extra code to create the buttons, and instead opted to create them graphically on the stage, you have passed references to them into the class file constructor. You also immediately pass these references to the local variables so you can access them in the scope of the class.

In order to instantiate the ButtonManager class and pass in the button instance references, return to the Main.as file and add the following line after the line that adds the Sounds.as class instance to the display list:

```
buts=new ButtonManager(butRW, butPlay, butPause, butStop, butFF);
```

Now let's add the button functionality.

Adding button functionality

You will start by adding event listeners to the ButtonManager.as class file constructor for each button to listen for MOUSE_DOWN events as soon as a button is pressed. As with the video player, you do not want to wait until the button is released to be notified, particularly for the fast-forward and rewind functions, which rely on the user pressing and holding down the button to execute them. The FF and RW buttons use a Timer class instance to continue to run while the button is pressed, and they have a release event handler, which allows you to stop them executing their timer when the user releases the mouse.

Add the following code to your ButtonManager.as class file constructor:

```
//Add button listeners
butRW.addEventListener(MouseEvent.MOUSE_DOWN, doRewind);
butRW.addEventListener(MouseEvent.CLICK, stopRewind);
butPlay.addEventListener(MouseEvent.MOUSE_DOWN, doPlay);
butFF.addEventListener(MouseEvent.MOUSE_DOWN, doFastForward);
butFF.addEventListener(MouseEvent.CLICK, stopFastForward);

butRW.enabled=false;
butFF.enabled=false;
butPause.enabled=false;
butStop.enabled=false;
```

You have disabled all of the buttons except for the play button. The other buttons will be enabled and disabled as logic dictates throughout the application's use. Also notice that the pause and stop buttons don't have event listeners added to them at this stage. Since these buttons don't need an event listener added to them until after the sound is playing, you have left it to the Play event handler to take care of this.

Now let's add the button event handlers to ButtonManager.as:

```
private function doRewind(evnt:MouseEvent):void{
  dispatchEvent(new MediaControlEvent("RW"));
}

private function stopRewind(evnt:MouseEvent):void{
  dispatchEvent(new MediaControlEvent("RWEND"));
}

private function doPlay(event:MouseEvent):void{
  butPause.addEventListener(MouseEvent.MOUSE_DOWN, doPause);
  butPause.enabled=true;
  butStop.addEventListener(MouseEvent.MOUSE_DOWN, doStop);
  butStop.enabled=true;
  butFF.enabled=true;
  butRW.enabled=true;
  dispatchEvent(new MediaControlEvent("PLAY"));
}

private function doPause(event:MouseEvent):void{
 if (pauseOn){
      butRW.enabled=true;
      butFF.enabled=true;
      butPlay.enabled=true;
      butStop.enabled=true;
      pauseOn=false;
} else {
      butRW.enabled=false;
      butFF.enabled=false;
```

```
                  butPlay.enabled=false;
                  butStop.enabled=false;
                  pauseOn=true;
            }
          dispatchEvent(new MediaControlEvent("PAUSE"));
      }

      private function doStop(event:MouseEvent) :void {
        butPause.removeEventListener(MouseEvent.MOUSE_DOWN, doPause);
        butPause.enabled=false;
        dispatchEvent(new MediaControlEvent("STOP"));
      }

      private function doFastForward(event:MouseEvent) :void {
        dispatchEvent(new MediaControlEvent("FF"));
      }
      private function stopFastForward(event:MouseEvent) :void {
        dispatchEvent(new MediaControlEvent("FFEND"));
      }
```

The Play event handler has some extra code. It adds the event listeners for the pause and stop buttons, and it enables all the other control buttons, now that their use is valid. The Stop event handler also has a little extra code. It removes the Pause event listener and disables the pause button.

You'll also notice that these functions are dispatching their own event: MediaControlEvent. This is the same class you used for the video player example in the previous chapter, and the reasoning for extending the Event class to create this class is the same as explained in that chapter: to allow for simple, modular, extendable event handling and registration for any classes that need to use the media control buttons. And as in the video player example, you're adding it to the ButtonManager class before it is created. Add the following function into the ButtonManager.as file:

```
//This function adds any external objects to the listener list
//for the mediaControl event
  public function addMediaControlListener(funcObj:Function):void{
    addEventListener(MediaControlEvent.CONTROL_TYPE, funcObj);
  }
```

It will register an external handler for any MediaControlEvent.CONTROL_TYPE events.

Now add a call to this function from the Main.as file. Add the following line to the end of the Main.as constructor:

```
buts.addMediaControlListener(soundManager.onControlCommand);
```

You have defined the Sound.as class function onControlCommand to handle the MediaControlEvent. CONTROL_TYPE events, which you'll add to the Sounds.as file next.

Save and close both the Main.as and ButtonManager.as files now. They are complete. The Main.as file should look like this:

```
package com.fas3.smc{

    import flash.display.MovieClip;
    import com.fas3.smc.Sounds;
    import com.fas3.smc.ButtonManager;
    import flash.text.TextField;
    import flash.display.SimpleButton;

    public class Main extends MovieClip {
        private var soundManager:Sounds;
        private var buts:ButtonManager;

        public function Main(){
            soundManager=new Sounds(movScrubber, txtStatus, ➡
txtHeadPosition, txtTrackLength, txtArtist, txtTitle, volumeSlider, ➡
panSlider);
            soundManager.loadSong("song1.mp3");
            addChild(soundManager);
            buts=new ButtonManager(butRW, butPlay, butPause, butStop, butFF);
            buts.addMediaControlListener(soundManager.onControlCommand);
        }

    }

}
```

The ButtonManager.as file should look like this:

```
Package com.fas3.smc{
    import flash.net.*;
    import flash.display.Sprite;
    import flash.display.SimpleButton;
    import flash.events.MouseEvent;
    import flash.events.EventDispatcher;
    import flash.events.Event;
    import com.fas3.smc.MediaControlEvent;

    public class ButtonManager extends Sprite{
        private var butRW:SimpleButton;
        private var butPlay:SimpleButton;
        private var butPause:SimpleButton;
        private var butStop:SimpleButton;
        private var butFF:SimpleButton;
        private var eventDispatcherButton:EventDispatcher;
            private var pauseOn:Boolean=false;

        //Simply instantiate your button manager class by passing it the
        //names of your Rewind, Play, Pause, Stop and Fast Forward
        //button instances
```

```
        public function ButtonManager(butRW:SimpleButton, butPlay: ➥
SimpleButton, butPause:SimpleButton, butStop:SimpleButton, ➥
butFF:SimpleButton){
        this.butRW=butRW;
        this.butPlay=butPlay;
        this.butPause=butPause;
        this.butStop=butStop;
        this.butFF=butFF;

        //Add button listeners
        butRW.addEventListener(MouseEvent.MOUSE_DOWN, doRewind);
        butRW.addEventListener(MouseEvent.CLICK, stopRewind);
        butPlay.addEventListener(MouseEvent.MOUSE_DOWN, doPlay);
        butFF.addEventListener(MouseEvent.MOUSE_DOWN, doFastForward);
        butFF.addEventListener(MouseEvent.CLICK, stopFastForward);

        butRW.enabled=false;
        butFF.enabled=false;
        butPause.enabled=false;
        butStop.enabled=false;
        }

    //This function adds any external objects to the listener list
    //for the mediaControl event
    public function addMediaControlListener(funcObj:Function):void{
        addEventListener(MediaControlEvent.CONTROL_TYPE, funcObj);
    }

    private function doRewind(evnt:MouseEvent):void{
        dispatchEvent(new MediaControlEvent("RW"));
    }

    private function stopRewind(evnt:MouseEvent):void {
        dispatchEvent(new MediaControlEvent("RWEND"));
    }

    private function doPlay(event:MouseEvent):void {
        butPause.addEventListener(MouseEvent.MOUSE_DOWN, doPause);
        butPause.enabled=true;
        butStop.addEventListener(MouseEvent.MOUSE_DOWN, doStop);
        butStop.enabled=true;
        butFF.enabled=true;
        butRW.enabled=true;
        dispatchEvent(new MediaControlEvent("PLAY"));
    }

    private function doPause(event:MouseEvent) :void {
        if (pauseOn){
```

```
                butRW.enabled=true;
                butFF.enabled=true;
                butPlay.enabled=true;
                butStop.enabled=true;
                pauseOn=false;
            } else {
                butRW.enabled=false;
                butFF.enabled=false;
                butPlay.enabled=false;
                butStop.enabled=false;
                pauseOn=true;
            }
            dispatchEvent(new MediaControlEvent("PAUSE"));
        }


        private function doStop(event:MouseEvent) :void {
          butPause.removeEventListener(MouseEvent.MOUSE_DOWN, doPause);
          butPause.enabled=false;
          dispatchEvent(new MediaControlEvent("STOP"));
        }

        private function doFastForward(event:MouseEvent) :void {
          dispatchEvent(new MediaControlEvent("FF"));
        }
        private function stopFastForward(event:MouseEvent) :void {
          dispatchEvent(new MediaControlEvent("FFEND"));
        }

      }
    }
```

The Sounds.as file still has some work to be done on it, which you'll handle next.

Handling button events

The ButtonManager MediaControlEvent.CONTROL_TYPE events are dispatched when any control button is pressed. Now you will add the event handlers to take action when they are notified of a button press. These event handlers go in the Sound.as file.

Open the Sounds.as class file and add the following function to it, to handle the MediaControlEvent. CONTROL_TYPE events:

```
    //----------------- CONTROL BUTTONS --------------------------

    public function onControlCommand(evt:MediaControlEvent) :void {
      switch(evt.command){
        //---- PAUSE ----
        case "PAUSE":
          if (pauseStatus){
```

```
              sc = snd1.play(playHeadPosition,1);
              restoreVolPan();
              timerSpectrum.start();
              pauseStatus=false;
            }else{
              timerSpectrum.stop();
              grFrequency.graphics.clear();
              storeVolPan();
              sc.stop();
              pauseStatus=true;
            }
            txtStatus.text=(txtStatus.text=="Playing")? "Paused" : "Playing";
        break;
        //---- PLAY ----
        case "PLAY":
          if (txtStatus.text!="Playing"){
            sc = snd1.play(0,1);
timerPlayHead.start();
            restoreVolPan();
            timerSpectrum.start();
            txtStatus.text="Playing";
            trackEnd=false;
          }
        break;
        //---- STOP ----
        case "STOP":
timerPlayHead.stop();
            txtStatus.text="Stopped";
            timerSpectrum.stop();
            grFrequency.graphics.clear();
            storeVolPan();
            sc.stop();
            movScrubber.movHead.width=1;
            txtHeadPosition.text="0:00";
        break;
        //---- RW ----
        case "RW":
          timerSpectrum.stop();
          grFrequency.graphics.clear();
          storeVolPan();
          sc.stop();
          timerRW.start();
          txtStatus.text="Rewind";
        break;
        //---- RW END ----
        case "RWEND":
          timerRW.stop();
```

```
        if(!trackStart){
          sc = snd1.play(playHeadPosition,1);
          txtStatus.text="Playing";
          restoreVolPan();
          timerSpectrum.start();
        }
      break;
      //---- FF ----
      case "FF":
        timerSpectrum.stop();
        grFrequency.graphics.clear();
        storeVolPan();
        sc.stop();
        timerFF.start();
        txtStatus.text="Fast Forward";
      break;
      //---- FF END ----
      case "FFEND":
        timerFF.stop();
        if(!trackEnd){
          sc = snd1.play(playHeadPosition,1);
          txtStatus.text="Playing";
          restoreVolPan();
          timerSpectrum.start();
        }
      break;
      default:
            trace("BUTTON COMMAND ERROR");
            break;
  }
 }
```

There are a number of conditional code segments in here, nearly all of which are based on the premise that you need to take note of the playhead position, the volume, and the pan settings before you stop the sound playing and execute fast-forward, rewind, pause, and so on, so that you can restart the sound playing with its previous settings still intact. For this, you use two functions: storeVolPan() and restoreVolPan(). Also, you will notice that the playhead timer is started and stopped on the start and stop buttons.

Add the following code to your Sounds.as file:

```
//Store volume and pan settings for reapplication
private function storeVolPan():void{
  playHeadPosition=sc.position;
  tempVol=stVolume.volume;
  tempPan=stVolume.pan;
}
```

```
//Restore pan and volume settings
private function restoreVolPan():void{
  stVolume.pan=tempPan;
  stVolume.volume=tempVol;
  sc.soundTransform=stVolume;
}
```

You have used a single switch/case statement to deal with every button press event, or delegate it as appropriate. Dispatching your own event allows you to send extra parameters in the dispatched object, and you are going to be interrogating it for a variable called command. This is a String that contains the type of command that a particular button fired off (such as STOP, RW, FF, or FFEND). Once a case has been made, it will set the status text field to reflect this change in status; record the volume, pan, and playhead positions; and execute the appropriate function(s) to carry out the command's native request.

The Pause case toggles between play and pause by using a pauseStatus Boolean variable, as the Sound class does not have an actual pause function. If you wanted to, you could extend the Sound class to include such a thing, almost exactly as you have done here.

The Play event restarts the sound file playing from the beginning but restores the volume and pan settings, in case they have been changed. It also starts the spectrum timer running to take the sound spectrum snapshot.

The Stop event stores the present user-defined volume and pan settings. It then stops the SoundChannel to which the Sound instance is assigned. Next, it does a little housekeeping by moving the playhead back to the beginning and making sure the numerical representation of the playhead is returned to zero. It also stops the sound spectrum timer and clears the sound spectrum sprite.

The FF/FFEND and RW/RWEND events also require special consideration. When the FF and RW buttons are pressed, they are required to fire off a Timer event to accommodate the need for the playhead increment or decrement for as long as the buttons are held down. They also stop the sound spectrum timer and clear the sound spectrum sprite.

Let's add the Timer declarations to the Sounds.as class file constructor now:

```
timerFF=new Timer(100, 0)
timerFF.addEventListener(TimerEvent.TIMER, this.runFF);
timerRW=new Timer(100, 0)
timerRW.addEventListener(TimerEvent.TIMER, this.runRW);
```

Now you need to write the functions they call. These Timer event handlers, which normally just increment or decrement the playhead, will also check for the exception that the playhead is equal to 0 (the beginning of the track) or to the total track length (the end of the track), and set the trackStart or trackEnd Boolean values to true to reflect whichever status has been achieved in such an event. These then do some housekeeping by resetting the numerical representation of the playhead, resetting the width of the scrub head movie clip, and setting the status text to notify the user that one of these exceptions has been reached. The users are at liberty to press the play button at this point in order to start playing the sound file again if they wish. Add the following code for these two functions to your Sounds.as file:

```
    //Fast Forward
    private function runFF(event:TimerEvent):void{
      if(playHeadPosition<trueChronoLength){
        playHeadPosition+=1000;
            movScrubber.movHead.width=((Math.floor(playHeadPosition) ➡
/trueChronoLength)*100)*4;
      }else{
        trackEnd=true;
        txtHeadPosition.text=txtTrackLength.text;
        txtStatus.text="End of track";
        movScrubber.movHead.width=400;
      }
    }

    //Rewind
    private function runRW(event:TimerEvent):void{
      if(playHeadPosition>1){
        playHeadPosition-=1000;
        movScrubber.movHead.width=((Math.floor(playHeadPosition) ➡
/trueChronoLength)*100)*4;
      }else{
        trackStart=true;
        txtHeadPosition.text="0:00";
        txtStatus.text="Start of track";
        movScrubber.movHead.width=1;
      }
    }
```

Upon releasing the FF or RW button, the associated timer is stopped, and a check is done to see if the trackEnd or trackStart Boolean was set to true. If not, the track is allowed to play from its newly incremented or decremented position, and the last-known volume and pan settings are applied.

Controlling the sound volume and panning

Now let's look at controlling the sound file's volume and panning. There is one important consideration before you start coding. If users have played the sound once and paused, stopped, or otherwise interacted with its timeline, they may well have set and reset the volume and pan settings. These settings need to be stored, recalled, and reapplied to the sound file when it is restarted or replayed. To the users, these are global settings, affecting any sound that they load and play, and they will not expect the volume or pan to change once they have been set. This will extend our basic button control functionality.

Now you need to control how loud the sound file plays back and the balance of volume from each speaker channel. You are going to be using the SoundTransform class for this, as explained earlier in the chapter. You will see you have already imported the class and defined an instance of it (called stVolume). Add the following line of code to the Sounds.as class file constructor:

```
    stVolume=new SoundTransform();
```

You also need some form of graphical volume and pan control mechanisms. For this example, you're using the Slider component (see Figure 8-7). I have already added two of these components to the demo FLA file: one for volume and one for panning, as shown in Figure 8-8.

Figure 8-7. The Slider component

Figure 8-8. The sliders in the final application

The parameters for the Slider components have been set as shown in Figure 8-9.

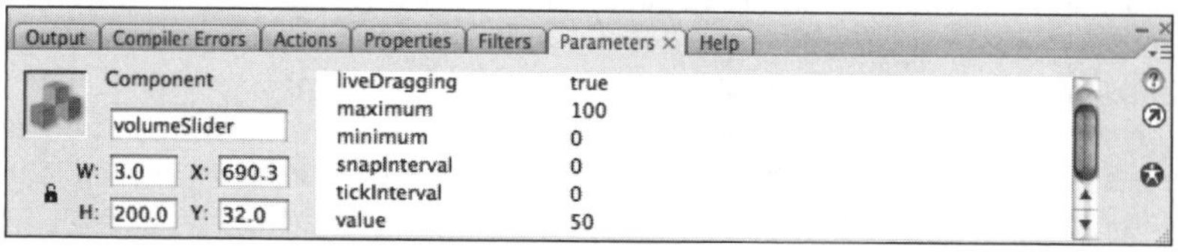

Figure 8-9. Slider component parameter settings

As you can see, I have set the scale from a minimum of 0 to maximum of 100, to give the user a percentage setting for the volume, and defaulted it to start at 50, so it will be in the middle range initially. The pan settings are only slightly different in that the SoundTransform.pan range is –1.0 to 1.0, so the minimum and maximum values are –100 and 100, respectively. The default value is 0, to start with the sound balanced.

I have called these instances volumeSlider and panSlider—not the best naming convention in the world, but you'll know what they are when I refer to them later. In order to use them, you just need to add event listeners to them.

Add the following lines to your Sounds.as class file constructor:

```
//Set volume controls
volumeSlider.addEventListener(SliderEvent.CHANGE, onVolSliderChange);
panSlider.addEventListener(SliderEvent.CHANGE, onPanSliderChange);
```

Add these functions to your Sounds.as class file also:

```
//Set volume
private function onVolSliderChange(evt:SliderEvent):void{
  stVolume.volume=(evt.value/100);
  sc.soundTransform=stVolume;
}

//Set pan
private function onPanSliderChange(evt:SliderEvent):void{
  stVolume.pan=(evt.value/100);
  sc.soundTransform=stVolume;
}
```

The event object that is returned to the event handler contains a value Number variable. This reflects the relative position in either the volume or pan range that you assigned, based on where the slider was set. This value needs to be converted into the SoundTransform class's native pan or volume range (1.0 through 1.0 or 0.0 through 1.0, respectively), so that it can be applied to the SoundTransform, and that, in turn, can be applied to the SoundChannel.

So now your Sounds.as class file is complete and should look like this:

```
package com.fas3.smc{
    import flash.media.Sound;
    import flash.media.SoundChannel;
    import flash.media.SoundLoaderContext;
    import flash.media.SoundTransform;
    import flash.media.SoundMixer;
    import flash.media.ID3Info;
    import flash.events.Event;
    import flash.utils.ByteArray;
    import flash.display.MovieClip;
    import flash.display.Sprite;
    import flash.net.URLRequest;
    import flash.text.TextField;
    import flash.utils.Timer;
    import flash.events.TimerEvent;
    import fl.controls.Slider;
    import fl.events.SliderEvent;
    import flash.filters.BitmapFilterQuality;
    import flash.filters.GlowFilter;
```

```
public class Sounds extends MovieClip {
        private var snd1:Sound;
        private var sc:SoundChannel;
        private var buffer:SoundLoaderContext;
        private var timerLoading:Timer;
        private var timerPlayHead:Timer;
        private var timerFF:Timer;
        private var timerRW:Timer;
        private var timerSpectrum:Timer;
        private var barWid:int = 200;
        private var barHi:int = 5;
        private var bytLoaded:int;
        private var bytTotal:int;
        private var pctLoaded:int;
        private var trueChronoLength:Number;
        private var txtStatus:TextField;
        private var txtTrackLength:TextField;
        private var txtHeadPosition:TextField;
        private var txtArtist:TextField;
        private var txtTitle:TextField;
        private var movScreen:MovieClip;
        private var movScrubber:MovieClip;
        private var multiplier:Number;
        private var nsMinutes:Number;
        private var nsSeconds:Number;
        private var pauseStatus:Boolean;
        private var playHeadPosition:Number;
        private var volumeSlider:Slider;
        private var panSlider:Slider;
        private var stVolume:SoundTransform;
        private var tempVol:Number=0.5;
        private var tempPan:Number=0;
        private var trackEnd:Boolean;
        private var trackStart:Boolean;
        private var baSpectrum:ByteArray;
        private var grFrequency:Sprite;
        private var w:uint = 1;
        private var spread:Number;
        private var glow:GlowFilter;


        //CONSTRUCTOR
        public function Sounds(movScreen:MovieClip, movScrubber: ➥
MovieClip, txtStatus:TextField, txtHeadPosition:TextField, ➥
txtTrackLength:TextField, txtArtist:TextField, txtTitle:TextField, ➥
volumeSlider:Slider, panSlider:Slider){
```

```
                   //Set movies and text fields to local references and
                   // to start positions and contents
                   this.movScreen=movScreen;
                   this.movScrubber=movScrubber;
                   this.txtStatus=txtStatus;
                   this.txtHeadPosition=txtHeadPosition;
             this.txtTrackLength=txtTrackLength;
             this.txtArtist=txtArtist;
             this.txtTitle=txtTitle;
             this.volumeSlider=volumeSlider;
             this.panSlider=panSlider;
             movScrubber.movLoaderBar.width=1;
             txtStatus.text="AWAITING LOCATION";

             buffer=new SoundLoaderContext(5000);//buffer size in ms
             stVolume=new SoundTransform();
             baSpectrum = new ByteArray();
             grFrequency = new Sprite();
             grFrequency.x = 0;
             grFrequency.y = 200;
             movScreen.movSpectrum.addChild(grFrequency);
             glow = new GlowFilter()

//Set volume controls
volumeSlider.addEventListener(SliderEvent.CHANGE, onVolSliderChange);
panSlider.addEventListener(SliderEvent.CHANGE, onPanSliderChange);

//Add Timers
timerLoading=new Timer(100, 0);
timerLoading.addEventListener(TimerEvent.TIMER, onLoading);
timerLoading.start();
timerPlayHead=new Timer(500, 0);
timerPlayHead.addEventListener(TimerEvent.TIMER, this.headPosition);
timerFF=new Timer(100, 0)
timerFF.addEventListener(TimerEvent.TIMER, this.runFF);
timerRW=new Timer(100, 0)
timerRW.addEventListener(TimerEvent.TIMER, this.runRW);
timerSpectrum=new Timer(100, 0);
timerSpectrum.addEventListener(TimerEvent.TIMER, onSpectrum);
//NB don't forget to stop the Timer when finished
    }

//--------------- Load song into Sound instance ----------------
public function loadSong(song:String):void{
snd1=new Sound(new URLRequest(song), buffer);
//Add event listeners for completion of loading and for ID3
//information
snd1.addEventListener(Event.ID3, id3Handler)
}
```

```
//---------------- Loader Timer handler ----------------------
private function onLoading(event:TimerEvent):void{
bytLoaded = snd1.bytesLoaded;
bytTotal = snd1.bytesTotal;
if ((bytTotal >= bytLoaded)&&(bytLoaded>0)){
if(txtStatus.text!="Playing"){
txtStatus.text="Loading";
}
movScrubber.movLoaderBar.width=((bytLoaded/bytTotal)*100)*4;
if(bytLoaded == bytTotal){
if(txtStatus.text=="Loading"){
txtStatus.text="Load Complete";
}
timerLoading.stop();
}
}
}


//---------------- HEAD POSITION & COUNT --------------------
private function headPosition(event:TimerEvent):void{
        multiplier=(1/(snd1.bytesLoaded/snd1.bytesTotal));
        trueChronoLength=snd1.length*multiplier;
        if(txtStatus.text=="Playing"){
           if(trueChronoLength>0){
                movScrubber.movHead.width=((Math.floor ➥
(sc.position)/trueChronoLength)*100)*4;
          }

        //Set timer display text field
        nsMinutes = Math.floor((sc.position/1000)/60);
        nsSeconds = Math.floor((sc.position/1000)%60);
        if (nsSeconds<10) {
            this.txtHeadPosition.text=nsMinutes.toString()+":➥
0"+nsSeconds.toString();
        }else{
            this.txtHeadPosition.text=nsMinutes.toString()+":➥
"+nsSeconds.toString();
        }
    }

        //Set track total length display text field
        var tlMinutes:int = Math.floor((trueChronoLength/ 1000)/60);
        if (tlMinutes<1){
            tlMinutes=0
        }
```

```
                var tlSeconds:int = Math.floor((trueChronoLength/ 1000)%60);
                if (tlSeconds<10) {
                        txtTrackLength.text=tlMinutes.toString()+":0"+ ↦
tlSeconds.toString();
                }else{
                        txtTrackLength.text=tlMinutes.toString()+":"+ ↦
tlSeconds.toString();
                }
            }

//---------------- ID3 information event handler ----------------
function id3Handler(event:Event):void {
            var song:Sound = Sound(event.target);
            //The ID3Info class translates the ID3 tags into more
            //legible calls for the information - e.g., TPE1 becomes
            //artist
            var songInfo:ID3Info = ID3Info(song.id3);
            for (var xx in songInfo){
                trace("ID3 - "+xx+" is "+songInfo[xx]);
            }
            txtArtist.text=songInfo.artist;
            txtTitle.text=songInfo.songName;
}


//----------------COMPUTE SPECTRUM -----------------------
private function onSpectrum(evt:Event):void{
        SoundMixer.computeSpectrum(baSpectrum, true);
//      SoundMixer.computeSpectrum(baSpectrum, false);
        grFrequency.graphics.clear();
        grFrequency.graphics.beginFill(0x00FF00);
        grFrequency.graphics.moveTo(0, 0);
        for (var i:int=0; i<512; i+=w) {
            spread = (baSpectrum.readFloat() * 150);
            grFrequency.graphics.drawRect(i, 0, w, -spread);
        }
        // Apply the glow filter to the gr graphic.
        glow.color = 0x009922;
        glow.alpha = 1;
        glow.blurX = 25;
        glow.blurY = 25;
        glow.quality = BitmapFilterQuality.MEDIUM;
        grFrequency.filters = [glow];
}
```

```
//--------------- CONTROL BUTTONS ---------------------------

public function onControlCommand(evt:MediaControlEvent):void{
    switch(evt.command){
        //---- PAUSE ----
        case "PAUSE":
            if (pauseStatus){
                //Play offset , number of loops:
                sc = snd1.play(playHeadPosition,1);
                restoreVolPan();
                timerSpectrum.start();
                pauseStatus=false;
            }else{
                timerSpectrum.stop();
                grFrequency.graphics.clear();
                storeVolPan();
                sc.stop();
                pauseStatus=true;
            }
            txtStatus.text=(txtStatus.text=="Playing")? "Paused" : "Playing";
        break;
        //---- PLAY ----
        case "PLAY":
            if (txtStatus.text!="Playing"){
                sc = snd1.play(0,1);//Play offset , number of loops
                timerPlayHead.start();
                restoreVolPan();
                timerSpectrum.start();
                txtStatus.text="Playing";
                trackEnd=false;
            }
        break;
        //---- STOP ----
        case "STOP":
            timerPlayHead.stop();
            txtStatus.text="Stopped";
            timerSpectrum.stop();
            grFrequency.graphics.clear();
            storeVolPan();
            sc.stop();
            movScrubber.movHead.width=1;
            txtHeadPosition.text="0:00";
        break;
        //---- RW ----
        case "RW":
            timerSpectrum.stop();
            grFrequency.graphics.clear();
            storeVolPan();
            sc.stop();
            timerRW.start();
            txtStatus.text="Rewind";
        break;
```

```
                    //---- RW END ----
                    case "RWEND":
                       timerRW.stop();
                       if(!trackStart){
                          //Play offset , number of loops:
                          sc = snd1.play(playHeadPosition,1);
                          txtStatus.text="Playing";
                          restoreVolPan();
                          timerSpectrum.start();
                       }
                    break;
                    //---- FF ----
                    case "FF":
                       timerSpectrum.stop();
                       grFrequency.graphics.clear();
                       storeVolPan();
                       sc.stop();
                       timerFF.start();
                       txtStatus.text="Fast Forward";
                    break;
                    //---- FF END ----
                    case "FFEND":
                       timerFF.stop();
                       if(!trackEnd){
                          //Play offset , number of loops:
                          sc = snd1.play(playHeadPosition,1);
                          txtStatus.text="Playing";
                          restoreVolPan();
                          timerSpectrum.start();
                       }
                    break;
                    default:
                       trace("BUTTON COMMAND ERROR");
                       break;
              }
       }
       //Fast Forward
       private function runFF(event:TimerEvent):void{
              if(playHeadPosition<trueChronoLength){
                 playHeadPosition+=1000;
                 movScrubber.movHead.width=((Math.floor(playHeadPosition) ➡
/trueChronoLength)*100)*4;
              }else{
                 trackEnd=true;
                 txtHeadPosition.text=txtTrackLength.text;
                 txtStatus.text="End of track";
                 movScrubber.movHead.width=400;
              }
       }
```

```
//Rewind
private function runRW(event:TimerEvent):void{
        if(playHeadPosition>1){
            playHeadPosition-=1000;
            movScrubber.movHead.width=((Math.floor(playHeadPosition)/ ➥
trueChronoLength)*100)*4;
        }else{
            trackStart=true;
            txtHeadPosition.text="0:00";
            txtStatus.text="Start of track";
            movScrubber.movHead.width=1;
        }
}

//Store volume and pan settings for reapplication
private function storeVolPan():void{
        playHeadPosition=sc.position;
        tempVol=stVolume.volume;
        tempPan=stVolume.pan;
}

//Reapply pan and volume settings
private function restoreVolPan():void{
        stVolume.pan=tempPan;
        stVolume.volume=tempVol;
        sc.soundTransform=stVolume;
}

//Set volume
private function onVolSliderChange(evt:SliderEvent):void{
        stVolume.volume=(evt.value/100);
        sc.soundTransform=stVolume;
}

//Set pan
private function onPanSliderChange(evt:SliderEvent):void{
        stVolume.pan=(evt.value/100);
        sc.soundTransform=stVolume;
}

}
}
```

Creating the custom event class

Now it's time to create the custom MediaControlEvent.as class. You will use this to fire off button interaction events. This is the same event class you used for the video player example in the previous chapter, so if you've already written it, just open the file again and save it to your audio project directory. If not, open a new ActionScript file and save it as MediaControlEvent.as, and put the following code in it:

```
package com.fas3.smc{
        import flash.events.Event;

        public class MediaControlEvent extends flash.events.Event {
            public static const CONTROL_TYPE:String = "headControl";
        public var command:String;

            public function MediaControlEvent( command:String ):void {
                super( CONTROL_TYPE);
            this.command = command;
            }
        }
}
```

This class simply extends the Event class, and works as described in the previous chapter.

And that completes this example. Save all your classes and publish your FLA file. You'll have a working MP3 player.

Summary

This chapter covered the basics of working with audio. You have learned how to do the following:

- Load an MP3 file or access the microphone
- Monitor and report on MP3 load and play status
- Read and display ID3 metadata
- Represent the sound data graphically using the sound spectrum
- Control MP3 loading and playback

You can experiment with the MP3 player you built in this chapter and see what else you can do with it. For example, you might add more aesthetically pleasing effects to the sound spectrum display. You could add a file list so you could browse the MP3 files and choose one to load. You could experiment with voice interaction and control. And you could create a multichannel sound mixer. The generic reference information presented in this chapter will be useful for pretty much any MP3-based ActionScript 3.0 project you want to try.

The next chapter covers the components that are available in ActionScript 3.0 and how they can help you quickly create standardized functional objects.

Chapter 9

WORKING WITH COMPONENTS

Todd Yard

This chapter covers the following topics:

- What components are in the context of ActionScript
- The benefits of working with components
- The makeup of the Flash component framework
- Scripting interactions with components
- The process of skinning components
- How to build your own components
- How to get more components

Up to this point in the book, you've been working with the objects in ActionScript that are built into the core language. These include objects like the display list items Sprite and MovieClip, and top-level objects like Array, String, and Number. For additional functionality, you've explored building your own classes from scratch or extending the existing classes, as in the iPod example in Chapter 3.

Sometimes, other developers have built additional functionality that you can use within your own projects. This functionality might be in the form of a class library from which you could create instances. Often, in the context of Flash and ActionScript, the additional functionality comes in the form of a special kind of class library built off the display list, providing drag-and-drop widgets to place in your applications or instantiate through code. These drag-and-drop widgets are called **components** in Flash lingo. If you understand what components are and what they can do, they can help speed up your development and add some pretty cool features to your projects.

> If you're a Flex user, note that this chapter is necessarily focused on the Flash CS3 IDE and its components framework. The Flex framework is a more robust and complex application framework that includes its own UI component classes—many more than are available by default in Flash. However, the concepts for scripting interaction between components is still applicable, and, perhaps more important, components can be developed using the graphical timeline in Flash CS3 for use within Flex.

Just what are components?

Components are items in your library just like any other movie clip symbol. In fact, all components must extend Sprite or MovieClip, and so are, by default, display objects that can be added to the display list. On that level, they are not much different from a graphic object drawn and then turned into a movie clip symbol. At that point in the game, each symbol instance can have different properties set—such as x, y, alpha, and rotation—all done visually on the stage in the IDE.

What makes components different and special is that in addition to the familiar display object settings, any number of additional parameters might be available for you to set in the IDE (through either the Parameters or Component Inspector panels). For example, the CheckBox component that comes with Flash CS3 has three additional parameters not standard to other sprites, but important for check boxes: label, labelPlacement, and selected.

So, in that light, components are extended sprites or movie clips that add specific functionality, usually for use within a UI. Components available with the standard installation of Flash CS3 include Button, CheckBox, ColorPicker, ComboBox, and many more. You can place instances of each type of component on the stage and configure them to act differently from other instances, so that two Button components could have two different labels, and three ComboBox components could have different lists of items.

> Although components are display objects and are generally UI widgets, that is not to say that they must be. A component might be nonrendering, meaning it would not draw any graphics within itself, and would simply provide additional functionality for a movie. In that case, it would be only a library item so that it could be dragged onto the stage and configured using the Parameters or Component Inspector panel, but at runtime it would be invisible, or perhaps purposely remove itself from the display list. We won't explore this nonrendering type of component in this chapter, but you should be aware that these are valid forms of components as well.

Accessing your components

To add a component to your Flash file, you can drag it in from the Components panel or simply double-click it in the Components panel, and it will be added to the center of the stage. You can open this panel by selecting Window ➤ Components from the main menu. One folder in the Components panel contains general UI controls, like Button, List, and Slider. The other folder contains controls for video playback, including the FLVPlayback component. With both of its folders expanded, this panel should appear as shown in Figure 9-1.

To add any of these components to your file, simply drag and drop the items onto your stage or directly into your Library. In either case, the components will then appear in your Library. You can drag additional instances from your Library, as opposed to having to access the Components panel again.

Some components are made of multiple subcomponents, so don't be surprised if by adding one component to your file you get several in your Library. For instance, if you add the ComboBox component to your Library, you'll find that the List and TextInput components come with it, as shown in Figure 9-2. This is one advantage to the modular style in which components are often created. With the ComboBox component added to your file, you can also create instances of the TextInput or List component without any additional file size cost. Nice!

Of course, you do not necessarily need to drag and drop component instances onto the stage to use them. Just as with any other symbol, once a component is in the Library, you can create a new instance by using the new keyword in ActionScript (hey, this is still an ActionScript book, right?), as long as it is set to be exported for ActionScript in the first frame, which all Flash CS3 components are by default. So, for instance, to create a new instance of the ComboBox class, you would use this code:

```
import fl.controls.ComboBox;

var combo:ComboBox = new ComboBox();
addChild(combo);
```

Adjusting parameters

Now you have components accessible in your Flash file through your Library, but how exactly can you configure an instance? Perhaps you've often wondered about the Parameters panel, which lies conspicuously next to the Properties panel at the bottom of the Flash IDE (I know it kept me up nights). Well, now you know the answer! When you have a component selected on the stage, the Parameters panel populates with all of the wonderful options available for editing through the IDE for

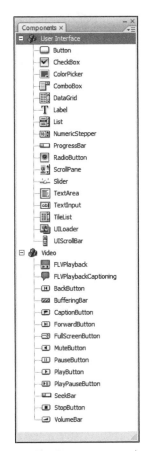

Figure 9-1. The Components panel, with its two folders expanded

Figure 9-2. A Flash file's Library after the ComboBox component has been dragged into it, bringing its subcomponents along

347

that component instance (there may be more available through ActionScript). Let's take a look at an example.

1. Create a new Flash file for ActionScript 3.0. Open the Components panel if it is not currently open (Windows ➤ Components).

2. Expand the User Interface folder in the Components panel and drag a Button component onto your stage. Notice that the button symbol now appears in your Library, along with the Component Assets folder, which contains the button symbol's skins (among other things).

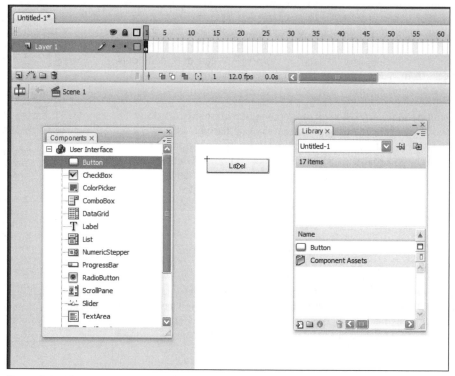

Figure 9-3. A Button component is added to the stage, and thus also appears in the Library.

3. Select the Button instance on the stage if it is not currently selected, and then open the Parameters panel. This panel should be tabbed with the Properties and Filters panels at the bottom of the Flash IDE if you have the default layout. If the Parameters panel is not there, open it by selecting Window ➤ Properties ➤ Parameters. Five parameters are available in the Parameters panel: emphasized, label, labelPlacement, selected, and toggle, as shown in Figure 9-4. The values in the left column of the grid are the names of the configurable properties. The values in the second column are the current values of the properties and are all editable.

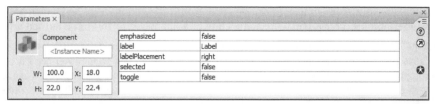

Figure 9-4. The available parameters for a Button instance, accessed through the Parameters panel

4. Click the cell that says Label in the second column, which is the current value of the `label` property. The word becomes highlighted and you can overwrite it with your own string. Type in **My Button** and press Enter.

Did you notice what happened on the stage? Your Button instance now has My Button as its label, giving you instant feedback to your change, as shown in Figure 9-5. This sweet little feature is called Live Preview, and it allows components to update themselves based on certain properties (unfortunately, some properties are not reflected; for instance, changing a skin does not update the skin of the Live Preview). Keep an eye on the instance on the stage as you edit to see how your changes are represented (or else the engineer who developed this fantastic feature will go cry in the corner).

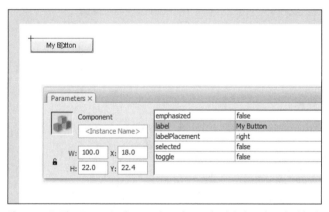

Figure 9-5. The Button's Live Preview shows the label updated with the new value.

5. Click the word false in the second column next to the `emphasized` property. This parameter does not offer an input field, but rather a list of only two options: true or false. Select true, and you will see the component update to emphasized.

6. Click the right value next to the `labelPlacement` property and select left from the list of four items. Nothing happens! In this case, the parameters here are a little misleading, as they show options that are applicable only to coded items. `labelPlacement` affects only Button instances that have icons (in which case, the `labelPlacement` parameter controls on which side of the icon the label is placed), and icons can be set only through ActionScript. So changing this value here does nothing, unless you write some code to add an icon to this or all Button instances.

7. Change the selected property from false to true. Again, nothing happens! In this case, it is because the selected property of a Button instance is directly tied to whether the button is set to toggle. A button that does not toggle cannot be selected. So if you change the toggle property to true as well, then you should see the Button instance change to show it is selected. If you test your movie, you should see that the instance starts out selected and can be toggled between states. Figure 9-6 shows the Parameters panel and component after making all these changes to the properties.

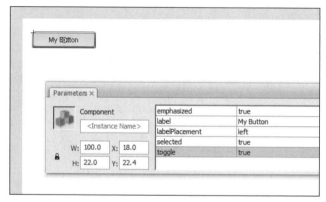

Figure 9-6. The Button instance with its selected, toggle, and emphasized properties set to true

Don't get frustrated by the Parameters panel. At this point, it pays to know where to find information about all of your components and why properties might not be working as expected. That information is available through the ActionScript 3.0 Language and Components Reference in your Flash Help (select Help ➤ Flash Help, or press F1). From there, open the All Classes folder, and you will see all ActionScript classes, including the components. You can browse each component's properties here (as well as methods, styles, and events, with sample code) to investigate just what is configurable and how.

You can set component properties from one more panel: the Component Inspector, accessed by selecting Window ➤ Component Inspector. As shown in Figure 9-7, this panel includes three tabs: Parameters, Bindings, and Schema. The Parameters tab offers pretty much the same options as the Parameters panel. I say "pretty much," since the Button instance has two additional properties to set: enabled and visible. Why the discrepancy? When creating a component, the developer decides which parameters to make inspectable. Although all of these inspectable parameters will appear in the Component Inspector, it is possible to limit the number of parameters that appear in the Parameters panel by using a special syntax. This might be a good option for parameters that are rarely changed, so that they appear in the Component Inspector when they are really needed, but otherwise do not clutter the more-often-used Parameters panel.

If you select either the Bindings or Schema tabs, you'll see that everything is disabled except for the plus icon. If you click this in either tab, you get a nice, friendly dialog box like the one shown in Figure 9-8, which explains these features are not available for ActionScript 3.0; they are available only for ActionScript 1.0 and 2.0.

Well, there you go! The component framework in Flash CS3 and ActionScript 3.0 was intentionally simplified from the previous version to make components more lightweight. This makes the framework easier to work with for developing applications and movies using the Flash graphical environment (with the thought that more complex application development that requires more advanced features would be done using the Flex framework). Two features to go were component binding and schemas. So with ActionScript 3.0, you won't have much use for the Component Inspector panel, other than to access the few extra properties it offers. For the examples in this chapter, you will set properties through the Parameters panel and put the Component Inspector panel to bed (by clicking its little close button).

Figure 9-7. The Component Inspector panel also allows you to set component parameters.

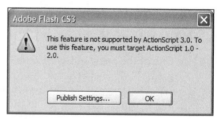

Figure 9-8. One of the few instances where features are removed from a previous version

Benefits of working with components

We have looked at what components are, how to add them to your files, and how to configure them. A big remaining question is why you would want to do such a thing. Well, here's a list:

- **Rapid prototyping**: Do you need to put an application together fast, fast, FAST? Components, with their ready-to-use, often complex functionality, make it a cinch to put together an interface of standard UI widgets in no time.

- **No need to reinvent the wheel**: OK, a button might not be a big deal to code in itself, but when you add on functionality like icons, labels, and toggling, it gets a lot more complex than you might expect. Others have coded it already. Why not leverage the work already done?

- **Easy to have minor differences in widgets**: You need one button with a label, another with a label and an icon. You have one check box with the label on the right, another with the label on the left, and another with its label twice as big as all other instances. These minor differences between instances can be handled by a properly coded component, while keeping base functionality and graphical appearance consistent among all instances.

- **Conforming functionality**: One complaint against Flash interfaces is the lack of conformity among different applications, potentially causing frustration for the users who must "learn" an interface before using it. Using standard components, such as those available in the Flash component framework, helps to reduce this potential frustration.

- **More OOP-like development**: OOP is something that you are already doing with ActionScript, perhaps without really being aware of it. As explained in Chapter 1, OOP is a method of programming where distinct, self-contained objects (think of Sprite and Array instances) interact with each other in a recommended pattern that maintains a separation of responsibility. You don't need to understand this fully or be a die-hard OOP proponent to know that by using self-contained widgets with clearly defined APIs, you are building in more of an OOP manner, which will make it easier to develop and maintain your code.

- **Something for everyone**: A lot of components are out there—not just the ones available with the standard Flash CS3 installation—that will do pretty much anything you could need. If you don't have the time to develop from scratch, chances are someone else already has. The "Using third-party components" section at the end of the chapter discusses where you might find more components to use.

Exploring the Flash component framework

One of the great add-ons to the Flash CS3 installation is the Flash component framework. You actually get both the ActionScript 2.0 (these are commonly referred to as V2 components) and ActionScript 3.0 components, but the former are available only for use with ActionScript 2.0 applications, as you might expect. Since we are in the middle of an ActionScript 3.0 book, we'll stick to the 3.0 versions.

The ActionScript 3.0 components come in two broad categories: UI and Video components, and both sets can be accessed from your Components panel.

UI components

The UI components consist of the following widgets:

- Button: This is the most common UI element, which allows a user to click for an action. The Button component also lets you set a label and/or icon, and allows for toggling behavior, meaning that the button can stay in one of two states: selected or unselected.

- CheckBox: Similar to the Button component set to toggle, this component has selected and unselected states, usually represented by a checkmark within a box (the name says it all, doesn't it?). A label, if added, is placed to the side of the box.

- ColorPicker: This component allows a user to set a color based on a pop-up swatch list of colors laid out in a grid. Alternatively, a color may be set by typing a hex value into a text field within the pop-up list. The close state of the ColorPicker shows a single swatch with the selected color.

- ComboBox: This is a drop-down list that displays a scrolling list of options, from which one can be selected. The selected option then appears displayed in the closed state of the component. A ComboBox instance can be set as editable, and the way a list item is rendered is completely configurable (meaning it does not need to be simply a text string, but can be an image, an image plus text, or anything you need to represent the data).

- DataGrid: Probably the most complex of the UI components, the DataGrid represents data in a scrolling grid of columns and rows, where each row is a line item with possibly multiple values laid out across columns, each of which represents a single value. Each column can have a different way to represent its data, so that one column might have all of its values as text, while another column might use images.

- Label: One of the simpler UI components, a Label is simply a text string that can be single- or multiple-line, and display regular or HTML text. The benefit of using Label components over TextField components is that the component framework makes it easy to change formatting across an entire application.

- List: The List component is useful for displaying arrays of values in a vertically laid out, scrollable region (the ComboBox, when open, displays a List instance). The way items are represented in the List component is completely configurable, just as in the ComboBox, so you are not limited to merely a list of text values.

- NumericStepper: This component allows a user to set a single number from an ordered set of numbers, through a text field or by clicking up/down arrows that change the value of the text field. You can configure the range of numbers represented and the interval between numbers.

- ProgressBar: When an application is loading external data or media, it is best to offer the user feedback on the progress of the loading process, and that is where the ProgressBar component comes in handy. This component displays a graphical representation of the state of the load, either in a determinate manner (for example, showing a percentage of the bytes loaded in) or in an indeterminate manner (for example, showing a looping animation to assure the user that something is occurring, though it does not represent a percentage of bytes).

- RadioButton: This component is like a CheckBox in a group. When there are multiple RadioButton instances grouped together (programmatically, not graphically), only one option within the group may be selected at one time. This is great if there are a small number of options from which only one may be selected, and one *must* be selected for validation. A good example of this is male/female options on a user registration page.

- ScrollPane: This component offers a way to display other display objects and externally loaded images within a scrollable region. You can use this if you need to limit the area in which a display object may be viewed, but you wish to allow the user to scroll to any area of that display object. This is useful not only for loaded images when there is limited screen real estate, but also for forms that contain many controls, where you need to scroll vertically.

- Slider: This component allows the user to select a numeric value by dragging a slider thumb either horizontally or vertically within a defined region. The range represented, the interval between numbers that can be selected (for instance, if you only want integers or if you want decimal values), and the tick marks are configurable.

- TextArea: This component is a useful multiline input field that can optionally display scrollbars. If you need a user to enter any moderately large amount of data, or you wish to display such data (you can set a TextArea instance to be noneditable), this is a great component to use.

- TextInput: This component is the little brother of the TextArea component, allowing only a single line of input. This is useful for when smaller amounts of data need to be entered, like a username, a password, or an e-mail address.

■ TileList: This component is most useful for displaying a scrollable grid of image data in a speci-fied number of columns and rows (you can also configure the component to display only a sin-gle scrollable row or column). Like the other list components (List, ComboBox, and DataGrid), the TileList allows you to configure the way that tiles are displayed, so if the default method of displaying a tile isn't what you need, you can create your own class to represent a tile in the manner required.

■ UIScrollBar: Scrollbars are ubiquitous and necessary in complex applications that are now com-monplace, so thank goodness that the Flash component framework includes its own. Use the UIScrollBar component when you need to scroll a visual region. Often, using the ScrollPane is easier for scrolling display objects that need to be masked, but the UIScrollBar is most useful for text fields that need to be scrolled when you don't want to deal with a TextArea component.

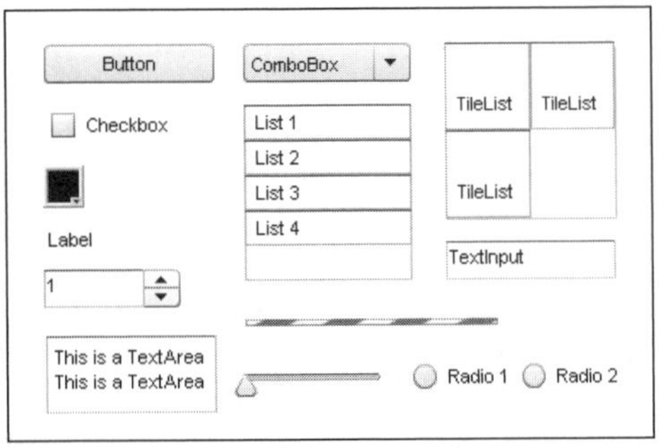

Figure 9-9 shows most of the UI components laid out on the stage.

Figure 9-9. The UI components on display

Video components

The video components are built a little differently than the UI components and are specifically tar-geted for playback and interaction with video. Really, only two of the video components are in the form of movie clip symbols with customizable parameters: FLVPlayback and FLVPlaybackCaptioning. The other components that appear in the Components panel under the Video folder—such as PlayButton, SeekBar, and VolumeBar—are skins that can be used to customize the controls of an FLVPlayback component. All you need to do is drag them to the stage, and they will automatically work with the FLVPlayback component; there is no parameter configurability.

Let's take a look at the two configurable video components. The FLVPlayback component is shown in Figure 9-10, but the FLVPlaybackCaptioning component is nonrendering, so it does not appear in the screenshot of the published SWF.

Figure 9-10. An FLVPlayback component with its selected control skins

■ FLVPlayback: This component fulfills almost all of your video playback needs. It can load and play both progressively downloaded and streaming video, and there are a wide vari-ety of customizable controls for such common functionality, such as play/pause toggling, volume control, back and for-ward buttons (when playing a list of videos), and a seek bar for showing the playhead position. Skins are all assigned from externally loaded SWFs and come with many different options, though these skins can also be changed directly to suit your needs, since you can modify the original FLA source (found in your Flash CS3 installation directory under FLVPlayback Skins/FLA/ActionScript 3.0).

- FLVPlaybackCaptioning: This component doesn't actually have any graphic representation, but instead adds functionality to an FLVPlayback component. Using an FLVPlaybackCaptioning component, you can specify XML to load with your video. This XML can list time codes in a single or multiple FLV files, text that should be shown at those times (represented in a format known as timed text), and the text formatting that should be applied. When the video plays back, the caption text will appear over it. Through code, you can have the text appear elsewhere by listening for change events and updating your own text display.

As mentioned previously, the remaining components in the Video folder in the Components panel are controls that can be used to build and skin your own layout for the FLVPlayback controls. The workflow for this would be to set the skins parameter of your FLVPlayback instance to None, then drag the desired controls from the Components panel to the stage in whatever configuration you need. The components are built in such a way that the FLVPlayback component and the controls will automatically plug in to each other, so that you do not need any additional code to wire up things. You are then free to lay out and skin the controls however you need. See the "Styling and skinning" section later in this chapter for more on skinning components.

Going behind the scenes

Now that we've explored briefly what is available for use with the Flash component framework, let's pop the hood and take a look at what's going on to make everything run so smoothly.

1. Create a new Flash ActionScript 3.0 file to start fresh.

2. With the Components panel open, drag a Button component to the stage. At this point, you should see the Button symbol in your Library as well as the Component Assets folder.

3. Generally, you should never need to go into this folder and can access all you need through the component symbols (or their instances) themselves. But what's the fun of looking under the hood if we honor that now? Open the Component Assets folder in your Library.

4. You will see three more folders: _private, ButtonSkins, and Shared. Expand ButtonSkins to see all of the—you guessed it—button skin symbols, as shown in Figure 9-11. You can enter editing mode for any of these symbols to change their graphical appearance. However, a better option for this is to double-click the component symbol or one of its instances, as you will learn in the "Styling and skinning" section later in this chapter.

5. Expand the Shared folder. You will see the focusRectSkin symbol. This symbol is used by many of the components to represent when they have keyboard focus. Several symbols will appear in this Shared folder, based on which

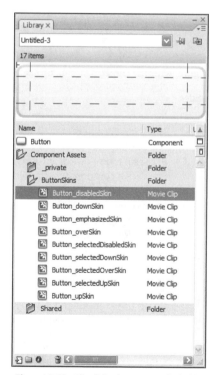

Figure 9-11. All of the button symbol skins are accessible in the Library.

components you have in your Library. The general rule is that any skin used by multiple components will appear here.

6. Expand the _private folder. You will see two symbols: Component_avatar and ComponentShim, as shown in Figure 9-12.

Figure 9-12. The contents of the _private folder in the expanded Component Assets folder

What are these goodies? The Component_avatar symbol is simply a rectangle that is used to size components in the IDE. Since components behind the scenes are just code, this graphic is used so that you can select and resize instances on the stage. At runtime, this graphic is removed from the display list in the component. (For all of you users of the V2 components, this serves the same functionality as BoundingBox_mc.)

The ComponentShim symbol is much more interesting. To speed up the compile time of a movie, the component classes have been precompiled into SWC files. However, SWC files are not editable in the IDE. So, to keep components precompiled for speed and encapsulation, and yet still offer access for editing skins, all component classes have been precompiled into the ComponentShim symbol. This means that the component symbol, such as Button, is not precompiled, so it can be edited, but all of the code that is used to define Button's functionality is precompiled into the ComponentShim symbol, along with all other UI components. This keeps the code tucked away and ensures faster compile times, yet still offers access to a component's skins by double-clicking the symbol or an instance.

That's pretty sweet! But if all of the component classes are compiled into the ComponentShim, why doesn't the file size increase enormously with the addition of a single component? After all, dragging a Button component into your file must also mean that you are getting DataGrid, TileList, and ScrollPane components, right? Actually, no. Much like when you include multiple import statements in your ActionScript referencing classes you do not use, the compiler knows not to include the unused component classes. Only if you include the additional components in your Library will you get the extra components compiled into your SWF, because each component's symbol in the Library is set to export for ActionScript.

Finding the files

If you use components a lot, would like to know better how they are put together, or need to make modifications, you should know where to find them in your file system.

First, you need to find the directory where you installed Flash. The default directory on Windows is C:\Program Files\Adobe\Adobe Flash CS3, On a Mac, it is Mac HDD:Library:Application Support: Adobe:Flash CS3. Within this directory, you should find a language-specific subdirectory, like en for

English. If you expand this, you will find Configuration and First Run directories. First Run will include files copied to your personal user directory the first time you launch Flash under a specific login. The Configuration directory is the one of interest now. Go ahead and expand that, and you should see subdirectories, as shown in Figure 9-13.

The two subdirectories of interest in this discussion of components are Components and Component Source.

Components directory

If you select the Components directory, you will see two FLAs and four subdirectories, as shown in Figure 9-14. Whatever is in this Components directory will appear in your Components panel in the Flash IDE. The two FLAs are named User Interface and Video, and correspond to the two folders in the Components panel you've already explored. The four subdirectories—Data, Media, User Interface, and Video—contain ActionScript 2.0 components that you will find in the Components panel while editing an ActionScript 2.0 document.

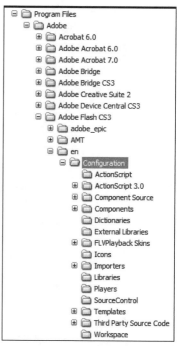

Figure 9-13. The Configuration directory in a default Flash CS3 installation

Figure 9-14. The Components subdirectory in a default Flash CS3 installation

If you want to open the User Interface FLA, you will need to copy it into another directory, since Flash already recognizes this FLA as being open in the Components panel and will not open a second instance. Let's do that now.

Select the User Interface.fla file in your file system and copy it to your clipboard. Select another directory, perhaps one associated with this chapter's files in your personal folders, and paste the file there. Next, double-click the FLA to open it in Flash. You will see the stage appear as shown in Figure 9-15.

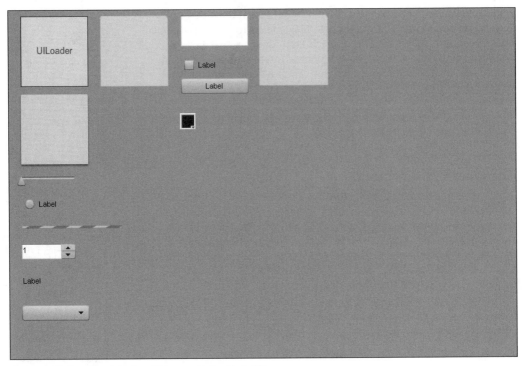

Figure 9-15. The User Interface FLA open in the Flash IDE

This FLA is merely a container for the components so that they appear in a single folder in the Components panel. If you ever needed to modify the default skins that appear for any components, as opposed to editing in each file in which you use a component, you might edit the skins in the User Interface.fla file. In addition, if you ever wanted to add a component to the User Interface folder in your Components panel, you could add it to this file. In those cases, though, you would save the file under a new name and copy it into the Components directory within your user directory for your Flash configuration. For instance, on a Windows machine, that Components directory is located at C:\Documents and Settings\<user>\Local Settings\Application Data\Adobe\Flash CS3\<language>\Configuration. Once you had done that and restarted Flash, a new folder would appear in your Components panel and would contain all of the modified components, but the original UI components would remain untouched.

Component Source directory

The second directory of interest in the Configuration directory is Component Source. Expand Component Source, and you will see both ActionScript 2.0 and ActionScript 3.0 directories. Expand the ActionScript 3.0 directory to find FLVPlayback, FLVPlaybackCaptioning, and User Interface subdirectories, as shown in Figure 9-16.

Select the User Interface directory and notice that it contains a ComponentShim.fla file. This is the file that includes all of the uncompiled component symbols for each class (not to be confused with the symbols that contain the skins).

Double-click the ComponentShim.fla file to open it in Flash. Notice that there is nothing on the stage, and no ActionScript in the timeline or document class specified. However, the Library contains a symbol for each of the UI component classes, and each of these is set to export for ActionScript in the first frame. It is this file that is used to create the compiled symbol, which is then included within each component. If you wanted to modify the component source or add more classes to the ComponentShim symbol that appears in each component, this is the file you would modify and recompile.

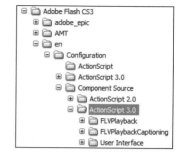

Figure 9-16. The Component Source directory contains all of the ActionScript source for the component classes.

Now, the ComponentShim is a great trick for helping the compile times in complex applications with many components (and, believe me, compile time can be a real pain in these circumstances), but what if you need access to that original source code that has been precompiled? Well, thankfully, Adobe has included the source for this purpose. Expand the fl subdirectory in the User Interface directory, and you will see all of the packages containing the ActionScript files that are used in the components, as shown in Figure 9-17.

Let's try modifying the source code to see how that might work.

1. Expand the fl directory and select the core directory within this. You should see two ActionScript files: InvalidationType.as and UIComponent.as, as shown in Figure 9-18. All UI components inherit from UIComponent, either directly or indirectly, so if you add a trace() statement within this class's constructor, you should see it appear in the Flash IDE's Output panel.

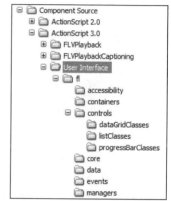

Figure 9-17. The ActionScript source code for all UI components is found in the User Interface directory in Configuration/Component Source/ActionScript 3.0.

Figure 9-18. The ActionScript classes found in the fl/core directory

2. Copy and rename UIComponent.as so that you have a backup, which is always a good idea when you are editing an original source file. Even though you will be adding only a single trace() statement, you want to be sure you can revert the file to its original condition, if necessary.

3. Double-click UIComponent.as so that it opens in Flash. Although it's 1,500 lines of ActionScript, a quick look will show that the majority of the file is comments, so it's not as complex as you might first fear. Find the constructor at line 459, and add the single line of code shown in bold.

```
public function UIComponent() {
  super();
  trace(this);
  instanceStyles = {};
  sharedStyles = {};
  invalidHash = {};
```

This will simply call the toString() method on the instance of the component that is being created and send the value to the Output panel.

4. Create a new Flash ActionScript 3.0 file and drag a Button component from Components panel on to the stage. Test your movie.

Nothing traces! Let's think this one through. You know that the components have a ComponentShim symbol that contains all of the precompiled component classes. Since the classes are precompiled, your trace() statement is not present (it wasn't there when the classes were first compiled). So in order to modify this code, does that mean you need to recompile the ComponentShim and replace it in your file?

Thankfully, the answer to that is no. There is a nice trick to precompiled code, and that is if the Flash compiler finds uncompiled ActionScript in the classpath while compiling your SWF, it will use these classes as opposed to the precompiled versions. All that means is that if you point to the component source code directory, when you test the movie, the Flash compiler will grab the uncompiled source and ignore the precompiled code, and thus the trace() statement will be run.

5. Select File ➤ Publish Settings. On the Flash tab, click the Settings button next to the ActionScript version drop-down list. This opens the ActionScript 3.0 Settings dialog box, as shown in Figure 9-19.

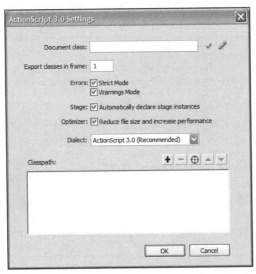

Figure 9-19. The ActionScript 3.0 Settings dialog box is where classpaths can be specified.

6. Click the button that looks like a target next to the Classpath: label. This opens a browse dialog box. Navigate your file system to select the Configuration/Component Source/ActionScript 3.0/ User Interface directory where the ActionScript source resides. Click OK, and the path will be entered into the Classpath list, as shown in Figure 9-20.

Figure 9-20. The path to the component source has been added to the classpath for the file.

7. Click OK to exit the ActionScript 3.0 Settings dialog box, and then click OK again to exit the Publish Settings dialog box. Test your movie again.

You should have noticed two things. First, the compiling of your movie should have taken slightly longer (not much, since there is just one component, but it might be noticeable). Second, the Output panel should have opened and traced [object Button]. So now you know that if you ever need to modify the component source, you can merely point to the source directory, and the compiler will grab the classes from there. Of course, as before, it is always recommended that you duplicate the original files before making any changes, so that you have a backup in case you need to restore the previous versions.

Scripting interaction

Now that you have some familiarity with the components and an idea of what is going on behind the scenes, it's time to plug some components together in a simple example. This will demonstrate how easy it is to work with the components and how they can be made to interact through ActionScript.

You will create a List instance that allows a user to add items to it though a TextInput instance and a Button instance. If an item is selected in the List instance, the user will be allowed to edit or delete the selected item. Such a control might be useful for any type of list that a user should be able to add

Figure 9-21. An example of multiple components working together to create a simple interface

to, such as a shopping cart, a buddy list, or a group of events. The end result will look like Figure 9-21.

Adding the components

You'll begin by adding the components to create the interface.

1. Create a new Flash ActionScript 3.0 file and save it as editableList.fla into a project directory for this chapter.

2. Select Modify ➤ Document from the main menu to open the Document Properties dialog box. Set the width of the file to **230 px** and the height to **200 px**. Change the Background color option to a light gray (#CCCCCC), as shown in Figure 9-22.

Figure 9-22. The document properties for the editableList.fla file

3. Open the Components panel if it's not currently open (Window ➤ Components). Drag the Button, Label, List, and TextInput components on to your stage from the User Interface folder.

4. Select the List instance on the stage. In the Property inspector, change its dimensions to 200 × 100 and set its position to (15, 15). Leave all of its default parameter settings, but give the instance the name names_li. The _li suffix makes it easy to see that the object is a List instance.

5. Select the TextInput instance. In the Property inspector, change its dimensions to 170 × 22 and set its position to (15, 120). Give it the instance name editName_ti (_ti for TextInput). Keep all of its default parameter settings.

6. Select the Button instance. In the Property inspector, change its dimensions to 22 × 22 and set its position to (193, 120). Give it the instance name deleteName_bn (_bn for Button). In the Parameters panel, set the label property to - (a minus sign).

7. Select the Label instance. In the Property inspector, change its dimensions to 200 × 20 with its position set to (15, 150). This instance does not need a name (you will not be manipulating it through ActionScript). In the Parameters panel, change its text property to **Enter a name to add to the list:**. Figure 9-23 shows the results so far.

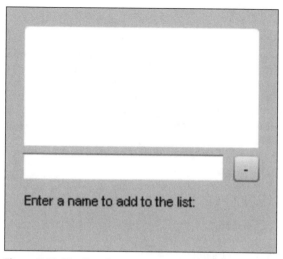

Figure 9-23. The first three components laid out on the stage

8. Drag another `TextInput` instance from your Library (Window ➤ Library) to the stage. Give it the dimensions 170 × 22 and the position (15, 170). Give it the instance name `addName_ti`. All of its parameters should remain at their defaults.

9. Drag another `Button` instance from the Library to the stage. Name it `addName_bn`. Make its dimensions the same as the other `Button` instance, 22 × 22, and set its position to (193, 170). In the Parameters panel, change its `label` property to + (a plus sign).

You are now finished with the interface itself, as shown in Figure 9-24. Using components makes it easy to lay out and align groups of components in the visual editor. Of course, to get those components to do anything useful, you'll need some ActionScript to wire everything together.

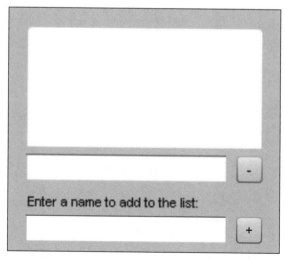

Figure 9-24. The completed component interface for the editable list

Adding the ActionScript

Create a new ActionScript file and save it as EditableList.as into a package directory com/foundationAS3/ch9 that is a subdirectory of where you saved the editableList.fla file from the previous steps. This will be the package structure for your ActionScript class.

In the ActionScript file, create the package structure, class declaration, and constructor for your EditableList class. Let's also include the imports you will need, including the controls classes that are included in your interface. Note that these controls are found in the f1 package, not the flash package that you have been previously using. The flash package contains all of the classes built into the Flash Player runtime. The f1 package contains classes provided for the Flash component framework that come with the Flash CS3 IDE installation.

```
package com.foundationAS3.ch9 {

  import fl.controls.Button;
  import fl.controls.List;
  import fl.controls.TextInput;

  import flash.display.Sprite;

  public class EditableList extends Sprite {

    public function EditableList() {
    }

  }

}
```

You will call an init() method from within the constructor in order to set up event listeners on all of your components. Add the lines in bold to the EditableList class.

```
package com.foundationAS3.ch9 {

  import fl.controls.Button;
  import fl.controls.List;
  import fl.controls.TextInput;

  import flash.display.Sprite;
  import flash.events.Event;
  import flash.events.MouseEvent;

  public class EditableList extends Sprite {

    public function EditableList() {
      init();
    }
```

```
private function init():void {
    addName_bn.addEventListener(MouseEvent.CLICK, onAddName);
    deleteName_bn.addEventListener(MouseEvent.CLICK, onDeleteName);
    editName_ti.addEventListener(Event.CHANGE, onNameChange);
    names_li.addEventListener(Event.CHANGE, onNameSelected);
}

private function onAddName(event:MouseEvent):void {
}

private function onDeleteName(event:MouseEvent):void {
}

private function onNameChange(event:Event):void {
}

private function onNameSelected(event:Event):void {
}

}

}
```

Since all the controls components are interactive display objects, they have the same event API that you have explored previously with Sprite. Each component may have additional events that are dispatched based on the type of component. For instance, the CHANGE event is dispatched from a List instance whenever the selection in the List instance changes. You will use this CHANGE event to update the other controls based on the selection. The CHANGE event is also dispatched from a TextInput instance when its text is changed. You will use this event from editName_ti to update the data in the List instance for the selected item.

First, though, you need to provide a way to enter items into the list. You will handle this in the onAddName() method, which will be called whenever addName_bn is clicked. Update the onAddName() method with the following bold lines.

```
private function onAddName(event:MouseEvent):void {
    var newItem:Object = {label:addName_ti.text};
    names_li.dataProvider.addItem(newItem);
    addName_ti.text = "";
}
```

A List instance has a dataProvider property through which all manipulation of the internal list data must be done. You can use the addItem() method of dataProvider to append items to the List instance's data. A new item needs at least a label property for display in the list, so you add a new item by creating an Object instance with one property: label. To this label property, you assign the value of the addName_ti instance's text property. Once addItem() has been called, you remove the text from addName_ti so that the user can enter a new item.

If you test your movie now and type a name in the bottom field and click the add button, that name should appear in names_li. Try adding several names to see them appear.

Next, let's allow someone to select an item in the list and be able to edit or remove that item. Removing items will be handled in onDeleteName(). Editing items will be handled in the onNameChange(). In order to make it easy for a user to edit a name, you'll populate the editName_ti TextInput instance with the label value of the currently selected item in the list. That will be taken care of in the onNameSelected() handler. Update your EditableList class with the following bold lines. Code not listed does not need to be changed.

```
private function onDeleteName(event:MouseEvent):void {
  names_li.dataProvider.removeItemAt(names_li.selectedIndex);
  editName_ti.text = "";
}

private function onNameChange(event:Event):void {
  var newItem:Object = {label:editName_ti.text};
  names_li.dataProvider.replaceItemAt(newItem, names_li.selectedIndex);
}

private function onNameSelected(event:Event):void {
  editName_ti.text = names_li.selectedItem.label;
}
```

When an item is selected in the list, the onNameSelected() handler will be called. This assigns the label from the currently selected item, found through the aptly named selectedItem property of List, to the text property of editName_ti.

If the user then types into editName_ti, adding or removing letters, the onNameChange() handler will be called (thanks to the CHANGE event fired by editName_ti). A new item is created using the current text in editName_ti. You then can use the list dataProvider's replaceItem() method to replace the value of the currently selected item with the new, updated item.

Finally, whenever the deleteName_bn button is clicked, it will dispatch a CLICK event, which will be handled by the onDeleteName() method. The dataProvider's removeItemAt() method is just what you need to remove the currently selected item. removeItemAt() takes an integer value representing the index of the item in the list to remove, which you can obtain through the selectedIndex property of List. Once the item is deleted, you remove the text from the editName_ti field as well.

At this point, you have a pretty nice little mini-application to create lists. One problem, though, is that the delete button can be clicked when no item has been selected. The same issue occurs with the editName_ti component. Also, items can be added to the list without any labels by clicking the add button without typing anything into addName_ti. You can take care of these problems by enabling and disabling controls based on the states of other controls. All of the controls have an enabled property, which actually comes from the UIComponent class from which they all descend. If this property is not true, then the component does not allow for interaction.

First, you want to disable the two buttons and editName_ti when the SWF launches. This will ensure that the only initial interaction allowed will be entering text into addName_ti. Add the following bold lines to the init() method to try this.

```
private function init():void {
    addName_bn.addEventListener(MouseEvent.CLICK, onAddName);
    addName_ti.addEventListener(Event.CHANGE, onNameEnter);
    deleteName_bn.addEventListener(MouseEvent.CLICK, onDeleteName);
    editName_ti.addEventListener(Event.CHANGE, onNameChange);
    names_li.addEventListener(Event.CHANGE, onNameSelected);

    addName_bn.enabled = false;
    deleteName_bn.enabled = false;
    editName_ti.enabled = false;
}
```

Unfortunately, if you test the movie, you will see that the buttons don't disable themselves as expected, although the text input field does. Well, that's no good. This is a problem with the constructor running before some internal code within the component, which is reenabling itself. To handle this, you will move your code into the next frame by setting up a handler for the ENTER_FRAME event and disabling the components then. Alter your code for the init() method to look like the following, which creates a new listener for the ENTER_FRAME event and moves the disabling code into that listener.

```
private function init():void {
    addName_bn.addEventListener(MouseEvent.CLICK, onAddName);
    addName_ti.addEventListener(Event.CHANGE, onNameEnter);
    deleteName_bn.addEventListener(MouseEvent.CLICK, onDeleteName);
    editName_ti.addEventListener(Event.CHANGE, onNameChange);
    names_li.addEventListener(Event.CHANGE, onNameSelected);
    addEventListener(Event.ENTER_FRAME, onNextFrame);
}

private function onNextFrame(event:Event):void {
    removeEventListener(Event.ENTER_FRAME, onNextFrame);
    addName_bn.enabled = false;
    deleteName_bn.enabled = false;
    editName_ti.enabled = false;
}
```

If you test the movie again, you should see the buttons are disabled. Now you need to handle when to enable those buttons.

The add button should be enabled whenever there is text entered into the addName_ti field. You can listen for this through the CHANGE event for the TextInput instance. Then the button should disable itself when the field is cleared. Add the following bold lines to handle these events.

```
private function init():void {
  addName_bn.addEventListener(MouseEvent.CLICK, onAddName);
  addName_ti.addEventListener(Event.CHANGE, onNameEnter);
  deleteName_bn.addEventListener(MouseEvent.CLICK, onDeleteName);
  editName_ti.addEventListener(Event.CHANGE, onNameChange);
  names_li.addEventListener(Event.CHANGE, onNameSelected);
  addEventListener(Event.ENTER_FRAME, onNextFrame);
}

private function onNextFrame(event:Event):void {
  removeEventListener(Event.ENTER_FRAME, onNextFrame);
  addName_bn.enabled = false;
  deleteName_bn.enabled = false;
  editName_ti.enabled = false;
}

private function onAddName(event:MouseEvent):void {
  var newItem:Object = {label:addName_ti.text};
  names_li.dataProvider.addItem(newItem);
  addName_ti.text = "";
  addName_bn.enabled = false;
}

private function onNameEnter(event:Event):void {
  addName_bn.enabled = addName_ti.text.length > 0;
}

private function onDeleteName(event:MouseEvent):void {
  names_li.dataProvider.removeItemAt(names_li.selectedIndex);
  editName_ti.text = "";
}
```

Now the add button will be enabled in the onNameEnter() method, which will be called when text is entered or edited in the addName_ti component. It will be disabled in the onAddName() method when a new item is added to the list and the addName_ti text is cleared.

The final step is enabling the delete button and the editName_ti component whenever an item can be edited or deleted. This will occur in the onNameSelected() handler. When an item is deleted, you need to disable these controls once again. Add the following bold lines, which should handle these occurrences.

```
private function onDeleteName(event:MouseEvent):void {
  names_li.dataProvider.removeItemAt(names_li.selectedIndex);
  deleteName_bn.enabled = false;
```

```
            editName_ti.text = "";
            editName_ti.enabled = false;
        }

        private function onNameChange(event:Event):void {
            var newItem:Object = {label:editName_ti.text};
            names_li.dataProvider.replaceItemAt(newItem, ➥
    names_li.selectedIndex);
        }

        private function onNameSelected(event:Event):void {
            editName_ti.text = names_li.selectedItem.label;
            editName_ti.enabled = true;
            deleteName_bn.enabled = true;
        }
```

Save the EditableList.as file and return to the editableList.fla file.

You now need to set the document class for this file to be the EditableList class you just created. In the Property inspector, set the document class to com.foundationAS3.ch9.EditableList.

Now test your movie. You should see your mini-application for creating and editing a list of names (as shown earlier in Figure 9-21), all through the use of Flash components and ActionScript to wire everything together.

If you get errors upon compiling, see if the error messages help you determine where the syntax of what you typed was incorrect. If you are unable to debug, compare your file with the EditableList.as file included with the files you downloaded for this chapter.

That's not a bad little app for a few pages' work! Imagine now if you had to code all those components yourself to build such an application, and how much longer such a task would take. There are times when that will be necessary and inevitable, but for the times it isn't, the components offer a great way to quickly implement an application consisting of UI controls.

Styling and skinning

One important thing to know about any component framework is how you might go about customizing the built-in components so that you can make the interfaces you create unique, with your own desired look and feel. Generally, altering items like colors and fonts within a component is referred to as **styling**, and changing the graphics used to produce the overall look of a component is called **skinning**. Let's look at what you can do within the Flash component framework to restyle and reskin for your needs.

Styling components

With the V2 components for ActionScript 2.0 from previous versions of Flash (these are also included in your CS3 installation if you create an ActionScript 2.0 file), the default skins had a large number of styles that could be set to control colors within the skins. This offered great color configurability for the default skins. However, many found the task of reskinning to be difficult, or at least not as easy as they would have liked.

With the ActionScript 3.0 components, the workflow for reskinning has been greatly simplified. This simplification has also resulted in the reduction of the number of styles that can be set for the default skins. Although the configurable styles vary from component to component, most styles can be generally separated into those for setting text properties and those for setting skin properties. Using styles to set individual colors within a skin is no longer supported; instead, you need to create new skins with the desired new colors. You'll learn how to create skins a little later in this chapter.

For now, let's concentrate on altering text properties across components using styles. You'll continue with the previous list example and change aspects of the text properties in order to achieve a slightly different look. To do this, you'll change styles globally for all components, change styles for all instances of a single component class, and change the style on a single component instance.

Setting up for changing styles

To begin, save the class file EditableList.as as StyledList.as in the same directory. You'll use this as a base file for testing your styling code. Also save the editableList.fla as styledList.fla and change the document class to StyledList. In StyledList, change the following bold code.

```
package com.foundationAS3.ch9 {

    import fl.controls.Button;
    import fl.controls.List;
    import fl.controls.TextInput;

    import flash.display.Sprite;
    import flash.events.Event;
    import flash.events.MouseEvent;

    public class StyledList extends Sprite {

        public function StyledList() {
            init();
        }
```

You'll create a new method called setStyles(), which you'll call from the init() method. To make things cleaner, you'll move all of the event listener code into its own method as well.

```
        public function StyledList() {
            init();
        }

        private function init():void {
            setStyles();
            addListeners();
        }
```

```
    private function setStyles():void {
    }

    private function addListeners():void {
      addName_bn.addEventListener(MouseEvent.CLICK, onAddName);
      addName_ti.addEventListener(Event.CHANGE, onNameEnter);
      deleteName_bn.addEventListener(MouseEvent.CLICK, onDeleteName);
      editName_ti.addEventListener(Event.CHANGE, onNameChange);
      names_li.addEventListener(Event.CHANGE, onNameSelected);
      addEventListener(Event.ENTER_FRAME, onNextFrame);
    }
```

To set styles for all components or all instances of a certain class, you need to use the Flash component framework's StyleManager class. Import this class at the top of the code, along with TextFormat, which you'll need for setting text formats for components.

```
    package com.foundationAS3.ch9 {

      import fl.controls.Button;
      import fl.controls.List;
      import fl.controls.TextInput;
      import fl.managers.StyleManager;

      import flash.display.Sprite;
      import flash.events.Event;
      import flash.events.MouseEvent;
      import flash.text.TextFormat;

      public class StyledList extends Sprite {
```

Now you can start setting some styles!

Setting styles for all components

To set styles for all components in the framework, use the StyleManager's setStyles() method. This takes the name of the style property to set and the value for that property. Let's first change the color of the text for all components to a blue to match the highlight color built into the skins. Add the lines in bold to achieve this.

```
    private function setStyles():void {
      // blue green text for all components' default state
      var format:TextFormat = new TextFormat("Arial", 10, 0x01578F);
      StyleManager.setStyle("textFormat", format);
    }
```

If you test your movie now, you should see blue text for all of the components, except for the disabled state of the buttons, which requires setting a different property: disabledTextFormat.

Setting a style for all instances of a component

Next, let's try changing a style for all instances of a single component. For this, you will use StyleManager's setComponentStyle() method, which takes the class of component for which you wish to set a style property, the name of the property, and the value for that property. Since you're using only plus and minus symbols for your buttons, let's boost up the point size of the text to make it more visible. For this, add the following lines in bold.

```
private function setStyles():void {
    // blue green text for all components' default state
    var format:TextFormat = new TextFormat("Arial", 10, 0x01578F);
    StyleManager.setStyle("textFormat", format);
    // blue green text for Button default state
    format = new TextFormat("Arial", 12, 0x01578F);
    StyleManager.setComponentStyle(Button, "textFormat", format);
    // light gray text for Button disabled state
    format = new TextFormat("Arial", 12, 0x999999);
    StyleManager.setComponentStyle(Button, "disabledTextFormat", format);
}
```

You set two properties here, textFormat and disabledTextFormat, so that the point size of the text doesn't change based on the state. Notice that you can assign a new TextFormat instance each time to the format variable once the previous value has been passed in the setComponentStyle() call. You can do this because the variable is simply storing a reference, and that reference is passed in the method call, not the variable itself. So you then can assign new references to the variable that can be passed in the subsequent calls. If you test the movie again, the text for the button labels should be increased by 2 points.

Setting the style for a single instance of a component

As a final step, let's change the color of just the deleteName_bn component so that its label is red when it is clickable, giving a bit of a visual warning that clicking the button causes a destructive action. To set the style on a single instance, you need to use the UIComponent class's setStyle() method, which, like StyleManager's setStyles(), takes a name of a style property and the value to set. Since all of the controls inherit from UIComponent, this method is available on each component instance. Add the following lines in bold.

```
private function setStyles():void {
    // blue green text for all components' default state
    var format:TextFormat = new TextFormat("Arial", 10, 0x01578F);
    StyleManager.setStyle("textFormat", format);
    // blue green text for Button default state
    format = new TextFormat("Arial", 12, 0x01578F);
    StyleManager.setComponentStyle(Button, "textFormat", format);
    // light gray text for Button disabled state
    format = new TextFormat("Arial", 12, 0x999999);
    StyleManager.setComponentStyle(Button, "disabledTextFormat", format);
```

```
    // red text for delete button default state
    format = new TextFormat("Arial", 12, 0xFF0000);
    deleteName_bn.setStyle("textFormat", format);
}
```

If you test your movie once more, you'll see that all components have blue text (unless disabled), the button instances have text at a slightly larger point size, and when the delete button is active, its label is red as opposed to blue. This is styling at work!

Skinning using the timeline

If you are used to the graphic tools in Flash, reskinning a component using the new ActionScript 3.0 components is a piece of cake—simpler than it has been in either of the two previous versions. Any component instance on the stage or symbol in the Library allows you to double-click it to enter into symbol-editing mode, where the different supported skins are made obvious. Figure 9-25 shows an example of entering symbol-editing mode by double-clicking the List symbol.

Entering symbol-editing mode for a component immediately takes you to frame 2 of the component's timeline, where graphic skins on the left are labeled with descriptive text on the right. If you want to edit any of the skins, double-click the desired skin to enter its symbol-editing mode. Figure 9-26 shows what you find if you enter symbol-editing mode by double-clicking List_Skin within the List symbol.

At this point within the List_Skin symbol, you have a simple vector graphic that you can edit directly to change shapes, colors, or both, and these changes will be reflected in every single List instance in your application. The horizontal and vertical dotted lines represent the slices for the scale9 grid. This grid determines how a graphic is resized, and it is a great enhancement over manually slicing components, as we had to do before the feature was introduced in Flash 8. Only the middle section of the grid is scaled both vertically and horizontally. The top and bottom rows are not scaled vertically, and the right and left columns are not scaled

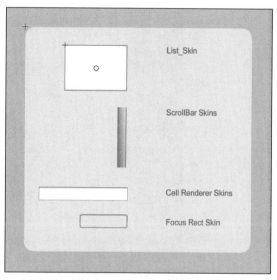

Figure 9-25. The skins that can be found within the List symbol

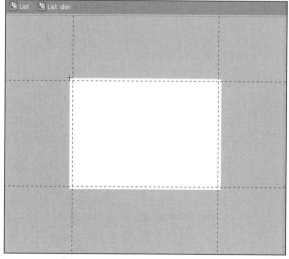

Figure 9-26. The List_Skin, which is the back graphic of the List component, in symbol-editing mode

373

horizontally. For more information about scale9 grids and how to create and use them, check out the Flash documentation.

Sometimes, a complex component contains nested components, which you need to navigate to in order to find the vectors to edit them. If you return to symbol-editing mode for the List symbol and double-click ScrollBar Skins, you should see something like Figure 9-27.

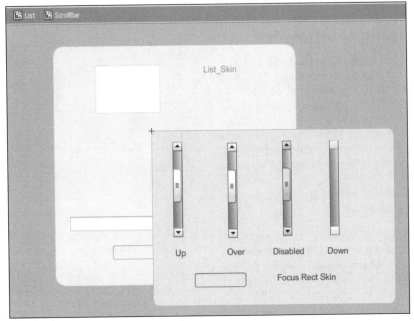

Figure 9-27. The ScrollBar skin accessed from within the List component

The ScrollBar is a complex symbol itself, so it contains a number of nested skins. You need to be aware that multiple components use the ScrollBar, so although you might be editing the ScrollBar symbol from within the List symbol, any component that uses these skins will be affected. The same holds true for editing of a global skin like the Focus Rect Skin, which appears within every single component. Editing this changes the skin that is used by all components that allow focus.

Let's do some timeline graphic editing to see how easy it is to change a skin in this manner. You will change the graphics for the TextInput component so it uses rounded corners like the Button component, as opposed to sharp corners. You'll need to edit both the enabled and disabled states.

1. Save styledList.fla as timelineSkinList.fla. The document class can remain the same, as you will not alter any code for this example; you will change only the Library graphics.

2. Double-click one of the TextInput instances on the main timeline's stage. You should enter symbol-editing mode and see the skins, as shown in Figure 9-28.

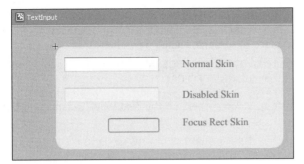

Figure 9-28. Symbol-editing mode for TextInput

3. Double-click the Normal Skin graphic (TextInput_upSkin) to enter its symbol-editing mode. You should see a graphic like the one shown in Figure 9-29.

Figure 9-29. Symbol-editing mode for the Normal Skin graphic within TextInput

4. Delete the graphics on the timeline and draw a rounded rectangle with a corner radius of 3 and a stroke of 1 pixel that is around 150 × 25 in its dimensions. You do not need to be exactly precise, as you can drag the scale9 dividers wherever they need to go to suit your graphic.

5. Make the fill of the rectangle white (#FFFFFF). Assign a linear gradient to the stroke with two color stops set to #6D6F70 and #D3D5D6. Use the Gradient Transform tool to rotate and scale the gradient so that it runs vertically down the component, moving from the darker color to the lighter color. The result should look like Figure 9-30.

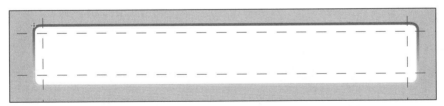

Figure 9-30. A new graphic is drawn for the skin using a rounded rectangle

6. Use the Selection tool to move the scale9 grid dividers to make sure that the corners do not get scaled in any resizing of the component; only the straight lines scale on resizing.

7. Now that the Normal Skin is complete, copy it to your clipboard.

8. Return to symbol-editing mode for the TextInput symbol. Double-click the Disabled Skin graphic (TextInput_disabledSkin) to enter its symbol-editing mode. Delete the graphic that is on its timeline, and then paste in place the graphic copied from the Normal Skin.

9. Alter the fill for the disabled state rectangle to #DBDBDB. Alter the gradient stroke so that the top color is #AFAFB0 and the bottom color is #CECECF.

Now test your movie. You should see nice rounded corners on the TextInput instances, in both the normal and disabled states.

Skinning using classes

Now it just doesn't seem right that we spend too much time in an ActionScript book doing edits in the timeline when we have this perfectly wonderful language to accomplish the same thing. Let's take a look at how you might use code to create and set skins for components, as opposed to editing graphic symbols in the Library.

First, it helps to remember that any symbol exported from the Library is done so as a class, whether you specify the class file to associate with the symbol or it is generated for you automatically behind the scenes. As such, any skin that is in the Library that a component instantiates at runtime is a class. There is nothing that requires that such a skin class needs to be in the Library, as long as it is available for a component to instantiate when it needs to draw itself. Therefore, you do not need to use pre-drawn graphics in the Library, but can draw the graphics through code in a custom class, as long you specify which class or classes a component should use for its skins.

In this next example, you'll create a new skin for the buttons in your list application, but instead of using the vector tools on the timeline, you'll create the graphics using ActionScript. The skins will be simple round graphics with a 1-point stroke. You'll create a different skin for each of the four states of the buttons: up, over, down, and disabled.

To begin, create a new ActionScript file and save it as StrokedCircle.as into a new skins subdirectory in the com/foundationAS3/ch9 directory (so the full path will be com/foundationAS3/ch9/skins).

Creating a skin for the button's up state

Next, enter the following code, which represents everything you will need to draw the up state for your buttons.

```
package com.foundationAS3.ch9.skins {

  import flash.display.Shape;

  public class StrokedCircle extends Shape {

    protected var _fillColor:uint = 0xE6E6E6;
    protected var _strokeColor:uint = 0x5C5C5C;

    public function StrokedCircle() {
      init();
    }
```

```
      protected function init():void {
        draw();
      }

      private function draw():void {
        graphics.lineStyle(1, _strokeColor);
        graphics.beginFill(_fillColor);
        graphics.drawCircle(25, 25, 25);
        graphics.endFill();
      }

    }

  }
```

At this point in the book, nothing here should come as a surprise to you. The class extends Shape, since it is merely drawing graphics into itself and does not need to allow for interactivity. You define two protected properties for the fill and stroke color. These are made protected so that child classes can set their own values for these colors. The constructor for the class simply calls the init() method, which is also made protected so that child classes can use it to set new values for the colors before the graphics are drawn, which is handled in the draw() method. That draw() method sets a line style of 1 point and draws a circle with a 25-pixel radius, which is really arbitrary, since the components will resize the skin as necessary by setting its width and height directly.

That is all you need to do to create a skin. Pretty easy, isn't it? If you think so, then you'll love the next steps. You need to create variations for the over, down, and disabled states, but you can use inheritance to leverage the drawing code you just wrote, and just have the child classes set new color values.

Creating skins for the button's other states

Create a new ActionScript file and save it as StrokedCircleOver.as into the same skins directory as StrokedCircle.as. Enter the following code.

```
package com.foundationAS3.ch9.skins {

  public class StrokedCircleOver extends StrokedCircle {

    override protected function init():void {
      _strokeColor = 0x0076C1;
      super.init();
    }

  }

}
```

Do you love it? A child class of StrokedCircle with a change of color needs only override the superclass's protected init() method (remember it is the protected access setting that lets a child class override the parent class's implementation). A new color is specified for the stroke color, and then the superclass's init() method is called. And that's it—the same skin shape with different colors.

For the down state of the button, create another new ActionScript file and save it into the same skins directory as the other two skins as StrokedCircleDown.as. Enter the following code.

```
package com.foundationAS3.ch9.skins {

  public class StrokedCircleDown extends StrokedCircle {

    override protected function init():void {
      _fillColor = 0xA7DCFE;
      _strokeColor = 0x0076C1;
      super.init();
    }

  }

}
```

This is pretty much the same as the StrokedCircleOver class, except in this case, both the fill and stroke color are overridden.

The final skin is for the disabled state of the button. Once more, create a new ActionScript file and save it into the skins directory as StrokedCircleDisabled.as. The following is the entirety of the class's code.

```
package com.foundationAS3.ch9.skins {

  public class StrokedCircleDisabled extends StrokedCircle {

    override protected function init():void {
      _fillColor = 0xE8E8E8;
      _strokeColor = 0xC2C3C5;
      super.init();
    }

  }

}
```

At this point, you have created four new skins for your buttons in separate class files. The skins all inherit from Shape, since they are only containers for drawn graphics and don't require any child objects or interactivity. All you need to do now is associate the classes with the relevant skin properties of the Button class.

Associating the skins with the buttons

Save the StyledList.as document class file created earlier as SkinnedList.as into the same directory. Let's first update the file with the new class name. You'll also import the skins package you just created, as you will need to reference the classes within the package to assign these classes to your Button instances.

```
package com.foundationAS3.ch9 {

  import fl.controls.Button;
  import fl.controls.List;
  import fl.controls.TextInput;
  import fl.managers.StyleManager;

  import flash.display.Sprite;
  import flash.events.Event;
  import flash.events.MouseEvent;
  import flash.text.TextFormat;

  import com.foundationAS3.ch9.skins.*;

  public class SkinnedList extends Sprite {

    public function SkinnedList() {
      init();
    }
```

All the rest of the code should remain unchanged.

Now you need to associate the skins you just created in the class files with the properties of the
Button class that determine which skin is used for which state. Just as with the text properties discussed earlier, this is all handled through the StyleManager and its setComponentStyle() method, if
you want to set skins for all instances of a component. If you want to change the skin on only a single
instance, you use UIComponent's setStyle(). In this case, you will change the skins for all Button
instances.

Within the setStyles() method of SkinnedList, add the following bold lines to associate the new
skin classes with the Button class.

```
        private function setStyles():void {
          // blue green text for all components' default state
          var format:TextFormat = new TextFormat("Arial", 10, 0x01578F);
          StyleManager.setStyle("textFormat", format);
          // blue green text for Button default state
          format = new TextFormat("Arial", 14, 0x01578F);
          StyleManager.setComponentStyle(Button, "textFormat", format);
          // light gray text for Button disabled state
          format = new TextFormat("Arial", 14, 0x999999);
          StyleManager.setComponentStyle(Button, "disabledTextFormat", format);
          // red text for delete button default state
          format = new TextFormat("Arial", 14, 0xFF0000);
          deleteName_bn.setStyle("textFormat", format);
          StyleManager.setComponentStyle(Button, "upSkin", StrokedCircle);
          StyleManager.setComponentStyle(Button, "overSkin", StrokedCircleOver);
          StyleManager.setComponentStyle(Button, "downSkin", StrokedCircleDown);
          StyleManager.setComponentStyle(Button, ➡
      "disabledSkin", StrokedCircleDisabled);
        }
```

Figure 9-31. The result of using ActionScript to reskin all Button instances

Each component class has different skin properties depending on the type and complexity of the component. The Button class itself has many more skin properties, but some of these deal only with Button instances that toggle or with icons. The four skin properties that define the four different states are all that you need to modify here. As you can see, the value for each skin property is actually a reference to the class itself that should be used to draw the button in that state.

If you test your movie now, you should see that the buttons have changed their appearance to a stroked circle with a solid fill, as shown in Figure 9-31. Using the StyleManager and a little ActionScript in the manner just demonstrated, it's easy to reskin your applications for each project.

Creating components from scratch

Sometimes you will need functionality that isn't provided by the default Flash components, and your best course of action may be to create a component specifically for your purpose. Creating a component is basically like creating a custom class, with only a few extra steps to plug the class into the Parameters panel so that its configurable parameters appear. This next example will demonstrate the process as you create a simple UI component for a dial interaction.

Creating the widget

Let's start by creating the symbol and graphics needed for the component. Remember that the whole purpose of a component is to allow for a visual widget that you can position and configure in the Flash IDE; otherwise, you could do the same without components using ActionScript alone. So creating the visual widget is a good place to begin.

1. Create a new Flash ActionScript 3.0 file and save it as dial.fla into your Chapter 9 project directory.

2. On the stage, draw a 30 × 30-pixel gray circle with no stroke. Use the Line tool to draw a 1-point line that is 15 pixels long. Align the line so that it is centered vertically within the circle and aligned to its right edge. The result should look like Figure 9-32.

Figure 9-32. The dial graphic created from a circle and a line

3. Select both the circle and line, and convert them into a movie clip symbol (press F8). Name it Dial_skin and make sure it is aligned in the center, as shown in Figure 9-33. Click OK.

4. In the Property inspector, name the Dial_skin instance still selected on the stage graphic. Convert this instance into a movie clip symbol as well (press F8 again), but this time, align the symbol in the top left and name it Dial. Select to export the symbol for ActionScript, but set its class to be com.foundationAS3. ch9.controls.Dial, as shown in Figure 9-34. Click OK. You will see an ActionScript Class Warning dialog box letting you know that there is no class found, but this is OK, as you will create the class in the next section.

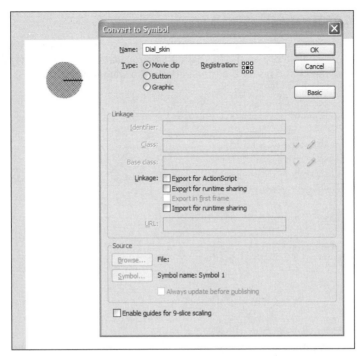

Figure 9-33. Creating a symbol from the graphics for the dial component

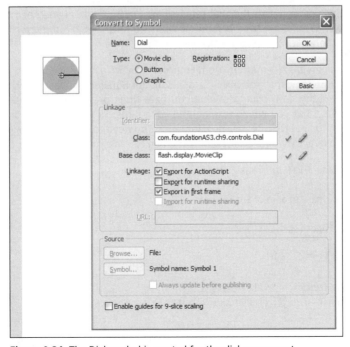

Figure 9-34. The Dial symbol is created for the dial component.

Writing the component code

Create a new ActionScript file and save it as Dial.as into a new controls subdirectory in the com/foundationAS3/ch9 directory, so the full path is com/foundationAS3/ch9/controls. Add the following code to start the class. This adds all the imports you will need, including Sprite, from which the Dial class inherits.

```actionscript
package com.foundationAS3.ch9.controls {

    import flash.display.Sprite;
    import flash.events.Event;
    import flash.events.MouseEvent;
    import flash.geom.Point;

    public class Dial extends Sprite {

        public function Dial() {
        }

    }

}
```

As mentioned previously, the Flash ActionScript 3.0 UI components all extend, either directly or indirectly, the UIComponent class (the FLVPlayback component, however, does not). Certainly, if you want to take advantage of the framework and what it offers, such as focus management and styling, you would want to extend UIComponent. But that requires a bit more work, as you need to build the component in particular ways and override certain methods. To keep things simple for this example, you will just extend Sprite, which is also perfectly valid.

First, you need to call an init() method from your constructor, as you have often done in classes in previous examples. You know that you have a graphic on the timeline of the symbol, and you will need to manipulate that graphic. You could do what you have done previously, and just code against the instance name graphic, but you would lose helpful code hints. So you will assign a reference to this graphic and cast that to Sprite for easier development. You need to use getChildByName(), since referencing the graphic directly would throw an error when turning your symbol into a component.

```actionscript
    public class Dial extends Sprite {

        private var _graphic:Sprite;

        public function Dial() {
            init();
        }

        private function init():void {
            _graphic = getChildByName("graphic") as Sprite;
        }
```

Now you can code using the private property _graphic and get those handy-dandy code hints as you type.

Next, you should handle the interaction with the dial.

Handling events

When users click the dial, they should be able to then rotate it. The obvious event to listen for is the MOUSE_EVENT that is fired when users click the dial. Add the following bold lines to handle this event.

```
private function init():void {
  _graphic = graphic;
  addEventListener(MouseEvent.MOUSE_DOWN, onClickDial);
}

private function onClickDial(event:MouseEvent):void {
}
```

Whenever the dial is clicked, the onClickDial() handler will run. Two things will need to happen after this point. First, as the user moves the mouse, the dial should rotate. Second, when the user releases the mouse, the dial should stop rotating. You can handle the former with the MOUSE_MOVE event, and set up a listener for this only after the user has clicked the dial. The second item is a little trickier, as you want to not only handle when the user releases the mouse while over the dial, but also if the user moves the mouse off the dial and releases. Adding a listener to the MOUSE_UP event fired by the dial is not enough to achieve this, as that does not account for whether the mouse is not over the dial when released. In order to account for both circumstances, you can listen to the stage's MOUSE_UP event, not the dial's.

Since MOUSE_UP is a bubbling event, eventually this event will reach the stage from any display object that causes it to be dispatched. Because of this, you can safely subscribe to this event to catch whenever the mouse is released, but you want to do this only if the user has first clicked the dial. So you'll add the listener only in the onClickDial() method. Add the following lines in bold to handle the mouse move and release events after the dial has been clicked.

```
private function onClickDial(event:MouseEvent):void {
  addEventListener(MouseEvent.MOUSE_MOVE, onRotateDial);
  stage.addEventListener(MouseEvent.MOUSE_UP, onReleaseDial);
}

private function onReleaseDial(event:MouseEvent):void {
  removeEventListener(MouseEvent.MOUSE_MOVE, onRotateDial);
  stage.removeEventListener(MouseEvent.MOUSE_UP, onReleaseDial);
}

private function onRotateDial(event:MouseEvent):void {
}
```

Now the flow is that when the user clicks the dial, onClickDial() is called. Two listeners are added to listen for when the mouse moves or when the mouse is released. When the mouse moves, onRotateDial() is called, where you'll handle rotating the graphic. When the mouse is released anywhere on the stage, onReleaseDial() is called, and the mouse move and released listeners are removed.

You have taken care of the events. Now you need to rotate the dial as the user moves the mouse.

Rotating the dial

In order to rotate the dial with mouse movement, you need to record the starting angle of the dial when it is first clicked. As the user moves the mouse, you can measure the angle of the mouse in relation to the center of the graphic and rotate the graphic accordingly, adjusting for the starting angle. The lines in bold take care of this.

```
public class Dial extends Sprite {

  private var _graphic:Sprite;
  private var _startRadians:Number;
  private var _startRotation:Number;

  public function Dial() {
    init();
  }

  private function init():void {
    _graphic = graphic;
    addEventListener(MouseEvent.MOUSE_DOWN, onClickDial);
  }

  private function onClickDial(event:MouseEvent):void {
    _startRotation = _graphic.rotation;
    var click:Point = new Point(mouseX-_graphic.x, mouseY-_graphic.y);
    _startRadians = Math.atan2(click.y, click.x);
    addEventListener(MouseEvent.MOUSE_MOVE, onRotateDial);
    stage.addEventListener(MouseEvent.MOUSE_UP, onReleaseDial);
  }

  private function onReleaseDial(event:MouseEvent):void {
    removeEventListener(MouseEvent.MOUSE_MOVE, onRotateDial);
    stage.removeEventListener(MouseEvent.MOUSE_UP, onReleaseDial);
  }

  private function onRotateDial(event:MouseEvent):void {
    var distance:Point = new Point(mouseX-_graphic.x, mouseY-_graphic.y);
    var radians:Number = Math.atan2(distance.y, distance.x) - _startRadians;
    var degrees:Number = radians*180/Math.PI;
    _graphic.rotation = _startRotation + degrees;
  }
```

Here, you save the starting rotation of the graphic in _startRotation. You also find the angle of the mouse click in relation to the center of the graphic using the Math.atan2() method, saving the results into _startRadians. The Math.atan2() method takes the distance on the y axis and the distance on the x axis, and determines the angle in radians based on these values.

Whenever the mouse moves after the dial is clicked, you find the current distance from the center of the graphic and convert this to an angle measured in radians as well, subtracting from this the starting radians value. At this point, you have an angle that measures the distance the mouse has moved from its initial click. You can convert this to degrees using the standard formula: degrees = radians × 180/PI. It is this degrees value that you can add to the initial starting rotation of the graphic to set a new rotation for the graphic based on the mouse position.

At this point, you have a working dial that can be clicked and turned, but it doesn't have much use unless you can know what the current value of the dial is and when it changes. Your next step is to set up a way to determine when the value changes and provide access to that value.

Getting and setting dial values

The value of the dial itself can easily and simply be the current rotation of the graphic, but to make the component useful in multiple environments, let's allow for a minimum and maximum value to be set.

Add the following new properties at the top of your code with the other property declarations.

```
public class Dial extends Sprite {

  private var _graphic:Sprite;
  private var _startRadians:Number;
  private var _startRotation:Number;
  private var _minValue:Number = 0;
  private var _maxValue:Number = 100;

  public function Dial() {
    init();
  }
}
```

Next, let's add getters and setters for these values at the bottom of the class definition.

```
private function onRotateDial(event:MouseEvent):void {
  var distance:Point = new Point(mouseX-_graphic.x, mouseY-_graphic.y);
  var radians:Number = Math.atan2(distance.y, distance.x) - _startRadians;
  var degrees:Number = radians*180/Math.PI;
  _graphic.rotation = _startRotation + degrees;
}

public function get minValue():Number {
  return _minValue;
}

public function set minValue(min:Number):void {
  _minValue = min;
}
```

```
    public function get maxValue():Number {
      return _maxValue;
    }

    public function set maxValue(max:Number):void {
      _maxValue = max;
    }


  }

}
```

Now, based on the minimum and maximum values (which you've defaulted to 0 and 100, respectively), you can provide a getter for the current value based on the current rotation of the graphic within the specified numeric range.

Add the following getter and setter for the current value of the dial.

```
    private function onRotateDial(event:MouseEvent):void {
      var distance:Point = new Point(mouseX-_graphic.x, mouseY-_graphic.y);
      var radians:Number = Math.atan2(distance.y, distance.x) - _startRadians;
      var degrees:Number = radians*180/Math.PI;
      _graphic.rotation = _startRotation + degrees;
    }

    public function get value():Number {
      var degrees:Number = _graphic.rotation;
      if (degrees < 0) degrees += 360;
      return degrees/360*(_maxValue-_minValue)+_minValue;
    }

    public function set value(num:Number):void {
      _graphic.rotation = (num-_minValue)/(_maxValue-_minValue)*360;
    }

    public function get minValue():Number {
      return _minValue;
    }

    public function set minValue(min:Number):void {
      _minValue = min;
    }
```

When the getter is called, you find the current rotation of the _graphic property, making it positive if it is negative (the rotation will fall between −180 and 180). You can then find where this lies as a percentage of 360 degrees. This percentage can be multiplied with the full range (maximum value minus the minimum value). If the minimum value is greater than 0, you can add this to your result.

Let's plug in some numbers to see how these equations work. If your minimum value is 0 and your maximum value is 100, and your dial is rotated exactly 180 degrees (halfway), then 180/360 will give you 0.5. This value multiplied by the full range (100 – 0 = 100) gives 50 (0.5 × 100). You add this to the minimum value (0), for a result of 50.

As another example, if the range is specified with a minimum of 100 and a maximum of 200, and the dial is rotated 120 degrees, you get a rotation percentage of roughly 0.33 (120/360), and this is multiplied by a range of 100 (200 – 100), which gives a result of around 33. This value added to the minimum value results in around 133.

When the setter for value is called, this formula is simply reversed.

When the value changes for the dial, you should dispatch an event so that listeners can be informed of the changes. You can take care of this in the onRotateDial() method. Add the following bold line to achieve this.

```
private function onRotateDial(event:MouseEvent):void {
  var distance:Point = new Point(mouseX-_graphic.x, mouseY-_graphic.y);
  var radians:Number = Math.atan2(distance.y, distance.x) - _startRadians;
  var degrees:Number = radians*180/Math.PI;
  _graphic.rotation = _startRotation + degrees;
  dispatchEvent(new Event(Event.CHANGE));
}
```

You have now created a working dial that you could use in any project by instantiating it through the code and setting its properties. To make it into a component, you simply need to specify which of its properties should appear in the Parameters panel as configurable properties. You do this through the use of metatags in the ActionScript.

Adding metatags

Metatags are special tags that are ignored by the compiler, but have special significance in the IDE. For components, there is an Inspectable tag that you can place in your ActionScript to inform the IDE of which properties should be accessible in the Parameters panel.

Add the following Inspectable metatags to your code.

```
public function get value():Number {
  var degrees:Number = _graphic.rotation;
  if (degrees < 0) degrees += 360;
  return degrees/360*(_maxValue-_minValue)+_minValue;
}

[Inspectable(defaultValue=0)]
public function set value(num:Number):void {
  _graphic.rotation = (num-_minValue)/(_maxValue-_minValue)*360;
}

public function get minValue():Number {
  return _minValue;
}
```

```
[Inspectable(defaultValue=0)]
public function set minValue(min:Number):void {
  _minValue = min;
}

public function get maxValue():Number {
  return _maxValue;
}

[Inspectable(defaultValue=100)]
public function set maxValue(max:Number):void {
  _maxValue = max;
}
```

Not too tough, is it? The only additional piece of information that you provide in this example is the default value you would like to have set. To find out more about the use of the Inspectable tag and what it allows, consult the Adobe documentation.

Your code is complete at this point, so save it and return to the dial.fla file you created at the beginning of the example.

Turning the symbol into a component

To turn your Dial symbol into a component, all you need to do is right-click it in the Library and select Component Definition. This opens the Component Definition dialog box, as shown in Figure 9-35.

Figure 9-35. The Component Definition dialog box

In the dialog box, enter the name of your ActionScript class into the Class text box: **com.foundationAS3.ch9.controls.Dial**, and then click OK. At this point, the symbol icon in the Library should change to the component symbol, as shown in Figure 9-36.

It's time now to test your component!

Testing the component

Let's try out the component in a little movie.

1. Select the Dial instance you have on the stage in dial.fla (if you have deleted it from the stage, simply drag a new instance from the Library) and look at the Parameters panel. You will see that your dial has three configurable parameters: maxValue, minValue, and value. You can keep the default values (or change them if you would like to see the result),

2. Name the instance of the component dial in the Property inspector.

3. Create a dynamic TextField instance next to the dial and name it dialValue. Turn on its background for better visibility.

4. Create a new layer on your timeline and select the first frame of this layer.

5. Open your Actions panel (press F9) and enter the following code.

```
dial.addEventListener(Event.CHANGE, onDialChange);
dialValue.text = String(Math.floor(dial.value));

function onDialChange(event:Event):void {
  dialValue.text = String(Math.floor(dial.value));
}
```

6. Test your movie. You should see something like Figure 9-37. Turning the dial should update the number within the text field to show the dial's current value.

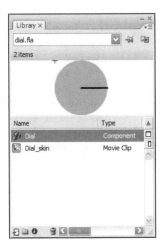

Figure 9-36. The Library gets a swanky new icon for the Dial component.

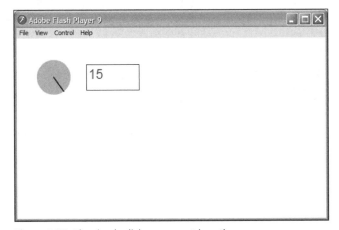

Figure 9-37. The simple dial component in action

389

And that's it for creating a component! Of course, you can do a lot more with it, such as limiting the range of movement and offering multiple states for rollover and disabled, but the basic functionality is there. You have seen how easy it is to turn a class into a component in your Library.

In this example, you've left this class uncompiled so that it is easy to go in and edit the graphic for a project. However, this simplified approach also means that you cannot have different skins for multiple dials in a single application. As explained earlier in the chapter, precompiling will also speed up compile times when you have many components. Finally, precompiling by turning a symbol into an SWC file automatically creates a Live Preview of your component. This wouldn't affect the sample component, but if you had a number of parameters that affected visual properties, the Live Preview feature is a great asset.

This has given you a little taste of what it takes to put together a component, and perhaps you will be encouraged to explore more and build your own component libraries for your projects. The work is in initially creating the components, but after you have done it once, the reuse of the components and the speed components can bring to your development are fantastic advantages.

> *There can be a whole lot more behind a component than what you saw here. First, components can be built on top of the Flash component framework to help manage things like skins and focus management. Live Previews can be built or enabled by precompiling the class into an SWC, and custom interfaces for setting component parameters can be built and used instead of the* Parameters *panel, which has limitations since it requires simple form input. Finally, after a component is built, it can be distributed using the Adobe Extension Manager so that the component can be installed by any user acquiring the extension and will appear in the* Component *panel along with the default components. Check out the Flash documentation as well as the Flash Developer Center (*http://www.adobe.com/devnet/flash/*) for more information about these topics.*

Using third-party components

Of course, sometimes you just don't have the time to create your own components. Thank goodness that someone else has probably already done it. Be sure to check out the Adobe Exchange (http://www.adobe.com/cfusion/exchange) for free components, as well as more complex components available for purchase.

A number of third-party sites also provide a wealth of components to shop through to see what might suit your needs, such as Flashloaded (http://www.flashloaded.com) and the Flash Components network (http://flashcomponents.net). Any of these sites, as well as the Flash documentation, should have instructions for installing the components. In any case, you will need the Adobe Extension Manager, which comes with the Flash CS3 installation. You can always check for updates at Adobe's site.

Summary

The goal of this chapter was to give you some insight into the power and flexibility of using the Flash components, the speed at which you can build applications that incorporate the framework, and how you might configure these components to create unique experiences for your users. You've also looked at how you might create your own components for your own needs and acquire ready-made components from third parties. The use of components can greatly increase your rate of production and ease your workflow, while encouraging you to work in an object-oriented manner by separating and containing functionality in individual objects.

In the next chapter, we put the IDE aside once more and dive right back into the code, exploring a powerful new ActionScript feature: regular expressions. If you ever need to do any string manipulation or searching through text, regular expressions will prove to be your best friends. You might want to take a break and interact a bit with your human friends first, though. Then come on back, turn the page, and we'll get into some really nifty programming.

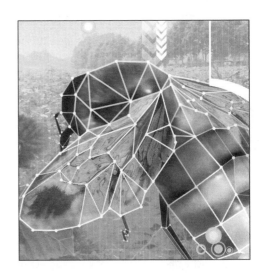

Chapter 10

REGULAR EXPRESSIONS

Steve Webster with Todd Yard

This chapter covers the following topics:

- What regular expressions are and why they are useful
- The anatomy of regular expressions
- How to use regular expressions in ActionScript 3.0
- Useful regular expressions
- Resources for more information about regular expressions

In this chapter, we're going to spend some time looking at regular expressions, one of the brand-new features introduced into ActionScript 3.0 that has helped make it a proper, grown-up programming language.

Regular expressions have often been considered something of a dark art, reserved for propeller-heads who eat Perl scripts for breakfast and go back for seconds. Seeing a regular expression in the wild, you would be forgiven for writing them off as incomprehensible gobbledygook. For example, take a look at the following regular expression:

```
^([a-zA-Z0-9._-]+)@([a-zA-Z0-9.-]+)\.([a-zA-Z]{2,4})$
```

Believe it or not, this pattern can be used to make sure that an e-mail address is valid.

By learning a few simple rules, it's possible to break down even complex regular expressions into understandable chunks. This chapter is all about learning those simple rules. I promise that by the end of this chapter, you will be able to break down the preceding regular expression and understand exactly what each part does.

Once you've mastered regular expressions, you'll find a whole bunch of uses for them in your ActionScript projects. They help you to solve a specific kind of problem that would otherwise require a lot of coding. In fact, regular expressions are not just part of ActionScript 3.0. You can use them in a number of different programming languages, from JavaScript to Java, from Perl to PHP, and beyond.

Why we need regular expressions

A **regular expression** is string of characters that describes a pattern that you can use to search a string. Those of you who have used ActionScript in previous versions might very well exclaim, "Hold on just a minute! Isn't that what the String.indexOf() method is for?" Well, yes, but regular expressions are like String;indexOf() on steroids.

String.indexOf(), for those not familiar with this method, returns the first position of a character or substring within a string. Here is an example of its syntax.

```
var bookTitle:String = "Foundation ActionScript 3.0";
var firstIndex:int = bookTitle.indexOf("n");
trace(firstIndex);  // outputs 3
```

As you can see, the first appearance of the character *n* is as the fourth letter in the string. The output is 3, since, as in arrays, the first index position is 0.

One of the first problems with String.indexOf() is that it returns only the first index of the particular substring. In the previous example, if you wanted to find all instances of *n*, you might use this script:

```
var bookTitle:String = "Foundation ActionScript 3.0";
var startIndex:int = 0;
var positionIndex:int;
var stringLength:uint = bookTitle.length;
var positions:Array = [];
while (startIndex < stringLength-1) {
  positionIndex = bookTitle.indexOf("n", startIndex);
  if (positionIndex > -1) {
    positions.push(positionIndex);
    startIndex = positionIndex + 1;
  } else {
    break;
  }
}
trace(positions);  // outputs 3,9,16
```

Well, that seems like a lot of work, doesn't it?

Another problem with using the String.indexOf() method to search for a string is that you have no control over whether the string you're searching for is matched against a whole word or part of a word. For example, consider the following variable:

```
var tongueTwister:String = ➥
"Peter Piper picked a peck of pickled peppers";
```

The variable tongueTwister contains the opening line of a particularly bothersome tongue twister. Now, let's say you wanted to see if this string contained the word *pick*. We, as humans, can look at the string and confirm that although the words *picked* and *pickled* are there, the word *pick* is nowhere to be seen. Nonetheless, if you use String.indexOf() to search the string, it will return a match:

```
trace(tongueTwister.indexOf("pick"));  // outputs 12
```

What's happening here is that String.indexOf() isn't searching for the word *pick*, it's searching for any consecutive sequence of characters containing the letters *p*, *i*, *c*, and *k*, in that order. The value of the tongueTwister variable contains this sequence of characters (twice, in fact), so the result is a match.

> *If your brain works faster than mine, at this stage, you might be thinking that you could just add a space on either side of the word you're searching for in the search string to get a whole-word match with String.indexOf(). That would work in this instance, but would fail if the word you were searching for was at the beginning or end of the string, or if it was nudged up against any pesky punctuation.*

Another potential problem with using String.indexOf() to search strings is that you must be very exact. Let's revisit the old chestnut of American English vs. British English. If you need to search a string of text for a word, and you aren't sure whether the author has used the English or American spelling, you'll need to search for both (*colour* vs. *color* in this example):

```
var entry:String = "Purple is my favourite colour";
if (entry.indexOf("color") > -1 || entry.indexOf("colour") > -1) {
  trace("We have a match!");
}
```

OK, I'll admit that this example doesn't seem too bad, but any amount of extra typing seems like it should be unnecessary for a word that differs by only a single letter.

What's the best way to get around the problems with String.indexOf()? Let me put it this way: this would be a very short chapter if regular expressions weren't the answer.

> *The examples for this chapter are presented so that users of the Flash IDE can copy the code directly into the timeline to test it. The same code can be wrapped in a document class, as was initially demonstrated in Chapter 2, so that it can be tested in both the Flash IDE and Flex Builder. For brevity's sake, the chapter text does not include all of the document class code and concentrates specifically on the regular expression syntax. However, this chapter's downloadable files include document classes for both Flash and Flex Builder users to use to run all the code included within the chapter.*

Introducing the RegExp class

In ActionScript 3.0, regular expressions are represented by the RegExp class. You can create a new RegExp object in two ways:

- By using the new keyword with the RegExp constructor. This is the same technique you've used to create instances of almost all the classes you've met thus far. The RegExp constructor takes two arguments: a string specifying the pattern to search for as a string, and a series of modifiers that change the way the regular expression behaves, also specified as a string.

  ```
  var myFirstRegExp:RegExp = new RegExp("pattern", "modifiers");
  ```

- By using a regular expression literal. A regular expression literal is similar to a string literal, except that it is delineated by forward slashes (/), with the patterns placed between the forward slashes and the modifiers placed after them:

  ```
  var myFirstRegExp:RegExp = /pattern/modifiers;
  ```

In terms of functionality, these two techniques are the same; they both create a new RegExp object with the specified pattern and modifiers. However, depending on which technique you choose and the characters in your pattern, you may need to slightly change how the pattern is specified. If you use the constructor technique, you'll need to make sure that any characters that have special meaning as a string are escaped using the backslash (\).

I personally tend to prefer regular expression literals, as they require less typing, and anything that reduces the wear and tear on my poor fingers has to be a good thing. When specifying your pattern as a regular expression literal, you'll need to escape the forward slashes and backslashes using a backslash character (much like you escape special characters in a string literal). You'll see examples of regular expression literals throughout this chapter.

Having said all that, sometimes you have no choice but to use the RegExp constructor. This is necessary when either the pattern or the modifiers for the regular expression (or both) come from the value of a variable, as explained in the "Using variables to build a regular expression" section later in this chapter.

The anatomy of a regular expression pattern

Now that you know how to create a RegExp object, it's time to look at how the pattern for a regular expression is built and exactly what you can do with it.

A very simple regular expression pattern might look something like this:

```
pick
```

Yes, it really is just a simple string of characters. This signifies a regular expression that will match the character sequence p, i, c, k, in that order.

If you're thinking that this is the same as the tongue-twister example you saw earlier, you're right. You can verify this by adapting the earlier example to use a regular expression instead of the String.indexOf() method.

```
var tongueTwister:String = ➥
"Peter Piper picked a peck of pickled peppers";
var pickRegExp:RegExp = /pick/;
trace(pickRegExp.test(tongueTwister));   // outputs true
```

Here, you're using the test() method of the RegExp object to see if the value of the tongueTwister variable matches the pattern you've defined. This method returns a Boolean value indicating whether the specified string contains the pattern: true for a match and false for no match. In this case, you should see the value true traced to the Output panel (or output to the console, if you are using Flex Builder).

To see exactly what is being matched, you can use the replace() method of the String object. The String.replace() method uses a regular expression to replace the text matched by a regular expression with the specified replacement string:

```
var tongueTwister:String = ➥
"Peter Piper picked a peck of pickled peppers";
var pickRegExp:RegExp = /pick/;
var replaced:String = tongueTwister.replace(pickRegExp, "MATCH")
// outputs: Peter Piper MATCHed a peck of pickled peppers
trace(replaced);
```

If you test this code, you should see the following in the Output panel:

```
Peter Piper MATCHed a peck of pickled peppers
```

You can tell that the pickRegExp regular expression matched the first occurrence of the string pick at the beginning of the word picked, which has been replaced by the string MATCH, the specified replacement string.

> *You might have noticed that the string* pick *that is part of the word* pickled *toward the end of the* tongueTwister *string wasn't replaced. Unless you tell it otherwise, a regular expression will stop searching when it finds the first occurrence of a string that matches the specified pattern. If you want it to continue and find all matches, you'll need to use the global modifier, which you'll learn about in the "Using the global modifier" section later in this chapter.*

In the previous regular expression example, the pattern is just made up of regular characters, and as you've discovered, that makes it as useless as String.indexOf() for solving the tongue-twister problem. However, regular expressions can also contain metacharacters, which add a lot more power and flexibility to string searches.

Introducing metacharacters

Metacharacters are characters that have special meaning in the regular expression pattern, and they make regular expressions a powerful tool. Table 10-1 contains a partial list of the metacharacters.

Table 10-1. Common metacharacters

Metacharacter	Description
\b	Matches a word boundary, which is a position between a word character (any alphanumeric or underscore character) and a nonword character
\d	Matches a single digit
\s	Matches any whitespace character such as a space, tab, or newline
\w	Matches any alphanumeric character or an underscore (_)

The metacharacters listed in Table 10-1 also have exact opposites, which can be specified using the uppercase version of the same letter. For example, to match any character that is not a digit, you can use the \D metacharacter. The word boundary metacharacter (\b) is a little trickier in this respect, in that you need to remember that it matches a position *between* two characters. Its opposite, \B, still matches a position between two characters, either two word characters or two nonword characters.

If you've been paying attention, you might have noticed that one of these metacharacters finally offers the solution to the tongue-twister problem from earlier. By placing a word boundary metacharacter (\b) on either side of the pick string, you can specify that you want it to match only as whole word:

    \bpick\b

Now the pattern will match only if there is a word boundary (anything that's not an alphanumeric character or an underscore) on either side of pick.

```
var tongueTwister:String = ➥
"Peter Piper picked a peck of pickled peppers";
var pickRegExp:RegExp = /\bpick\b/;
trace(pickRegExp.test(tongueTwister));  // outputs false
```

That gives an output of false, which is the desired result, since the string being tested does not contain the word *pick*. Now we can put away this pesky problem and peruse other possibilities in programming.

Using anchors to restrict the position of matches

Like their heavy-chained nautical counterparts, **anchors** can restrict the action of your regular expression. Up to this point, the regular expression examples have been free as a bird—free to hunt the entire search string for a match. Anchors allow you to specify where in the string to look for a match to the pattern: at the beginning, at the end, or both.

Take the following variable, which gives the recipe for a good story.

```
var goodStory:String = "beginning, middle and end";
```

Let's say that you wanted to match the word *beginning*, but only if it appeared at the beginning of the string. You could indicate that as part of your pattern by preceding it with the start-of-string anchor, which is represented by a caret (^).

```
^beginning
```

This matches the string beginning, but only if it is the first thing in the string being searched.

The start-of-string anchor has a counterpart called the end-of-string anchor, which is represented by a dollar sign ($). You would use this anchor if you wanted the pattern to match only if it appeared at the end of the string. The end-of-string anchor goes at the end of the pattern:

```
end$
```

This, you might have guessed, matches the string end, but only if it is the last thing in the string being searched.

Finally, you can use a combination of both anchors to specify that the pattern should match the entire string:

```
^beginning, middle and end$
```

This would match the string beginning, middle and end, but only if the search string contained exactly that string and nothing else. Let's see how that works in an example.

```
var goodStory0:String = "beginning, middle and end";
var goodStory1:String = "beginning, middle and end with epilogue";

var myRegExp:RegExp = /^beginning, middle and end$/;

trace( myRegExp.test( goodStory0 ) );  // outputs true
trace( myRegExp.test( goodStory1 ) );  // outputs false
```

This example tries to match the exact string beginning, middle and end. Since the first recipe contains this exactly, running test() on this string returns true. The second recipe does not end with the specified string end, so returns false when tested.

Providing alternatives using alternation

In the examples so far, every character specified in the regular expression patterns must match in order for the string as a whole to be considered a match. **Alternation** allows you to specify a number of alternative patterns to be matched, by separating the strings with a pipe, or vertical bar, symbol (|). As an example, the following pattern will match either the word *one* or *two*.

```
one|two
```

You could use alternation to solve the earlier spelling problem to match either *color* or *colour*, as follows:

```
var entry:String = "Purple is my favourite colour";
var colorRegExp:RegExp = /color|colour/;
if (colorRegExp.test(entry)) {
  trace("We have a match!");
}
```

You can specify as many alternatives as you like:

```
one|two|three|four|five|six|seven|eight|nine|ten
```

Alternation operates on the entire pattern. You can force the alternation to act only on a particular part of the pattern using groups, which are covered in the "Grouping patterns" section later in this chapter.

Using character classes and character ranges

Character classes allow you to specify that, instead of a specific character, you would like one of a number of characters to be matched at a given position in a pattern. You create a character class by wrapping the characters to be matched in square brackets. For example, if you wanted a regular expression to match any of the vowels in the English alphabet, you could create a character class like this:

```
[aeiou]
```

This pattern will match only a single character, but that character can be any one of those specified in the character class. You can use the character class as part of a larger expression:

```
b[aeiou]g
```

This pattern would match *bag*, *beg*, *big*, *bog*, and *bug*.

Specifying each character that could possibly match is all well and good, but what if you wanted to match any letter of the alphabet? You would end up with the following:

```
[abcdefghijklmnopqrstuvyxyz]
```

Thankfully, this can be rewritten much more efficiently as a **character range**. A character range in a character class is specified as two characters separated by a hyphen (–). The following pattern is equivalent to the previous example:

```
[a-z]
```

You can also combine character ranges in a single character class by specifying them one after another. To match any alphanumeric digit, you could use the following pattern:

```
[a-zA-Z0-9]
```

The characters in a character class don't need to be alphanumeric. For example, you might want to construct a pattern to match any of the standard punctuation characters:

    [.,;:'!?]

The only symbols you need to be wary of when using a character class are the hyphen and the opening and closing square brackets. A hyphen can be specified only as either the first or the last character in the character class, so as not to be confused with a character range. If you want to include square brackets in the class, escape them with backslashes.

    [\[\]-]

Simple, no?

Matching any character using the dot metacharacter

Sometimes you want your patterns to be extremely flexible. The **dot metacharacter**, represented by a period or full-stop symbol (.), will match any single character in the string, without caring what that character is. The only exception to this rule is that, by default, it will not match a newline character (you'll find out how to alter this behavior in the "Using the dotall modifier" section later in this chapter).

Let's say that you wanted to match any string that was exactly five characters long, but you didn't care which five characters they were. You could construct a pattern that consisted solely of five dot metacharacters:

    .....

This would match *hello*, *knife*, *a bag*, and even *&^%$£*—any string that is five characters in length, provided that none of those characters were a newline.

As with all the other metacharacters, if you want to match a period character literally in your pattern, you need to escape it with a backslash:

    ActionScript [123]\.0

This expression would match *ActionScript 1.0*, *ActionScript 2.0*, or *ActionScript 3.0*.

Note that the period symbol has no special meaning when specified as part of a character class, so there's no need to escape it.

Matching a number of occurrences using quantifiers

So far, each character in the regular expression patterns you've seen has matched exactly one character in the string being searched. However, in a regular expression, you can use **quantifiers** to determine how many times a given character should be matched. Table 10-2 shows the available quantifiers.

Table 10-2. Regular expression quantifiers

Quantifier	Description
?	Matches zero or one occurrence of the preceding character
*	Matches zero or more occurrences of the preceding character
+	Matches one or more occurrences of the preceding character

We'll look at each one of these quantifiers in turn.

Matching zero or one occurrence

Earlier you saw an example of the `String.indexOf()` method, showing that it wasn't ideal for matching a word when you weren't quite sure of its spelling. The specific example was matching the British English or American English spelling of the word *colour*. If your memory is as bad as mine, here's a little refresher of the rather awkward solution using `String.indexOf()`:

```
var entry:String = "Purple is my favourite colour";
if (entry.indexOf("color") > -1 || entry.indexOf("colour") > -1) {
  trace("We have a match!");
}
```

You then saw a way to solve this problem using a regular expression with alternation, but that wasn't much of an improvement:

```
var entry:String = "Purple is my favourite colour";
var colorRegExp:RegExp = /color|colour/;
if (colorRegExp.test(entry)) {
  trace("We have a match!");
}
```

You still need to specify the majority of the letters in the word twice. What you really need is a way to specify that the letter *u* is optional in the word *colour*, and does not need to be present in the string in order for it to match. Using the zero-or-one quantifier, represented by a question mark (?), you can do just that:

```
colou?r
```

You can now rewrite the code to use the regular expression:

```
var entry:String = "Purple is my favourite colour";
var colorRegExp:RegExp = /colou?r/;
if (colorRegExp.test(entry)) {
  trace("We have a match!");
}
```

Matching zero or more occurrences

If you want to say that a given character can appear zero or more times, use the zero-or-more quantifier, which is represented by an asterisk (*). Like the zero-or-one quantifier, this quantifier is placed after the character you want to be matched zero or more times in the string.

For example, the following pattern will match any word beginning with *i* and ending with *s*, with zero or more other characters in between. (Remember that \w matches any alphanumeric character and \b specifies the beginning or end of the word.)

    \bi\w*s\b

This would match the words *is*, *insulates*, and *inconsistencies* with equal aplomb.

Matching one or more occurrences

The ? and * quantifiers allow zero occurrences of a given character. However, you may need to specify that there should be at least one occurrence. In such cases, use the one-or-more quantifier, which is represented by the plus sign (+). As with the other quantifiers, you place this symbol after the character that you want to match in the string.

Modifying the earlier example, you can say that you want to match any word beginning with *i* and ending with *s*, but that there must be at least one character between them, by replacing the * quantifier with a + quantifier.

    \bi\w+s\b

This pattern would still match *insulates* and *inconsistencies*, but would no longer match *is*, because there is no letter between the *i* and the *s*.

How to prevent greedy quantifiers

By default, the * (zero-or-more) and + (one-or-more) quantifiers are greedy. They'll consume as much as they possibly can and leave only what is left for the rest of the pattern to match. I feel a demonstration of the problem coming up:

```
var compassPoints:String = "Naughty elephants squirt water";
var firstWordRegExp:RegExp = /\b.+\b/;
trace(compassPoints.replace(firstWordRegExp, "MATCH"));
```

Here, you want to match a word boundary (\b), followed by one or more non-newline characters (.+), followed by another word boundary (\b). You might reasonably expect that Naughty would be replaced by MATCH. What you actually get in the Output panel is the following:

    MATCH

What happened to the rest of the string? The answer is that the .+ portion of the regular expression ate every last bit of it. The word boundaries that were matched were the very beginning of the string and the very end of the string, and the rest was consumed by the greedy quantifier, because the dot metacharacter matches any non-newline character, including whitespace characters.

To put the quantifiers on a diet and stop them from being so greedy, you can add a question mark (?) just after the quantifier symbol.

```
var compassPoints:String = "Naughty elephants squirt water";
var firstWordRegExp:RegExp = /\b.+?\b/;
trace(compassPoints.replace(firstWordRegExp, "MATCH"));
```

This might seem a little confusing at first, since the question mark is also the symbol for the zero-or-one quantifier. However, when it is placed after either the * or + quantifier, it forces that quantifier to consume as few characters as possible, while allowing the entire pattern to be matched.

```
MATCH elephants squirt water
```

If only it were that easy to correct the appetite of human beings, I could give up my extortionate gym membership.

Another way to solve the problem is by restricting which characters are allowed to appear between the word boundaries:

```
var compassPoints:String = "Naughty elephants squirt water";
var firstWordRegExp:RegExp = /\b\w+\b/;
trace(compassPoints.replace(firstWordRegExp, "MATCH"));
```

Now, instead of matching one or more non-newline characters (using the . metacharacter) surrounded by word boundaries, the expression will match only one or more characters that can make up a word (using the \w sequence, which matches only alphanumeric characters and underscores) surrounded by word boundaries.

You'll often find that there are many ways to make your regular expression patterns more specific. Be pragmatic, and don't be afraid to experiment to see which approach works best for you.

Being more specific with bounds

Sometimes being able to specify that you want zero or one or more occurrences of a character isn't specific enough. You might want to specify that you want at least four occurrences of this character, or between two and six occurrences of that character. While you could do this by stringing together some of the quantifiers you've already met, it wouldn't be pretty.

```
\b\w\w\w?\w?\w?\w?\b
```

This pattern will match words of two to six characters, but you would be forgiven for taking a while to work that out.

Thankfully, you can use a **bound** in your regular expression patterns to specify how many characters should be matched. Like quantifiers, bounds are placed after the character that you want to be affected, and they are denoted by curly braces ({}).

The simplest example of a bound specifies exactly how many occurrences should be matched. The following pattern matches words of exactly two characters:

```
\b\w{2}\b
```

You can also specify a maximum number of occurrences to be matched. The following pattern matches words of between two and six characters:

```
\b\w{2,6}\b
```

Finally, you can leave off the maximum value (keeping the comma) to specify that you want at least the minimum number of occurrences to match, but without an upper limit. The following pattern matches words of at least two characters:

```
\b\w{2,}\b
```

Beware that bounds that can match a variable number of characters (those that have a maximum value specified or that are unlimited) are greedy by default. Just like the * and + quantifiers, they will consume as many occurrences as possible while allowing the rest of the pattern to match. You can demonstrate this by going back to the earlier example and replacing the + quantifier with a bound looking for two or more occurrences of a non-newline character:

```
var compassPoints:String = "Naughty elephants squirt water";
var firstWordRegExp:RegExp = /\b.{2,}\b/;
trace(compassPoints.replace(firstWordRegExp, "MATCH"));
```

This will produce the same result as using the + quantifier, namely that the entire string will be replaced by MATCH.

If you want a bound to be lazy rather than greedy, just append a question mark after the closing curly brace, just as with the quantifiers:

```
var compassPoints:String = "Naughty elephants squirt water";
var firstWordRegExp:RegExp = /\b.{2,}?\b/;
trace(compassPoints.replace(firstWordRegExp, "MATCH"));
```

This results in just the first word being replaced.

Grouping patterns

Using the quantifiers with single characters is incredibly restrictive. What if you wanted to apply a quantifier or a bound to a sequence of characters? You would group them using parentheses, as in this example:

```
b(an)+a
```

This matches the letter *b*, followed by one or more occurrences of the sequence *an*, followed by the letter *a*, which would include the word *banana*.

```
var myFavoriteFruit:String = "banana";
var bananaRegExp:RegExp = /b(an)+a/;
trace(bananaRegExp.test(myFavoriteFruit));  // outputs true
```

Of course, it would also include the sequence *banananananananana*, since the pattern specifies one or more occurrences of *an*. If you wanted to be more restrictive, you could use a bound instead:

```
var myFavoriteFruit:String = "banana";
var bananaRegExp:RegExp = /b(an){2}a/;
trace(bananaRegExp.test(myFavoriteFruit));  // outputs true
```

No more banananananananana for you.

Groups are also useful when using alternation. As you saw earlier, the alternation operator (|) acts on the entire pattern, rather than just the preceding character (as is the case with the quantifiers). Consider the following expression:

```
\bb(oa|iscui)t\b
```

This would match both *boat* and *biscuit*, as the parentheses limit the alternation between the substrings *oa* and *iscui* between the opening *b* and closing *t*.

Accessing matched strings with backreferences

In addition to allowing you to organize your patterns, groups let you extract certain pieces of information from a regular expression. When you enclose either part or all of a pattern in a group, the portion of the string matched by that group, referred to as a **capture group**, is available later in the pattern via a **backreference**.

A backreference is a numeric reference to a capture group preceded by a backslash (\), starting at 1 for the first group and counting up to a maximum of 99.

Working out the index of your group can be quite troublesome, particularly if you have nested groups (groups within groups) in your pattern, but a simple rule of thumb should see you through: count the number of unescaped opening parentheses, starting from the left side of your pattern up to and including the group you want to target. The number you end up with will be the index of the backreference to that group.

A simple example might make this a little clearer. Suppose you wanted to search through a piece of text with HTML tags and find any references to headings. You could use the dot metacharacter and quantifiers to write the pattern, like this:

```
<h[1-6]>.*?</h[1-6]>
```

This would do the job of matching valid heading tags, but it would also match strings with mismatched opening and closing heading tags:

```
var invalidHtmlText:String = "<h1>A mismatched example</h6>";
var headingRegExp:RegExp = /<h[1-6]>.*?<\/h[1-6]>/;
trace(headingRegExp.test(invalidHtmlText));  // outputs true
```

According to the pattern, the value of the invalidHtmlText variable is perfectly valid. It has an opening header tag with a level of 1 through 6 (<h[1-6]>), some text (.*?), and then a closing heading tag with a level of 1 through 6 (<\/h[1-6]>). Nothing in the pattern says that the opening and closing tags must be of the same level. Just in case the expressions are still looking uncomfortably foreign to you, here is a more detailed breakdown:

<h	Matches literally the characters <h
[1-6]	Matches any one digit 1 through 6
>	Matches literally the character >
.	Matches any one character
*	Matches zero or more occurrences of the preceding character (which, because it is a period, means any character)
?	Prevents the preceding qualifier from being greedy, meaning it will match only the minimal number of characters to fulfill the expression's requirements
<\/h	Matches literally the characters </h (note the need to escape the forward slash)
[1-6]	Matches any one digit 1 through 6
>	Matches literally the character >

> *Notice that when translating the pattern to an ActionScript 3.0 regular expression literal, you need to escape the forward slash in the closing heading tag. This is necessary because regular expression literals are delineated by forward slashes, and you need to tell the ActionScript compiler that this forward slash is part of the pattern and not the end delimiter.*

To solve this problem, you need a way to tell the regular expression engine that whatever number was used to open the tag should also be used to close the tag. You can do this by wrapping the portion of the pattern that matches the contents of the opening tag in parentheses, and then using a back-reference in the closing tag to specify that they must match.

```
var invalidHtmlText:String = "<h1>A mismatched example</h6>";
var validHtmlText:String = "<h1>A matching example</h1>";
var headingRegExp:RegExp = /<(h[1-6])>.*?<\/\1>/;
trace(headingRegExp.test(invalidHtmlText));  // outputs false
trace(headingRegExp.test(validHtmlText));  // outputs true
```

Running this example will confirm that only the valid HTML text will match the regular expression.

Using backreferences with the String.replace() method

Backreferences can also be used in the replacement string that is passed to the `String.replace()` method. When used in this context, backreferences are specified slightly differently, using a $ (dollar sign), instead of a backslash, followed by the capture group index.

To demonstrate replacing using regular expressions and backreferences, let's imagine that you have loaded in HTML text dynamically to populate a `TextField` instance. Although a `TextField` instance can be populated with HTML text, it understands only the most basic HTML tags. One of the tags not understood is <strong>, which needs to be converted to a <b> tag to display properly in a text field. To go through a string and replace all occurrences of the <strong> tag and its contents with the <b> tag with the *same* contents, you can use this code:

```
var htmlText:String = "<strong>This text is important</strong>";
var strongRegExp:RegExp = /<strong>(.*?)<\/strong>/;
var replaced:String = htmlText.replace(strongRegExp, "<b>$1</b>");
trace(replaced);  // outputs: <b>This text is important</b>
```

Here, the backreference $1 refers to the capture group containing the match for (.*?). Remember that the full match for the entire expression is both the opening and closing <strong> tags and the contents between. This full match is replaced by the opening and closing <b> tags enclosing whatever characters are contained in the first capture group denoted by the parentheses. In the example, the matched characters for the capture group are This text is important, so the backreference $1 includes these characters, and you can use this backreference to insert these characters into your final string.

You can also use the special index 0 (zero) to make use of the part of the search string that was matched by the whole pattern.

Using backreferences after the pattern has been matched

One of the methods of the RegExp object we've not yet explored is the exec() method. This is similar to the test() method in that it executes the regular expression against the specified string, but rather than just returning true for a match, you actually get some useful information.

The exec() method returns an Object containing the groups that were matched, stored by group index, including the part of the string matched by the entire pattern at index 0, as well as two other special properties:

- input: The string that was passed to the method
- index: The position within the string in which the matched substring was found

Returning to the example in the previous section, you can see what this means in practice:

```
var htmlText:String = "<strong>This text is important</strong> ➥
while this text is not as important";
var strongRegExp:RegExp = /<strong>(.*?)<\/strong>/;
var matches:Object = strongRegExp.exec(htmlText);
for (var i:String in matches) {
  trace(i + ": " + matches[i]);
}
```

Running this example will result in the following text in the Output panel:

```
0: <strong>This text is important</strong>
1: This text is important
input: <strong>This text is important</strong> ➥
while this text is not as important
index: 0
```

As you can see, the array of capture groups contains two indexes. First, the entire matched substring is found in the first index (0). The second index (1) contains the matched group denoted by parentheses. In addition, the whole string being searched is contained in the input property. Finally, index traces as 0, since the matched substring begins at the first character in the string through which you were searching.

Understanding the e-mail regular expression pattern

As I promised, you can now make sense of the e-mail validation regular expression pattern presented at the beginning of the chapter.

^([a-zA-Z0-9._-]+)@([a-zA-Z0-9.-]+)\.([a-zA-Z]{2,4})$

Let's break down each of its parts. First, notice that the whole pattern in enclosed in start and end anchors (^ and $, respectively).

^([a-zA-Z0-9._-]+)@([a-zA-Z0-9.-]+)\.([a-zA-Z]{2,4})**$**

This means that the pattern will match only if the entire string being searched matches the pattern. If you omitted these anchors, the pattern would match a string that contained a valid e-mail address somewhere within it. This might be what you want if you are trying to extract all e-mail addresses from a larger string, but it's not correct for validating an e-mail address.

Moving on, you can see that there is a group toward the beginning of the expression containing a character range.

^**([a-zA-Z0-9._-]+)**@([a-zA-Z0-9.-]+)\.([a-zA-Z]{2,4})$

This group contains a character class that matches any alphanumeric character, a period, an underscore, or a hyphen. This character class then has the one-or-more quantifier applied to it, to indicate that you want to match as many of these characters in a row as possible. This will match the mailbox name portion of an e-mail address. It is grouped for readability only, but that could be useful later on if you wanted to reference the mailbox name using a backreference.

Next comes an @ symbol. This has no special meaning in the pattern and is treated as a literal character.

^([a-zA-Z0-9._-]+)**@**([a-zA-Z0-9.-]+)\.([a-zA-Z]{2,4})$

This matches the @ character that separates the mailbox name from the domain name in an e-mail address.

Following that is another group containing a character range.

^([a-zA-Z0-9._-]+)@**([a-zA-Z0-9.-]+)**\.([a-zA-Z]{2,4})$

This group is almost identical to the first, except that the character range does not contain an underscore character. since it would be invalid in a domain name. Again, the pattern looks for one or more occurrences of the character range (which is why you use the + quantifier).

Next is an escaped period.

^([a-zA-Z0-9._-]+)@([a-zA-Z0-9.-]+)\.([a-zA-Z]{2,4})$

Remember the period needs to be escaped if you want to match it literally, because it has special meaning within a regular expression pattern. Without the preceding backslash, it matches any non-newline character.

The final part of the regular expression pattern is another group.

^([a-zA-Z0-9._-]+)@([a-zA-Z0-9.-]+)\.**([a-zA-Z]{2,4})**$

This group consists of a character class matching an uppercase or lowercase letter and a bounds operator, indicating that you want between two and four characters that match that class. This matches the top-level domain (com, net, org, uk, and so on) for the domain name portion of the e-mail address.

Changing regular expression behavior with modifiers

We've been concentrating on patterns for so long that you might have forgotten the other element to regular expressions: **modifiers**. Modifiers are used to change the behavior of the entire regular expression or just some of the metacharacters within a pattern. ActionScript 3.0 supports the modifiers listed in Table 10-3.

Table 10-3. Regular expression modifiers

Modifier	Property	Description
i	ignoreCase	Specifies that the entire pattern is case-insensitive
g	global	Specifies that the pattern should be matched as many times as possible throughout the string being searched instead of just once
m	multiline	Allows the start-of-string and end-of-string anchors to additionally match the start and end of a line, respectively
s	dotall	Allows the dot metacharacter to match newline characters
x	extended	Specifies that whitespace in the pattern should be ignored

The modifiers are separate from the pattern in a regular expression, and are specified either as a string passed as the second argument to the RegExp constructor or after the second forward slash in a regular expression literal. You can specify more than one modifier (it doesn't make sense to specify the same modifier more than once). A regular expression using all of the available modifiers (more power, MORE POWER) would look something like this:

/pattern/igmsx

And if you use all of those modifiers, you're writing more complex regular expressions than I've ever needed.

Once the modifiers have been configured for a RegExp object, you can test to see which ones have been set by using the equivalent property names, as specified in Table 10-3:

```
var globalRegExp:RegExp = /abc/g;
trace(globalRegExp.global);  // outputs true
```

The properties are read-only Boolean values, so the preceding example would output true to the Output panel.

Let's now look at each of the modifiers in turn to see how they affect your patterns.

Using the case-insensitive modifier

Using the i (case-insensitive) modifier allows you to specify that any alphabetic character in your pattern should match both the uppercase and lowercase versions in the string being searched. This means that an *a* in the pattern would match either an *a* or an *A*.

```
var colorRegExp:RegExp = /colou?r/i;
trace(colorRegExp.test("colour"));  // outputs true
trace(colorRegExp.test("Color"));   // outputs true
trace(colorRegExp.test("COLOUR"));  // outputs true
```

Using the case-insensitive modifier, you could reduce the number of characters in the e-mail validation pattern by eliminating all the uppercase character ranges:

```
/^([a-z0-9._-]+)@([a-z0-9.-]+)\.([a-z]{2,4})$/i
```

Unfortunately, the case-insensitive modifier has no effect on non-English characters, such as *è* and *È*. For those occasions when you want to perform a case-insensitive match on a string containing non-English characters, you'll need to use character classes or alternation instead.

Using the global modifier

The g (global) modifier allows you to use the exec() method to find more than one occurrence of your entire pattern in the specified search string. For example, without the global modifier, multiple calls to the exec() method in the following example result in the same word being matched every time:

```
var compassPoints:String = "Naughty elephants squirt water";
var wordRegExp:RegExp = /\b\w+\b/;
trace(wordRegExp.exec(compassPoints));  // outputs Naughty
trace(wordRegExp.exec(compassPoints));  // outputs Naughty
trace(wordRegExp.exec(compassPoints));  // outputs Naughty
trace(wordRegExp.exec(compassPoints));  // outputs Naughty
```

This is because the RegExp object is being reset after each exec() method is called. You can change this behavior with the global modifier:

```
var compassPoints:String = "Naughty elephants squirt water";
var wordRegExp:RegExp = /\b\w+\b/g;
trace(wordRegExp.exec(compassPoints));  // outputs Naughty
trace(wordRegExp.exec(compassPoints));  // outputs elephants
trace(wordRegExp.exec(compassPoints));  // outputs squirt
trace(wordRegExp.exec(compassPoints));  // outputs water
```

This time, the RegExp object remembers the position at the end of the previous match. The next time exec() is called, it begins its search from where it left off previously.

The global modifier also changes the behavior of the String.match() method. Normally, this method would return an array containing exactly one element, consisting of the first substring that was matched by the specified regular expression.

```
var compassPoints:String = "Naughty elephants squirt water";
var wordRegExp:RegExp = /\b\w+\b/;
trace(compassPoints.match(wordRegExp));  // outputs Naughty
```

This example would output the following to the Output panel:

```
Naughty
```

However, if you use the global modifier, the array returned from the String.match() call will contain one element for each time the pattern was matched throughout the entire string.

```
var compassPoints:String = "Naughty elephants squirt water";
var wordRegExp:RegExp = /\b\w+\b/g;
// outputs Naughty,elephants,squirt,water
trace(compassPoints.match(wordRegExp));
```

The revised example would output the following to the Output panel:

```
Naughty,elephants,squirt,water
```

The final method affected by the global modifier is the String.replace() method. I trust you can work out what the following example does.

```
var compassPoints:String = "Naughty elephants squirt water";
var wordRegExp:RegExp = /\b\w+\b/g;
// outputs MATCH MATCH MATCH MATCH
trace(compassPoints.replace(wordRegExp, "MATCH"));
```

Using the multiline modifier

The m (multiline) modifier changes the behavior of the start-of-string and end-of-string anchors such that they will also match the start and end of a line in a string, respectively. When combined with the global modifier, this makes it easy to construct a regular expression to take a string containing multiple lines and convert them into list items:

```
var list:String = "one\ntwo\nthree\nfour";
var singleLineRegExp:RegExp = /^(.*?)$/mg;
trace(list.replace(singleLineRegExp, "<li>$1</li>"));
```

This example will produce the following output:

```
<li>one</li>
<li>two</li>
<li>three</li>
<li>four</li>
```

Notice how the newlines are still present. They weren't actually consumed by the anchors and so were not replaced by the replacement string.

Using the dotall modifier

The dot metacharacter normally matches any character in a string with the exception of newlines. Using the s (dotall) modifier means that the dot metacharacter will match any character in the string being searched, including newlines. This is a subtle shift, but a useful one.

Going back to the <strong> tag example, only by allowing newlines to be recognized with other characters would the following expression be able to find the <strong> tag spread across multiple lines. Try the following both with and without the dotall modifier.

```
var htmlText:String = "<strong>This text\nis important</strong>";
var strongRegExp:RegExp = /<strong>(.*?)<\/strong>/s;
var replaced:String = htmlText.replace(strongRegExp, "<b>$1</b>");
trace(replaced);
```

Using the extended modifier

Using the x (extended) modifier allows you to format your regular expression pattern using whitespace without actually affecting the pattern itself. This is generally used to aid readability of a pattern. For example, you could use whitespace to separate the various parts of the e-mail validation pattern like so:

```
/^   ([a-z0-9._-]+)   @   ([a-z0-9.-]+)   \.   ([a-z]{2,4})   $/ix
```

> In my experience, the extended modifier is rarely (if ever) used. If other developers pick up your code, they may well presume that the whitespace is part of the pattern, and only when they look at the modifiers (if they look at them at all) will they realize that the whitespace has no meaning. There are some instances where using the extended modifier makes sense, such as when you have a really long regular expression. If you use it, make sure that you add in a comment before the regular expression to point it out.

Using variables to build a regular expression

Another, perhaps better, option for breaking up long regular expressions to make them more readable is to build up the expression using variables. In order to use variables to construct a regular expression, you must use the RegExp constructor as opposed to a regular expression literal. Consider the following example.

```
var localName:String = "^([a-z0-9._-]+)";
var domain:String = "([a-z0-9.-]+)";
var topLevel:String = "([a-z]{2,4})$";
var emailValidator:RegExp = ➡
new RegExp(localName + "@" + domain + "\\." + topLevel, "i");
var email:String = "someAddress@someserver.com";
trace( emailValidator.test(email) );  // outputs true
```

This example breaks out each of the groups and assigns them to variables, then constructs the regular expression and passes it in the RegExp constructor (note that because the backslash for the period is within a string, you need to escape that backslash with another backslash so that it is read literally and not ignored). Whether this is more readable than including the expression in a literal declaration is debatable.

```
var emailValidator:RegExp = ➡
/^([a-z0-9._-]+)@([a-z0-9.-]+)\.([a-z]{2,4})$/i;
var email:String = "someAddress@someserver.com";
trace( emailValidator.test(email) );  // outputs true
```

At the very least, you have options as to how you want to represent your regular expressions and can decide what works best for you and your group.

Useful regular expressions

Table 10-4 shows a list of regular expression patterns that you might find useful in your projects. See if you can work out how they do what they do. (Note that these regular expression patterns do not include any boundaries, so if you want to ensure that these are not matched within other words, you should include the \b metacharacter.)

Table 10-4. Common regular expressions

Matches	Regular expression
US Social Security number	\d{3}-\d{2}-\d{4}
24-hour time with optional seconds (hh:mm[:ss])	`([01][0-9]|2[0-3]):([0-5][0-9])(:([0-5][0-9]))?
US date (mm/dd/yyyy)	`(0?[1-9]|1[012])/(0?[1-9]|[12][0-9]|3[01])/([0-9]{4})

Matches	Regular expression
UK date (dd/mm/yyyy)	`` `(0?[1-9]|[12][0-9]|3[01])/(0?[1-9]|1[012])/([0-9]{4}) ``
E-mail address	`([a-z0-9._-]+)@([a-z0-9.-]+)\.([a-z]{2,4})`
URL	`(\w+)://([^/:]+)(:\d*)?([^?# ]*)(\?[^# ]*)?(#[^ ]*)?`

Many of the regular expression patterns in Table 10-4 could be written differently or more accurately. Half of the job in creating the pattern for a regular expression is finding the right balance between clarity and accuracy. The official regular expression to validate an e-mail address is more than 6,000 characters long and is almost completely incomprehensible to mere mortals. The version presented here is 42 characters long, much more understandable, and good enough in all but the most exceptional cases.

Regular expression resources

I hope this chapter has given you an insight into regular expressions, but there's no way it could possibly tell the whole story. If you have a taste for regular expressions and would like to explore some of the more esoteric features, you could do no better than getting yourself a copy of Jeffrey Friedl's *Mastering Regular Expressions* (O'Reilly). This book will tell you everything you ever wanted to know and more about regular expressions, and then mess with your head with a look at how regular expression engines work and how to best optimize your patterns to squeeze every last ounce of performance out of them. Be warned that by the time you've finished this book, you will either be institutionalized or a fully paid-up member of the propeller-head club.

For those of you who are averse to institutionalization, you might want to check out Tony Stubblebine's excellent *Regular Expression Pocket Reference* (O'Reilly). Any developers who use regular expressions more than once a year should have a copy of this reference on their desk.

If you're in a fix and you can't quite work out how to build a regular expression to suit your needs, chances are that someone has solved the problem before. If they have, it's probably listed on the Regular Expression Library website (http://www.regexlib.com), which contains a searchable list of regular expression patterns that have been contributed by visitors to the site. The collection is ever-growing and driven by the community, so if you find aw solution to a problem that isn't already listed, you can contribute that to the developer community through this site.

Summary

We've covered a lot of ground in this chapter. If you're still reading this, you should give yourself a pat on the back (and extra pats if you read it all in one sitting.) We started off by looking at what regular expressions are and why they are useful. Next, we spent a long time wading through the various features of a regular expression pattern and how they can be used in a variety of practical examples, using the various regular expression capable methods along the way. We then looked at the modifiers that can be applied to a regular expression and how they affect the way in which a pattern is matched. Finally, you saw some commonly used regular expressions and were directed to some resources for learning more about regular expressions.

Regular expressions offer an amazing amount of power for searching through and manipulating string data in ActionScript. Actually, a lot in programming comes down to manipulating strings and other types of data. In the next chapter, we'll look at using XML, one of the most useful ways of storing and passing data back and forth with the server. See you on the next page, when you're ready to add yet another powerful tool to your ActionScript toolkit.

Chapter 11

USING XML

Sean McSharry

This chapter covers the following topics:

- What XML and E4X are
- How XML can be used with ActionScript 3.0
- The different methods of constructing XML

Extensible Markup Language (XML) is a simple, tag-based, descriptive language that can be created in any text editor. XML allows users to describe complex, hierarchical data in simple, logical terms. It has become popular because it makes data portable, and disparate development languages and operating systems are transparent to the solution.

XML has some simple structural rules and structural terminology, and can be quite complex. However, to use XML with ActionScript, you need to adhere to only the basic structural rules when creating it. You can write your own XML file or, as is often the case, you can access other applications' XML data sources.

If you have written XML parsers in ActionScript in the past, you probably iterated through the incoming XML object to access the data you needed. This was a little time-consuming, and many of us wrote parsers that we kept and improved so that we could use them again in each project that read an XML file. Some of you may have had the foresight to use the XPath API. This allowed you to drill down to the exact piece of data you were looking for in the XML document, and even to do filtered searches on it. For those of you who have used the XPath API, the new method of interrogating XML, called ECMAScript for XML (E4X), will be familiar, but it is even more powerful than XPath and allows dot-notation access. E4X is also much easier and quicker to use than a traditional XML parser. Additionally, E4X automatically ignores whitespace (carriage returns, tabs, spaces, and line feeds between XML elements).

In this chapter, you'll learn how to use E4X, but let's back up and start with some XML basics.

Understanding XML and E4X

XML is a hierarchical data structure made up of various defined components. The **XML document** is the XML file, or your entire data structure. The **XML tree** is the XML hierarchical structure, which shows the structure of an XML file and gives you an indication of how it may be traversed.

XML document components

Let's review the main XML document components: the root node, elements, attributes, and text nodes.

Root node

All XML documents must have a **root node**. This is the first and last node in an XML document or tree (the opening and closing node). Usually, the root node will have a fairly descriptive name, matching the data's purpose. So if the XML document described TV channels and their associated programs, like an electronic program guide (EPG), the root node might appear like so:

```
<EPG>
```

Elements

An XML **element** is a unit of XML data, delimited by tags. An XML element can enclose other elements. All XML elements must have matching opening and closing tags, which are hierarchically balanced. This is wrong:

```
<person>
     <name>Sean
<person>
```

Correct XML has a matching closing element tag that begins with /, like this:

```
<person>
     <name>Sean</name>
</person>
```

Another way is to open and close an element in one go. You can create the opening element tag with the / at the end, like so:

```
<person/>
```

Attributes

Essentially, **attributes** are data nodes within the opening element tag. These are often the topic of much debate.

Those who argue against using attributes say that the same information could be represented in the text node of an element (discussed next). Also, if you need to represent more than one piece of information, some suggest that you should create separate child elements to represent the data in a more hierarchical structure that more faithfully reflects the convention of XML.

The argument for using attributes is that no further hierarchical element creation is necessary, and this could save XML development time and make it more maintainable.

The arguments both for and against using attributes are valid, and you will need to decide for yourself. What I can tell you is that tests have shown that attributes are processed faster by ActionScript than text node information. Also, it is considered appropriate to use attributes for smaller related pieces of information about the element, whereas larger pieces of information, such as descriptive text paragraphs, are better suited to text nodes.

So, a contact element might contain attributes like this:

```
<person>
        <name id="Sean" location="London" age="21 again"/>
</person>
```

This element has both an opening and close tag in one (the / at the end). This is because it quite legitimately contains all its information in its attributes.

Text nodes

A **text node** is the optional textual content that sits between the opening and closing tags in an XML element. In ActionScript 2.0, a text node was referred to as an *element value*. Text nodes are entirely optional. They are useful if you have large sections of text or if you need to represent special characters in your XML, as attributes cannot do this as well. An example of both of these conditions is if you wanted to have descriptive text about a given person but wanted to allow a third party to format it for HTML inside the XML, without needing to worry about how ActionScript would interpret these HTML tags (special characters). Here's an example:

```
<person>
    <name id="Sean" location="London" age="21 again"> <![CDATA[
    <b>Sean McSharry</b> :
    An author from the foED stables, Sean has become one of their
    most prolific writers <i>but</i> he's quite mad.]]></name>
</person>
```

While the statement is quite untrue (I am not prolific), you will notice the CDATA tag in the text node that encapsulates it. This allows for special characters to be used with impunity, by reading them literally, instead of interpreting them.

E4X

E4X is a standard maintained by Ecma International (see http://www.ecma-international.org/publications/standards/Ecma-357.htm). It allows you to interface with the XML through simple, intuitive, dot-syntax notational methods.

E4X gives you advanced search and filtering control. You're going to love it. You'll see examples of using E4X throughout this chapter.

Accessing an XML file

You can write your own XML file for your ActionScript project, or, as is often the case, you can draw XML information from a server back-end via Remote Procedure Call (RPC), calling PHP, Java, C# pages, or some other technology to return an XML object. You may also use an XML socket server to push XML information to your application from the back-end.

Creating an XML object

Before you can do anything with XML, you need to create an XML object. Here is how to create an XML object in ActionScript:

```
Private var xmlObject:XML;
```

Once you have an XML object, there are many ways to populate it. More often than not, you will be reading an existing external XML file or source in to your XML object (even if it's one you created yourself). Populating an XML object internally is far less common. So, let's start by looking at how to access an external XML file.

Loading an XML file

For this chapter's example, you will load in a list of channels and programs for a TV EPG. You will find the XML file used in this example in the code you downloaded for this chapter, in a file called EPG.xml.

The following is the XML you'll be using. I've kept it simple, as the XML is less important than the code you will use to manipulate it.

```
<EPG>
<Channel id="BBC1">
<Program id="6am News" starttime="6:00">The breaking headlines </Program>
<Program id="Good Morning Britain" starttime="6:15">Stories from ➡
around the UK</Program>
<Program id="EastEnders" starttime="8:00" >Catch up with Albert ➡
Square</Program>
</Channel>
<Channel id="ITV">
```

```
<Program id="Healthy Eating" starttime="6:00">Meals even our kids ➡
will eat</Program>
<Program id="News" starttime="6:35">News roundup of the morning's ➡
events</Program>
<Program id="Cartoons" starttime="6:50" >Keep the kids occupied</ ➡
Program>
<Program id="Breakfast" starttime="7:00">Topical conversation, News</ ➡
Program>
</Channel>
<Channel id="Channel 4">
<Program id="Scooby Doo" starttime="6:00">Watch the kids solve ➡
mysteries</Program>
<Program id="Big Brother" starttime="6:30">Catch up with the ➡
housemates </Program>
<Program id="Big Breakfast" starttime="7:15" >Everything you need in ➡
the morning</Program>
</Channel>
</EPG>
```

Now let's set up the ActionScript to load in the XML:

```
var urXML:URLRequest;
var ulXML:URLLoader;

//Connect to the XML file
urXml = new URLRequest("EPG.xml");
//Instantiate loader
ulXml = new URLLoader(urXml);
//Add event listener for load complete
ulXml.addEventListener(Event.COMPLETE, xmlLoaded);
//Load XML into loader object
ulXml.load(urXml);
```

Here, you have first added the code to create a URLRequest instance for the XML file. Then you created a URLLoader instance to load it and an event listener to handle the data once it has finished loading. Finally, you execute the load() function on the URLLoader instance. It's easy, and even longhand,
it can be done in four lines of code. Once URLLoader has fired the COMPLETE event, the XML needs to
be handed off to an XML object. This should be defined like so:

```
private var xmlEPG:XML;
```

So the handler function should look like this:

```
private function xmlLoaded(evt:Event){
xmlEPG = new XML(ulXml.data);
}
```

Getting XML from a remote source

XML can also come from other external sources. It can be returned to you from an RPC, from a PHP call, or from a .NET call on the back-end, for example. Making the call and assigning the return value should be as simple as this:

```
this.urlSendVars.sendAndLoad("http://www.pokercoder.com/php/reg.php", ➥
this.urlResultVars, "GET");
```

One more option for receiving external XML data is to use an XML socket server. This is also a push technology, which means that your application doesn't need to poll for information or updates. Instead, it connects once and remains connected to the remote socket server. The socket server pushes updates to your application as it gets them or as it is programmed to.

So now that you have your XML data, you need to read what's in it.

Reading the XML

Reading the XML is when you really begin to use E4X. You're going to like it, I guarantee. For this example, you will use the EPG.xml file. As you can see, this file gives you all of the XML elements and nodes that were introduced earlier in the chapter. So let's look at how to address this information.

Reading the root node

In truth, you will probably never refer to the root node directly by name. However, when you assign the XML source to an XML object, that object becomes the root node. So xmlEPG becomes the root node when the onCOMPLETE event handler calls the handler function and assigns the returned XML data to the XML object:

```
xmlEPG = new XML(ulXml.data);
```

If you want to check this, just add the following line to the end of the event handler code:

```
trace("Root node = "+xmlEPG.name());
```

You'll see that it outputs the EPG root node name, which is, of course, EPG. This is essential for allowing you to reference any other data in your XML.

Reading elements in an XML tree

Now we will look at interrogating the elements. It's also a good opportunity to introduce XMLList objects.

> Technically, you don't need the elements themselves. They are usually more of a reference point in order to extract the data from text nodes or attributes that populate them.

What is an XMLList object and how does it differ from an XML object? An XML object is a single root object. There is only one top-level node: the root node. Usually, this contains a full hierarchical family of XML elements. The XMLList object differs only in that it can contain more than one top-level XML object or element, You could consider it either as having no root node or having multiple root nodes, where each top-level element constitutes a root node.

Suppose that you want to see all the program information for the ITV channel in your XML file. Your E4X assignment could look like this:

```
var xmlITV:XMLList = xmlEPG.Channel[1].children();
trace("Channel ITV = "+xmlITV);
```

This code interrogates the root node for all the child nodes that live under the second Channel node. Notice that in E4X-formatted XML interrogation, you can still use the child/children syntax that is associated with more traditional XML parsing methods. The trace() statement in the code will display all of the ITV channel Program nodes as an XMLList:

```
Channel ITV = <Program id="Healthy Eating" starttime="6:00">Meals ➥
even our kids will eat</Program>
<Program id="News" starttime="6:35">News roundup of the morning's ➥
events</Program>
<Program id="Cartoons" starttime="6:50">Keep the kids occupied </Program>
<Program id="Breakfast" starttime="7:00">Topical conversation, News </Program>
```

You can be more specific if, for example, you want just the first child node of the second channel:

```
var xmlITV:XMLList = xmlEPG.Channel[1].child(0);
trace("Channel ITV = "+xmlITV);
```

This will return the actual text node of the specified element as it interprets that you have interrogated a single element:

```
Channel ITV = Meals even our kids will eat
```

You'll learn more about accessing text nodes in the "Reading text nodes" section later in this chapter.

So, how easy is that? It gives me goose bumps.

Now let's say you want to read the attributes of a specific node, rather than just return an XMLList.

Reading an XML element's attributes

It would be nice if reading attributes were as easy and logical as reading an element. Well, it is! But first you need to be able to access the attributes. To do this, you use a specific syntax: the @ symbol. The following is the basic code required to read the id attribute of the xmlEPG.Channel[1].child(0) element:

```
var xmlITV:XMLList = xmlEPG.Channel[1].child(0).@id;
trace("Channel ITV Program id = "+xmlITV);
```

This code returns the id attribute information:

```
Channel ITV Program id = Healthy Eating
```

This works great if you know where the ITV and specific Program nodes live (xmlEPG.channel[1].child(0)). But often you won't have access to see the XML file or source, or you won't want to be so specific. You will always be given the schema in one form or another, so that you know the hierarchical structure of the XML you are receiving, but that doesn't tell you where specific data resides. Also, needing to know where the ITV channel node (or any other node) lives in advance has little time-saving benefit or convenience over traditional XML parsing. It would be much more useful if you could just interrogate the XML for any Program node that contained a specific id attribute of ITV. Well, thanks to E4X, you can do exactly that kind of intelligent search.

Searching XML

So far, you can interrogate a node's attributes, and you can get the program title information from the program's id attribute. Now you want to interrogate so that you can get the program title information from specific programs on specific channels.

Imagine that you don't know where the ITV channel element is in the XML document and you want to know what the first program on ITV (chronologically) is called. You shouldn't need to know where that specific channel node is in relation to its siblings to get that information. You know its id attribute is ITV. Shouldn't that be enough? From this information, you can indeed perform a search on any XML or XMLList object to see which program is coming next on the ITV channel. This is quite a practical search, and E4X makes it quick and easy to perform. Once again, this would be a normal request of any EPG.xml data:

```
var xmlITV:XMLList = xmlEPG.Channel.(@id == "ITV").child(0).@id;
trace("ITV next program = "+xmlITV);
```

You are still referencing the attributes using the @ symbol. However, here you have made an in-line comparative call, asking it to return any id information from the first child (Program) node of any Channel XMLList where the Channel's id attribute equals ITV, and you have traced the results. This trace returns the following:

```
ITV next program = Healthy Eating
```

While this *is* a search, E4X allows you to do far more compound, intelligent searches. For example, if you were searching through the program list of a particular channel, say ITV, you might reasonably want to extract information by start time rather than position in the Program nodes. Let's say you're looking for a start time of 6 a.m. You can write your search code like this:

```
var xmlITV:XMLList = xmlEPG.Channel.(@id == "ITV").Program. ➡
(@starttime == "6:00").@id;
trace("ITV at 6am = "+xmlITV);
```

Here, you are extending your previous code, which returned the program name (the Program node's id attribute), to return the same data but based on any Program node whose starttime attribute is equal to 6am and that is showing the ITV Channel id attribute in its parent Channel node. Not surprisingly, this returns the following trace information:

```
ITV at 6am = Healthy Eating
```

Now let's say you want to base your search on *any* program starting at 6 a.m. on all channels. This requires a very small change to the last piece of code:

```
var xmlITV:XMLList = xmlEPG.*.Program.(@starttime == "6:00").@id;
trace("ITV at 6am = "+xmlITV);
```

All you've done is to replace the Channel node interrogation with a wildcard symbol (*), and presto, the trace shows this:

```
Programs starting at 6am = 6am NewsHealthy EatingScooby Doo
```

Although this is not a very good representation of the data, as all three returned program id attributes are concatenated together in one unsightly string, it does highlight the results.

Searching for an attribute or element at any level

The previous example worked well, but for the sake of argument, let's say you don't even know where the Program node is to be found hierarchically. And once again, let's assume that you want to find out what programs start at 6 a.m. on every channel. In the real world, you may know that there are Program nodes that contain the program titles and start times, but you might not want to worry about the infrastructure of the XML source code in order to extract that information.

In my experience, it is entirely possible for the data model to be modified or redesigned after coding has begun. There are many reasons for such changes. Suffice it to say, none of them are brought about by someone spending a reasonable amount of time properly planning the schema requirements. It would be nice if you could account for such changes in advance, or at least easily respond when you must reactively counter them. Thankfully, E4X comes to the rescue again.

Suppose some bright spark has just realized that he needs to split up the different days of the EPG. Instead of having thought this through before writing a functional specification, he is now forced to make a panicked knee-jerk decision to fix the XML. So he just adds in a Day tag. This is a bad solution to the problem, but, believe me, it happens more often than you might think, so you will likely encounter such situations. This changes the original EPG.xml file by putting the Program nodes down one level, inside a new tag called Day:

```
<EPG>
<Channel id="BBC1">
<Day id="Monday">
<Program id="6 oclock News" starttime="6:00">The breaking headlines </Program>
<Program id="Good Morning Britain" starttime="6:15">Stories from ➡
around the UK</Program>
<Program id="EastEnders" starttime="8:00" >Catch up with Albert Square</Program>
</Day>
</Channel>
```

```
<Channel id="ITV">
<Day id="Monday">
<Program id="Healthy Eating" starttime="6:00">Meals even our kids ➥
will eat</Program>
<Program id="News" starttime="6:35">News roundup of the morning's ➥
events</Program>
<Program id="Cartoons" starttime="6:50" >Keep the kids occupied </Program>
<Program id="Breakfast" starttime="7:00">Topical conversation, News </Program>
</Day>
</Channel>
<Channel id="Channel 4">
<Day id="Monday">
<Program id="Scooby Doo" starttime="6:00">Watch the kids solve ➥
mysteries</Program>
<Program id="Big Brother" starttime="6:30">Catch up with the ➥
housemates </Program>
<Program id="Big Breakfast" starttime="7:15" >Everything you need in ➥
the morning</Program>
</Day>
</Channel>
</EPG>
```

These changes have programming implications. Try your XML call to collect the list of programs starting at 6 a.m.:

```
var xmlSixAM:XMLList = xmlEPG.*.Program.(@starttime == "6:00").@id;
trace("Programs starting at 6am = "+xmlSixAM);
```

This will now return the following:

```
Programs starting at 6am =
```

As you can see, the * wildcard no longer works. You could modify the XMLList assignment to reflect the new structure, but there is no guarantee that the data won't be modified again. You need a way to automatically search down through the full XML path until you find the Program node, so that you can carry out the same interrogation no matter where this node resides. And here is that code, care of E4X:

```
var xmlSixAM:XMLList = xmlEPG..Program.(@starttime == "6:00").@id;
trace("Programs starting at 6am = "+xmlSixAM);
```

At a glance, this may look no different from the previous code, but look again. Where the root node ends, there is a double set of periods (..) before the Program node. This tells the compiler to search through any and all levels of the XML document, from the root node down, for a Program node. Then you check its starttime attribute, check if it is set to 6am, and if it is, return its id attribute, which gives the name of the program. This will trace the contents of the entire returned XMLList, like so:

```
Programs starting at 6am = 6am NewsHealthy EatingScooby Doo
```

Obviously, this is not how you would interrogate the XMLList once it is populated, as it returns a fairly unusable and nondelimited list of values. However, it does show exactly what data it holds.

> *The double-period notation is comparatively processor-intensive. You should consider if it is the appropriate solution for your needs. To use this method for every search would be very poor convention.*

You can call specific entries in the XMLList by using the array position syntax, like so:

```
trace("Programs starting at 6am = "+xmlSixAM[2]);
```

The [2] represents the array position in the XMLList. In this instance, the trace would return one program:

```
Programs starting at 6am = Scooby Doo
```

Of course, in the real world, you would be collecting a list of channels and then iteratively going through the returned XMLList to display all the programs starting at the same time on those channels.

Reading text nodes

You can access text nodes as either XML or Strings—it's your choice. Reading text nodes technically requires that you convert the XML text node to a String, and to adhere to good convention, I suggest you do exactly that. However, ActionScript automatically makes that cast conversion for you if you omit it. Here's a simple example of interrogating the text node as an XML format:

```
var xmlTextNode:XMLList = xmlEPG.Channel.Day.Program;
trace("text = "+xmlTextNode.*[0]);
```

This returns the following:

```
text = The breaking headlines as they come in
```

Obviously, this is a very simple example, and in real-life terms, it's probably of no value. A more realistic use of this approach would be as follows:

```
var xmlString:String = xmlEPG.Channel.(@id == "ITV").Day.(@id == ➡
"Monday").Program.(@id == "Breakfast");
trace("Breakfast text = "+xmlString);
```

Here, you are searching through the Channel nodes for any channel with the id attribute of "ITV", and then extracting the text node of any of those that have a Day node with the id attribute of "Monday" and have "Breakfast" in their Program node's id attribute. This will trace the following:

```
Breakfast text = Topical conversation, News, Weather, Sports, Fashion and Gossip
```

You've read in the XML data and interrogated it in many ways. E4X allows a lot of logical scope to do this. Now it's time to see how it assists in modifying an existing node, element, or attribute or creating new ones.

Modifying XML

E4X makes it easy to add elements to an XML object using ActionScript, as well as remove them. Let's see how that works.

Adding elements to an XML object

Adding an element to your XML is a common requirement. For example, in the sample XML, you may need to add another Channel element and its associated elements and attributes. Take another look at the XML document:

```
<?xml version="1.0" encoding="ISO-8859-1"?>
<EPG>
    <Channel id="BBC1">
        <Day id="Monday">
            <Program id="6 oclock News" starttime="6:00">The ➡
breaking headlines</Program>
            <Program id="Good Morning Britain" starttime="6:15"> ➡
Stories from around the UK</Program>
            <Program id="EastEnders" starttime="8:00" >Catch up with ➡
Albert Square</Program>
        </Day>
    </Channel>
    <Channel id="ITV">
        <Day id="Monday">
            <Program id="Healthy Eating" starttime="6:00">Meals even ➡
our kids will eat</Program>
            <Program id="News" starttime="6:35">News roundup of the ➡
morning's events</Program>
            <Program id="Cartoons" starttime="6:50" >Keep the kids ➡
occupied</Program>
            <Program id="Breakfast" starttime="7:00">Topical ➡
conversation, News</Program>
        </Day>
    </Channel>
    <Channel id="Channel 4">
        <Day id="Monday">
            <Program id="Scooby Doo" starttime="6:00">Watch the kids ➡
solve mysteries</Program>
            <Program id="Big Brother" starttime="6:30">Catch up with ➡
the housemates</Program>
            <Program id="Big Breakfast" starttime="7:15" >Everything ➡
you need in the morning</Program>
        </Day>
    </Channel>
</EPG>
```

Oops, BBC2 seems to be missing! Let's fix that now.

First, create your new XML object that will be added to the existing root node:

```
var xmlBBC2:XML = <Channel/>;
```

You could build the XML all in one go, like so:

```
var xmlBBC2:XML = <Channel id="BBC2">
                    <Day id="Monday">
                            <Program id="➡
University Challenge" starttime="6:00">Are you smart enough?</Program>
                    </Day>
                            </Channel>
```

But often you will build an XML element as you go along, so let's treat the additions and modifications as separate requirements.

In this new XML object, <Channel> is now the root node. However, it is very important to be aware that each node, element, and attribute is added to the existing XML document as the lastChild, among its peers, by default. If you want to avoid more complex hierarchical-based additions, I suggest you give the order of addition some thought before commencing.

You can add all the hierarchical elements in one go when defining a final text node, like so:

```
var BBC2.Day.Program = "program description"
```

It is also possible to do this when defining a final attribute:

```
var BBC2.Day.Program.@id = "program name"
```

Though you have not specified any text node or attribute for the Day node, it is created by default as part of the XML path to the Program node. This is very useful, as it means you can target your final text node or attribute without needing to write many lines of code for the definition of all the intervening nodes. This allows for the creation of quite complex XML trees from just a few lines of code.

You can continue to add attributes and text nodes; however, you need to be aware of what happens when you add same-named sibling nodes. Suppose you have created the following XML:

```
<Channel id="BBC2">
        <Day id="Monday">
                        <Program id="University Challenge" ➡
starttime="6:00">Are you smart enough?</Program>
                </Day>
        </Channel>
```

Now let's say you want to add another sibling Program node:

```
var BBC2.Day.Program = "Live snooker from Wembley"
trace(xmlBBC2.toXMLString());
```

If you expect E4X to simply add a next child sibling Program node to the existing Day node, then you are in for a big surprise when you publish it:

```
<Channel id="BBC2">
        <Day id="Monday">
                    <Program id="University Challenge" ➡
starttime="6:00"> Live snooker from Wembley </Program>
            </Day>
        </Channel>
```

As you can see, it has simply replaced the text node of the existing Program node. The same would be true if you tried this with attributes. And if your goal was to *replace* a node, this is how that could be accomplished.

If we want to add a sibling node with the same name, the correct syntax is as follows:

```
var BBC2.Day.Program[1] = "Live snooker from Wembley"
trace(xmlBBC2.toXMLString());
```

Now you will see the new extra sibling node:

```
<Channel id="BBC2">
        <Day id="Monday">
            <Program id="University Challenge" starttime="6:00">Are ➡
you smart enough?</Program>
            <Program>Live snooker from Wembley </Program>
        </Day>
</Channel>
```

Next, you need to add new attribute nodes to finish the second program entry. You might code the following:

```
varBBC2.Day.Program[1].@id = "Snooker Finals";
varBBC2.Day.Program[1].@starttime = "6:45";
```

Your XML should trace like so:

```
<Channel id="BBC2">
        <Day id="Monday">
            <Program id="University Challenge" starttime="6:00">Are ➡
you smart enough?</Program>
            <Program id="Snooker Finals" starttime="6:45">Live ➡
snooker from Wembley </Program>
        </Day>
</Channel>
```

This is how to *create same-name sibling nodes*.

Removing elements and attributes from an XML object

E4X, once again, makes removing elements and attributes incredibly simple. For this purpose, you use the delete command, and follow all previously described protocols and syntax for dealing with elements and attributes.

So, if you wanted to delete the second Program node you just added in the previous section, your code would look like this:

```
delete xmlBBC2.Day.Program[0]
```

Attributes can be deleted in the same way:

```
delete xmlBBC2.Day.Program[0].@id
```

This might be a good time to talk about deleting a text node:

```
delete xmlBBC2.Day.Program[0].*
```

And this demonstrates that you can use the wildcard (*) with delete. You can also use the double period and any other previously mentioned search or location syntax to carry out most E4X commands.

Summary

In this chapter, you have worked through XML and E4X in reasonable detail. I suggest further reading and experimentation on your part. For example, *Foundation XML for Flash* by Sas Jacobs (friends of ED, 2005) is devoted to the subject of using XML with Flash (although it doesn't cover ActionScript 3.0).

E4X is a huge step forward and incredibly easy to use. It will make working with XML quick and powerful. I can't say enough good things about E4X.

In this and the previous chapters, you've learned all about ActionScript 3.0. In the next chapter, you'll put it all together in a .single, real-world application

Chapter 12

CASE STUDY: CREATING A DYNAMIC IMAGE VIEWER

Todd Yard

We've covered so much ground throughout this book—from the core elements of the ActionScript language, through advanced coding features like graphic creation and dynamic loading of data, all the way to the use of components and class libraries to extend functionality. Now it's time to pull all of that knowledge together into a single, real-world application that shows what you can accomplish easily with your newly acquired ActionScript skills. This will help to solidify the concepts that you have been absorbing over the past couple hundred pages (and you'll create something pretty cool and useful, to boot!).

In just a single project, you'll use many of the skills taught in the past 11 chapters. This chapter's example demonstrates the following:

- How to use a document class to act as the main entry point for an application
- How to lay out and configure components in the IDE
- How to style and customize components
- How to take advantage of the ActionScript 3.0 event model
- How to use the Drawing API to dynamically create graphics
- How to apply graphic filters through ActionScript
- How to modify the display list at runtime
- How to load and parse XML

- How to load and display images
- How to set and retrieve properties from object instances
- How to use loops and conditional constructs
- How to create and instantiate custom classes
- How to extend a class and use inheritance

And that's just a high-level list. You will use plenty of supporting skills to reach the end goal. These include manipulating strings and numbers, using numeric and object operators (including casting objects), applying access modifiers and data type assignment, and exercising a whole list of syntactical skills that should be almost second nature to you by this point. That's one of the great things about applying your ActionScript knowledge: the more you code, the easier it becomes. Then you can spend less time worrying about the lower-level tasks and more time concentrating on the overall application and how to approach different problems in more elegant ways.

An overview of the image viewer

Loading and displaying images is a common task in a front-end application, whether it is explicitly for display of media files or images are loaded and used to render the GUI. This makes an image viewer a great practical application for your ActionScript skills.

This chapter's case study is an interface built using the Flash ActionScript 3.0 components and tied together with ActionScript. The ActionScript loads an external XML file containing image information, such as the name and path to the file, and a thumbnail representation of the file.

The data, once loaded, will be rendered in one of two forms: a text list or a thumbnail grid. Clicking an item in either list will load the relevant image and display it within a scrolling pane. A slider will allow users to zoom into the image. The scrolling pane will allow not only for scrolling, but also for panning the image by clicking and dragging. The completed application appears in Figure 12-1.

When we get to the ActionScript, you'll see that you won't need a large number of classes or a huge amount of code to achieve the goal for this application, since a good portion of the UI logic is encapsulated in the components themselves (which is a great reason to be using the components in the first place). For this project, you will create the following classes:

- An ImageViewer document class, which will kick everything off and handle events from the components
- An ImageData class, which will take care of the loading and formatting of external data
- An ImageHolder class, which will wrap your image-loading code and take care of some simple transition animation
- An Image class, which will hold the metadata for a single image
- A very simple SimpleImageCell class, which will extend the ImageCell class used by the TileList component in order to control the rendering of the images in the TileList instance

You'll start by building the interface.

Figure 12-1. The finished image viewer application

Laying out the interface

Let's begin the project by laying out the interface for the application using the drag-and-drop components in the Flash CS3 IDE. Before you do this, I would like to point out that it is certainly possible to
use components in your applications without placing them on stage. The following would attach and
position a Label instance.

```
var label:Label = new Label();
label.x = 50;
label.y = 100;
label.text = "This is a Label instance.";
addChild(label);
```

There is nothing wrong with this approach. In fact, many would even argue it is better, since it is easier to manage and develop code stored in external files than to manage FLAs and objects in the timeline. However, visually positioning and configuring items allows you to easily align and tweak your
interface without needing to constantly recompile your SWF. Also, it certainly is great for quickly creating prototypes of your interfaces, so that is the approach you will use here. If, once you are happy
with the appearance of an application, you wish to move the component instantiation, placement, and
configuration directly into the code, it is not a difficult process.

So, let's get started.

1. Create a new Flash ActionScript 3.0 document and save it into a Chapter 12 project directory
   as imageViewer.fla.

2. Use the Document Properties dialog box (Modify ➤ Document) to change the dimensions to
   600 × 350 and to set the background color to #CCCCCC, as shown in Figure 12-2.

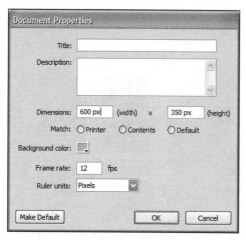

Figure 12-2. The document property settings for the image viewer

3. Open the Components panel if it is not already open (Window ➤ Components). From this panel, drag into your file's Library (Window ➤ Library) the following components from the User Interface folder: Label, List, RadioButton, ScrollPane, Slider, and TileList. Your Library should look like Figure 12-3.

Figure 12-3. The image viewer library with all required components

4. In the main timeline, create five new layers, for a total of six layers. Name the six layers, top to bottom, **radios**, **list**, **tilelist**, **slider**, **labels**, and **scrollpane**. The timeline should look like Figure 12-4.

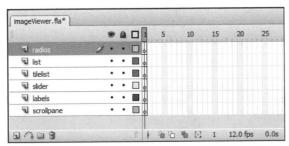

Figure 12-4. The image viewer's timeline with six layers ready for component placement

5. Drag an instance of the ScrollPane component from your Library into the scrollpane layer. This will be used to display all loaded images and allow for panning of those images. Using the Parameters panel, position the instance at (10, 40) and set its dimensions to 400 × 300. Name the instance imagePane_sp. In the parameters data grid, set the scrollDrag property to true. This property, when true, allows a user to pan an image in the scrolling pane by clicking and dragging. The result of these settings is shown in Figure 12-5.

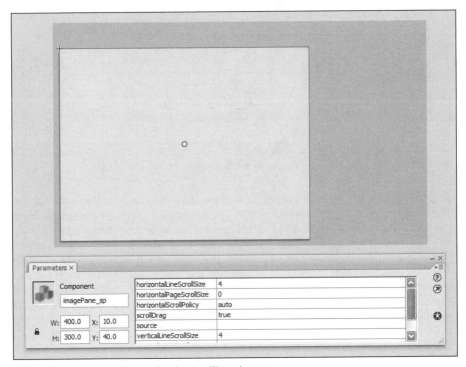

Figure 12-5. The properties set for the ScrollPane instance

6. Drag an instance of the Label component from the Library into the labels layer. Name the instance title_lbl. In the Parameters panel, position it at (10, 13) and change its dimensions to 250 × 22. In the parameters data grid, set the text property to **Choose an image at right**. Notice that the Live Preview automatically updates with this new text.

7. Drag another instance of the Label component into the labels layer. Set this instance at (280, 15) and alter its dimensions to 50 × 20. This instance does not require a name (you will not be manipulating it through ActionScript), but change its text property in the parameters data grid to **zoom:**. The result of placing and configuring both labels is shown in Figure 12-6.

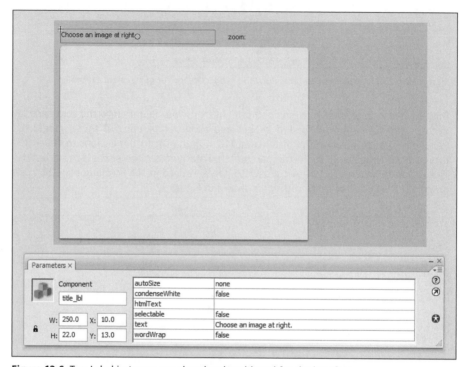

Figure 12-6. Two Label instances are placed and positioned for the interface.

8. Drag an instance of the Slider component into the slider layer and position it at (325, 22). Name the instance zoom_sl. Its dimensions can remain at their defaults. For its parameters, set liveDragging to true. This will send change events while the slider is being dragged, as opposed to waiting until the slider is released. Set its minimum property to 1, while leaving the maximum at 10. minimum and maximum control the range of values available to the slider. Since this slider will be setting the scale of your image, you don't want its value to go below 1, which is 100%. Give the instance a snapInterval setting of .1, which will force its value to be in increments of 0.1. Finally, set both tickInterval and value to 1. tickInterval will set tick marks on the component (you should see them appear in the Live Preview), and value determines the initial value, which you set to 1, or 100% scale for the image. The result of all these settings is shown in Figure 12-7.

9. Going in layer order, the next component to configure is the TileList, which will be used to display a grid of thumbnails that the user can click to load an image. Drag an instance from your Library and place it in the tilelist layer. Use the Parameters panel to position it at (420, 40), to set its dimensions to 170 × 300. Name the instance thumbnails_tl. Leave all of its parameters at their default values. The stage, with the TileList instance sized and positioned, should look like Figure 12-8.

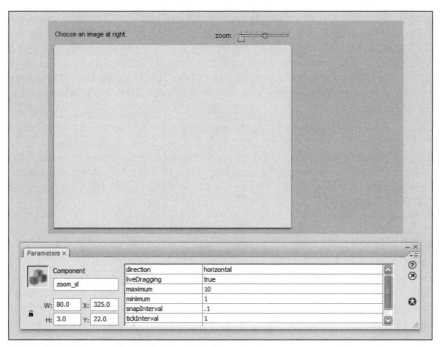

Figure 12-7. The properties set for the Slider instance

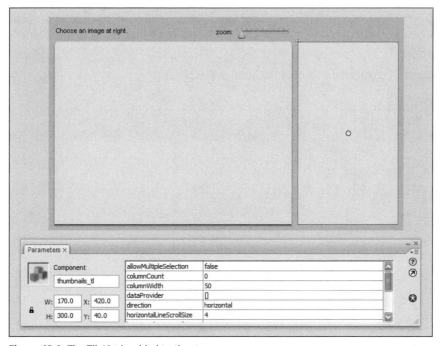

Figure 12-8. The TileList is added to the stage.

10. Drag an instance of List from the Library into the list layer. Like the TileList instance, this will be used to show data from which the user can choose, but the List instance will display this data as a list of text. You will code the interface to show the user only one of the two lists, and allow the user to toggle between the views. Because of this, the List instance's size and position should match exactly that of the TileList instance, so position it at (420, 40) and set its dimensions to 170 × 300. Name the instance names_li. Leave all of its parameters at the default values.

> *Here is a good example of why it is good practice to utilize the timeline layer options in Flash to organize your UI elements. By creating a new layer for each element, or at least type of element, it is easy to toggle visibility or lock certain layers to provide easier access to different elements. Because the TileList and List instances share the same position on the stage, selecting one or the other would be difficult if they were not separated by layers.*

11. Drag two instances of the RadioButton component from the Library to the radios layer. You will use these buttons to allow the user to toggle between the two different list views.

12. Place one RadioButton instance at (420, 13) and set its dimensions to 90 × 22. Name this instance thumbnails_rb. In the parameters data grid, set its label to **thumbnails** and its groupName to **listView**. This groupName parameter will tie the two radio buttons together.

13. Set the second RadioButton instance at (520, 13) and set its dimensions to 80 × 22. Give it the instance name names_rb. In the Parameters panel, set its label to **names** and its groupName to **listView**. Since both instances share the same groupName, only one of the two instances will be selectable at a time, and selecting one will automatically deselect the other.

You may have noticed that you did not set either radio button as selected. You will set the initial selection through code, which will cause an event to fire. You can catch that event to set the initial state of the interface as well.

The final interface, completed in the IDE, is shown in Figure 12-9.

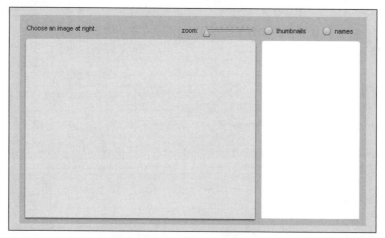

Figure 12-9. The completed interface with all of the components laid out and configured on the stage

With the interface complete, you are ready to write some code to plug everything together and load data into it.

Creating the document class

First, you will take care of creating the document class that will be your entry point for the application and centralize all of the logic.

Create a new ActionScript file and save it as ImageViewer.as into a new com/foundationAS3/ch12 directory that is within the Chapter 12 project directory you created for the imageViewer.fla file in the previous section. Within this file, you'll add the package, class, and constructor information. You'll also set up the standard call to an init() method.

```
package com.foundationAS3.ch12 {

  import flash.display.Sprite;

  public class ImageViewer extends Sprite {

    public function ImageViewer() {
      init();
    }

    private function init():void {
    }

  }

}
```

I truly believe that here, in the depths of Chapter 12, there is nothing in the preceding code that should surprise you!

In previous examples that included objects set in the IDE, you've seen how those objects can be directly referenced in the ActionScript code of the document class without error. However, the problem with this approach is that it doesn't provide all that cool code hinting and code completion as you develop. In order to enable this, you'll assign references to your timeline objects to typed properties of your class. Add the following bold lines to your ImageViewer class.

```
package com.foundationAS3.ch12 {

  import flash.display.Sprite;

  import fl.containers.ScrollPane;
  import fl.controls.Label;
  import fl.controls.List;
  import fl.controls.RadioButton;
  import fl.controls.Slider;
  import fl.controls.TileList;
```

```
       public class ImageViewer extends Sprite {

         private var _imagePane_sp:ScrollPane;
         private var _title_lbl:Label;
         private var _thumbnails_rb:RadioButton;
         private var _names_rb:RadioButton;
         private var _thumbnails_tl:TileList;
         private var _names_li:List;
         private var _zoom_sl:Slider;

         public function ImageViewer() {
           init();
         }

         private function init():void {
           assignComponentReferences();
         }

         private function assignComponentReferences():void {
           _imagePane_sp = imagePane_sp;
           _title_lbl = title_lbl;
           _thumbnails_rb = thumbnails_rb;
           _names_rb = names_rb;
           _thumbnails_tl = thumbnails_tl;
           _names_li = names_li;
           _zoom_sl = zoom_sl;
         }

       }

     }
```

First, you import all the necessary controls classes at the top of the code. Then each component instance you need to reference is given a private property and typed to the appropriate class. Finally, within the init() method, you call a new assignComponentReferences() method, which simply assigns each component instance reference to the typed private property. Notice that you are using the underscore prefix for all of the private properties. This is to differentiate them from the public instance names for the components that you set in the IDE.

Now as you type within this class, you should get helpful code hints popping up to speed your development. Give it a try, At the end of the init() method, type _zoom_sl.. As you type the dot operator, a pop-up window with all of Slider's public methods and properties should appear. Very nice! (Make sure you delete this line after you run this test!)

When users interact with the components, you need to account for those events and act accordingly. Add the following bold lines to your code for this purpose.

```
package com.foundationAS3.ch12 {

  import flash.display.Sprite;
  import flash.events.Event;

  import fl.containers.ScrollPane;
  import fl.controls.Label;
  import fl.controls.List;
  import fl.controls.RadioButton;
  import fl.controls.Slider;
  import fl.controls.TileList;

  public class ImageViewer extends Sprite {

    private var _imagePane_sp:ScrollPane;
    private var _title_lbl:Label;
    private var _thumbnails_rb:RadioButton;
    private var _names_rb:RadioButton;
    private var _thumbnails_tl:TileList;
    private var _names_li:List;
    private var _zoom_sl:Slider;

    public function ImageViewer() {
      init();
    }

    private function init():void {
      assignComponentReferences();
      assignHandlers();
    }

    private function assignComponentReferences():void {
      _imagePane_sp = imagePane_sp;
      _title_lbl = title_lbl;
      _thumbnails_rb = thumbnails_rb;
      _names_rb = names_rb;
      _thumbnails_tl = thumbnails_tl;
      _names_li = names_li;
      _zoom_sl = zoom_sl;
    }

    private function assignHandlers():void {
      _thumbnails_rb.addEventListener(Event.CHANGE, onListViewChange);
      _thumbnails_tl.addEventListener(Event.CHANGE, onImageSelected);
      _names_li.addEventListener(Event.CHANGE, onImageSelected);
      _zoom_sl.addEventListener(Event.CHANGE, onZoom);
    }
```

```
        private function onListViewChange(event:Event):void {
        }

        private function onImageSelected(event:Event):void {
        }

        private function onZoom(event:Event):void {
        }

    }

}
```

Within the init() method, you call another new method, assignHandlers(), which adds four event listeners. The first event listener is for one of your radio buttons to handle toggling the list view between displaying thumbnails and text. Why is this needed for only one of the two radio buttons? Because of the way the two radio buttons are wired, if one is selected, the other is deselected, and its CHANGE event is fired. So no matter which of the two in the interface is clicked, you need to listen for the CHANGE event on only one of them. In fact, if you listened for both, you would receive multiple events.

The next two listeners are for the two different lists: your List and TileList instances. Selection in either list will result in the same action, namely loading an image, so you give the same event handler to both.

The final event listener is set up for when the slider· is moved. This event will call an appropriately named onZoom() method within this class.

All three handlers are added at the end of the code, though each is currently empty. And, of course, remember to import the Event class at the top.

Without image data yet available in your code, you cannot yet fill in the onImageSelected() or onZoom() methods. You can toggle the list view based on the radio button selection, though. For that, add the following bold code.

```
package com.foundationAS3.ch12 {

  import flash.display.Sprite;
  import flash.events.Event;

  import fl.containers.ScrollPane;
  import fl.controls.Label;
  import fl.controls.List;
  import fl.controls.RadioButton;
  import fl.controls.Slider;
  import fl.controls.TileList;

  public class ImageViewer extends Sprite {

    private var _imagePane_sp:ScrollPane;
    private var _title_lbl:Label;
    private var _thumbnails_rb:RadioButton;
    private var _names_rb:RadioButton;
```

```
  private var _thumbnails_tl:TileList;
  private var _names_li:List;
  private var _zoom_sl:Slider;

  public function ImageViewer() {
    init();
  }

  private function init():void {
    assignComponentReferences();
    configureComponents();
    assignHandlers();
  }

  private function assignComponentReferences():void {
    _imagePane_sp = imagePane_sp;
    _title_lbl = title_lbl;
    _thumbnails_rb = thumbnails_rb;
    _names_rb = names_rb;
    _thumbnails_tl = thumbnails_tl;
    _names_li = names_li;
    _zoom_sl = zoom_sl;
  }

  private function configureComponents():void {
    _names_rb.selected = true;
  }

  private function assignHandlers():void {
    _thumbnails_rb.addEventListener(Event.CHANGE, onListViewChange);
    _thumbnails_tl.addEventListener(Event.CHANGE, onImageSelected);
    _names_li.addEventListener(Event.CHANGE, onImageSelected);
    _zoom_sl.addEventListener(Event.CHANGE, onZoom);
  }

  private function onListViewChange(event:Event):void {
    _thumbnails_tl.visible = _thumbnails_rb.selected;
    _names_li.visible = !_thumbnails_rb.selected;
  }

  private function onImageSelected(event:Event):void {
  }

  private function onZoom(event:Event):void {
  }

 }

}
```

You are going to need more component initialization as you develop further, so here you create a configureComponents() method and call it from within the init() method. All that you need to configure at this time is which radio button is selected, and you default this to _names_li by setting its selected property. Setting this will automatically cause the CHANGE event to fire on _thumbnails_rb, which will result in onListViewChange() being called.

Within onListViewChange(), you set the visibility of the two list components based on which radio button is selected. If _thumbnails_rb is selected, then _thumbnails_tl will be visible and _names_li will not. If _thumbnails_rb is not selected, then the opposite will occur.

At this point, you should be able to test your movie. Right now, the only testable functionality will be the toggling of the list views, but you should give that a try to ensure that all of your syntax is correct before going further. Return to imageViewer.fla and in the Property inspector, enter com.foundationAS3.ch12.ImageViewer as the document class name. Test the movie.

Loading image data

Now that your document class is effectively hooked up to all the components, you need to get some image data to display into your application. For this project, you will load the data from an XML file that is stored relative to the SWF, which is a common approach. Take a look at the XML file that you will be using, which is included in the files you downloaded for this chapter (unless you really feel like typing all that XML!).

```
<?xml version="1.0" ?>
<images>
  <image>
    <name>Audrey holding her baby doll.</name>
    <file>images/baby.jpg</file>
    <thumb>images/thumbs/baby.jpg</thumb>
  </image>
  <image>
    <name>The first trip to the beach.</name>
    <file>images/beach.jpg</file>
    <thumb>images/thumbs/beach.jpg</thumb>
  </image>
  <image>
    <name>Building (and destroying) a fort.</name>
    <file>images/fort.jpg</file>
    <thumb>images/thumbs/fort.jpg</thumb>
  </image>
  <image>
    <name>Prodigy?</name>
    <file>images/piano.jpg</file>
    <thumb>images/thumbs/piano.jpg</thumb>
  </image>
  <image>
    <name>A personal pool party.</name>
    <file>images/pool.jpg</file>
```

```
        <thumb>images/thumbs/pool.jpg</thumb>
    </image>
    <image>
        <name>So seemingly innocent...</name>
        <file>images/sleeping.jpg</file>
        <thumb>images/thumbs/sleeping.jpg</thumb>
    </image>
</images>
```

The root node of the XML is <images>. This contains a number of <image> child nodes. Each of these <image> child nodes contains data for a single image in <name>, <file>, and <thumb> child nodes. Your job will be to load in this XML and make it usable by your components. Copy this XML file and the images folder into same directory as imageViewer.fla.

The first thing you will do for handling of this external data is create a class on the ActionScript side that will hold the data for a single image. Create a new ActionScript file and save it into the same directory as ImageViewer.as. The following is the entirety of the class (nice and simple!).

```
package com.foundationAS3.ch12 {

    public class Image {

        private var _name:String;
        private var _file:String;
        private var _thumb:String;

        public function Image(name:String, file:String, thumb:String) {
            _name = name;
            _file = file;
            _thumb = thumb;
        }

        public function get name():String {
            return _name;
        }

        public function get file():String {
            return _file;
        }

        public function get thumb():String {
            return _thumb;
        }

    }

}
```

This class has three private properties that map exactly to the <image> node in the XML, with public getters to access each of these properties. Setting the properties is handled in the constructor, which takes the three values as arguments.

Loading the XML

Now that you have defined the class that will represent the data, your next task is to load the data and create the necessary Image instances. It is often a good idea to move all code that deals with loading and parsing of data into its own class or classes. This way, if ever you need to change how the data is loaded—for instance, switch from a static XML file to a web service—you do not need to worry about how that change might affect other parts of your code. Abstracting functionality into separate classes that can encapsulate the code to hide the implementation is a common technique in OOP and one that makes sense for most objects. You'll follow that methodology by creating an ImageData class that will load the XML and prepare it for use by other classes.

Create a new ActionScript file and save it into the same directory as Image.as and ImageViewer.as. Add the following code, which creates the necessary package and class structure, and provides a public method that will kick off the loading of the external data.

```
package com.foundationAS3.ch12 {

  import flash.events.Event;
  import flash.events.EventDispatcher;
  import flash.net.URLLoader;
  import flash.net.URLRequest;

  public class ImageData extends EventDispatcher {

    private static const DATA_FILE:String = "images.xml";

    private function onXMLLoaded(event:Event):void {
    }

    public function load():void {
      var loader:URLLoader = new URLLoader();
      loader.addEventListener(Event.COMPLETE, onXMLLoaded);
      loader.load(new URLRequest(DATA_FILE));
    }

  }

}
```

This class extends the EventDispatcher class, so that you can broadcast events for an ImageData instance, which is necessary to let other classes know when data has loaded and is ready.

Within the public load() method, you use a URLLoader instance to load in an external XML file, the path to which is stored in the constant DATA_FILE. URLLoader's load() method requires that the parameter passed in is a URLRequest instance. Before you call load(), though, you set up a listener for when the XML has completed loading. It is also a good idea to set up listeners for load errors, but for simplicity, this example doesn't include those listeners.

Parsing the data

To handle the parsing of the data upon completion, add the following lines in bold.

```
public class ImageData extends EventDispatcher {

  private static const DATA_FILE:String = "images.xml";

  private var _data:Array;

  private function onXMLLoaded(event:Event):void {
    _data = [];
    var loader:URLLoader = event.target as URLLoader;
    var xml:XML = new XML(loader.data);
    var images:XMLList = xml.child("image");
    var numImages:uint = images.length();
    var image:XML;
    for (var i:uint = 0; i < numImages; i++) {
      image = images[i] as XML;
      _data.push(
        new Image(
          image.child("name").toString(),
          image.child("file").toString(),
          image.child("thumb").toString()
        )
      );
    }
    dispatchEvent(new Event(Event.COMPLETE));
  }

  public function load():void {
    var loader:URLLoader = new URLLoader();
    loader.addEventListener(Event.COMPLETE, onXMLLoaded);
    loader.load(new URLRequest(DATA_FILE));
  }
```

onXMLLoaded() will be called when the XML has successfully loaded. This is a little more complex than methods you have dealt with thus far in this chapter, so let's break it down bit by bit.

Within this method, you create a new Array instance and assign it to the _data property, which you declared at the top of the class. You then find the data within the URLLoader instance that dispatched the event and pass this to the XML constructor to get the data as XML.

```
var loader:URLLoader = event.target as URLLoader;
var xml:XML = new XML(loader.data);
```

At this point, you can use E4X syntax, which was discussed in Chapter 11, to find all the nodes with the name image and assign this resulting XMLList to the images variable.

```
var images:XMLList = xml.child("image");
```

451

Using the length() method of XMLList to determine the number of images, you can then loop through each XML object in the XMLList and create a new Image instance for each one.

```
var numImages:uint = images.length();
var image:XML;
for (var i:uint = 0; i < numImages; i++) {
```

To create the Image instances, you take advantage of a little more E4X syntax. First, you grab a reference to the XML object in the images XMLList and assign this reference to the variable image.

```
image = images[i] as XML;
```

You then create a new Image instance and pass the string values for the name, file, and thumb child nodes of the image XML to the Image constructor.

```
new Image(
    image.child("name").toString(),
    image.child("file").toString(),
    image.child("thumb").toString()
)
```

The child() method of XML actually returns an XMLList, but if the list has only one item, you can refer to it as a single XML object (pretty sly, but an extremely useful feature). Calling toString() on an XML object will return the node value for that object. The result of all this is that by calling image.child("name").toString(), you get just the text value within the <name> node.

Finally, the new Image() call returns a reference to the Image instance (as is the case whenever using the new operator). so you can push this reference directly into the _data array.

```
_data.push(
    new Image(
        image.child("name").toString(),
        image.child("file").toString(),
        image.child("thumb").toString()
    )
);
```

Once all the Image instances have been created and pushed into the _data array, you dispatch an event so that other objects can listen and act accordingly when the data is ready.

```
dispatchEvent(new Event(Event.COMPLETE));
```

That's easily the most complex code you will see in this chapter, so if you got through that and everything made sense, give yourself a pat on the back and know that it's all downhill from here!

Accessing the data

To finish the ImageData class, you need to provide two ways of getting the information from the class. You know that the application needs to display the images in the TileList instance and the names in the List instance. Let's make it easy for the document class and let the ImageData class take care of formatting the data to be passed to the different components.

First, add a getNameData() method that returns an array that holds the image names and references to the Image objects. This will be perfect for any lists that need to display just the text data, like your List instance. Add the following bold lines.

```
public function load():void {
  var loader:URLLoader = new URLLoader();
  loader.addEventListener(Event.COMPLETE, onXMLLoaded);
  loader.load(new URLRequest(DATA_FILE));
}

public function getNameData():Array {
  var nameData:Array = [];
  var numImages:uint = _data.length;
  var image:Image;
  for (var i:uint = 0; i < numImages; i++) {
    image = _data[i] as Image;
    nameData.push({label:image.name, data:image});
  }
  return nameData;
}

  }

}
```

Here, you create a new Array instance, nameData, and then loop through all of the Image instances stored in _data. For each Image instance, you push into the nameData variable an object with two properties: label and data. label holds the name of the image, and data holds a reference to the Image itself. The resulting nameData array is returned from the method.

Now you'll add a getThumbData() method that works similarly to getNameData(), but will return the information that will be used by your TileList instance, or any list that needs to display image data. Add the following bold lines.

```
public function getNameData():Array {
  var nameData:Array = [];
  var numImages:uint = _data.length;
  var image:Image;
  for (var i:uint = 0; i < numImages; i++) {
    image = _data[i] as Image;
    nameData.push({label:image.name, data:image});
  }
  return nameData;
}
```

```
        public function getThumbData():Array {
          var thumbData:Array = [];
          var numImages:uint = _data.length;
          var image:Image;
          for (var i:uint = 0; i < numImages; i++) {
            image = _data[i] as Image;
            thumbData.push({label:"", source:image.thumb, data:image});
          }
          return thumbData;
        }

    }

  }
```

The structure is similar to getNameData(). In this case, for each iteration of the loop, you create a new object with three properties: label, source, and data. Once again, data will hold a reference to an Image instance. source will hold the path to the thumbnail image. You pass an empty string to label, as you don't want the labels to appear in your TileList, and the easiest way to manage that is to not pass in labels for the tiles. The resulting thumbData is returned from this method.

That finishes the ImageData class. Housing all loading and parsing of data in this class means that if you needed a different implementation for loading data, you could change the code without any ill effects on other classes that use this data. Additionally, dividing responsibilities among multiple classes with specific purposes keeps the code more manageable.

Displaying images

With data being loaded into the application and formatted for the lists, you can add the code necessary to initiate this process and tie the results to your components. This will be handled in your main ImageViewer class.

Return to ImageViewer.as and add the following code to instantiate the ImageData class and have it load in the XML.

```
    package com.foundationAS3.ch12 {

      import flash.display.Sprite;
      import flash.events.Event;

      import fl.containers.ScrollPane;
      import fl.controls.Label;
      import fl.controls.List;
      import fl.controls.RadioButton;
      import fl.controls.Slider;
      import fl.controls.TileList;
      import fl.data.DataProvider;
```

```
public class ImageViewer extends Sprite {

  private var _imagePane_sp:ScrollPane;
  private var _title_lbl:Label;
  private var _thumbnails_rb:RadioButton;
  private var _names_rb:RadioButton;
  private var _thumbnails_tl:TileList;
  private var _names_li:List;
  private var _zoom_sl:Slider;
  private var _images:ImageData;

  public function ImageViewer() {
    init();
  }

  private function init():void {
    assignComponentReferences();
    configureComponents();
    assignHandlers();
    loadImageData();
  }

  private function assignComponentReferences():void {
    _imagePane_sp = imagePane_sp;
    _title_lbl = title_lbl;
    _thumbnails_rb = thumbnails_rb;
    _names_rb = names_rb;
    _thumbnails_tl = thumbnails_tl;
    _names_li = names_li;
    _zoom_sl = zoom_sl;
  }

  private function configureComponents():void {
    _names_rb.selected = true;
  }

  private function assignHandlers():void {
    _thumbnails_rb.addEventListener(Event.CHANGE, onListViewChange);
    _thumbnails_tl.addEventListener(Event.CHANGE, onImageSelected);
    _names_li.addEventListener(Event.CHANGE, onImageSelected);
    _zoom_sl.addEventListener(Event.CHANGE, onZoom);
  }

  private function loadImageData():void {
    _images = new ImageData();
    _images.addEventListener(Event.COMPLETE, onDataLoaded);
    _images.load();
  }
```

455

```
private function onDataLoaded(event:Event):void {
  _images.removeEventListener(Event.COMPLETE, onDataLoaded);
  _thumbnails_tl.dataProvider = new DataProvider(_images.getThumbData());
  _names_li.dataProvider = new DataProvider(_images.getNameData());
}

private function onListViewChange(event:Event):void {
  _thumbnails_tl.visible = _thumbnails_rb.selected;
  _names_li.visible = !_thumbnails_rb.selected;
}

private function onImageSelected(event:Event):void {
}

private function onZoom(event:Event):void {
  }
 }

}
```
}

Figure 12-10. The interface with thumbnails displayed in the TileList instance, with the data loaded from external XML

Here, you add one more private property, _images, which will hold a reference to the ImageData instance. Then, within the init() method, you call a new method, loadImageData(). This new method instantiates a new ImageData instance and assigns it to your _images property. You add an event listener for when the data has loaded and call ImageData's public load() method to initiate the loading of the external data.

The onDataLoaded() method handles the event that fires when the data is ready in the ImageData instance. When this fires, you first remove the listener, and then you assign DataProvider instances to the two different lists (remember to import the DataProvider class at the top of the code). To populate the dataProviders, you call the two methods that you created in ImageData—getThumbData() and getNameData()—and pass the results to the DataProvider constructor.

If you test your movie now, you should see the List instance populate with the image names. If you click the thumbnails radio button, the thumbnail images appear in the TileList instance, as shown in Figure 12-10.

Handling image selection

Now you need to handle what happens when an item is selected in one of the lists. This will be taken care of in the onImageSelected() method, which is the handler for the lists' CHANGE events.

Fill in the onImageSelected() method in ImageViewer with the following bold lines.

```
private function onImageSelected(event:Event):void {
    var image:Image = event.target.selectedItem.data as Image;
    var index:int = event.target.selectedIndex;
    _thumbnails_tl.selectedIndex = index;
    _names_li.selectedIndex = index;
    _title_lbl.text = image.name;
    _imagePane_sp.source = image.file;
}
```

When an item in either list is clicked, the event will cause this method to fire. You can reference the list clicked by using event.target. The selected item within that list can be obtained through the selectedItem property (thank goodness, or thank good design, that both lists have the same properties, or interface). Items in the list will have a data property that will hold a reference to the relevant Image instance. Remember that the arrays you pass to the dataProviders have this reference. These lines are in the ImageData class when you form the arrays:

```
nameData.push({label:image.name, data:image});
```

```
thumbData.push({label:"", source:image.thumb, data:image});
```

Because the Image instances can be found in the selected item's data property, you can cast this to Image in your onImageSelected() handler.

```
var image:Image = event.target.selectedItem.data as Image;
```

In the next lines, you find the index of the selected item in the clicked list and make sure that both lists set this index as selected, so that if the user toggles to the other view, the other list shows the same selection.

```
var index:int = event.target.selectedIndex;
_thumbnails_tl.selectedIndex = index;
_names_li.selectedIndex = index;
```

In the next and last two lines of the method, you assign the name of the image to the text property of the _title_lbl label and set the source for the ScrollPane instance to the image file. The result, as can be seen in Figure 12-11, is that an image loads into the pane and can be scrolled, and the name of the same image appears in the label above.

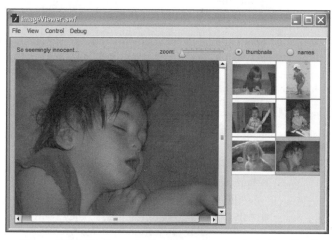

Figure 12-11. The image loads when an item is selected in either list.

457

Scaling an image

As a final step for the initial working interface, let's hook up the zoom slider so that dragging the slider will change the scale of the loaded image.

Add the following bold lines to your code to enable zooming of the images.

```
private function onImageSelected(event:Event):void {
    var image:Image = event.target.selectedItem.data as Image;
    var index:int = event.target.selectedIndex;
    _thumbnails_tl.selectedIndex = index;
    _names_li.selectedIndex = index;
    _zoom_sl.value = 1;
    _title_lbl.text = image.name;
    _imagePane_sp.source = image.file;
}

private function onZoom(event:Event):void {
    if (_imagePane_sp.content) {
        _imagePane_sp.content.scaleX = ➥
_imagePane_sp.content.scaleY = _zoom_sl.value;
        _imagePane_sp.update();
    }
}
```

Easy enough, isn't it? In the onZoom() method, if there is currently content in the pane, you set the scaleX and scaleY properties of that content to be the current value of the slider, and then call the update() method of ScrollPane so that the scrollbars adjust to the new content size. You also add a line to the onImageSelected() method so that when a new image is loaded, you reset the zoom level to 1.

Test your movie now. You should see image data loaded and displayed in your two lists, which you can display with the radio button toggle. When a list item is clicked, the image appears in the scrolling pane with its name above, and it can be scaled using the slider instance.

That's not bad output for your work thus far! However, you can make this application more sleek and aesthetically pleasing with a few graphic enhancements.

Adding graphic enhancements

To enhance the look of the image viewer application, you'll make four adjustments:

- Make the label for the image stand out from the other labels for the components.
- Improve the look of the thumbnails within the TileList instance so that they don't seem so crammed together.
- Add drop shadows to the lists, so they conform with the look of the scrolling pane, which has a drop shadow beneath it by default.
- Create a more gentle transition when an image is loaded by adding animation.

Changing the image label

You can make the image label stand out by changing the TextFormat instance for the label itself. In the ImageViewer class, add the following bold line to assign a new TextFormat to _title_lbl and make its text larger.

```
private function configureComponents():void {
  _names_rb.selected = true;
  _title_lbl.setStyle("textFormat", new TextFormat("Arial", 14));
}
```

Make sure that in addition to adding this line, you import flash.text.TextFormat with the rest of the class imports at the top of the class.

```
import flash.display.Sprite;
import flash.events.Event;
import flash.text.TextFormat;
```

Test your movie, and you'll see the result of these changes, as shown in Figure 12-12.

Figure 12-12. The title for an image is made bigger through the use of a TextFormat applied to a style.

Improving the thumbnail layout

Next, you'll improve the thumbnail layout by making the thumbnails larger and adding some space around them.

Add the following bold lines to ImageViewer to make the tiles in the TileList larger to fill the space horizontally.

```
private function configureComponents():void {
  _thumbnails_tl.columnWidth = 85;
  _thumbnails_tl.rowHeight = 70;
  _names_rb.selected = true;
  _title_lbl.setStyle("textFormat", new TextFormat("Arial", 14));
}
```

Now let's create more padding around the images within each cell. To accomplish this, you will create a new cell renderer for tiles that will have this new padding setting. Creating a new cell renderer for a list is a simple procedure and allows you to customize exactly how list items appear.

Create a new ActionScript file and save it as SimpleImageCell.as into the same directory as ImageViewer.as. Add the following code, which is by far the easiest class you have created this book!

```
package com.foundationAS3.ch12 {

    import fl.controls.listClasses.ImageCell;

    public class SimpleImageCell extends ImageCell {

        public function SimpleImageCell() {
            super();
            setStyle("imagePadding", 5);
        }

    }

}
```

The class extends ImageCell, which a TileList instance will use by default. Within the constructor, you set the imagePadding style property, which is supported by ImageCell, to 5 pixels. All that you need to do now is assign this cell renderer to your tile list.

Return to ImageViewer and add the following bold line to the configureComponents() method.

```
private function configureComponents():void {
    _thumbnails_tl.columnWidth = 85;
    _thumbnails_tl.rowHeight = 70;
    _names_rb.selected = true;
    _title_lbl.setStyle("textFormat", new TextFormat("Arial", 14));
    StyleManager.setComponentStyle(TileList, "cellRenderer", SimpleImageCell);
}
```

In order for this to compile, you will need to import the StyleManager class at the top of your code.

```
import fl.containers.ScrollPane;
import fl.controls.Label;
import fl.controls.List;
import fl.controls.RadioButton;
import fl.controls.Slider;
import fl.controls.TileList;
import fl.data.DataProvider;
import fl.managers.StyleManager;
```

With the new cell renderer applying its 5-pixel padding, you should see something like Figure 12-13 when you test the movie.

Figure 12-13. A custom cell renderer is used to apply padding around the thumbnail images.

Adding drop shadows

Next, you'll add drop shadows beneath the lists to match the shadow of the scrolling pane. To create a shadow, you need a shape. One option is to apply a drop shadow to both list components, since either one or the other is visible at all times. Another option, if you want to ensure that the shadow remains consistent between the two, is to draw a new shape under the lists and use this shape to create the shadow. Let's take the latter approach.

To create the shape and its shadow, add the following bolded lines to the ImageViewer class.

```
package com.foundationAS3.ch12 {

  import flash.display.Shape;
  import flash.display.Sprite;
  import flash.events.Event;
  import flash.filters.DropShadowFilter;
  import flash.text.TextFormat;

  import fl.containers.ScrollPane;
  import fl.controls.Label;
  import fl.controls.List;
  import fl.controls.RadioButton;
  import fl.controls.Slider;
  import fl.controls.TileList;
  import fl.data.DataProvider;
  import fl.managers.StyleManager;

  public class ImageViewer extends Sprite {

    private var _imagePane_sp:ScrollPane;
    private var _title_lbl:Label;
    private var _thumbnails_rb:RadioButton;
    private var _names_rb:RadioButton;
    private var _thumbnails_tl:TileList;
    private var _names_li:List;
    private var _zoom_sl:Slider;
    private var _images:ImageData;

    public function ImageViewer() {
      init();
    }

    private function init():void {
      assignComponentReferences();
      configureComponents();
      drawListShadow();
      assignHandlers();
      loadImageData();
    }
```

```
private function assignComponentReferences():void {
  _imagePane_sp = imagePane_sp;
  _title_lbl = title_lbl;
  _thumbnails_rb = thumbnails_rb;
  _names_rb = names_rb;
  _thumbnails_tl = thumbnails_tl;
  _names_li = names_li;
  _zoom_sl = zoom_sl;
}

private function configureComponents():void {
  _thumbnails_tl.columnWidth = 85;
  _thumbnails_tl.rowHeight = 70;
  _names_rb.selected = true;
  _title_lbl.setStyle("textFormat", new TextFormat("Arial", 14));
  StyleManager.setComponentStyle(TileList, "cellRenderer", SimpleImageCell);
}

private function drawListShadow():void {
  var shadowShape:Shape = new Shape();
  shadowShape.x = _names_li.x;
  shadowShape.y = _names_li.y;
  shadowShape.graphics.beginFill(0);
  shadowShape.graphics.drawRect(0, 0, _names_li.width, _names_li.height);
  shadowShape.graphics.endFill();
  shadowShape.filters = [
    new DropShadowFilter(2, 90, 0, 1, 4, 4, .7, 1, false, false, true)
  ];
  addChildAt(shadowShape, 0);
}

private function assignHandlers():void {
  _thumbnails_rb.addEventListener(Event.CHANGE, onListViewChange);
  _thumbnails_tl.addEventListener(Event.CHANGE, onImageSelected);
  _names_li.addEventListener(Event.CHANGE, onImageSelected);
  _zoom_sl.addEventListener(Event.CHANGE, onZoom);
}
```

In the drawListShadow() method, which you call from the init(), a new Shape instance is created. This can be a Shape, rather than a Sprite, since you don't need to allow for any interactivity. This shape is placed at the same screen position as the List instance. Then a solid, black rectangle is drawn within the shape, with a width and height to equal the List instance as well. You then create a new DropShadowFilter instance with some settings that mimic the look of the drop shadow used by the scrolling pane. The most important setting to note is the final true, which specifies that the shape itself will not be visible; only the shadow that the shape produces appears, which is great, since you want only the shadow!

The final line of the method adds the shape to the display list at the bottom of the stack. This places the shape below the two list instances, effectively creating a shadow for both. Test your movie to see the result, which should look something like Figure 12-14.

Creating an animated transition

The final enhancement is to have loaded images animate in order to create a smoother transition. To accomplish this, you will create a new class to handle the loading and animation of an image specifically.

Create a new ActionScript file and save it as ImageHolder.as into the same directory as ImageViewer.as. Add the following code, which takes care of loading an image.

Figure 12-14. A drop shadow is added on a new shape below the list instances.

```
package com.foundationAS3.ch12 {

  import flash.display.Loader;
  import flash.display.LoaderInfo;
  import flash.display.Sprite;
  import flash.events.Event;
  import flash.net.URLRequest;

  public class ImageHolder extends Sprite {

    public function ImageHolder(file:String) {
      loadImage(file);
    }

    private function loadImage(file:String):void {
      var loader:Loader = new Loader();
      loader.contentLoaderInfo.addEventListener(Event.COMPLETE, onImageLoaded);
      loader.load(new URLRequest(file));
    }

    private function onImageLoaded(event:Event):void {
      var loaderInfo:LoaderInfo = event.target as LoaderInfo;
      loaderInfo.removeEventListener(Event.COMPLETE, onImageLoaded);
      addChild(loaderInfo.content);
      dispatchEvent(new Event(Event.COMPLETE));
    }

  }

}
```

This class extends Sprite so that you can add other display objects (namely, the loaded image) to it and allows for event dispatching. The constructor for the class takes a path to an image, which is subsequently passed to loadImage().

loadImage() creates a new Loader instance and passes the path to the file, wrapped in a URLRequest instance, to the Loader's load() method. To be informed when the image has loaded completely, you need to add an event listener, but not to Loader itself. You add the listener to the LoaderInfo instance, which can be found in the contentLoaderInfo property of Loader. You pass onImageLoaded as the handler for the COMPLETE event. Note that it is a good idea to handle load errors as well as successful loads, but that handling is omitted here for brevity and simplicity.

In the onImageLoaded() method, you first remove the event listener, and then add the image that was loaded as a child of this ImageHolder instance. This image can be found in the content property of the LoaderInfo instance. Finally, you dispatch a COMPLETE event to inform listeners that the image has loaded.

At this point, you have not added your animation, but you have enough structure in place to ensure that your image loading is working as expected. You just need to return to ImageViewer to add the necessary lines of code to use this ImageHolder class for all the image loading.

Return to ImageLoader and add or edit the following bold lines in order to use the ImageHolder class to load and display images in the scrolling pane.

```
private function onImageSelected(event:Event):void {
    var image:Image = event.target.selectedItem.data as Image;
    var index:int = event.target.selectedIndex;
    _thumbnails_tl.selectedIndex = index;
    _names_li.selectedIndex = index;
    _zoom_sl.value = 1;
    _title_lbl.text = image.name;
    var imageHolder:ImageHolder = _imagePane_sp.source as ImageHolder;
    if (imageHolder) {
        imageHolder.removeEventListener(Event.COMPLETE, onImageLoaded);
    }
    imageHolder = new ImageHolder(image.file);
    imageHolder.addEventListener(Event.COMPLETE, onImageLoaded);
    _imagePane_sp.source = imageHolder;
}

private function onImageLoaded(event:Event):void {
    var imageHolder:ImageHolder = event.target as ImageHolder;
    imageHolder.removeEventListener(Event.COMPLETE, onImageLoaded);
    _imagePane_sp.refreshPane();
}

private function onZoom(event:Event):void {
    if (_imagePane_sp.content) {
        _imagePane_sp.content.scaleX = _imagePane_sp.content.scaleY = _zoom_sl.value;
        _imagePane_sp.update();
    }
}
```

In the onImageSelected() method, you no longer pass the image file path directly to the scrolling pane. Instead, you pass an ImageHolder instance. Before this is done, though, you check to see if the scrolling pane's current source is an ImageHolder instance, which will be the case for all but when the first image is selected to load. If the ImageHolder instance exists, then you make sure to remove a previously added event listener. You do this to ensure that if a user clicks quickly and repeatedly on items in the lists, you don't have errant event listeners waiting to be fired when they are no longer needed.

```
var imageHolder:ImageHolder = _imagePane_sp.source as ImageHolder;
if (imageHolder) {
    imageHolder.removeEventListener(Event.COMPLETE, onImageLoaded);
}
```

After this initial check and cleanup, a new ImageHolder instance is created and passed the path to the image file to load. You add a listener to receive notification of when the image has completed loading, and then set the source of the scrolling pane to be the new ImageHolder instance.

```
imageHolder = new ImageHolder(image.file);
imageHolder.addEventListener(Event.COMPLETE, onImageLoaded);
_imagePane_sp.source = imageHolder;
```

You add the listener so that when an image has completed loading, you can refresh the scrolling pane, allowing its scrollbars to adjust for the size of the loaded image. If you do not do this, the scrolling pane will reset its scrollbars only when its source property is set, which occurs before the image has completed loading and its size is unknown. The refreshing is therefore handled in the event listener for the COMPLETE event of ImageHolder.

If you test your movie now, the image will appear as before with no apparent change. Don't worry—that's good! You haven't added the transition animation yet, and the fact that the image loads as before shows you've set up your loading code correctly.

What you've done is separate the code for loading an image into its own class in order to make it easier in the future (or in the next step) to modify that code without needing to worry about the internal workings of other classes, namely your main ImageViewer document class. It is good practice in OOP to separate responsibilities into individual, independent classes, creating a more modular structure that allows for easier debugging, maintenance, modification, and reuse. Next, you will add lines to ImageHolder to produce a transition effect. If you wish to alter the transition in the future, you can modify the code within this class, and the transition will update without you needing to alter code anywhere else.

Return to the ImageHolder class and finish it with the code that will animate the alpha property of the instance from 0 to 1 once the image loads.

```
package com.foundationAS3.ch12 {

    import flash.display.Loader;
    import flash.display.LoaderInfo;
    import flash.display.Sprite;
    import flash.events.Event;
    import flash.net.URLRequest;
```

```
public class ImageHolder extends Sprite {

  public function ImageHolder(file:String) {
    alpha = 0;
    loadImage(file);
  }

  private function loadImage(file:String):void {
    var loader:Loader = new Loader();
    loader.contentLoaderInfo.addEventListener(Event.COMPLETE, onImageLoaded);
    loader.load(new URLRequest(file));
  }

  private function onImageLoaded(event:Event):void {
    var loaderInfo:LoaderInfo = event.target as LoaderInfo;
    loaderInfo.removeEventListener(Event.COMPLETE, onImageLoaded);
    addChild(loaderInfo.content);
    addEventListener(Event.ENTER_FRAME, onEnterFrame);
    dispatchEvent(new Event(Event.COMPLETE));
  }

  private function onEnterFrame(event:Event):void {
    alpha += 0.1;
    if (alpha >= 1) {
      alpha = 1;
      removeEventListener(Event.ENTER_FRAME, onEnterFrame);
    }
  }

}

}
```

In the constructor of the class, you set alpha to 0. Once the image loads, within the onImageLoaded()
handler, you set up a new listener for the ENTER_FRAME event dispatched by every sprite, each frame
of the movie. Each time this onEnterFrame() handler is called, you increment alpha by 0.1. Once the
alpha value reaches 1, you remove the event listener, since the animation is completed.

> *The approach shown here will produce a linear animation (which, in this case,
> means the alpha increases by the same amount each iteration) that is depend-
> ent on the frame rate of the movie, since it is using an ENTER_FRAME event.
> Because it is tied to the frame rate, the fade in will occur much more quickly in
> a movie set at 30 frames per second (fps) than one at 12 fps. If you wanted to
> have more control over the total time for the animation, or wanted to more
> easily use custom easing equations for less of a linear effect, you might want to
> look at ActionScript 3.0's built-in Timer class, which works independently from
> a movie's frame rate.*

Test your movie and see the final result, with images animating in upon load. Not too much extra code has given you a much smoother application.

Summary

How was that? Not a bad little project for a single chapter! Applying many of the skills presented throughout the earlier chapters, you were able to create an application that loads external data in XML form and displays that data in list views that, when clicked, cause images to load and animate into a pannable, zoomable pane.

The Flash ActionScript 3.0 components were used extensively, with styles and properties and even a custom cell renderer to configure and customize instances. Event listening and dispatching were used throughout to inform the interrelated classes of when things need to occur. You dynamically created graphics and applied filters, and used ActionScript to create an animated transition for the images, which are all loaded from external sources.

At a higher level, you created custom classes, taking advantage of inheritance to extend the core ActionScript classes, to manage your application and provide much of its functionality. At a lower level, you used an entire arsenal of ActionScript language elements—from variables to operators, statements to expressions, functions to loops to conditionals—all to create the application that serves a very real and functional purpose.

You deserve many kudos, as a new ActionScript developer, for getting to this point in the book and in your programming education, and for being able to apply such a wealth of new knowledge!

If you are interested in Flex—what it can offer and how it utilizes ActionScript—keep on turning these pages. All of your ActionScript knowledge is immediately applicable to Flex. In the next two chapters, you'll learn just what Flex adds to the mix and create a Flex application to explore its capabilities, using both the Flex framework and the core ActionScript classes with which you are already familiar.

If Flash is your game and Flex is for another day, then congratulations on reaching this point! There is much more to ActionScript that you can discover, and the best way to do that is to experiment, play, and have fun with the language and what it can offer. Take advantage of the wealth of free tutorials, blogs, forums, and open source code presented by others equally excited by ActionScript and its capabilities. And never stop learning, as there is never a point when there isn't something new to learn and wow you. Good luck!

For all you Flexers, see you at the turn of the page!

Chapter 13

GETTING STARTED WITH FLEX 2

Steve Webster

This chapter covers the following topics:

- What Flex 2 is and how it relates to Flash
- How to install and use the Flex 2 SDK
- How to install and use Flex Builder 2
- How to create a simple Flex 2 application with both the Flex SDK and Flex Builder 2

Before you dig into this chapter, I have a confession to make: there isn't enough space in this book to teach you everything there is to know about Flex 2. It's not all bad, though. Instead of trying to cover the entire world of Flex in a couple chapters, I'm going to show you enough of Flex to give you a comfortable grounding and get you started.

> If you decide that you want to go ahead and master Flex 2, friends of ED has just the book for you: The Complete Guide to Flex with ActionScript 3 by Charles E. Brown (ISBN 1590597338).

Introducing Flex 2

Put simply, Flex 2 is a family of products that makes it easier for developers to create so-called rich Internet applications (RIAs).

If you think back to the discussion of Flash ActionScript 3.0 components in Chapter 9, you'll recall that it took quite a bit of work to create a relatively simple application. The components were designed to be easy to skin and use streamlined code so movies would not have as much overhead and would load more quickly. A lot of the complexity in the previous version of the Flash components was removed for these reasons.

Flex 2, on the other hand, has been designed from the ground up with application development in mind. The components are more robust, and Flex 2 has a large framework of classes designed to manage more complex graphic user interfaces (GUIs). The Flex 2 framework is heavier than its Flash sibling's framework, it's not quite as easy to configure graphically, and it doesn't have a timeline to create more expressive content natively (although you can import other SWFs for that purpose). But Flex 2 blows everything else away if you want to create desktop-style applications on the Internet.

Understanding rich Internet applications

The term *rich Internet application* is bandied about a lot at the moment, but it's hard to find a concrete definition of what an application must have or do to qualify as an RIA. In lieu of anything more official, I'm going to tell you what I think defines an RIA.

Macromedia (who later merged with Adobe) invented the term *rich Internet application* back in March 2002, giving a name to a concept that had already existed for some time under various guises. The concept is a simple one: an application that is delivered over the Internet but behaves more like a desktop application.

Instead of the traditional web application model, where all the data and processing are held on the server and what you see in your web browser is just a static representation of the data, RIAs handle some of the data and processing themselves. This means that they can give the user instant feedback on operations, rather than needing to wait for the server to respond.

The ability to process data on the client and give the user instant feedback also means that some of the idioms traditionally found in desktop software can be re-created on the Web. Features such as drag-and-drop, table sorting, and tree controls are all common in the latest crop of RIAs.

Meet the (Flex) family

As I mentioned earlier, Flex 2 is not a single product. Rather, it's a family of products and technologies that work together to give you the platform to create truly engaging RIAs.

The Flex framework

The most important part of Flex 2 is the **Flex framework**, which is a collection of ActionScript 3.0 classes on top of which applications are built. When you hear developers talking about how Flex is great, they're usually talking about the Flex framework. It is the primary reason that application development is so quick and easy with Flex.

The Flex framework classes include UI components (buttons, data grids, and so on), layout containers, data formatting and validation libraries, and a whole lot more. The next chapter explores a number of parts of the Flex framework to give you a taste of what Flex is all about.

Flash Player 9

Flex is part of the Adobe Flash Platform, which is a collection of technologies with the Flash Player at its core. This means that users don't need to download yet another browser plug-in to view your applications—they just need Flash Player 9. By the time this book hits the shelf, more than 90% of regular web users will have Flash Player 9 installed. That's more than enough to start developing Flex applications targeted at the wider Internet population (and not just us web geeks). In fact, the likes of YouTube and MySpace were already deploying content for Flash Player 9 when Flash Player 9 adoption was hovering around the 40% mark.

Targeting the Flash Player also means that your applications will be cross-platform out of the box, opening your application to audiences on Windows, Mac OS X, and Linux without you having to lift a finger. And that's nice.

One downside of the reliance on the Flash Player is that your applications will run within a security sandbox and won't be able to write to files on the local file system. For this reason, Flex applications tend to be distributed, where data is stored on a central server and accessed over the Internet. This need not dash any of your hopes of writing the next version of Microsoft Word as a Flex application though. Adobe AIR provides a runtime environment for your Flex applications that has access to the local file system. See the "Adobe AIR" section coming up shortly for more information about this capability.

MXML

ActionScript 3.0 may well be perfect for providing the functionality of a Flex application, but it's not the ideal medium for creating UIs. If you've ever had to use the Document Object Model (DOM) in JavaScript to create HTML elements, you have some idea of how painful creating UIs using ActionScript 3.0 can be.

Thankfully, Flex includes an XML-based markup language called Multimedia Extensible Markup Language (MXML), which provides a structured way to define your UIs. You can think of MXML as the XHTML of the Flex world. It allows you to lay out your application and specify its various states, as well as how and when to transition between those states.

Having said all that, MXML is about more than just UIs. You can also include script and style blocks to determine the behavior and appearance of your applications. Script blocks can either contain

ActionScript 3.0 code or link to external ActionScript 3.0 files. Style blocks use CSS syntax to define styles for interface controls, and like the script blocks, can either contain the style data or link to an external CSS file.

You can also create nonvisual objects that link to web services or other external data sources, and use the magic of data binding to render the data using the UI components included as part of the Flex framework. In fact, using the HTTPService class and data binding, you could create a Flex application that consumes a web service (such as a Flickr photostream) and display the data to the user without needing to write a single line of ActionScript 3.0 code!

Flex 2 Software Development Kit

Once you have your ActionScript 3.0 and MXML files, you'll need something to turn those files into an SWF file that can be loaded into the Flash Player. The Flex 2 Software Development Kit (SDK) includes the entire Flex framework, the mxmlc compiler for compiling Flex applications, the compc compiler for compiling components, and a command-line debugger to help you root out problems in your applications.

The Flex 2 SDK is free for both commercial and noncommercial purposes, and is available from the Adobe website (http://www.adobe.com/products/flex/sdk). It contains everything you need to start writing Flex applications today, and without spending a single penny. Now that's what I call a bargain.

Later in the chapter, in the "Building your first Flex 2 application" section, you'll build a simple application using the Flex 2 SDK so you can see how to use the compiler.

Flex Builder 2

Creating and maintaining large applications using nothing but a text editor and the Flex 2 SDK is perfectly acceptable, but it's not the most efficient use of your time.

Flex Builder 2 is an integrated development environment (IDE) designed to help you build Flex 2 applications more quickly and easily than if you were using the simple tools provided as part of the SDK. It includes a visual interface builder that makes it easy to create and edit the MXML files for your interfaces, a code editor that understands both MXML and ActionScript 3.0 code, and an integrated debugger to help you find and fix bugs within applications.

If you want to use Flex Builder 2, you'll need to purchase a license from Adobe, but you can download the free 30-day trial from http://www.adobe.com/products/flex if you just want to play around.

To demonstrate how much simpler it is to create applications with Flex Builder 2 as opposed to the Flex 2 SDK, you'll create the same application using both tools.

Flex Data Services

Flex Data Services is an enterprise-level product that makes it easy for your application to communicate with a central server and vice versa. Distributed RIAs (applications that store data on a central server) require a middle tier to act as an intermediary between the data store (probably a database) and the application itself, and Flex Data Services helps fill this role.

> *Flex Data Services isn't the only option for the middle tier of a distributed RIA. You could use PHP, ASP, or any number of other server-side programming languages to roll your own, or even use a third-party solution.*

The services that Flex Data Services provides include data synchronization, automatic paging of results, the ability to push data from the server to the application, and collaborative features.

If you're interested in exploring Flex Data Services, you can download the free Flex Data Services Express and find out more information about it on the Adobe website (http://www.adobe.com/products/flex/dataservices). Also consider picking up a copy of *The Complete Guide to Flex with ActionScript 3* by Charles E. Brown (friends of ED, 2007).

Adobe AIR

The final part of the Flex 2 puzzle is Adobe AIR (the acronym stands for Adobe Integrated Runtime, and yes, that means its full title is the redundant Adobe Adobe Integrated Runtime), which is a cross-platform (Windows and Mac OS X) runtime environment. AIR was still being developed as this book went to print, available for trial at Adobe Labs (http://labs.adobe.com/technologies/air/).

AIR allows you to build and deploy RIAs using a mixture of Flash 9, Flex 2, HTML, JavaScript, and PDF files that can be installed and run from the user's desktop rather than their web browser. In addition to allowing RIAs to run on the desktop, an AIR application has full access to the local file system and is able to integrate with features of the host operating system such as the clipboard, windowing system, and the network API.

AIR is available for free, meaning that anyone can create desktop applications using Flex 2 without spending any hard-earned cash. Consider it an early or late birthday present from Adobe (unless it's actually your birthday today, in which case, happy birthday).

Getting started with the Flex 2 SDK

In this section, we'll get you up and running with the Flex 2 SDK. First you'll download and install the SDK, and then you'll create your first Flex application.

Installing the Flex 2 SDK

The Flex 2 SDK is available as a free download from the Adobe website. Go to http://www.adobe.com/products/flex/sdk and click to download the Flex 2 SDK. If you haven't downloaded anything from the Adobe website before, you'll be asked to register.

Once the `.zip` file has downloaded, you'll need to extract the contents somewhere sensible on your computer. The steps to do this differ greatly depending on which operating system you're using, so follow the steps under the appropriate heading in this section.

Windows XP/Vista

If you're using Windows XP or Vista, first extract the contents of the Flex 2 SDK .zip file into a folder named flex in the root of your C: drive. Next, you need to add the c:\flex\bin directory to the system path, as follows:

1. From the Start menu, right-click My Computer and select Properties from the menu.

2. In the System Properties dialog box, select the Advanced tab, as shown in Figure 13-1. Click the Environment Variables button.

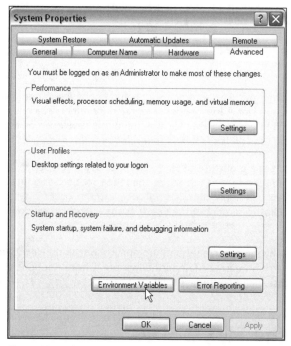

Figure 13-1. The Advanced tab of the System Properties dialog box

3. Under System variables, scroll down the list until you find an entry for Path, select that entry, and then click the Edit button.

4. In the Edit System Variable dialog box, shown in Figure 13-2, scroll to the end of the text in the list box under System variables and add ;c:\flex\bin to the end. Don't omit the semicolon at the beginning—it's used to separate multiple values for the Path variable, and without it you won't be able to use the mxmlc compiler.

5. Click OK in all the open dialog boxes to accept the changes you've made.

6. To test that everything worked, open the Command Prompt window by selecting Start ➤ All programs ➤ Accessories ➤ Command Prompt. In the window, type **mxmlc**, and then press the Enter key. You should see the output shown in Figure 13-3.

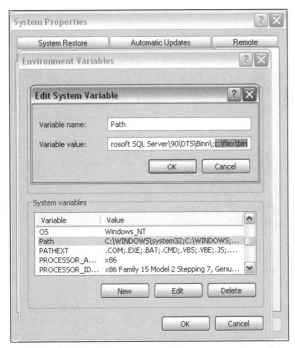

Figure 13-2. Adding the c:\flex\bin directory to the system path

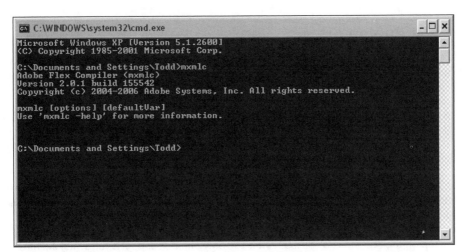

Figure 13-3. Verifying that mxmic is installed on Windows XP/Vista

If you got a message saying that mxmlc is not a recognized command, try repeating the preceding steps.

Mac OS X

If you're using Mac OS X, follow these steps to install the Flex 2 SDK:

1. Extract the contents of the Flex 2 SDK .zip file into a folder named flex in your home folder.

2. Open a Terminal window by double-clicking the Terminal.app file in the Applications folder within the Utilities folder.

3. If you're using Mac OS X 10.2 or earlier, type the following line, and then press Enter:

   echo 'setenv PATH ~/flex/bin:$PATH' >> ~/.tcshrc.

   If you're using Mac OS X 10.3 or later, type the following line, and then press Enter:

   echo 'export PATH=~/flex/bin:$PATH' >> ~/.bash_profile

4. To test that the change has taken effect, quit and reopen Terminal.app, type **mxmlc**, and press Enter. You should see output showing that the mxmlc compiler is installed.

If you got message telling you the mxmlc command could not be found, try repeating the preceding steps.

Linux

If you're using a Linux distribution on a daily basis, you probably know better than I do where you want to put your downloaded applications. I suggest somewhere like /usr/local/flex, but feel free to extract the files wherever you choose. Once that's done, all you need to do is to edit your .profile file and add the /usr/local/flex/bin directory to the PATH environment variable, or whatever the equivalent is for the shell you're using.

Finding a suitable editor

After you have the Flex 2 SDK installed, you'll need a text editor to edit the ActionScript 3.0 and MXML files. You have several options, depending on whether you're using Mac OS X or Windows as your operating system of choice.

If you're using Microsoft Windows, I suggest a great open source editor called FlashDevelop, which is designed specifically for working with Flash and Flex 2 projects. Download it from http://www.flashdevelop.org. Be sure to download and configure the extras for ActionScript 3.0 and MXML code completion, as explained on the site.

For Mac OS X, there is no one good solution, so you'll need to make do with a decent programmer's editor, such as BBEdit or TextWrangler from Bare Bones Software (http://www.barebones.com), or TextMate from MacroMates (http://macromates.com/). These editors can be used to edit ActionScript 3.0 and MXML files, but you won't get any of the fancy code hinting that you get with FlashDevelop on the PC. And currently, BBEdit is the only one that supports full syntax highlighting for ActionScript 3.0 files.

Building your first Flex 2 application

As I mentioned earlier, you're going to create a really simple application using the Flex 2 SDK, and then re-create it later in the chapter using Flex Builder 2. It's really worth following this tutorial through, even if you plan on using Flex Builder 2 to create all your applications, because I'm going to cover some basic information about the Flex framework and MXML here that won't be repeated later.

The application you're going to create is a reader for the blog on the foundationAS3.com website. Oh, and you're going to do it without writing a single line of ActionScript code, just to show off how powerful MXML can be. The end result is going to look something like Figure 13-4.

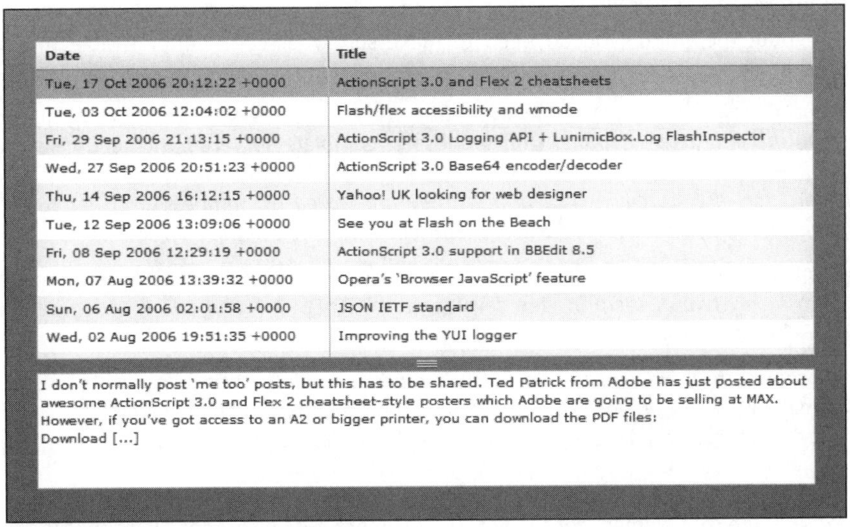

Date	Title
Tue, 17 Oct 2006 20:12:22 +0000	ActionScript 3.0 and Flex 2 cheatsheets
Tue, 03 Oct 2006 12:04:02 +0000	Flash/flex accessibility and wmode
Fri, 29 Sep 2006 21:13:15 +0000	ActionScript 3.0 Logging API + LunimicBox.Log FlashInspector
Wed, 27 Sep 2006 20:51:23 +0000	ActionScript 3.0 Base64 encoder/decoder
Thu, 14 Sep 2006 16:12:15 +0000	Yahoo! UK looking for web designer
Tue, 12 Sep 2006 13:09:06 +0000	See you at Flash on the Beach
Fri, 08 Sep 2006 12:29:19 +0000	ActionScript 3.0 support in BBEdit 8.5
Mon, 07 Aug 2006 13:39:32 +0000	Opera's 'Browser JavaScript' feature
Sun, 06 Aug 2006 02:01:58 +0000	JSON IETF standard
Wed, 02 Aug 2006 19:51:35 +0000	Improving the YUI logger

I don't normally post 'me too' posts, but this has to be shared. Ted Patrick from Adobe has just posted about awesome ActionScript 3.0 and Flex 2 cheatsheet-style posters which Adobe are going to be selling at MAX. However, if you've got access to an A2 or bigger printer, you can download the PDF files:
Download [...]

Figure 13-4. The RSS reader you'll build

The layout has a table containing all the items from the RSS feed of the foundationAS3.com blog, with the summary of the selected item shown in the area below. The two areas are separated by a draggable divider, so that users can decide how much space they want to give to the listing and to the summary.

So, let's build the RSS reader.

1. Decide where you want to keep your projects. If you have been moving progressively through this book, you probably have created project directories for each chapter. You can do the same here and create a Chapter 13 directory. Wherever you choose to create your projects, create a new directory within it named RSSReader.

2. Within the RSSReader directory, create two subdirectories, named src and bin.

> *Although step 2 isn't strictly necessary, it's good to keep your files organized in this way. The src directory will contain any MXML and ActionScript 3.0 files. The final SWF file will be output into the bin directory. In larger applications, you might also have components, libraries, and assets directories containing other files related to the project.*

3. Fire up your chosen text editor, create a new blank file, and save it in the src directory with the name RSSReader.mxml.

4. Now you can start writing the MXML for your RSS reader application. Because MXML is a type of XML, you need to start the MXML file with the **XML declaration**.

```
<?xml version="1.0" encoding="utf-8"?>
```

The version attribute specifies the version of the XML specification that this document uses. Since there is only one version of XML at this time, the value of this attribute will be 1.0. The value of the encoding attribute signifies the character encoding used in the MXML file. In this case, you've used utf-8, since that character set supports all characters in all countries throughout the world (you do need to make sure your code editor is able to save UTF-8 encoded files).

> If all this character-encoding stuff sounds like complete nonsense, then count yourself lucky—you're not quite a geek yet. The short version goes something like this: when characters are stored in a computer, they are stored as numbers, and determining which number is used for a particular character is the job of the character encoding.
>
> Many different character encodings are available, but you're really likely to come across only two of them in Flex development: ISO-8859-1 and UTF-8. Of those, only UTF-8 properly supports multilingual content.
>
> Of course, in order to translate those numbers back into their respective characters, somehow you need to include information about which character encoding is used, and that's what the encoding attribute of the XML declaration is all about.

5. Next, add the root element for the MXML document. When creating Flex applications, this will always be an <mx:Application> element:

```
<?xml version="1.0" encoding="utf-8"?>
<mx:Application xmlns:mx="http://www.adobe.com/2006/mxml">
</mx:Application>
```

This is the root tag of the MXML document, much like the <html> tag in an XHTML document. The xmlns:mx attribute is required by the XML standard, and it basically uniquely identifies the mx namespace that the Flex 2 framework uses. These namespaces are similar to the namespaces in ActionScript 3.0. You need to make sure you get the value of this attribute right, or you'll upset the mxmlc compiler.

6. You're now at the stage where you have a perfectly valid Flex application. It doesn't actually do anything, but that's beside the point. Let's make sure everything is okay before moving on by compiling the application using the mxmlc command-line compiler. Open a Command Prompt window (Windows) or Terminal window (Mac) and navigate to the RSSReader directory you created in step 1.

7. In Windows, type the following line, and then press Enter:

```
mxmlc src\RSSReader.mxml -output=bin\RSSReader.swf
```

In Mac OS X or Linux, type the following line, and then press Enter:

```
mxmlc src/RSSReader.mxml -output=bin/RSSReader.swf
```

Make sure there are no errors.

8. Open the RSSReader.swf file in the bin directory with your web browser. You should see absolutely nothing but a blue-green gradient background.

9. If you got all that working, it's time to add the remainder of the MXML in the RSSReader.mxml file. I'm not going to go over every little detail here; you'll explore more details of MXML tags in the next chapter. But have a look and see if you can get a general feel for how the structure of the MXML translates into the UI shown in Figure 13-4. I've added some comments to help you.

```
<?xml version="1.0" encoding="utf-8"?>
<mx:Application xmlns:mx="http://www.adobe.com/2006/mxml"
  layout="vertical" creationComplete="feed.send()">
    <!-- The HTTPService item is used to load the RSS data from -->
    <!--  the specified URL -->
    <mx: HTTPService id="feed" url="http://foundationas3.com/feed"/>
    <mx:VDividedBox width="100%" height="100%">
      <!-- DataGrid control populated with entries from the feed -->
      <!-- using data binding -->
      <mx:DataGrid id="entries" dataProvider= ➡
"{feed.lastResult.rss.channel.item}" width="100%" height="66%">
        <mx:columns>
          <mx:DataGridColumn dataField="pubDate" headerText="Date"/>
          <mx:DataGridColumn dataField="title" headerText="Title"/>
        </mx:columns>
      </mx:DataGrid>
      <!-- TextArea control bound to the description property of -->
      <!-- the selected item from the entries DataGrid -->
      <mx:TextArea htmlText="{entries.selectedItem.description}" ➡
width="100%" height="34%"/>
    </mx:VDividedBox>
</mx:Application>
```

Basically, what you have here is an HTTPService object with an ID of the feed that fetches the RSS data from the foundationAS3.com website and stores it. This information is displayed in the DataGrid using the magic of data binding, which essentially means that whenever the data source is updated, any component bound to that data source will automatically be updated. The same technique is used to show the description of the currently selected item in DataGrid in the TextArea control.

10. Return to the Command Prompt window (Windows) or Terminal window (Mac). You should still be in the RSSReader directory. In Windows, type the following line, and then press Enter:

```
mxmlc src\RSSReader.mxml -output=bin\RSSReader.swf
```

In Mac OS X or Linux, type the following line, and then press Enter:

```
mxmlc src/RSSReader.mxml -output=bin/RSSReader.swf
```

Make sure there are no errors.

11. Open the RSSReader.swf file in the bin directory with your web browser. You should see something like Figure 13-4. If you got a bunch of funny looking errors instead, double-check your MXML file with the one provided in the files you downloaded for this chapter from the friends of ED website.

Now that you've worked with the free Flex 2 SDK, let's turn our attention to the commercial Flex 2 IDE—Flex Builder 2.

Getting started with Flex Builder 2

Installing Flex Builder 2 is actually a bit of a no-brainer. For both Windows and Mac OS X, a lovely installer wizard guides you through the process. All you need to do is to download the installer from the Adobe website at http://www.adobe.com/products/flex/flexbuilder (again, registering if necessary), and then double-click the installer file once it had downloaded to begin the installation.

Sadly, Adobe has no plans to make Flex Builder 2 available for Linux, so if you're using Linux, you're stuck with the Flex 2 SDK.

Understanding the Flex Builder 2 interface

Flex Builder 2 is a powerful IDE for Flex 2 applications, built on top of the Eclipse open development platform (http://www.eclipse.org). It's available both as a stand-alone application and as a plug-in for the Eclipse IDE. Unfortunately, this power means that Flex Builder 2 isn't the easiest of applications to get comfortable with, although if you use Eclipse for other types of projects, using it for Flex will be a natural transition. If you have never used Eclipse, it can be a bit of a daunting environment. Thankfully, the first thing you see when you launch the application is the Flex Start Page, which contains links to samples and tutorials to get you started, as shown in Figure 13-5.

The Flex Builder 2 interface is contextual, which means that it adapts to suit the task you're performing at a given time. Even when you've just started the IDE, you can still see some of the elements that will be useful to you once you start creating applications.

On the top-left side of the Flex Builder 2 screen is the Navigator panel, which lists all the Flex projects that you have created. If this is the first time you've started Flex Builder 2, your projects list will be completely empty. You'll remedy that in a moment.

Below the Navigator panel is the Outline panel, which will show you an outline of the MXML or ActionScript 3.0 document you're working on at the moment and allow you to quickly jump to various points of interest.

Below the Flex Start Page panel is the Problems panel. This is where any compiler warnings and errors will show up, giving you a description of each item, and the filename and line number in which the error or warning occurred. Double-clicking an entry in this list will take you directly to the line of code causing the problem.

That's about all there is to see of the Flex Builder 2 IDE without actually creating a new Flex 2 project, so let's get going.

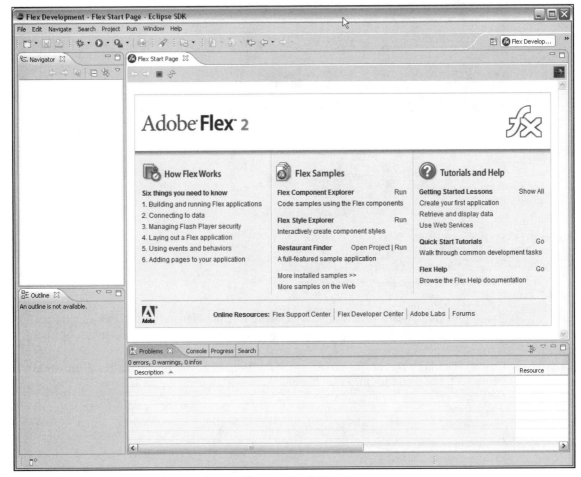

Figure 13-5. The Flex Start Page appears when you first start Flex Builder 2.

Building your first Flex Builder 2 application

As I mentioned earlier, you're going to create the exact same RSS reader application as you just did with the Flex SDK, but do it Flex Builder 2 style. You'll still need to get your hands dirty with a bit of manual MXML authoring, but by the time you've finished this example, the benefits of having a fully integrated IDE over the simple SDK should be clear.

Creating a new Flex project

You begin by creating a new project in Flex Builder 2.

1. Select File ➤ New ➤ Flex Project from the main menu. This will launch the New Flex Project wizard, as shown in Figure 13-6.

Figure 13-6. Choosing a new Flex project type

2. You can see from the list here that you can create several different types of Flex applications. Since you're going to be consuming an XML service, a basic project is good enough, so click Next to continue.

3. On the following page of the wizard, enter **RSSReader** as the project name, as shown in Figure 13-7, and then click the Finish button.

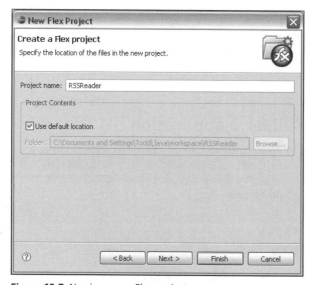

Figure 13-7. Naming a new Flex project

You'll now see your new RSSReader project in the Navigator panel in the top left of the Flex Builder 2 interface, as shown in Figure 13-8.

The bin directory is where the final SWF file will be stored, and that directory also contains a variety of SWF, JavaScript, and HTML files to make it easy for you to deploy your Flex applications with the minimum of fuss. The JavaScript and HTML files are generated from templates in the html-template directory. Note that there is no src directory, as you used with the command-line compiler. The main MXML file for a Flex application needs to be included in the root directory of the project. If you were creating additional source files, either ActionScript or MXML, you would create a src directory in which to place these files (though this is completely optional).

Figure 13-8. The RSSReader project appears in the Navigator panel.

The RSSReader.mxml file has been created and opened in the Source view of the MXML editor panel, as shown in Figure 13-9, ready for you to start building the application.

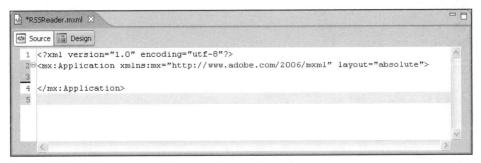

Figure 13-9. The RSSReader.mxml file open in Source view

Working in Design view

Click the Design button within the MXML editor panel to switch to Design view. This shows a general preview of what the project will look like when it is compiled, which for now is just a blue-green background, as shown in Figure 13-10.

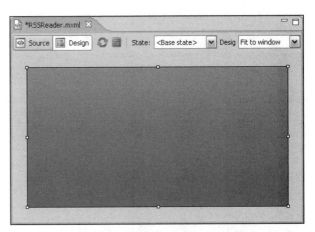

Figure 13-10. Initial Flex Builder project in Design view

483

The small bounding box with drag handles shows the item you currently have selected. Over on the right side are two new panels:

Figure 13-11. The States panel

- The States panel (see Figure 13-11) allows you to define a number of states for the UI of your application, so that you can alter the layout or content of your Flex application programmatically at runtime.

- The Flex Properties panel is like the Property inspector in Flash CS3, in that it displays the properties for whatever item you have currently selected in the MXML document and allows you to change their values. In Figure 13-12, it's showing the properties of the mx:Application object.

You might also have noticed a new Components tab added to the same panel as the Outline tab on the left side of the Flex Builder interface, as shown in Figure 13-13. This contains an organized list of all the UI controls, containers, navigators, and other components that you can add to your Flex application.

Before you add any components to your application, you need to configure the main mx:Application container to lay out its children vertically.

1. In the Flex Properties panel under Layout, select vertical from the Layout drop-down list, as shown in Figure 13-14.

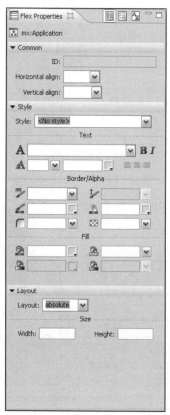

Figure 13-12. The Flex Properties panel

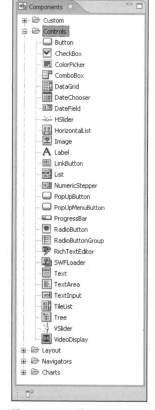

Figure 13-13. The Components panel

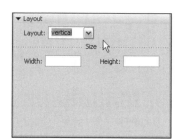

Figure 13-14. Setting the layout to vertical

2. The first component you need to add to your application is a VDividedBox control, which is in the Layout folder in the Component tab. The VDividedBox control lays out items vertically with a drag bar between items, allowing the user to be able to resize the height of the items. Select the VDividedBox entry and drag it over the blue-green box of the application preview in the center of the Flex Builder 2 interface and then drop it. When you do this, you'll see a dialog box asking what size the VDividedBox should be, as shown in Figure 13-15.

3. Enter 100% for both width and height, and then click OK.

4. Next find the DataGrid control in the Controls folder in the Components panel and drag it onto the VDividedBox outline in the application preview. You should see a horizontal blue line appear where the DataGrid component will be inserted, so you know it's within the VDividedBox, as shown in Figure 13-16.

Figure 13-15. Inserting a VDividedBox component

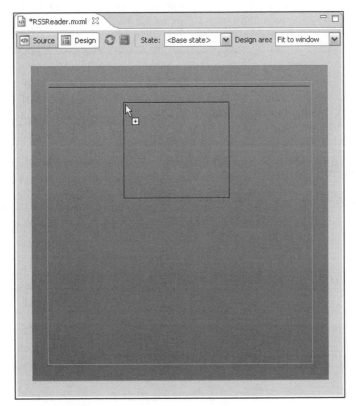

Figure 13-16. Adding a DataGrid component

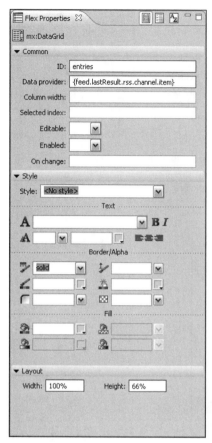

Figure 13-17. Setting the DataGrid properties

5. Using the Flex Properties panel, set the following properties of the DataGrid component (see Figure 13-17):

- ID: **entries**
- Data provider: **{feed.lastResult.rss.channel.item}**
- Width: **100%**
- Height: **66%**

Don't worry about the fact that the DataGrid control has three columns and you only want two. There's no way to manipulate the columns of a data grid through the visual editor, so that's one of the things you'll need to handle manually later.

6. Save your project. You will see an error listed in the Problems panel, as shown in Figure 13-18. It's complaining that it can't find something named feed, which you referenced when setting the Data provider property for the DataGrid control. If you remember back to the Flex 2 SDK example, feed is the ID of the HTTPService object. This is something else you can't solve in the visual view, since the HTTPService class is nonvisual.

7. Drag a TextArea component onto the bottom edge of the DataGrid control so that you have a horizontal blue line just below the DataGrid control, as shown in Figure 13-19.

This means that the TextArea component will be inserted below the DataGrid component in the VDividedBox component. Set the TextArea control's width to 100% and height to 34% using the Flex Properties panel. Unless Adobe has fixed this bug, your TextArea will probably disappear from the visual view completely after doing this. I don't know why it does that, but it's certainly annoying. Don't worry—your TextArea is still there, I promise.

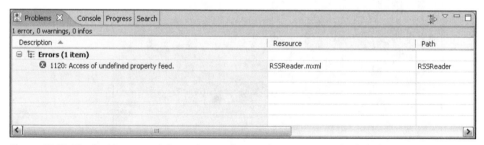

Figure 13-18. The Problems panel shows that a referenced property can't be found.

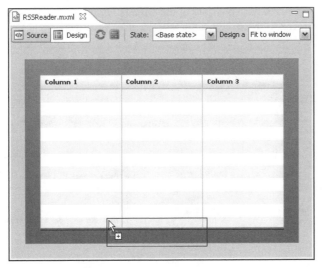

Figure 13-19. Adding a TextArea component

Working in Source view

Now switch back to Source view by clicking the Source button at the top of the page. You'll see that Flex Builder 2 has been hard at work creating your MXML for you, as shown in Figure 13-20. All you need to do now is finish off the bits that it couldn't handle.

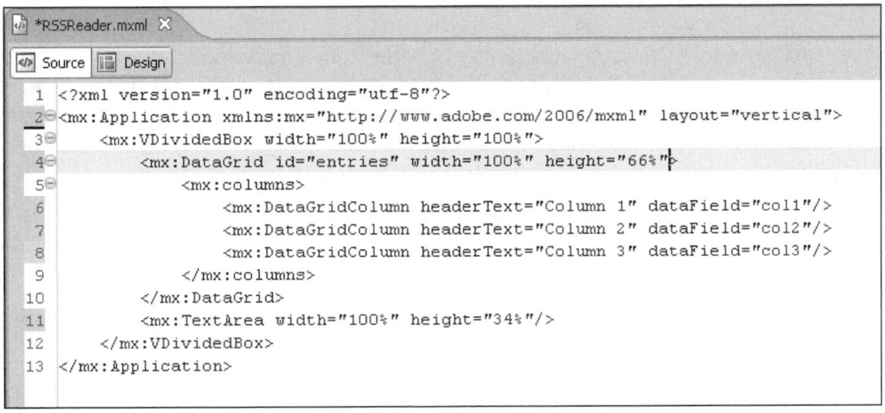

```
1  <?xml version="1.0" encoding="utf-8"?>
2  <mx:Application xmlns:mx="http://www.adobe.com/2006/mxml" layout="vertical">
3      <mx:VDividedBox width="100%" height="100%">
4          <mx:DataGrid id="entries" width="100%" height="66%">
5              <mx:columns>
6                  <mx:DataGridColumn headerText="Column 1" dataField="col1"/>
7                  <mx:DataGridColumn headerText="Column 2" dataField="col2"/>
8                  <mx:DataGridColumn headerText="Column 3" dataField="col3"/>
9              </mx:columns>
10         </mx:DataGrid>
11         <mx:TextArea width="100%" height="34%"/>
12     </mx:VDividedBox>
13 </mx:Application>
```

Figure 13-20. The MXML file created by Flex Builder 2

1. First, let's modify the columns for the data grid. Delete one of the three columns, since you will need only two. Then change the headerText of the first column to Date and set the dataField to pubDate. pubDate is the name of the property of the items in the data grid that will be displayed in that column. Date will be what is displayed in the column header. For the second column, change the headerText to Title and the dataField to title.

487

2. Next, let's handle that error. As a child of the <mx:Application> tag, insert an <mx:HTTPService> tag. Notice how the MXML editor automatically gives you suggestions after you start typing, as shown in Figure 13-21.

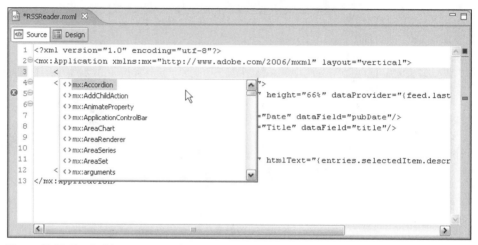

Figure 13-21. Flex Builder 2's MXML editor suggests tags after you begin typing.

You can use the keyboard to navigate up and down the list of suggestions, pressing the Enter key when you find the one you need. Add an id attribute with the value feed, and a url attribute with the value http://foundationAS3.com/feed, and then close the element. Save the file. Once Flex Builder 2 is finished compiling your project, the error should disappear from the Problems panel.

3. Add an attribute named htmlText to the <mx:TextArea> tag with a value of {entries.selectedItem.description} to bind its contents to the description property of the currently selected item in the entry's data grid. This means that whenever the selection in the data grid changes, it will automatically update the text in the text area. Sweet automation!

4. The only thing left to do is to add the creationComplete attribute to the <mx:Application> tag with a value of feed.send(). This invokes the send() method of the HTTPService instance you've named feed when the application fires its creationComplete event after all of its children have been created.

5. Save the file, and then click the Run button (the green play button) in the main toolbar to launch your RSS reader application.

Summary

Phew! We've covered a lot of ground for such a short chapter, so I'll keep the summary short. You should now have enough of an idea about what Flex is to start exploring more in depth in the next chapter. And you've built a semi-useful application to boot.

I'll see you in the next chapter when you're hungry for more.

Chapter 14

FLEX BY EXAMPLE

Steve Webster

In this chapter, you're going to put into practice all that you've learned about Flex 2 in the previous chapter and ActionScript 3.0 throughout this book. Here, you'll develop the simple RSS reader application you built in Chapter 13 as a full-featured feed reader application. You'll see that although the Flex framework and the MXML markup language are extraordinary, powerful tools on their own, you need to add ActionScript to create truly robust, complex applications.

This chapter demonstrates the following:

- How to conceptualize and plan a Flex project
- How to create a new Flex project in Flex Builder
- How to import and take advantage of external class libraries
- How to lay out a UI using MXML
- How to use controls and layout classes in the Flex framework
- How to use data binding to wire components together
- How to create pop-up dialog boxes
- How to create custom classes for use within a Flex application
- How to create and dispatch custom events
- How to use web services to load data
- How to save data between sessions using SharedObject

You'll see how all of the ActionScript skills you've learned throughout this book can be applied to Flex development.

Planning the application

Before you rush headlong into building this application (yes, I saw you reaching for your mouse), you need to identify exactly what you want it to do and roughly how you want it to look. Proper planning of a large application is an important step during your development process, helping you to identify potential problems, ensure consistent architecture, and provide better visibility (both for you and your clients) of what you will be building.

Because planning is so important to creating a good application, I'm going to dispense a few personal opinions about how a project should be developed. I'm not going to teach you the "right" way to do it (which is just as well, because there is no right way to do it, whatever the fat-cat consultants or hip Extreme Programming gurus might tell you). The point is to get you thinking about how to develop an application—from an initial idea to the finished article.

Let's walk through the five main steps of planning an application:

- Gather the requirements.
- Create the functional specification.
- Design the UI.
- Design the Interaction.
- Design the data and logic.

Gathering the requirements

The first step in planning an application is to identify the requirements. In a real-world project, this can mean anything from an informal chat with the people who will be using your application to a full-blown, official requirements-gathering process. The aim in both cases is the same: make sure your application is useful to the people who are going to be using it every day. Now, that's not to say that you must try to implement every little feature that each user says he wants. Part of the headache of the requirements-gathering process is that, most of the time, what your users think they want isn't what they really want, and you need to work hard to decipher their requests into a feasible requirement. You also have a responsibility to include only the features that will be useful to a significant portion of your user base. This means that some features will not make the cut, even though they may be good ideas.

So, what are the requirements for the application you'll build in this chapter? Since this is a practice application, I get to set the requirements. And since I'm being informal, I can just list what the application should do:

- Support multiple feeds, allowing the user to add and remove feeds
- Support the most common feed formats
- Allow the user to manually refresh feeds

- Automatically refresh feeds every 5 minutes
- Show the user the number of articles in a given feed
- Provide a way for the user to view the website associated with the feed
- Remember the user's feed between sessions

Of course, this list could include even more features, but I want to keep version 1.0 of this application manageable, so these requirements will do just fine for now. At the end of chapter, I'll leave you with a few ideas of where you could take this application if you feel like tinkering.

When deciding on what you want your application to do, it's worth giving some thought to the things you won't be able to do. In the case of the feed reader application, limitations are imposed by the Flash Player in which the application will run.

One limitation relates to storage. Although you want to store the user's feed list, the only local storage medium available to a Flex application is a local `SharedObject`, which is limited in terms of how much content it can hold. This means that you won't be able to store the list of articles fetched from each feed, as would be the case in a normal feed reader application, so when the application is restarted the history of articles in the feed will be lost. (Note that you could use Adobe AIR, introduced in the previous chapter, to build an application that has direct access to the file system.)

The other main limitation is imposed by the Flash Player's security sandbox. The Flash Player can't load XML data from another domain without express permission in the form of a `crossdomain.xml` file. This file, which is hosted on the server delivering the data, specifies other domains whose files, like SWFs, may access that data. This won't be a problem during development because you'll be running the application locally, which thankfully means it won't be subject to this particular security restriction. However, it does mean that you won't be able to upload this application and have it work for every feed.

> *You could host the application remotely by creating a server-side proxy script to fetch the feed data on behalf of the application. Such a proxy would be hosted on the same domain as your application SWF and would load the data from the remote domain. Since the application SWF would need to communicate with only the proxy script, hosted on the same domain, there would be no security restriction in the Flash Player. Adobe has examples of this available at* http://kb.adobe.com/selfservice/viewContent.do?externalId=tn_16520#proxy.

The Flash Player imposes other limitations, such as not being able to interface with the web browsers to have your application configured as the default feed reader, but these are relatively minor in comparison to the two just discussed.

Creating the functional specification

Now that you know what your application needs to do (and what it does not need to do), you can start thinking about how it should work. The essence of the process is to convert the requirements you've gathered into tangible, measurable features.

In a more formal setting, this would involve drawing up a functional specification document, which would be circulated to all interested parties so that everyone knows exactly what is being built. Such a document could run to hundreds or thousands of pages, depending on the complexity of your application, and it may need to go through several rounds of revisions before everyone is happy with it.

However, for the sample application, you'll just flesh out the requirements gathered in the previous step into a list of features, with some basic details of how each feature will work.

- **Feed reading**:
  - The users will be able to view a list of the feeds to which they have subscribed, with the list showing the title of the feed and the number of articles it contains.
  - The users will be able to see the date and title of the articles for a given feed, and the title and excerpt for a given article.
  - The users will be able to visit the website associated with a given feed, and they will be able to go to the page for an individual entry if they want to read more than the excerpt.

- **Subscription management**:
  - The users will be able to manage their feed subscriptions from within the application. When subscribing to a feed, the users will be able to specify the URL from the feed. This URL will then be used to fetch the feed data, and the feed title will be extracted from the metadata that is part of the feed data.
  - The system will support the following feed formats: RSS 1.0, RSS 2.0, and Atom 1.0.
  - The format of a feed will be automatically detected so that the users do not need to know the type of a given feed when subscribing.

- **Refreshing feeds**:
  - When the application is started, each feed in the user's subscription list will be refreshed, fetching the latest articles. The feeds will be refreshed automatically every 5 minutes.
  - A user will be able to manually refresh a given feed or all feeds in the subscription list.
  - When refreshing a feed, any old articles that no longer appear in the feed data will be kept until the end of the session.

Designing the UI

Once you have the functional specification, you can start to think about the user experience. You want your application to be as easy to use as possible (in line with one of the application requirements), so you're going to stick to a single screen.

Now, you don't need to go into a whole lot of detail here. You're not worried about the look and feel of the application. You just need to know what the major UI elements are and roughly where they sit on the screen. With that in mind, and having looked at some other feed reader applications for inspiration, I came up with the layout shown in Figure 14-1.

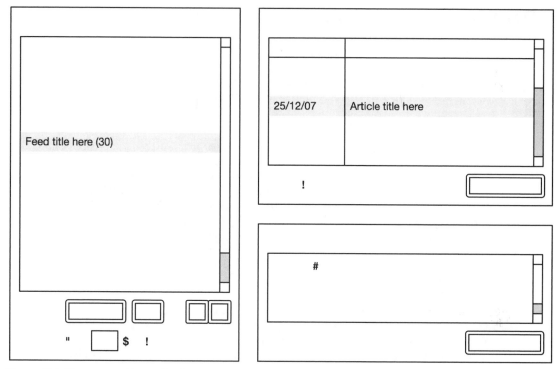

Figure 14-1. The proposed layout for the RSS application

On the left is the list of feeds to which the user has subscribed, with the number of unread articles in brackets after the title of the feed. Below the list is a button to add a new subscription (labeled with a + sign) and another button to remove the selected subscription (labeled with a – sign). Also included in this area are controls for refreshing the feeds, either manually or automatically at a specified interval.

In the top-right area is the list of articles in the selected feed, displayed in a scrollable grid showing the date and the title of the article. Beneath that is a label to tell the user when the feed was last checked for updates and a Visit website button, which will take the user to the website associated with the feed.

Below the article list are the title and excerpt from the selected article, with a label telling the user when the article was posted and a button that will take the user to the full article.

Although you can probably guess which containers and controls from the Flex framework you might use to build this, it's a little too early in the planning stage to be thinking about the implementation. There's still one crucial step left that may have an impact on how you build the UI.

Designing the interaction

Interaction design means deciding how the application will behave in response to user input. The user interaction for this application is going to be as simple as the interface.

For the sample application, the interaction is implied by the UI design. However, in a more formal project, interaction design is a crucial step to getting your application right.

If you're going to be doing interaction design as part of your job, I suggest getting hold of a copy of About Face 2.0: The Essentials of Interaction Design *by Alan Cooper and Robert M. Reimann (Wiley, 2003). This book will help you to determine what your potential users want from the UI and aid you in avoiding the most common pitfalls when designing a UI. This book was written with desktop application development in mind, but since RIA development is all about bringing desktop-style applications to the Web, most of the concepts discussed in this book apply equally well to our line of work.*

Designing the data and logic

At this stage, you would normally look at designing the data entities (using UML or entity relationship diagrams) and the logic of the application (using UML or flowcharts), but this isn't a book on software design, and that topic is way too big for me to do it any justice in a page or two. Take a look at the UML website (`http://www.uml.org`) for the UML specification and an introduction to its use, plus its benefits for application development.

Setting up the project

So now we get down to the fun stuff: using the Flex framework to build the application. In order to get a feel for MXML you won't be using the Design view in Flex Builder, but you will be using the Flex Builder 2 IDE to set up and manage the project to save the bother of messing too much with the command line. If you are using the free Flex 2 SDK, the ActionScript and the MXML covered here will be exactly the same. You will just need to manually create the directories and files, and compile through the command line (consult Adobe's documentation for instructions on compiling through the command line).

If you are using Flex Builder and are a fan of its Design view, it's still a good idea to get to know MXML and how to write it on your own. You can't accomplish everything from the Design view, and someday you'll need to roll up your sleeves and get busy with the underlying code. When that day comes, you'll be glad you took the time to understand MXML. Using the Design view and checking the generated MXML is a great way to become familiar with the markup language.

You're going to build the application in an incremental fashion, testing new features as you go. This means that you'll get the basics working first, and then build on those step by step until you have the finished application. Building an application in this way means that you can spot any problems early, rather than waiting until the very end to compile and test, only to find that the most basic things aren't working.

The first step in building the application is setting up the project. With Flex Builder open, select File ➤ New ➤ Flex Project from the menus to open the New Flex Project dialog box, as shown in Figure 14-2. Leave the radio button for Basic selected and click the Next button.

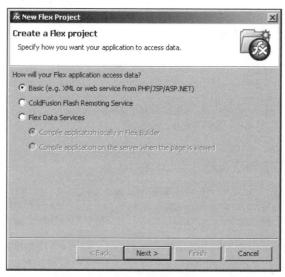

Figure 14-2. The New Flex Project dialog box in Flex Builder

In the next dialog box, enter **IrisReader** as the project name. Uncheck Use default location and create a project directory specifically for this chapter, following the same convention as you have for the examples in previous chapters, as shown in Figure 14-3. Click Finish to create the new project.

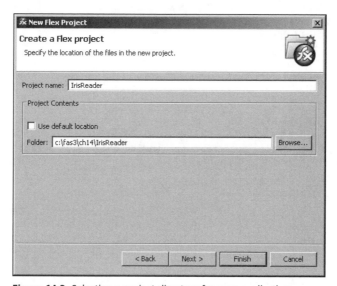

Figure 14-3. Selecting a project directory for your application

At this point, you have a project structure set up with the root directory containing your main MXML file, IrisReader.mxml, and a number of properties files, which you will not edit. In addition, three sub-directories have been created:

- settings: This directory contains Eclipse preferences, which you will not edit.
- bin: This directory contains all of the files needed to deploy your application, including HTML for embedding the SWF; JavaScript for player detection, writing the SWF to the page, and history management; and the SWFs themselves, both normal and debug versions.
- html-template: This directory contains the files that are used to produce the output in the bin directory, with tokens that can be replaced, based on your application. For instance, if you set the background color or width and height in your MXML, these values can be written into your HTML in the bin directory using the template in the html-template directory.

Creating the basic UI

Now that you have set up the project, you can start to build the UI. In Flex, this generally means starting with the container components that will control the layout of your application. Let's take the wireframe from Figure 14-1 and break that down into a hierarchy of Flex 2 containers, as shown in Figure 14-4.

As you can see, Panel containers (the boxed elements with title bars) separate the different elements of the UI, encapsulated in a combination of HDividedBox and VDividedBox containers. These containers position items horizontally or vertically, respectively, and provide a means to drag to resize the internal elements, giving the UI maximum flexibility.

You should be in Source view of the IrisReader.mxml file. Begin by changing the layout attribute of the <mx:Application> element to vertical. Then add an HDividedBox container with both width and height attributes set to 100%.

```
<mx:Application xmlns:mx=http://www.adobe.com/2006/mxml layout="vertical">
  <mx:HDividedBox width="100%" height="100%">
  </mx:HDividedBox>
</mx:Application>
```

Within the HDividedBox, add a Panel container with a title of Subscriptions, a width of 40%, and a height of 100%.

```
<mx:Application xmlns:mx="http://www.adobe.com/2006/mxml" layout="vertical">
  <mx:HDividedBox width="100%" height="100%">
    <mx:Panel title="Subscriptions" width="40%" height="100%">
    </mx:Panel>
  </mx:HDividedBox>
</mx:Application>
```

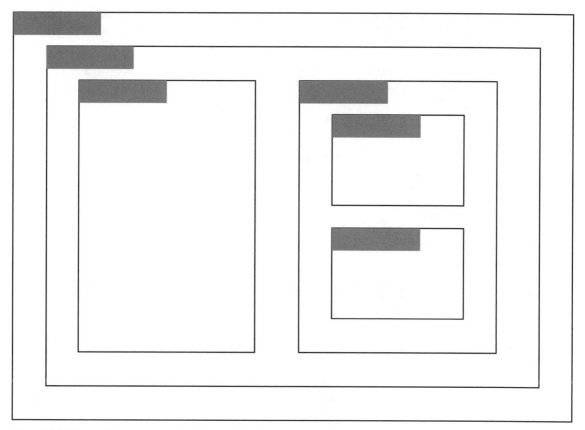

Figure 14-4. The container components in the application

As a sibling of the Panel, add a VDividedBox with a width of 60% (so it occupies the remainder of the width of the HDividedBox parent) and a height of 100%.

```
<mx:Application xmlns:mx="http://www.adobe.com/2006/mxml" layout="vertical">
  <mx:HDividedBox width="100%" height="100%">
    <mx:Panel title="Subscriptions" width="40%" height="100%">
    </mx:Panel>
    <mx:VDividedBox width="60%" height="100%">
    </mx:VDividedBox>
  </mx:HDividedBox>
</mx:Application>
```

Finally, add two Panel containers as children of the VDividedBox, with titles of Articles and Article from top to bottom, and both with 100% width and 50% height (so they take up half the VDividedBox each).

```
<mx:Application xmlns:mx="http://www.adobe.com/2006/mxml" layout="vertical">
  <mx:HDividedBox width="100%" height="100%">
    <mx:Panel title="Subscriptions" width="40%" height="100%">
    </mx:Panel>
    <mx:VDividedBox width="60%" height="100%">
      <mx:Panel title="Articles" width="100%" height="50%">
      </mx:Panel>
      <mx:Panel title="Article" width="100%" height="50%">
      </mx:Panel>
    </mx:VDividedBox>
  </mx:HDividedBox>
</mx:Application>
```

If you now switch to the Design view, you should see something like Figure 14-5.

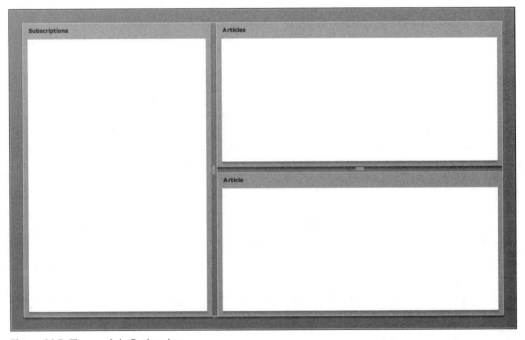

Figure 14-5. The panels in Design view

If you don't see all three panels, there's a chance that Design view has fallen out of sync with Source view. This seems to happen randomly with Flex Builder when using the divided box components. Thankfully, Adobe has provided a handy Refresh button in the Design view to bring it up to date. The Refresh button is just to the right of the Source and Design buttons. If clicking that a few times doesn't solve the problem, double-check that your source code matches what is shown here.

Creating basic feed integration

With the very basic UI created, you can turn your attention to loading feeds. One of the requirements for the application is support for RSS 1.0, RSS 2.0, and Atom 1.0 syndication formats.

The proper approach for feed integration is to abstract the common functionality from all three feed formats into a set of classes, and specialize those classes for each individual feed format. Creating these classes would be a lot of work and wouldn't necessarily teach you anything about building Flex applications (the whole point of this chapter). Thankfully, Adobe has already done the hard work for you with its XML syndication library, which is available from Adobe Labs.

Installing the XML syndication library

The XML syndication library provides code that parses the XML feed formats into ActionScript objects that you can handle natively in your application. All you need to do is download this library and integrate it into your project.

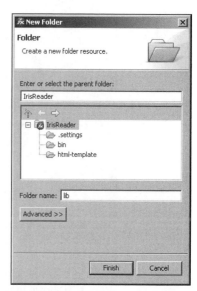

1. The XML syndication library is available through Google's code repository. Visit http://code.google.com/p/as3syndicationlib/ and download the featured .zip file.

2. Extract the .zip file to your desktop. The file of interest is xmlsyndication.swc, in the bin directory of the extracted files. In the doc directory, you'll find API documentation for the XML syndication library, which is worth reviewing, as you're going to be using several of these classes and interfaces in the feed reader application.

3. Right-click (Control-click for Mac OS X) the IrisReader project in Flex Builder's Navigator panel and select New ➤ Folder. Name the folder lib, as shown in Figure 14-6, and then click Finish. I use this folder to hold any third-party libraries that my Flex application uses.

Figure 14-6. Creating a new folder in Flex Builder

4. Right-click (Control-click for Mac OS X) the new lib folder and select Import. Select File system from the Select screen of the Import window. as shown in Figure 14-7, and then click Next.

5. Click the Browse button at the top right of the File system screen. Find and select the bin directory from the files extracted in step 2. and then click OK (Windows) or Choose (Mac OS X).

Figure 14-7. Choosing to import resources from the file system

501

6. Select the bin directory on the left side of the File system screen of the Import window, and check the check box next to the xmlsyndication.swc entry on the right side, as shown in Figure 14-8.

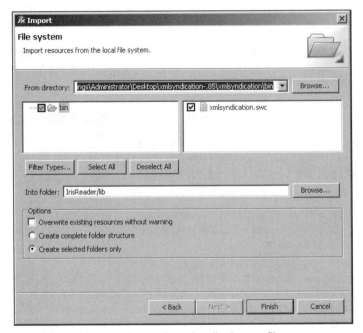

Figure 14-8. Choosing to import the xmlsyndication.swc file

7. Click the Finish button in the Import window to import the xmlsyndication.swc file into your project, as shown in Figure 14-9.

Figure 14-9.
The xmlsyndication.swc file imported into the project's working directory

8. Now you need to tell Flex Builder that you want this file compiled as part of your project. Right-click (Windows) or Control-click the IrisReader project in the Navigator panel and select Properties from the context menu.

9. Select Flex Build Path from the left side of the Properties for IrisReader window, and then select the Library path tab on the right side, as shown in Figure 14-10.

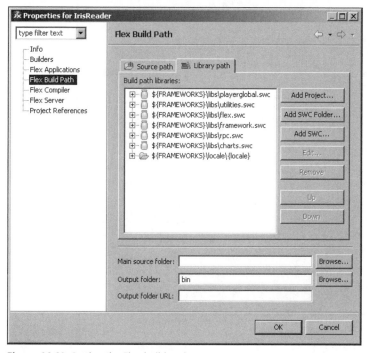

Figure 14-10. Setting the Flex build path

10. Click the Add SWC button, and then click the Browse button in the Add SWC dialog box. Select the xmlsyndication.src file within the lib directory of your main project directory, as shown in Figure 14-11. Then click OK (Windows) or Choose (Mac OS X).

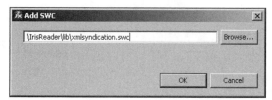

Figure 14-11.
Adding the xmlsyndication.src file to the build path

11. Your Library path tab should look like Figure 14-12. Click OK in the Properties for IrisReader window to close it.

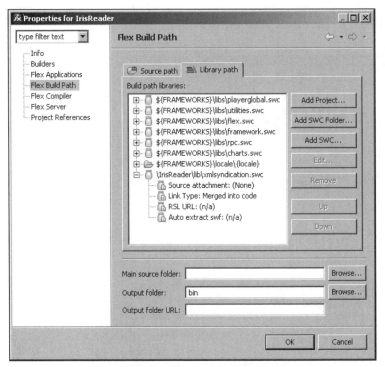

Figure 14-12. Completed Flex build path

If you're using Flex SDK 2, you can just create a lib directory in your chosen project directory and copy the xmlsyndication.swc file into that directory. Then all you need to do is add the xmlsyndication.swc file to the library-path option of the mxmlc compiler, which you can do as part of your compile command. In Windows, type this:

```
mxmlc -library-path+=lib\xmlsyndication.swc -output bin\
IrisReader.swf src\IrisReader.mxml
```

In Mac OS, type this:

```
mxmlc -library-path+=lib/xmlsyndication.swc -output bin/
IrisReader.swf src/IrisReader.mxml
```

Creating the Subscription class

You're going to encapsulate all the information about a subscribed feed in a class named Subscription. The following is the bare minimum information that your feed class will need to contain:

- The URL of the feed
- The title of the title (derived from the feed data)
- The URL of the feed's website (derived from the feed data)
- A list of articles for the feed
- The date the feed was last checked

Armed with this information, you can sketch out the skeleton of your Subscription class.

Right-click (Windows) or Control-click (Mac OS X) the IrisReader project in the Navigator panel and select New ➤ ActionScript Class to open the New ActionScript Class wizard. Enter **com.foundationAS3.ch14. irisreader** in the Package text box and **Subscription** in the Name text box, as shown in Figure 14-13. Click Finish to create the class file and necessary package directories, as shown in Figure 14-14. Flex Builder will automatically open the file, ready for editing.

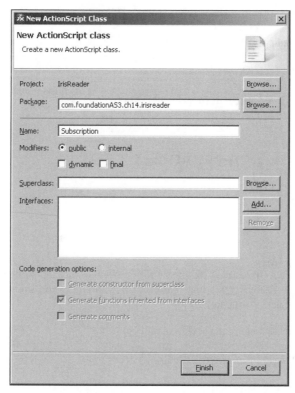

Figure 14-13. Creating the new Subscription class

Figure 14-14. The project directory structure in the Navigator panel showing the new class

If you're a pedant like me, reformat the generated ActionScript 3.0 file so that the opening braces are at the end of the previous line. This is an optional step, and plenty of coders would debate which is the better style (for instance, the Flex source uses next line, but Adobe's ActionScript documentation uses same line). In the code presented here, I'm going to assume you've made this change. You should now have a class that looks like this:

```
package com.foundationAS3.ch14.irisreader {

  public class IrisFeedReader {
  }

}
```

Now you can start to add the properties you need, beginning with feedURL, which is obviously going to be a String. At the moment, I can't see any reason why the URL of the feed will need to be changed from outside the Subscription class, so let's make it private with a public getter function and have the initial value passed through in the constructor.

```
package com.foundationAS3.ch14.irisreader {

  public class Subscription {

    private var _feedURL:String;

    public function Subscription(feedURL:String) {
      _feedURL = feedURL;
    }

    public function get feedURL():String {
      return _feedURL;
    }

  }

}
```

The other properties—title, url, articles, and lastChecked—will need to be visible from outside the Subscription class, but only for reading. With that in mind, let's add them as private variables, with each having a simple getter function.

```
package com.foundationAS3.ch14.irisreader {

  import mx.collections.ArrayCollection;

  public class Subscription {
```

```
private var _feedURL:String;
private var _title:String;
private var _url:String;
private var _articles:ArrayCollection;
private var _lastChecked:Date;

public function Subscription(feedURL:String) {
  _feedURL = feedURL;
  _articles = new ArrayCollection();
}

public function get feedURL():String {
  return _feedURL;
}

public function get title():String {
  return _title;
}

public function get url():String {
  return _url;
}

public function get articles():ArrayCollection {
  return _articles;
}

public function get lastChecked():Date {
  return _lastChecked;
}

  }

}
```

Notice that you're using an ArrayCollection for the articles property rather than a simple Array. This means that you can take advantage of data binding, which is available in the Flex framework's ArrayCollection class, when dealing with the articles list (if you need to), and maybe save yourself a few lines of code later on. You're also initializing the articles property in the constructor so that it's ready to be filled with articles from the feed.

Testing the Subscription class

You have a way to go with the Subscription class, but I get nervous if I go too long without at least testing to check that a class compiles without errors. With that in mind, let's add some script to the IrisReader.mxml file that imports the Subscription class and creates a new instance of it.

Switch to the IrisReader.mxml document in Flex Builder and add an <mx:Script> element after the <mx:Application> tag. This element will allow you to write ActionScript directly into your MXML file.

Add an import statement for the Subscription class, and then create a private variable to hold your test instance. Since you're here, you may as well make that variable an ArrayCollection that will hold all the Subscription objects for your application—there's no sense in adding extra work for yourself, now is there?

```
<mx:Application xmlns:mx="http://www.adobe.com/2006/mxml" layout="vertical">
  <mx:Script>
    <![CDATA[
      import com.foundationAS3.ch14.irisreader.Subscription;
      import mx.collections.ArrayCollection;

      private var _subscriptions:ArrayCollection;
    ]]>
  </mx:Script>
  <mx:HDividedBox width="100%" height="100%">
    <mx:Panel title="Subscriptions" width="40%" height="100%">
    </mx:Panel>
    <mx:VDividedBox width="60%" height="100%">
      <mx:Panel title="Articles" width="100%" height="50%">
      </mx:Panel>
      <mx:Panel title="Article" width="100%" height="50%">
      </mx:Panel>
    </mx:VDividedBox>
  </mx:HDividedBox>
</mx:Application>
```

Again, you've used an ArrayCollection, rather than a simple Array, for its data-binding benefits.

Finally, you need to write the code to initialize the _subscriptions variable and feed it an instance of the Subscription class. This function needs to run once the application is ready to go, so you'll tie it into the creationComplete event of the Application class. You can add a listener for this event directly within the MXML tag for the Application. The handler for the event will be passed an instance of FlexEvent, so you'll import that class as well.

```
<mx:Application xmlns:mx="http://www.adobe.com/2006/mxml" ➥
layout="vertical" creationComplete="onCreationComplete(event)">
  <mx:Script>
    <![CDATA[
      import com.foundationAS3.ch14.irisreader.Subscription;
      import mx.collections.ArrayCollection;
      import mx.events.FlexEvent;

      private var _subscriptions:ArrayCollection;
```

```
            private function onCreationComplete(event:FlexEvent):void {
              _subscriptions = new ArrayCollection();
              _subscriptions.addItem( ➥
      new Subscription("http://foundationas3.org/feed"));
            }
          ]]>
        </mx:Script>
        <mx:HDividedBox width="100%" height="100%">
          <mx:Panel title="Subscriptions" width="40%" height="100%">
          </mx:Panel>
          <mx:VDividedBox width="60%" height="100%">
            <mx:Panel title="Articles" width="100%" height="50%">
            </mx:Panel>
            <mx:Panel title="Article" width="100%" height="50%">
            </mx:Panel>
          </mx:VDividedBox>
        </mx:HDividedBox>
      </mx:Application>
```

With that done (and once you save any changes to the project files), you'll see any compile errors in the Problems panel. If you do see errors, don't fret. Just double-click each error to go to the appropriate line in the source code and see if you can figure out what's wrong.

Loading the data

Let's continue adding functionality to the Subscription class. You still need some way of retrieving the feed data, and you need to make use of the Adobe XML syndication library to process that feed data into something you can use in your application.

> Don't forget to keep saving your files as you proceed, so that Flex Builder can compile your application after each step. Not only will that prevent you from losing too much work should Flex Builder crash, it will detect any errors in your code early, so you can fix them right away.

You'll use the HTTPService class of the Flex framework to load the feed data, so the first thing you need is a private variable of this type that gets initialized with the feed URL in the constructor function.

```
package com.foundationAS3.ch14.irisreader {

  import mx.collections.ArrayCollection;
  import mx.rpc.http.HTTPService;

  public class Subscription {
```

509

```
                private var _feedURL:String;
                private var _title:String;
                private var _url:String;
                private var _articles:ArrayCollection;
                private var _lastChecked:Date;
                private var _service:HTTPService;

                public function Subscription(feedURL:String) {
                  _feedURL = feedURL;
                  _articles = new ArrayCollection();

                  _service = new HTTPService();
                  _service.url = _feedURL;
                }
           . . .
            }
```

By default, the HTTPService class returns its data as an Object, but the XML syndication library will deal only with either an XML object or a string containing the XML data. With that in mind, you need to change the resultFormat property of the _service object to HTTPService.RESULT_FORMAT_E4X so you get the data back in the desired format.

```
           . . .
            public function Subscription(feedURL:String) {
              _feedURL = feedURL;
              _articles = new ArrayCollection();

              _service = new HTTPService();
              _service.url = _feedURL;
              _service.resultFormat = HTTPService.RESULT_FORMAT_E4X;
            }
           . . .
```

Next, you need to add event listeners to the _service object to detect when a response is received from the server and to handle any errors that might occur.

```
            package com.foundationAS3.ch14.irisreader {

            import mx.collections.ArrayCollection;
            import mx.rpc.http.HTTPService;
            import mx.rpc.events.FaultEvent;
            import mx.rpc.events.ResultEvent;
              . . .
                public function Subscription(feedURL:String) {
                  _feedURL = feedURL;
                  _articles = new ArrayCollection();
```

```
            _service = new HTTPService();
            _service.url = _feedURL;
            _service.resultFormat = HTTPService.RESULT_FORMAT_E4X;
            _service.addEventListener(ResultEvent.RESULT, onServiceResult);
            _service.addEventListener(FaultEvent.FAULT, onServiceFault);
        }

        private function onServiceResult(event:ResultEvent):void {
        }

        private function onServiceFault(event:FaultEvent):void {
        }
    . . .
    }
```

With that done, you can turn your attention to fleshing out the onServiceResult() event handler method of the Subscription class. Here is where you use the XML syndication library you went to all that bother to integrate into your project.

Within the generic package of the library, the FeedFactory class analyzes the feed data and parses it into the appropriate object. This class has two static methods: getFeedByString(), for dealing with a String containing XML data, and getFeedbyXML(), for dealing with an XML object. Both functions return an object that implements the IFeed interface (which is also part of the generic package).

> *Interfaces* *are constructs in object-oriented languages that specify a group of methods that a class must implement. This is often described as a "contract" for a class that the class must fulfill. The reason to do this is so that objects of different classes that have different superclasses can all implement a common, known interface. This allows other objects to call methods that are guaranteed to be defined on those classes implementing the interface. The methods in an interface do not contain any body, and therefore have no functionality. The methods exist only to specify which methods a class implementing the interface must define.*
>
> *For example, suppose that you have a* Farmer *class, and a* Farmer *instance must feed both its* Chicken *instances and its* Pig *instances.* Chicken *extends* Bird, *while* Pig *extends* Mammal. *In the case of this farm, the inheritance stops there, without a grand* Animal *class from which all the animals extend. How can the farmer be guaranteed that both the chickens and the pigs will act the same way? An interface solves this problem.*
>
> *You define an interface named* IFeedable *(interfaces usually have a capital I prefix) that specifies an* eat() *method.* Pig *and* Chicken *implement* IFeedable, *which will require them to define an* eat() *method. Then, if the farmer had an array of animals, and that array contained only classes that implemented* IFeedable, *it would not matter whether an index contained a pig or a chicken or whatever—the interface could be used to allow for the* eat() *method to be called without a compile-time error, as in the following code.*
>
> ```
>     for each (animal:IFeedable in animals) {
>       animal.eat();
>     }
> ```

> *Because an interface can be used for a data type just as a class can be used, the* animal
> *variable can be cast to the interface, so* eat() *can be called successfully.*
>
> *Consider needing to check whether an animal actually had an* eat() *method, and having
> to use loose typing with* Object, *and you will begin to appreciate the value of interfaces.*
>
> ```
> for each (animal:Object in animals) {
>   if (animal.hasOwnProperty("eat")) {
>     animal.eat();
>   }
> }
> ```

Import all classes from the com.adobe.xml.syndication.generic package, and add a call to the FeedFactory.getFeedByXML() method in the onServiceResult event handler to parse the resulting XML into a local IFeed object.

```
package com.foundationAS3.ch14.irisreader {

  import mx.collections.ArrayCollection;
  import mx.rpc.http.HTTPService;
  import mx.rpc.events.FaultEvent;
  import mx.rpc.events.ResultEvent;
  import com.adobe.xml.syndication.generic.*;
. . .
    private function onServiceResult(event:ResultEvent):void {
      var feed:IFeed = FeedFactory.getFeedByXML(event.result as XML);
    }
. . .
```

You can now expand the onServiceResult() handler to use the information contained in your feed object, starting with pulling the feed title and URL out of the object's metadata property.

```
. . .
private function onServiceResult(event:ResultEvent):void {
  var feed:IFeed = FeedFactory.getFeedByXML(event.result as XML);

  _title = feed.metadata.title;
  _url = feed.metadata.link;
}
. . .
```

Next, you need to loop through the items array of the feed and add any new items to the articles collection of our Subscription object.

Each element of the items array is an object that implements the IItem interface. This interface has a date property, which is a Date object representing the time the article was posted. All you need to do is compare this date to the lastChecked property of your Subscription object to see if the article is new.

```
. . .
    private function onServiceResult(event:ResultEvent):void {
      var feed:IFeed = FeedFactory.getFeedByXML(event.result as XML);

      _title = feed.metadata.title;
      _url = feed.metadata.link;
      for each (var item:IItem in feed.items) {
        if (lastChecked == null || item.date.getTime() > lastChecked.getTime()) {
          articles.addItem(item);
        }
      }
    }
}
. . .
```

Notice that you add an extra check to the conditional to ensure that lastChecked exists before you call the getTime() method. If lastChecked didn't exist, which would happen when the class is first initialized, then calling getTime() would throw an error.

For this event handler, you need to set the lastChecked property to the current date, so that the next time you refresh the feed, you deal only with articles that have subsequently been added to the feed.

```
. . .
    private function onServiceResult(event:ResultEvent):void {
      var feed:IFeed = FeedFactory.getFeedByXML(event.result as XML);

      _title = feed.metadata.title;
      _url = feed.metadata.link;
      for each (var item:IItem in feed.items) {
        if (lastChecked == null || item.date.getTime() > lastChecked.getTime()) {
          articles.addItem(item);
        }
      }

    _lastChecked = new Date();
}
. . .
```

Now you need to add a public refresh function that can be called to refresh the feed by calling the send() method of the _service object. You also need to call this function internally from the constructor function to fetch the initial feed data.

```
. . .
    public function Subscription(feedURL:String) {
      _feedURL = feedURL;
      _articles = new ArrayCollection();

      _service = new HTTPService();
      _service.url = _feedURL;
      _service.resultFormat = HTTPService.RESULT_FORMAT_E4X;
```

```
      _service.addEventListener(ResultEvent.RESULT, onServiceResult);
      _service.addEventListener(FaultEvent.FAULT, onServiceFault);

    refresh();
  }
. . .
    private function onServiceFault(event:FaultEvent):void {
    }

    public function refresh():void {
      _service.send();
    }

    public function get feedURL():String {
      return _feedURL;
    }
. . .
```

Allowing Subscription instances to be used for data binding

The last thing you need to do with the Subscription class is to prepare it so that it can be used as the source for data binding. This involves marking the relevant parts of the class for data binding and dispatching appropriate events when you change the values.

Since the properties of the Subscription class are read-only, you'll need to manually dispatch propertyChange events to enable them to be used as the source of data-binding expressions. This also means that you need your class to extend EventDispatcher so you can dispatch the necessary events.

Import the EventDispatcher class from the flash.events package and change the class definition so that the Subscription class extends EventDispatcher.

```
. . .
  import mx.rpc.events.ResultEvent;
  import com.adobe.xml.syndication.generic.*;
  import flash.events.EventDispatcher;

public class Subscription extends EventDispatcher {
  . . .
```

Add the [Bindable] metadata tag just before the class definition. This tag informs the Flex compiler that the class will broadcast a change event that can be used for data binding.

```
. . .
  import mx.rpc.events.ResultEvent;
  import com.adobe.xml.syndication.generic.*;
  import flash.events.EventDispatcher;

  [Bindable]
  public class Subscription extends EventDispatcher {
  . . .
```

Since you have a lot of properties that need to dispatch the propertyChange event, let's create a helper function so you don't need to keep repeating the event-dispatching code. This function needs the name of the property that changed, the old value, and the new value, so it can create the PropertyChangeEvent object.

```
. . .
    import mx.rpc.events.ResultEvent;
    import mx.events.PropertyChangeEvent;
    import com.adobe.xml.syndication.generic.*;
    import flash.events.EventDispatcher;

    [Bindable]
    public class Subscription extends EventDispatcher {
. . .
    public function refresh():void {
      _service.send();
    }

    private function notifyPropertyChange(
      name:String,
      oldValue:Object,
      value:Object
    ):void {
      if (value !== oldValue) {
        dispatchEvent(PropertyChangeEvent.createUpdateEvent( ⇒
this, name, oldValue, value));
      }
    }

    public function get feedURL():String {
. . .
```

Notice that the value parameters for this function are of type Object so that they can be passed data of any type. Within the function, you're comparing the old and new values to make sure they are not the same before creating and dispatching the event, since you don't want to invoke the data-binding mechanism if nothing has changed.

Now you need to give each read-only property a private function that you can use to update the value, and then call the notifyPropertyChange() function with the appropriate values. Let's start with feedURL.

```
. . .
    public function get feedURL():String {
      return _feedURL;
    }
    private function setFeedURL(value:String):void {
      var oldValue:Object = _feedURL;
      _feedURL = value;
      notifyPropertyChange("feedURL", oldValue, value);
    }
. . .
```

Here, the setFeedURL() function first stores the old value of the _feedURL property before overwriting it with the value passed it. It then passes the name of the public property along with both these values to the notifypropertyChange function to invoke the data-binding mechanism.

Now add the remaining public properties.

```
. . .
    public function get title():String {
      return _title;
    }
    private function setTitle(value:String):void {
      var oldValue:Object = _title;
      _title = value;
      notifyPropertyChange("title", oldValue, value);
    }

    public function get url():String {
      return _url;
    }
    private function setURL(value:String):void {
      var oldValue:Object = _url;
      _url = value;
      notifyPropertyChange("url", oldValue, value);
    }

    public function get articles():ArrayCollection {
      return this._articles;
    }
    private function setArticles(value:ArrayCollection):void {
      var oldValue:Object = _articles;
      _articles = value;
      notifyPropertyChange("articles", oldValue, value);
    }

    private var _lastChecked:Date;
    public function get lastChecked():Date {
      return this._lastChecked;
    }
    private function setLastChecked(value:Date):void {
      var oldValue:Object = _lastChecked;
      _lastChecked = value;
      notifyPropertyChange("lastChecked", oldValue, value);
    }
. . .
```

Lastly, change the code in the onServiceResult() event handler to use these new functions rather than directly setting the private variable values. This will mean that the appropriate data-binding events will be dispatched and any associated UI controls will be updated.

```
. . .
      private function onServiceResult(event:ResultEvent):void {
        var feed:IFeed = FeedFactory.getFeedByXML(event.result as XML);

        setTitle(feed.metadata.title);
        setURL(feed.metadata.link);
        for each (var item:IItem in feed.items) {
          if (lastChecked == null || item.date.getTime() > lastChecked.getTime()) {
            articles.addItem(item);
          }
        }

        setLastChecked(new Date());
      }
. . .
```

That's it. You're finished with the Subscription class. It's time to turn your attention to hooking up the UI.

Creating the subscriptions list

The list of feeds that a user has subscribed to will be displayed in a simple List control. You already have a private _subscriptions property of the IrisReader.mxml file that will hold the user's Subscription objects, so all you need to do is to create a List control within the Subscriptions panel and bind it to the _subscriptions ArrayCollection.

Add a [Bindable] metatag just before the definition of the _subscriptions variable in the code block in the IrisReader.mxml file. While you're there, add a few more Subscription objects to the _subscriptions collection so that you can see more than one feed.

```
. . .
<mx:Script>
  <![CDATA[
    import mx.collections.ArrayCollection;
    import com.foundationas3.irisreader.Subscription;

    [Bindable]
    private var _subscriptions:ArrayCollection;

    private function onCreationComplete(event:FlexEvent):void {
      _subscriptions = new ArrayCollection();
      _subscriptions.addItem(new Subscription("http://foundationas3.com/feed"));
      _subscriptions.addItem(new Subscription("http://dynamicflash.com/feed"));
      _subscriptions.addItem( ➥
new Subscription("http://weblogs.macromedia.com/mxna/xml/rss.cfm"));
    }
  ]]>
</mx:Script>
. . .
```

Within the Subscriptions `<mx:Panel>` element, add a `List` control with its `dataProvider` property bound to the `_subscriptions` variable. Use `title` as the `labelField`, and set it `width` and `height` to 100%.

```
. . .
<mx:Panel title="Subscriptions" width="40%" height="100%">
  <mx:List id="subscriptionsList" dataProvider="{_subscriptions}" ➡
    labelField="title" width="100%" height="100%"/>
</mx:Panel>
. . .
```

You've given the `List` control an `id` of `subscriptionsList` here because, at some point in the future, you're going to need to get the currently selected entry from that control in order to populate the Articles panel's data grid (shown in Figure 14-1). Any controls you need to refer to from other parts of the code should have `id` attributes. It's possible to refer to them without using IDs, but that's a painful process.

If you test your application now, you should see a list of feeds in the left panel, as shown in Figure 14-15. Once they have loaded, you'll see their titles.

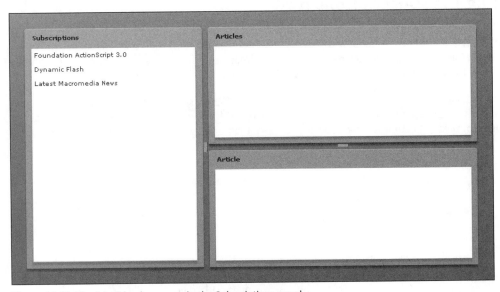

Figure 14-15. The list of feeds appears in the Subscriptions panel.

Before you get drunk on the power of data binding, you should know that a couple of things are amiss here: before the feed data has loaded, each `Subscription` object is shown as [object Subscription] (yuck), and you're not displaying the total number of articles in each feed.

To set these misdemeanors right, you will need to tell the `List` control how you want the label for each item to be rendered, by using a custom label function.

Remove the labelField attribute from the List control and replace it with a labelFunction attribute with a value of renderSubscriptionsListLabel.

```
. . .
<mx:Panel title="Subscriptions" width="40%" height="100%">
  <mx:List id="subscriptionsList" dataProvider="{_subscriptions}"
    labelFunction="renderSubscriptionsListLabel"
    width="100%" height="100%"/>
</mx:Panel>
. . .
```

Now you need to create the renderSubscriptionsListLabel() function in the <mx:Script> block. Label-renderer functions get passed the object for a given item in the list and should return a String of the label to be displayed. In this case, you want to test to see if the title of the Subscription object passed in is null, and if it is, display the feedURL property instead of the title. In any case, you also want to add the number of items in the feed after the URL or title in brackets. That all translates into a function that looks like this:

```
. . .
<mx:Script>
  <![CDATA[
    import mx.collections.ArrayCollection;
    import com.foundationas3.irisreader.Subscription;

    [Bindable]
    private var _subscriptions:ArrayCollection;

    private function onCreationComplete(event:FlexEvent):void {
      _subscriptions = new ArrayCollection();
      _subscriptions.addItem(new Subscription("http://foundationas3.com/feed"));
      _subscriptions.addItem(new Subscription("http://dynamicflash.com/feed"));
      _subscriptions.addItem( ➥
new Subscription("http://weblogs.macromedia.com/mxna/xml/rss.cfm"));
    }

    private function renderSubscriptionsListLabel( ➥
subscription:Subscription):String {
        var title:String = subscription.title;
        if (title == null) {
          title = subscription.feedURL;
        }
        title += " (" + subscription.articles.length + ")";
        return title;
    }
  ]]>
</mx:Script>
. . .
```

If you test the application now, you should see the feed URLs displayed in lieu of titles before the feed data is loaded, and each entry shows the number of items in that feed in brackets, as shown in Figure 14-16.

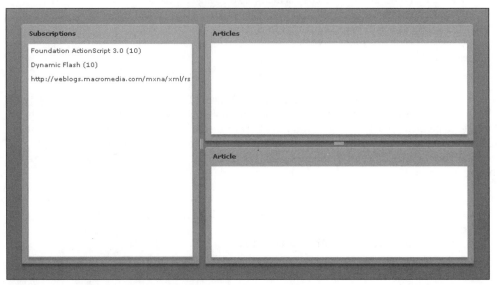

Figure 14-16. The list of feeds fixed to show URLs before data is loaded and the number of items in each feed

You'll come back to the Subscriptions panel later on to add the additional controls shown in Figure 14-1. Now let's get the basics of the other panels working.

Creating the articles data grid

From the wireframe you can see that the articles for a feed are displayed in a DataGrid control with two columns, showing the date and title of each article. You're going to use data binding to display the articles from the Subscription object currently selected in the subscriptions list.

Within the Articles <mx:Panel> element, add a 100% width and height DataGrid control with two columns. displaying the date and title properties of each item in the articles collection.

```
. . .
<mx:Panel title="Articles" width="100%" height="50%">
  <mx:DataGrid id="articlesGrid" width="100%" height="100%">
    <mx:columns>
      <mx:DataGridColumn dataField="date" headerText="Date"/>
      <mx:DataGridColumn dataField="title" headerText="Title"/>
    </mx:columns>
  </mx:DataGrid>
</mx:Panel>
. . .
```

Once again, you've given this control an id attribute so you can refer to it later in the code (specifically, for populating the Article panel with information about the currently selected entry in the data grid).

Next, add a dataProvider property to the DataGrid object with the value shown:

```
. . .
<mx:Panel title="Articles" width="100%" height="50%">
  <mx:DataGrid id="articlesGrid" width="100%" height="100%"
    dataProvider="{subscriptionsList.selectedItem.articles}" >
    <mx:columns>
      <mx:DataGridColumn dataField="date" headerText="Date"/>
      <mx:DataGridColumn dataField="title" headerText="Title"/>
    </mx:columns>
  </mx:DataGrid>
</mx:Panel>
. . .
```

Go ahead and test your application now. Once the feeds have loaded, select each one in turn and marvel once again at the magic of data binding. Figure 14-17 shows an example.

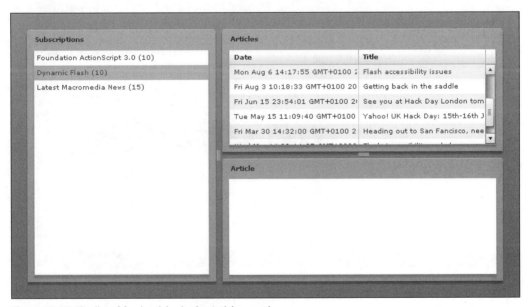

Figure 14-17. The list of feed articles in the Articles panel

But look again, and you'll see that something is not quite right with the way the application is working. According to the wireframe shown in Figure 14-1, the title of the Articles panel should change to be the title of the currently selected item in the subscriptions list. Luckily, you can use data binding to get around that, too.

Change the value of the title attribute of the Articles Panel component to match the following:

```
. . .
<mx:Panel title="{subscriptionsList.selectedItem.title}"
  width="100%" height="50%">
  <mx:DataGrid id="articlesGrid" width="100%" height="100%"
    dataProvider="{subscriptionsList.selectedItem.articles}" >
    <mx:columns>
      <mx:DataGridColumn dataField="date" headerText="Date"/>
      <mx:DataGridColumn dataField="title" headerText="Title"/>
    </mx:columns>
  </mx:DataGrid>
</mx:Panel>
. . .
```

Test the application again, and the results should look something like Figure 14-18.

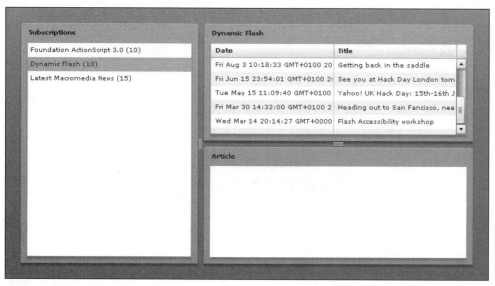

Figure 14-18. The Articles panel shows the title of the feed selected in the subscriptions list.

You still have a little work to do on the Articles panel. The date format looks a little funky, and you're missing the last updated timestamp and a button to take the user to the website. But for now, let's move on to populating the Article panel.

Populating the Article panel

The majority of the Article panel is taken up by a TextArea control that displays the excerpt of the currently selected item in the articlesGrid control. Let's add that now.

Add a 100% width and height TextArea control as a child of the Article <mx:Panel> container, and set the editable property to false (since there's no sense in allowing the user to change what's displayed in this control).

```
. . .
<mx:Panel title="Article" width="100%" height="50%">
  <mx:TextArea id="excerptTextArea" editable="false"
    width="100%" height="100%"/>
</mx:Panel>
. . .
```

Yet again, you've added an id attribute, and you should know why by now.

Set the htmlText property of the new TextArea control to be bound to the excerpt.value property of the currently selected item in the articlesGrid control.

```
. . .
<mx:Panel title="Article" width="100%" height="50%">
  <mx:TextArea id="excerptTextArea" editable="false"
    width="100%" height="100%"
    htmlText="{articlesGrid.selectedItem.excerpt.value}" />
</mx:Panel>
. . .
```

You've used excerpt.value because excerpt is an object with several properties. In this case you're interested in only the value property, so you read that directly. Flex Builder will warn you that it won't be able to detect assignments to the value property, and there's nothing you can do about that, since it's an internal part of the XML syndication library, which doesn't seem to have been built with data binding in mind. However, it doesn't affect the functionality of the completed application.

You know that the title of the Article panel should be the title of the currently selected item from the articlesGrid control, so let's set up that next. Change the value of the title attribute of the Article panel to be bound to the title property of the currently selected item from the articlesGrid control.

```
. . .
<mx:Panel title="{articlesGrid.selectedItem.title}"
  width="100%" height="50%">
  <mx:TextArea id="excerptTextArea" editable="false"
    width="100%" height="100%"
    htmlText="{articlesGrid.selectedItem.excerpt.value}" />
</mx:Panel>
. . .
```

Now test your application's newfound ability to display the excerpt from the selected item in the Article panel. The result should look something like Figure 14-19.

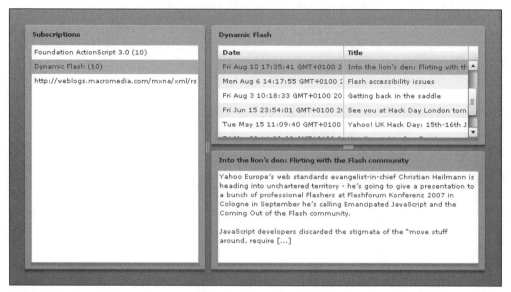

Figure 14-19. The Article panel shows an excerpt of the article selected in the Articles list.

Go ahead and take a break. When you're ready, you'll start fine-tuning the panels.

Completing the Subscriptions panel

Although your application is technically working, you still have a way to go to satisfy the requirements drawn up earlier in the chapter. The most glaring omission at the moment is that the subscriptions are hard-coded, which is no good unless you fancy recompiling the application every time you want to add or remove a feed. Let's fix that now.

Allowing users to subscribe to a feed

If you glance back at the application's UI in Figure 14-1, you'll see add/remove buttons below the list of subscribed feeds, which allow the users to manage their subscriptions. The section on interaction design mentioned that a dialog box should be shown when the user clicks the add button, but the dialog box wasn't part of the original wireframe. Figure 14-20 shows how that dialog box should appear.

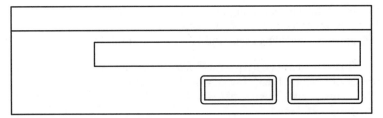

Figure 14-20. The dialog box for adding a feed

This is a very simple dialog box with a Label, a TextArea, and a couple of Button controls, all neatly wrapped in a TitleWindow container. You need to create this as a component that you can then reference in your application to be opened as a modal window.

Laying out the SubscribeDialog component

Let's begin by creating the new component and setting up its basic layout.

Right-click (Windows) or Control-click (Mac OS X) the IrisReader project in the Navigator panel of Flex Builder and select New ➤ MXML Component from the context menu. In the New MXML Component dialog box, enter **SubscribeDialog** in the Filename text box and pick TitleWindow from the Based on drop-down list. Select vertical from the Layout drop-down list, and enter **300** in the Width text box. Clear the value from the Height text box (so that the height of the dialog box will be based on its content). Your dialog box should look like Figure 14-21. Click Finish to create the component.

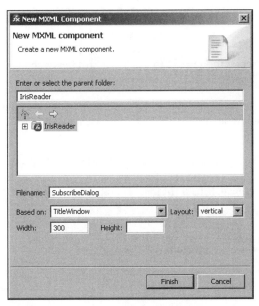

Figure 14-21. Creating the SubscribeDialog component

Now you have a new MXML file containing the values you selected for the TitleWindow container. In that file, set the title property of the TitleWindow container to "Subscribe to feed". Then add a 100% width HBox container containing Label and TextInput controls with the following configurations:

```
<mx:TitleWindow xmlns:mx="http://www.adobe.com/2006/mxml"
  title="Subscribe to feed" layout="vertical" width="300">
  <mx:HBox width="100%" verticalAlign="middle">
    <mx:Label text="Feed URL"/>
    <mx:TextInput id="feedURL" width="100%"/>
  </mx:HBox>
</mx:TitleWindow>
```

Add another HBox as a sibling of the previous one. It contains the two Button controls for the dialog box.

```
<mx:TitleWindow xmlns:mx="http://www.adobe.com/2006/mxml"
  title="Subscribe to feed" layout="vertical" width="300">
  <mx:HBox width="100%" verticalAlign="middle">
    <mx:Label text="Feed URL"/>
    <mx:TextInput id="feedURL" width="100%"/>
  </mx:HBox>
  <mx:HBox width="100%" horizontalAlign="right">
    <mx:Button id="okButton" label="OK"/>
    <mx:Button id="cancelButton" label="Cancel"/>
  </mx:HBox>
</mx:TitleWindow>
```

Now the main layout for the SubscribeDialog component is complete.

Wiring up the buttons

Next, you need to add the necessary buttons to the Subscriptions panel and wire up the subscribe button so that it opens the SubscribeDialog component you just created.

Switch back to the IrisReader.mxml file and add a ControlBar container below the List control in the Subscriptions <mx:Panel> container, containing the subscribe and unsubscribe buttons:

```
. . .
<mx:Panel title="Subscriptions" width="40%" height="100%">
  <mx:List id="subscriptionsList" dataProvider="{_subscriptions}"
    labelFunction="renderSubscriptionsListLabel"
    width="100%" height="100%"/>
  <mx:ControlBar>
    <mx:Button id="subscribeButton" label="+"/>
    <mx:Button id="unsubscribeButton" label="-"/>
  </mx:ControlBar>
</mx:Panel>
. . .
```

To make the subscribe button open the dialog box, you need to add a click event handler for the subscribeButton component. While you're there, you may as well do the same for the unsubscribeButton component. Have them call functions named subscribe and unsubscribe, respectively. You'll create those functions next.

```
. . .
<mx:Panel title="Subscriptions" width="40%" height="100%">
  <mx:List id="subscriptionsList" dataProvider="{_subscriptions}"
    labelFunction="renderSubscriptionsListLabel"
    width="100%" height="100%"/>
  <mx:ControlBar>
    <mx:Button id="subscribeButton" label="+"
      click="subscribe(event)"/>
    <mx:Button id="unsubscribeButton" label="-"
      click="unsubscribe(event)"/>
  </mx:ControlBar>
</mx:Panel>
. . .
```

Create the subscribe() and unsubscribe() functions, adding them to the bottom of the <mx:Script/> block in the IrisReader.mxml file.

```
    . . .
      return title;
    }

    private function subscribe(event:MouseEvent):void {
    }

    private function unsubscribe(event:MouseEvent):void {
    }
  ]]>
</mx:Script>
. . .
```

Import the PopUpManager class from the mx.managers package and use it in the subscribe() function to create a modal window from your SubscribeDialog component. You'll also call PopUpManager's centerPopUp() method to center the dialog box within the application window.

```
. . .
import mx.events.FlexEvent;
import mx.managers.PopUpManager;
. . .
private function subscribe(event:MouseEvent):void {
  var dialog:SubscribeDialog = PopUpManager.createPopUp(this, ➥
SubscribeDialog, true) as SubscribeDialog;
  PopUpManager.centerPopUp(dialog);
}
. . .
```

If you test the application now and click the new subscribe button in the Subscriptions panel, you should see the dialog box you just created pop up in the center of the screen, as shown in Figure 14-22.

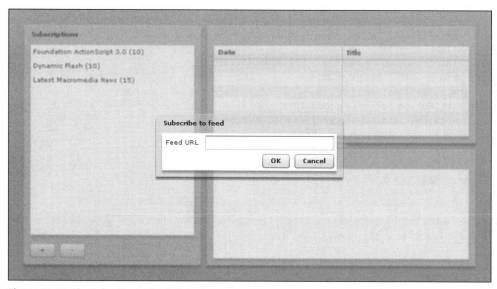

Figure 14-22. The Subscribe to feed dialog box

This dialog box doesn't actually do much at the moment. You can't even close it once it has been opened. But it's a start.

Next, you need to wire up the OK and Cancel buttons so they at least close the dialog box. You can do that by using various methods of the PopUpManager class in response to the button clicks.

Switch back to the SubscribeDialog.mxml file in Flex Builder and add in an <mx:Script> element at the top. Then import the PopUpManager class from the mx.managers package.

```
<mx:TitleWindow xmlns:mx="http://www.adobe.com/2006/mxml"
  title="Subscribe to feed" layout="vertical" width="300">
  <mx:Script>
    <![CDATA[
      import mx.managers.PopUpManager;

    ]]>
  </mx:Script>
  <mx:HBox width="100%" verticalAlign="middle">
```

To close the dialog box, you need to use the PopUpManager.removePopUp() method, passing a reference to this so it knows which window to close. You'll do this in click event handlers for the two buttons.

```
<mx:TitleWindow xmlns:mx="http://www.adobe.com/2006/mxml"
  title="Subscribe to feed" layout="vertical" width="300"
  <mx:Script>
    <![CDATA[
      import mx.managers.PopUpManager;

      private function onOKButtonClick(event:MouseEvent):void {
        PopUpManager.removePopUp(this);
      }

      private function onCancelButtonClick(event:MouseEvent):void {
        PopUpManager.removePopUp(this);
      }
    ]]>
  </mx;Script>
  <mx:HBox width="100%" verticalAlign="middle">
  . . .
  <mx:HBox width="100%" horizontalAlign="right">
    <mx:Button id="okButton" label="OK"
      click="onOKButtonClick(event)"/>
    <mx:Button id="cancelButton" label="Cancel"
      click="onCancelButtonClick(event)"/>
  </mx:HBox>
</mx:TitleWindow>
```

With that done, you should now be able to close the dialog box by clicking either the OK or Cancel button.

That's not the end of the story, however. You still need to be able to get the feed URL from the dialog box and create a new Subscription object for it when the user clicks the OK button.

Getting the feed

To get the new feed, you'll create an Event class to hold the feed URL and dispatch this event when the dialog box is being closed. Then you will have the main IrisReader class listen for this event being dispatched and act accordingly.

Right-click (Windows) or Control-click (Windows) the IrisReader project in the Navigator panel and select New ➤ ActionScript Class from the context menu. In the New ActionScript Class dialog box, enter details for a class named SubscribeDialogEvent in the com.foundationAS3.ch14.irisreader.events package, with Event as the superclass, as shown in Figure 14-23. Click Finish to create the new class.

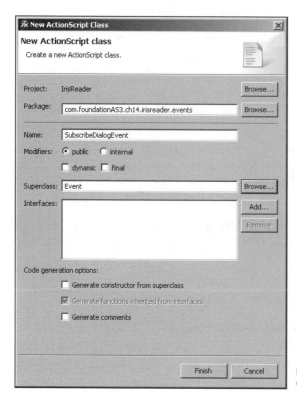

Figure 14-23.
Creating the SubscribeDialogEvent class

In the newly created SubscribeDialogEvent.as file, add a constructor function that accepts the event type and feed URL, both as Strings, as well as the bubbles and cancelable properties, and passes these to the superclass Event constructor.

```
package com.foundationAS3.ch14.irisreader.events {

    import flash.events.Event;

    public class SubscribeDialogEvent extends Event {

        public function SubscribeDialogEvent(
            type:String,
            feedURL:String,
            bubbles:Boolean=false,
            cancelable:Boolean=false
        ) {
            super(type, bubbles, cancelable);
        }

    }

}
```

Create a read-only feedURL property, and modify the constructor to store the feedURL parameter in this property.

```
package com.foundationAS3.ch14.irisreader.events {

  import flash.events.Event;

  public class SubscribeDialogEvent extends Event {

    private var _feedURL:String;

    public function SubscribeDialogEvent(
      type:String,
      feedURL:String,
      bubbles:Boolean=false,
      cancelable:Boolean=false
    ) {
      super(type, bubbles, cancelable);
      _feedURL = feedURL;
    }

    public function get feedURL():String {
      return _feedURL;
    }

  }

}
```

Finally, add a public static constant to represent the event type. The constant name is completely arbitrary but is generally a verb, so let's call it SUBSCRIBE. You also need to override Event's clone() method, which should be done for any child class of Event.

```
package com.foundationAS3.ch14.irisreader.events {

  import flash.events.Event;

  public class SubscribeDialogEvent extends Event {

    public static const SUBSCRIBE:String = "subscribe";
    private var _feedURL:String;

    public function SubscribeDialogEvent(
      type:String,
      feedURL:String,
      bubbles:Boolean=false,
      cancelable:Boolean=false
    ) {
```

```
        super(type, bubbles, cancelable);
        _feedURL = feedURL;
      }

      override public function clone():Event {
        return new SubscribeDialogEvent(type, feedURL, bubbles, cancelable);
      }

      public function get feedURL():String {
        return _feedURL;
      }

    }

  }
```

Next, modify the onOKButtonClick() method of the SubscribeDialog to dispatch your new event before the dialog box is closed, passing the text from the feedURL control as the feedURL parameter.

```
. . .
      import mx.managers.PopUpManager;
      import com.foundationAS3.ch14.irisreader.events.SubscribeDialogEvent;

      private function onOKButtonClick(event:MouseEvent):void {
        dispatchEvent(new SubscribeDialogEvent( ➥
SubscribeDialogEvent.SUBSCRIBE, feedURL.text));
        PopUpManager.removePopUp(this);
      }
. . .
```

In the subscribe() method in the IrisReader.mxml file, you need to listen for the subscribe event of the SubscribeDialog, and when it has fired, add a new Subscription object to the _subscriptions array using the feedURL that is included as part of the event data.

```
. . .
      import mx.managers.PopUpManager;
      import com.foundationAS3.ch14.irisreader.events.SubscribeDialogEvent;

      [Bindable]
      private var _subscriptions:ArrayCollection;
. . .
```

```
    private function subscribe(event:MouseEvent):void {
        var dialog:SubscribeDialog = PopUpManager.createPopUp(this, ⇒
SubscribeDialog, true) as SubscribeDialog;
        PopUpManager.centerPopUp(dialog);
        dialog.addEventListener(SubscribeDialogEvent.SUBSCRIBE, ⇒
onSubscribeDialogSubscribe);
    }

    private function unsubscribe(event:MouseEvent):void {

    }

    private function onSubscribeDialogSubscribe( ⇒
event:SubscribeDialogEvent):void {
        _subscriptions.addItem(new Subscription(event.feedURL));
    }
    . . .
```

That's all that needs to be done to allow users to add their own subscriptions. Give it a try using feed URLs from your favorite blogs or news sites. Figures 14-24 and 14-25 show an example of adding a subscription.

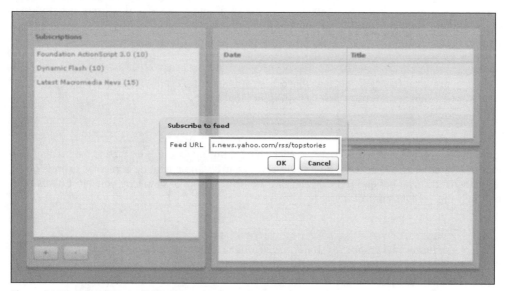

Figure 14-24. Subscribing to Yahoo! News feed

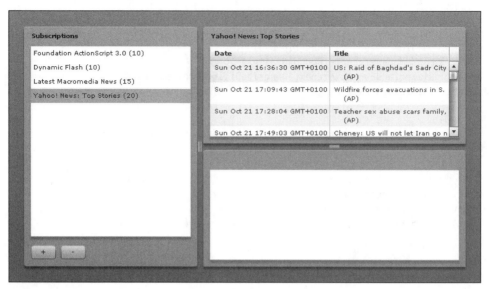

Figure 14-25. Yahoo! News has been added to the subscriptions list

Before moving on to the unsubscribe functionality, you need to tidy up a couple of subscription areas. First, a number of hard-coded subscriptions are in the application, and now that users can add their own subscriptions, you can get rid of the hard-coded ones. Change the init() method of the IrisReader.mxml file to remove the creation of the three Subscription objects.

```
. . .
        private function onCreationComplete(event:FlexEvent):void {
          _subscriptions = new ArrayCollection();
        }
. . .
```

Another slight problem is that the user can click the OK button in the Subscribe to feed dialog box without having entered a feed URL. You could solve that by implementing a regular expression to check that what the user has entered is a valid URL, but for the sake of simplicity, you'll just disable the OK button if the feedURL control is empty.

> *If this were a production-quality application being developed for a client, I would definitely make sure the URL entered was a valid URL. Depending on the requirements, I might even go so far as loading the contents of the URL to check that it is a valid feed before allowing the user to click the OK button.*

In the SubscribeDialog.mxml file, bind the enabled property of the OK button using a data-binding expression to check that the length of the feedURL control's text property is greater than zero.

```
<mx:Button id="okButton" label="OK" click="onOKButtonClick(event)" ➥
  enabled="{feedURL.text.length > 0}"/>
```

Allowing users to unsubscribe from a feed

Now that users can subscribe to a feed, they'll need some way of unsubscribing if the feed becomes boring (or, like mine, dormant for long periods of time). You already have a button in the Subscriptions panel for this purpose, and it's wired up to the unsubscribe method. So, all you need to do is to remove the selected item in the list from the _subscriptions collection when this button is clicked.

In the IrisReader.mxml file, modify the unsubscribe() method to remove the currently selected item in the subscriptionsList control from the _subscriptions collection.

```
    . . .
        private function unsubscribe(event:MouseEvent):void {
          _subscriptions.removeItemAt(subscriptionsList.selectedIndex);
        }
    . . .
```

You're removing the selected item by index in the list because the ArrayCollection class doesn't have a removeItem method. It just has a removeItemAt method.

To tidy up, you want the unsubscribe button enabled only if there is something selected in the _subscriptions list. To handle this, bind the enabled property of the unsubscribeButton using a data-binding expression that checks the selectedItem property of the subscriptionsList control to make sure it's not null.

```
    . . .
    <mx:Button id="unsubscribeButton" label="-"click="unsubscribe(event)"
      enabled="{subscriptionsList.selectedItem !== null}"/>
    . . .
```

Users can now add and remove subscriptions at their leisure. However, if they restart the application, all of their subscriptions are lost. Since one of the requirements was that the application remember the subscriptions list between sessions, let's tackle that now.

Saving the subscriptions list between sessions

As a Flex developer, you have basically two choices for data storage: store the data on the client in a local SharedObject or store it on the server using one of the variety of remote communication protocols that Flex supports. Since this section of the book is about Flex application development, you're going to go with the former approach. Local SharedObjects aren't without their limitations, though. They're the Flash equivalent of browser cookies, and like cookies, they can store only a limited amount of information. With this in mind, the plan is to store only a list of URLs for the user's subscriptions list, rather than the Subscription objects themselves and all the articles they contain.

Let's start by creating a function to save the subscriptions list to a local SharedObject.

In the IrisReader.mxml file, import the SharedObject class from the flash.net package, and then create a new function named saveData() that initially loads the local SharedObject named IrisReader.

```
import mx.managers.PopUpManager;
import com.foundationAS3.ch14.irisreader.events.SubscribeDialogEvent;
import flash.net.SharedObject;
. . .
private function unsubscribe(event:MouseEvent):void {
  _subscriptions.removeItemAt(subscriptionsList.selectedIndex);
}

private function saveData():void {
  var so:SharedObject = SharedObject.getLocal("IrisReader");
}
. . .
```

Create a new feedURLs array, and then loop through all the Subscription objects in the _subscriptions collection and add the feedURL property of each to the feedURLs array.

```
. . .
private function saveData():void {
  var so:SharedObject = SharedObject.getLocal("IrisReader");
  var feedURLs:Array = new Array();
  for each (var subscription:Subscription in _subscriptions) {
    feedURLs.push(subscription.feedURL);
  }
}
. . .
```

Finally, add the feedURLs array to the data property of the so object and call the flush() method to write the data to disk.

```
. . .
private function saveData():void {
  var so:SharedObject = SharedObject.getLocal("IrisReader");
  var feedURLs:Array = new Array();
  for each (var subscription:Subscription in _subscriptions) {
    feedURLs.push(subscription.feedURL);
  }
  so.data.feedURLs = feedURLs;
  so.flush();
}
. . .
```

With that done, you need an equivalent function to get the feed URLs from the SharedObject and re-create the _subscriptions collection. Create a function named loadData() that initially clears the _subscriptions collection and then loads the local SharedObject named IrisReader.

```
. . .
        so.data.feedURLs = feedURLs;
        so.flush();
    }

    private function loadData():void {
      _subscriptions.removeAll();
      var so:SharedObject = SharedObject.getLocal("IrisReader");
    }
. . .
```

After checking to make sure the feedURLs array exists as part of the SharedObject's data (which is necessary because it won't exist the first time the user uses the application), loop through all the entries and create a Subscription object for each one, adding it to the _subscriptions collection.

```
. . .
    private function loadData():void {
      _subscriptions.removeAll();
      var so:SharedObject = SharedObject.getLocal("IrisReader");
      if (so.data.feedURLs) {
        for each (var feedURL:String in so.data.feedURLs) {
          _subscriptions.addItem(new Subscription(feedURL));
        }
      }
    }
. . .
```

With these functions ready to go, you'll load the data when the application starts and save the data whenever it changes. Loading the subscriptions list when the application starts can be taken care of in the handler for the application's creationComplete event. Saving the data can be done whenever a new feed is added or removed in the onSubscribeDialogSubscribe() and unsubscribe() methods.

Add a call to the loadData() method just after the initialization of the _subscriptions collection in the onCreationComplete() method of the IrisReader.mxml file.

```
. . .
    private function onCreationComplete(event:FlexEvent):void {
      _subscriptions = new ArrayCollection();
      loadData();
    }
. . .
```

Next, add calls to saveData() in both the onSubscribeDialogSubscribe() and unsubscribe() methods.

```
    . . .
        private function unsubscribe(event:MouseEvent):void {
          _subscriptions.removeItemAt(subscriptionsList.selectedIndex);
          saveData();
        }
    . . .
        private function onSubscribeDialogSubscribe( ➥
    event:SubscribeDialogEvent):void {
            _subscriptions.addItem(new Subscription(event.feedURL));
            saveData();
        }
    . . .
```

And that's another feature you can check off your list. If you run the application now, subscribe to a few feeds, and then restart the application, you should see your feed list reloaded. Nice.

At this point, you're almost finished the Subscriptions panel, with one last feature to add.

Refreshing the subscriptions list

Of course, the users will want to see updates to their feeds. Let's take care of that now.

Automatically refreshing the subscriptions list

The big feature the feed reader application is missing is automatic checking of the subscriptions list and fetching of new articles. Users won't want to need to repeatedly click a refresh button just to see if there have been any updates to their favorite feeds. Let's get the feed to automatically refresh itself every 5 minutes.

Create a function named refreshAll() in the IrisReader.mxml file that loops through all the Subscription objects in the _subscriptions collection and calls their refresh methods.

```
    . . .
          }
        }

        private function refreshAll(event:Event):void {
          for each (var subscription:Subscription in _subscriptions) {
            subscription.refresh();
          }
        }

        private function onSubscribeDialogSubscribe( ➥
    event:SubscribeDialogEvent):void {
            _subscriptions.addItem(new Subscription(event.feedURL));
            saveData();
        }
    . . .
```

Now create a new private variable named refreshTimer to hold the Timer object and initialize the timer in the onCreationComplete() function. While you're there, add an event listener for the TimerEvent.TIMER event.

```
. . .
        import com.foundationAS3.ch14.irisreader.events.SubscribeDialogEvent;
        import flash.net.SharedObject;
        import flash.utils.Timer;
        import flash.events.TimerEvent;

        [Bindable]
        private var _subscriptions:ArrayCollection;
        private var _refreshTimer:Timer;

        private function onCreationComplete(event:FlexEvent):void {
          _subscriptions = new ArrayCollection();
          loadData();

          _refreshTimer = new Timer(5 * 60 * 1000);
          _refreshTimer.addEventListener(TimerEvent.TIMER, onRefreshTimer);
          _refreshTimer.start();
        }
. . .
```

Now add the onRefreshTimer() event handler function, which just needs to call the refreshAll() method you wrote earlier.

```
. . .
        private function refreshAll(event:Event):void {
          for each (var subscription:Subscription in _subscriptions) {
            subscription.refresh();
          }
        }

        private function onRefreshTimer(event:TimerEvent):void {
          refreshAll(event);
        }
. . .
```

That handles automatic refreshing. Now let's allow for manual updates,

Manually refreshing the subscriptions list

You can finish the Subscriptions panel by adding some buttons to allow the users to manually refresh the selected feed or all feeds in their subscriptions list.

In the IrisReader.mxml file, add a Label and two Button controls to the ControlBar container within the Subscriptions Panel component and give them appropriate labels. Add a 100% width Spacer to push the subscription buttons over to the right side of the control bar.

```
<mx:Panel title="Subscriptions" width="40%" height="100%">
  <mx:List id="subscriptionsList" dataProvider="{_subscriptions}"
    labelFunction="renderSubscriptionsListLabel"
    width="100%" height="100%"/>
  <mx:ControlBar>
    <mx:Label text="Refresh: "/>
    <mx:Button label="Selected"/>
    <mx:Button label="All"/>
    <mx:Spacer width="100%"/>
    <mx:Button id="subscribeButton" label="+"
      click="subscribe(event)"/>
    <mx:Button id="unsubscribeButton" label="-"
      click="unsubscribe(event)"
      enabled="{subscriptionsList.selectedItem !== null}"/>
  </mx:ControlBar>
</mx:Panel>
```

Add a click handler to the All button, which calls the refreshAll() function you created earlier.

```
<mx:Button label="All" click="refreshAll(event)"/>
```

Add a click handler to the Selected button, which calls a function named refreshSelected() (you'll create that in a moment). While you're there, bind the enabled property of this button using a data-binding expression to check that the selectedItem property of the subscriptionsList control isn't null.

```
<mx:Button label="Selected" click="refreshSelected(event)"
  enabled="{subscriptionsList.selectedItem !== null}"/>
```

Create the refreshSelected() function, which needs to cast the selectedItem property of the subscriptionsList control as a Subscription object and then call its refresh method.

```
private function refreshAll(event:Event):void {
  for each (var subscription:Subscription in _subscriptions) {
    subscription.refresh();
  }
}

private function refreshSelected(event:Event):void {
  (subscriptionsList.selectedItem as Subscription).refresh();
}
```

If you test your application, you should be able to refresh all subscriptions or just the selected feeds using the buttons you've just added, which are shown in Figure 14-26.

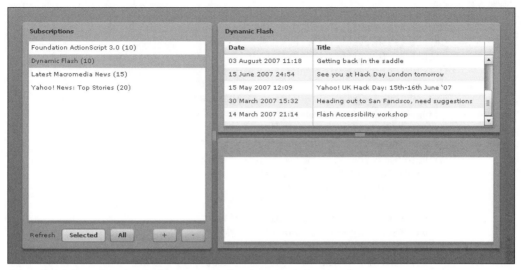

Figure 14-26. The Selected and All buttons added to the Subscriptions panel

You'll be glad to know that you're now finished with the Subscriptions panel. However, you could make some improvements, as I'll suggest at the end of the chapter.

Completing the Articles and Article panels

The hard work is complete. Now you just need to add some finishing touches to the Articles and Article panels.

Finishing the Articles panel

The Articles panel is actually very nearly complete. If you look at the original UI design (Figure 14-1), all that's missing is a label showing when the feed was last checked and a button to take users to the website for the feed.

However, before you get to those items, you have a little housework to do. The display formats for the dates in the application are not what you would call human-friendly. To make the dates prettier, you need to create a DateFormatter object and use this to render all the dates in the application.

Add a new private DateFormatter variable to the IrisReader.mxml file and initialize this variable in the init method to use DD MMM YYYY HH:MM as its format. This will display dates in a format like 25 Dec 2007 18:47.

```
. . .
        import flash.utils.Timer;
        import flash.events.TimerEvent;
        import mx.formatters.DateFormatter;

        [Bindable]
        private var _subscriptions:ArrayCollection;
        private var _refreshTimer:Timer;
        private var _dateFormatter:DateFormatter;

        private function onCreationComplete(event:FlexEvent):void {
          _subscriptions = new ArrayCollection();
          _loadData();

          _dateFormatter = new DateFormatter();
          _dateFormatter.formatString = "DD MMM YYYY HH:NN";

          _refreshTimer = new Timer(5 * 60 * 1000);
          _refreshTimer.addEventListener(TimerEvent.TIMER, onRefreshTimer);
          _refreshTimer.start();
        }
. . .
```

Now create a new private function that accepts a string and returns that string formatted using your
DateFormatter instance.

```
. . .
        private function onCreationComplete(event:FlexEvent):void {
          _subscriptions = new ArrayCollection();
          _loadData();

          _dateFormatter = new DateFormatter();
          _dateFormatter.formatString = "DD MMM YYYY HH:NN";

          _refreshTimer = new Timer(5 * 60 * 1000);
          _refreshTimer.addEventListener(TimerEvent.TIMER, onRefreshTimer);
          _refreshTimer.start();
        }

        private function formatDate(date:String):String {
          return _dateFormatter.format(date);
        }
. . .
```

Add a `ControlBar` container to the `Articles` panel containing a `Label` and a `Text` control. Bind the text property of the `Text` control to the `lastChecked` property of the currently selected `Subscription` object in the `subscriptionsList` control, formatting it by calling your new `formatDate()` method.

```
. . .
      <mx:Panel title="{subscriptionsList.selectedItem.title}"
        width="100%" height="50%">
        <mx:DataGrid id="articlesGrid" width="100%" height="100%"
          dataProvider="{subscriptionsList.selectedItem.articles}" >
          <mx:columns>
            <mx:DataGridColumn dataField="date" headerText="Date"/>
            <mx:DataGridColumn dataField="title" headerText="Title"/>
          </mx:columns>
        </mx:DataGrid>
        <mx:ControlBar>
          <mx:Label text="Last checked:"/>
          <mx:Text text= ➡
  "{formatDate(subscriptionsList.selectedItem.lastChecked)}"/>
        </mx:ControlBar>
      </mx:Panel>
. . .
```

That takes care of the last-checked date display and format, as shown in Figure 14-27, but what about the values in the Date column of the `articlesGrid` control? You can use a custom label function to render these dates using the same `DateFormatter` object.

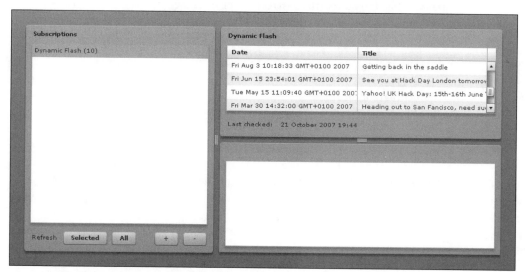

Figure 14-27. The last-checked date properly formatted

Set the labelFunction property of the DataGridColumn instance representing the Date column of the articlesGrid control to renderArticlesGridDate(). While you're there, set the width of the column to 150, since you won't need so much space for the date once it has been property formatted.

```
. . .
        <mx:DataGrid id="articlesGrid" width="100%" height="100%"
          dataProvider="{subscriptionsList.selectedItem.articles}">
          <mx:columns>
            <mx:DataGridColumn dataField="date" headerText="Date"
              labelFunction="renderArticlesGridDate" width="150"/>
            <mx:DataGridColumn dataField="title" headerText="Title"/>
          </mx:columns>
        </mx:DataGrid>
. . .
```

Now create the renderArticlesGridDate() function to return the formatted date. Label-renderer functions for DataGrid controls receive references to the item currently being rendered and the DataGridColumn in question. In this case. the current item will be an IItem object from the com.adobe.xml.syndication.generic.IItem package, which has a date property that you need to format. You need to feed this date to the format method of your DateFormatter object and return the resultant string.

```
. . .
        import flash.events.TimerEvent;
        import mx.formatters.DateFormatter;
        import com.adobe.xml.syndication.generic.IItem;
. . .
        private function formatDate(date:String):String {
          return _dateFormatter.format(date);
        }

        private function renderArticlesGridDate(
          item:IItem,
          column:DataGridColumn
        ):String {
          return _dateFormatter.format(item.date);
        }
. . .
```

Test the application again to see the prettier dates in all their glory, as shown in Figure 14-28.

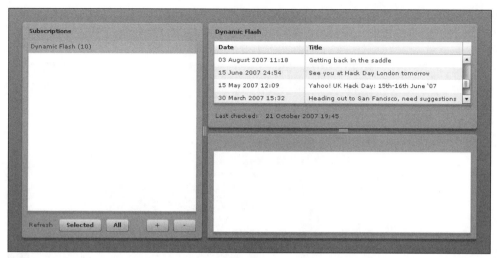

Figure 14-28. The Articles panel shows formatted dates.

Now that you have pretty dates all round, you just need to add the Visit site button. In the ControlBar for the Articles panel, add a 100% width Spacer and a Button control with a label of "Visit site" and click handler of visitSelectedSite(). Bind the enabled property of the button using a data-binding expression to check that there is something selected in the subscriptionsList control.

```
. . .
        <mx:ControlBar>
          <mx:Label text="Last checked:"/>
          <mx:Text text= ➡
  "{formatDate(subscriptionsList.selectedItem.lastChecked)}"/>
          <mx:Spacer width="100%"/>
          <mx:Button label="Visit site"
            click="visitSelectedSite(event)"
            enabled="{subscriptionsList.selectedItem !== null}"/>
        </mx:ControlBar>
. . .
```

Now create the visitSelectedSite() function, which should use the url property of the selected Subscription object in the subscriptionsList control to open a new window to the site using the built-in navigateToURL() function.

```
. . .
        private function refreshSelected(event:Event):void {
          (subscriptionsList.selectedItem as Subscription).refresh();
        }

        private function visitSelectedSite(event:Event):void {
          var subscription:Subscription = ➡
  (subscriptionsList.selectedItem as Subscription);
          navigateToURL(new URLRequest(subscription.url));
        }
. . .
```

That's all there is to it. If you test the project now, you'll see the Visit site button, as shown in Figure 14-29. You can click it to visit the site referenced in the metadata of your subscribed feeds.

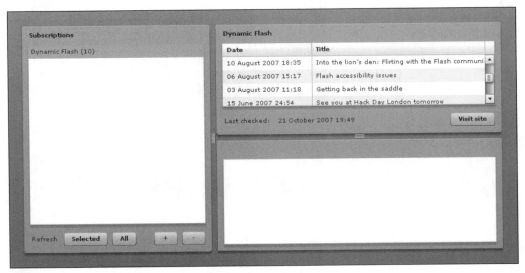

Figure 14-29. The Visit site button added to the Articles panel

With that, you've finished your work on the Articles panel and can turn your attention to the Article panel.

Finishing the Article panel

As with the Articles panel, the Article panel needs very little to satisfy the application's requirements. It's missing a label to show the date of the currently selected item in the Articles panel and a button to take users to the URL associated with the item so they can read the rest of the article.

Let's start with the article date. Add a ControlBar to the Articles panel in the IrisReader.mxml file, containing a Label and a Text control. Bind the text property of the Text control to the date property of the currently selected item in the articlesGrid control, passing that through the DateFormatter object so it's nice and pretty.

```
. . .
<mx:Panel title="{articlesGrid.selectedItem.title}"
  width="100%" height="50%">
  <mx:TextArea id="excerptTextArea" editable="false"
    width="100%" height="100%"
    htmlText="{articlesGrid.selectedItem.excerpt.value}" />
  <mx:ControlBar>
    <mx:Label text="Posted:"/>
```

```
            <mx:Text text= ➡
 "{formatDate(articlesGrid.selectedItem.date)}"/>
            </mx:ControlBar>
        </mx:Panel>
 . . .
```

Figure 14-30 shows the date added to the Article panel.

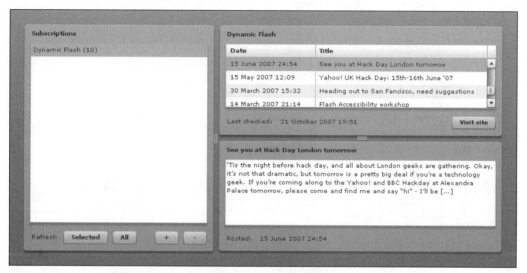

Figure 14-30. The date appears at the bottom of the Article panel.

Well, that was easy. Now you just need to add in and wire up the Read more button.

In the ControlBar for the Article panel, add a 100% width Spacer and a Button control with a label of "Read more" and click handler of readSelectedArticle(). Bind the enabled property of the button using a data-binding expression to check that there is something selected in the articlesGrid control.

```
    . . .
        <mx:ControlBar>
          <mx:Label text="Posted:"/>
          <mx:Text text= ➡
 "{formatDate(articlesGrid.selectedItem.date)}"/>
          <mx:Spacer width="100%"/>
          <mx:Button label="Read more"
            click="readSelectedArticle(event)"
            enabled="{articlesGrid.selectedItem !== null}"/>
        </mx:ControlBar>
    . . .
```

Now create the readSelectedArticle() function, which should use the link property of the selected IItem object in the articlesGrid control to open a new window to the site using the built-in navigateToURL() function.

```
    . . .
        private function visitSelectedSite(event:Event):void {
            var subscription:Subscription = ➡
    (subscriptionsList.selectedItem as Subscription);
            navigateToURL(new URLRequest(subscription.url));
        }

        private function readSelectedArticle(event:Event):void {
            var item:IItem = (articlesGrid.selectedItem as IItem);
            navigateToURL(new URLRequest(item.link));
        }
```

And now you can relax. You have finally nailed down the final feature of our feed reader application, as shown in Figure 14-31. Save your changes, run the project, and bask in the reflective glow of your achievement.

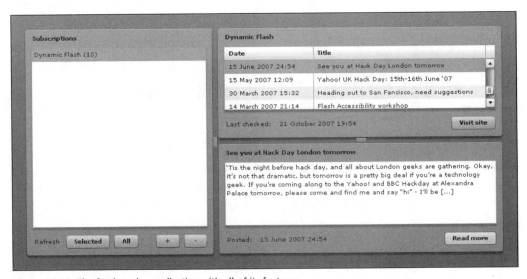

Figure 14-31. The feed reader application with all of its features

Improving the feed reader

While putting this chapter together, I made a conscious decision to omit some features that you would want to have in a high-quality feed reader application. That's not to say that the application you've built is useless. In fact, I'm using this application every day to keep an eye on the feeds that I subscribe to in a simple and unobtrusive way. However, the application would be even more useful if it had some of the following features:

- **User-specified refresh interval**: Currently, the feeds are refreshed every 5 minutes. This may be too frequent (or not frequent enough) for some users, so allowing them to specify their own interval (using a `Slider` or a `NumberStepper`, for example) would be a good idea. You would need to save their interval along with the subscriptions list in the local `SharedObject`; otherwise, the users would need to reset this value every time they started the application, which wouldn't be ideal.

- **Control columns in the `Articles` panel**: The `Articles` panel could contain more information about an item. Some extra fields may be important to users, so allowing them to specify which fields are visible (and in what order) would be a good idea.

- **The ability to organize subscriptions into folders**: Subscriptions can get a bit overwhelming if you've subscribed to hundreds of feeds, so the ability to add folders to the subscriptions list would be ideal. This would involve swapping the `List` control for a `Tree` control, and you would need to tweak how you get the data into it in the first place.

- **Reading list support**: You could add the ability to read Outline Processor Markup Language (OPML) files, which contain lists of feeds supplied by someone else. This would involve extending the Adobe XML syndication library to add support for OPML files. OPML files can contain folders, so the feature suggested in the previous item would be good to go with this one.

Summary

I hope that this chapter has been a bit of an eye-opener about the power of Flex framework when coupled with your own ActionScript for rapidly building high-quality, complex web applications. We started from the conceptualization stage and went all the way through full implementation, utilizing the built-in UI, utility, and management classes in Flex to wire together a set of common widgets to display remote data in an intuitive, straightforward manner that is both easy to use and aesthetically pleasing.

Flex in itself is a fantastic tool, but it can go only so far. It takes extra knowledge of the underlying ActionScript 3.0 language to truly bring out its full potential. The topics presented in this book—from the basic constructs of ActionScript all the way through event handling, graphic creation, and remote communication—can all be applied when developing Flex applications.

And remember, the Flex framework is built on ActionScript. The source code is available to peruse to gain insight into how some of its powerful features were implemented. Use it to learn further. Build your own classes that suit your own needs. The beauty of ActionScript is that it can be used to accomplish so many varied tasks, ranging from scripting animation, to building games, to creating full-blown e-commerce and social media sites.

Take advantage of ActionScript's potential and create what you want to create.

INDEX

Numbers and symbols

A